D0205283

HANDBOOK
FOR LITURGICAL STUDIES

I

Introduction to the Liturgy

THE PONTIFICAL LITURGICAL INSTITUTE

HANDBOOK
FOR LITURGICAL STUDIES

VOLUME I

Introduction to the Liturgy

ANSCAR J. CHUPUNGCO, O.S.B.

EDITOR

A PUEBLO BOOK

The Liturgical Press   Collegeville Minnesota

A Pueblo Book published by The Liturgical Press

Design by Frank Kacmarcik, Obl.S.B.

Library of Congress Cataloging-in-Publication Data

Handbook for liturgical studies / Anscar J. Chupungco, editor.
    p.   cm.
"A Pueblo book."
Includes bibliographical references and index.
Contents: v. 1. Introduction to the liturgy.
ISBN 0-8146-6161-0
   1. Liturgics—Study and teaching.   2. Catholic Church—Liturgy-
-Study and teaching.   I. Chupungco, Anscar J.
BV176.H234   1997
264—dc21   97-20141
                                                CIP

Contents

Introduction

This handbook, in five volumes, represents a complete course of liturgical studies which the Pontifical Liturgical Institute offers to professors and students of liturgy in universities and seminaries and to other persons engaged in liturgical ministry. It is offered as model, source, and reference.

The handbook is marked by the following traits. First, its orientation is theological, though not in the style of systematic or dogmatic treatise. Rather, the materials contained in the liturgical *ordo*, history, and tradition are examined as sources and components of the theology of liturgy. Second, the handbook pays greater attention to the role played by human sciences in the liturgy. These sciences include psycho-sociology, anthropology, linguistics, and the arts. Third, in the handbook pastoral and spiritual considerations are given appropriate treatment in the light of liturgical principles. A handbook with an international readership cannot pretend to provide concrete pastoral application, but it can suggest general models based on the meaning and purpose of the liturgy. Fourth, the materials from the East and the non-Roman West are integrated with the Roman, thus allowing the reader to acquire a comprehensive vision of Christian worship. And fifth, the contents of the handbook are arranged in such a way that the entire work can serve as a model for a complete liturgy course in theological faculties.

These traits differentiate the handbook from its predecessor *Anamnesis* (its volume on oriental liturgies is lacking), which the Pontifical Liturgical Institute published in the course of several years.

The five volumes cover all the basic themes that should form part of liturgical study.

Forty-two authors have contributed to this handbook. They come from Asia, Africa, Latin America, North America, and Eastern and Western Europe. A good number are professors and alumni of the Pontifical Liturgical Institute. The rest are authors with whom the institute shares the same approach to the study of liturgy. There are of course many more who could have been invited to contribute to this handbook.

In a common project such as this handbook the reader will note differences in the method and style of exposition. It is to be expected that each author who specializes in an area will stress points of particular and personal interest in his or her research. Such differences are a welcome trait of the handbook: *varietas delectat*. Yet the differences have not endangered the basic cohesiveness of each volume and of the entire handbook. On the contrary they, like inlaid bits of materials in a mosaic, present a cohesive view of the meaning, purpose, and actualization of Christian worship. Every author in the handbook draws her or his material from liturgical tradition and from ancient, medieval, and modern sources. The method of interpreting and explaining such material may of course differ from one author to another, but the reader should realize that there is no single method for a scientific study. Finally, amidst differences among authors in method, style of exposition, and sensitivity to topics the reader will sense an underlying spirit of fidelity to the Church, to its doctrine, to its traditions, and to its mission in today's world. Authors may expound their personal opinions, but the parameter is always fidelity to the Church.

Through editorial work unnecessary repetitions have been avoided and lacunae have been minimized. In reading these volumes one should keep in mind that they are not intended to serve as a dictionary of liturgy or a quick-reference manual, but a handbook for a liturgy course. And a liturgy course should not only hand out information but also form the attitude and mind of the student. Formation more than mere information should be the aim of liturgical study. Thus, it is important to pay attention to the gradual unfolding of the material from volume I to volume V as well as to the methodology, historical setting, theological and spiritual doctrines, and the pastoral concerns present in the handbook. In truth the study of these volumes should lead not only to a scientific understanding of the liturgy but also and above all to a deeper appreciation of its theological and spiritual riches. Or perhaps one can rephrase this by saying that the scientific study of the liturgy should lead to that active and spiritually fruitful participation in the ecclesial celebration of Christ's mystery desired by Vatican II.

A special word of gratitude goes to Fr. Adam Somorjai, O.S.B., for his competent and patient assistance in the difficult work of editing the materials.

The following also contributed to the shaping of the idea of the new handbook: Prof. Adrien Nocent, O.S.B., Prof. Crispino Valenziano, Prof. Matias Augé, C.M.F., Prof. Cassian Folsom, O.S.B., and Fr. Mario Ravizzoli, O.S.B.

Anscar J. Chupungco, O.S.B.
Editor

Abbreviations

A	*Ambrosius.* Milan, 1925–.
AAS	*Acta Apostolicae Sedis.* Rome, 1909–.
AB	*Analecta Bollandiana.* Brussels, 1882–.
ACC	Alcuin Club Collections. London, 1899–.
ACW	Ancient Christian Writers. New York, 1946–.
A.Dmitr	A. Dmitrievskij, *Opisanie liturgiceskich rukopisej hransjascih-sja v bibliotekach pravoslavnago Vostoka,* I–II. Kiev, 1895, 1902.
AGreg	Analecta Gregoriana. Rome, 1930–.
AL	Analecta liturgica. Rome (see SA).
ALW	*Archiv für Liturgiewissenschaft.* Regensburg. 1950–.
AMS	*Antiphonale Missarum Sextuplex*
Anàmnesis	*Anàmnesis: Introduzione storico-teologica alla liturgia.* Edited by the professors at the Pontificio Istituto Liturgico S. Anselmo, Rome, under the direction of S. Marsili and others. Casale Monferrato, 1974ff. Vol. 1, *La liturgia: Momento nella storia della salvezza.* Turin, 1974. Vol. 2, *La liturgia: Panorama storico generale.* Casale, 1978. Vol. 3/1, *La liturgia: I sacramenti. Teologia e storia della celebrazione.* 1986. Vol. 3/2: *La liturgia eucaristica: Teologia e storia della celebrazione.* Casale Monferrato, 1983. Vol. 5, *Liturgia delle ore.* 1990. Vol. 6, *L'anno liturgico: Storia, teologia e celebrazione.* Genoa, 1988. Vol. 7, *I sacramentali e le benedizioni.* 1989.
ASE	*Annali di storia dell'esegesi.* Bologna.
AST	Analecta sacra Tarraconensia. Barcelona, 1925–.
BA	Bibliothèque Augustinienne. Oeuvres de S. Augustin. Paris, 1949–.
BAR	S. Parenti and E. Velkovska, *L'eucologio Barberini gr. 336* (BELS 80). Rome, 1995.
BEL	Bibliotheca Ephemerides liturgicae. Rome, 1932–.
BELS	Bibliotheca Ephemerides liturgicae Subsidia. Rome, 1975–.
Bugnini	A. Bugnini, *The Reform of the Liturgy: 1948–1975.* Collegeville, Minn., 1990.
ButLitEc	*Bulletin de littérature ecclésiastique.* Toulouse, 1899–1936.
CAO	*Corpus antiphonalium officii.* Rome, 1963–1979.

CBL	Collectanea biblica Latina. Rome.
CCL	Corpus Christianorum. Series Latina. Turnhout, 1954–.
CCCM	Corpus Christianorum Continuatio Mediaevalis. Turnhout, 1971–.
CL	*Communautés et liturgies*. Ottignies, Belgium.
CLLA	*Codices liturgici Latini antiquiores*. Freiburg/Schweiz,. 1968.
Conc	*Concilium*. Edinburgh.
CPG	*Clavis Patrum Graecorum*. Turnhout, 1974–.
CSEL	Corpus scriptorum ecclesiasticorum Latinorum. Vienna, 1886.
CSIC	Consejo superior de investigaciones científicas. Madrid, 1940–1941.
DACL	*Dictionnaire d'archeologie chrétinne et liturgie*. Paris, 1907–1953.
DB	*Rituale Romanum: De benedictionibus* (Kaczynski). Vatican City, 1984.
DMP	*Directorium de Missis cum pueris—Directory for Masses with Children* (*EDIL1* ##3115-3169, pp. 968–980; *DOL* ##2134-2188, pp. 676–688).
DOL	International Commission on English in the Liturgy, *Documents on the Liturgy 1963–1979: Conciliar, Papal and Curial Texts*. Collegeville, Minn., 1982.
DPAC	*Dizionario patristico e di antichità cristiane*. 3 vols. Casale Monferrato, 1983–1988.
DS	H. Denzinger and A. Schönmetzer, *Enchiridion symbolorum*. 32nd ed. Freiburg, 1963.
DSp	*Dictionnaire de spiritualité ascétique et mystique*. Paris, 1932–.
DSPB	*Dizionario di spiritualità biblico-patristica*. Turin, 1993.
DV	Vatican II, *Dei Verbum* (Dogmatic Constitution on Divine Revelation)
EDIL1	*Enchiridion documentorum instaurationis liturgicae 1* (1963–1973). Ed. R. Kaczynski. Turin, 1976.
EDIL2	*Enchiridion documentorum instaurationis liturgicae 2* (1973–1983). Ed. R. Kaczynski. Rome, 1988.
EO	*Ecclesia Orans*. Rome, 1984–.
EP 1961	A.-G. Martimort, *L'Église en prière: Introduction à la liturgie*. Paris, 1961.
EP 1983	*L'Église en prière*, 1983.
EphLit	*Ephemerides liturgicae*. Rome, 1887–.
EstTrin	*Estudios trinitarios*
FCh	Fontes Christiani. Freiburg.

FOP	Faith and Order Papers. Geneva.
FS	Festschrift
GCS	Die griechischen christlichen Schriftsteller der ersten drei Jahrhunderte. Leipzig.
GeV	*Sacramentarium Gelasianum Vetus*
GrH	*Sacramentarium Gregorianum Hadrianum*
HBS	Henry Bradshaw Society. London, 1891–.
HDG	*Handbuch der Dogmengeschichte*
HGK	*Handbuch der Kirchengeschichte*
HJ	*Heythrop Journal.* Oxford, 1960–.
HS	*Hispania sacra.* Madrid, 1948–.
IEHE	*Instituto español de historia eclesiástica.* Rome.
IGMR	*Institutio generalis Missalis Romani—General Instruction of the Roman Missal (EDIL1,* ##1381-1736, pp. 469–546; *DOL* ##1376-1731, pp. 465-533).
Irén	*Irénikon.* Chevetogne, 1926–.
Jungmann	J. A. Jungmann, *Missarum sollemnia.* 2 vols. Casale Monferrato, 1963.
JAC	*Jahrbuch für Antike und Christentum.* Münster, 1958–.
JLw	*Jahrbuch für Liturgiewissenschaft.* Münster, 1921–1941, 1973–1979.
JThS	*Journal of Theological Studies.* London, 1900–1905; Oxford, 1906–1949; n.s. Oxford, 1950–.
LeV	*Lumière et vie.* Lyon, 1951–.
LJ	*Liturgisches Jahrbuch.* Münster, 1951–.
LL	A. Nocent, "I libri liturgici." *Anàmnesis 2: La liturgia: Panorama storico generale.*
LO	Lex Orandi. Paris, 1944–.
LQF	Liturgie- (until 1957: geschichtliche) wissenschaftliche Quellen und Forschungen. Münster, 1909–1940; 1957–.
LThk	*Lexikon für Theologie und Kirche.* Freiburg, 1957–1965.
MD	*La Maison-Dieu.* Paris, 1945–.
MEL	Monumenta Ecclesiae liturgica. Paris, 1890–1912.
MGH	Monumenta Germaniae historica. Berlin, 1826.
MHS	Monumenta Hispaniae sacra. Madrid, 1946–.
ML	C. Vogel, *Medieval Liturgy: An Introduction to the Sources.* Washington, 1986.
MR1570	*Missale Romanum* ex decreto Sacrosancti Concilii Tridentini restitutum Pii V Pont. Max. iussu editum (various editions; here *Missale Romanum* ex decreto Sacrosancti Concilii

	Tridentini restitutum Summorum Pontificum cura recognitum. Editio XIX iuxta typicam. Turin–Rome, 1961).
MR1975	*Missale Romanum* ex decreto Sacrosancti Oecumenici Concilii Vaticani II instauratum auctoritate Pauli Pp. VI promulgatum. Editio typica altera. Vatican City, 1975.
MS	*Medieval Studies.* Toronto–London, 1938–.
MuS	*Musicam sacram. EDIL1* ##733-801, pp. 275–291; *DOL* ##4122-4190, pp. 1293–1306.
NBA	Nuova biblioteca Agostiniana. Rome.
NDL	*Nuovo dizionario di liturgia.* Rome, 1984.
NHL	*Neues Handbuch der Literaturwissenschaft.* Frankfurt-am-Main.
Not	*Notitiae.* Vatican City, 1965–.
NRT	*Nouvelle revue théologique.* Louvain, 1869–.
OCA	Orientalia christiana analecta. Rome, 1935–.
OCP	*Orientalia christiana periodica.* Rome, 1935–.
OE	Vatican II, *Orientalium ecclesiarum* (Drecree on the Catholic Oriental Churches)
OLM	*Ordo lectionum Missae—Lectionary for Mass:* Introduction, 2nd ed. *EDIL2* ##4057-4181, pp. 337–370; *LD*, pp. 135–176.
PDOC	*Petit dictionnaire de l'Orient chrétien*
PG	Patrologia Cursus Completus: Series Graeca. Paris, 1857–1866.
Ph	*Phase: Revista de pastoral liturgica.* Barcelona, 1961–.
PL	Patrologia Cursus Completus: Series Latina. Paris, 1844–1855.
PRG	*Pontificale Romano-Germanicum*
QL	*Questions liturgiques.* Louvain, 1911–.
RAC	*Reallexikon für Antike und Christentum.* Stuttgart, 1950–.
RB	*Revue biblique.* Paris, 1892–.
RBén	*Revue bénédictine.* Maredsous, 1884–.
RCT	*Revista catalana de teología.* Barcelona, 1976–.
RED	Rerum ecclesiasticarum documenta. Rome, 1954.
RET	*Revista Española de teología.* Madrid, 1940–.
Rev Lit et Monastique	*Revue de liturgie e monastique.* Maredsous, 1911–1940.
RG	*Revue grégorienne.* Paris, 1911–.
RHE	*Revue d'histoire ecclésiastique.* Louvain, 1900–.
Righetti	*Manuale di storia liturgica.* Vol. 1 (2nd ed., 1950); vol. 2 (2nd ed., 1955); vol. 3 (1949); vol. 4 (1953). Milan.
RL	*Rivista liturgica.* Praglia-Finalpia, 1914–.

RSPT	*Revue des sciences philosophiques et théologiques*. Paris, 1907–.
RSR	*Recherches de science religieuse*. Paris, 1910–.
SA	Studia Anselmiana. Rome, 1933–.
SAEMO	*Sancti Ambrosii Episcopi Mediolanensis Opera*
SC	Vatican II, *Sacrosanctum Concilium* (Constitution on the Sacred Liturgy)
ScC	*Scuola cattolica*. Milan, 1873–.
SCA	Studies in Christian Antiquity. Washington, 1941–.
SCh	Sources chrétiennes. Paris, 1941–.
SE	*Sacris erudiri*. Steenbruge, 1948–.
SF	Spicilegium Friburgense. Freiburg, 1957.
SFS	Spicilegii Friburgensis Subsidia
SL	*Studia liturgica*. Rotterdam, 1962.
ST	Studi e testi. Vatican City, 1900–.
StudPad	*Studia patavina*. Padua, 1954.
ThS	*Theological Studies*. Woodstock, 1940–.
TQ	*Theologische Quartalschrift*. Tübingen, 1819–.
TRE	*Theologische Realenzyklopädie*. Berlin, 1947–.
TS	*Typologie des sources du moyen âge occidental*
TTZ	*Trierer theologische Zeitschrift*. Trier, 1945–.
TU	Texte und Untersuchungen zur Geschichte der altchristlichen Literatur. Berlin, 1882–.
TuA	Texte und Arbeite. Beuron, 1917–.
UR	Vatican II, *Unitatis redintegratio* (Decree on Ecumenism)
VC	*Vigiliae Christianae*. Amsterdam, 1947–.
Ve	*Sacramentarium Veronense*
ViSpi	*Vie spirituelle*. Paris, 1947–.
WUNT	Wissenschaftliche Untersuchungen zum Neuen Testament. Tübingen, 1950.
Wor	*Worship*. Collegeville, Minn., 1951–. Formerly *Orate Fratres*, 1926–1951.
ZAW	*Zeitschrift für Alttestamentliche Wissenschaft*. Berlin, 1881–.
ZRG RA	*Zeitschrift der Savigny-Stiftung für Rechtsgeschichte (Romantische Abteilung)*. Weimar.

Part I

Preliminary Notions

Anscar J. Chupungco, O.S.B.

1

A Definition of Liturgy

EVOLUTION OF THE WORD "LITURGY"

The word "liturgy" is etymologically derived from the Greek words λαός (people) and ἔργον (work). Thus the immediate meaning of the compound word λειτουργία is public works or state projects. Indirectly it also refers to the public office one undertakes. In the course of time, during the Hellenistic period, the word acquired a broader meaning to include the work done by slaves for their masters and even the small acts of service one did for one's friends.

The Septuagint employs the word λειτουργία as many as 170 times to designate the levitic cult. It is not easy to explain how a secular word came to be used for the sacred rites of Israel. Perhaps this had something to do with the classical meaning of the word which signifies official function held by society's nobility. It fits the definition of the levitic cult as a divine institution entrusted to the care of Israel's nobility, the levitic priests.

The words λειτουργία, λειτουργεῖν, and λειτουργός appear fifteen times in the New Testament and refer variably to a secular function of magistrates (Rom 13:6), the Old Testament priestly office of Zechariah (Luke 1:23), Christ's sacrificial or priestly offering whereby he became the λειτουργός of the sanctuary (Heb 8:2), the spiritual sacrifice of Christians (Rom 15:16), and the cultic celebration of the Christians who "made liturgy to the Lord" at Antioch (Act 13:2).[1]

The early Christian writers retained this cultic meaning of liturgy. This seems to be the sense of *Didaché* 15,1 which affirms that bishops

[1] S. Marsili, "Liturgia," 33–44.

and deacons also perform the λειτουργία of prophets and teachers. The *Apostolic Tradition* 10 claims that clerical ordination is *propter liturgiam*. For the Churches in the East, which have consistently kept this usage, λειτουργία means the sacred rites in general and the eucharistic celebration in particular. This second meaning is referred to when we speak of the liturgy of St. John Chrysostom, of St. Basil, of St. James, of St. Mark, etc. The Latin Church, on the other hand, used terms like *officia divina, opus divinum*, and *sacri* or *ecclesiae ritus*. The use of the word *liturgia* in the context of the Mass did not appear in the Latin West until the sixteenth century, thanks to renaissance writers like G. Cassander, J. Pamelius, and J. Bona. For the other forms of worship the old Latin terms continued to be employed. The word appeared for the first time in official Latin documents during the pontificate of Gregory XVI (+1846).

LITURGY IN *MEDIATOR DEI* AND *SACROSANCTUM CONCILIUM*

The encyclical *Mediator Dei*, no. 25, defines liturgy as "the public worship which our Redeemer as head of the Church renders to the Father, as well as the worship which the community of the faithful renders to its Founder, and through him to the heavenly Father. In short, it is the worship rendered by the Mystical Body of Christ in the entirety of its head and members."[2] This definition has profoundly influenced *SC* 7 which speaks of the liturgy as "an exercise of the priestly office of Jesus Christ," as "the whole public worship performed by the Mystical Body of Jesus Christ, that is, by the Head and his members," and as "an action of Christ the Priest and of his Body which is the Church."

A more comprehensive definition of the liturgy by *SC* 7 includes the basic concept of the presence of Christ in the celebrations of the Mass, the sacraments, the word of God, and the divine office. At Mass Christ himself "now offers through the hands of the priests, who formerly offered himself on the cross." Quoting a saying from St. Augustine, the Constitution affirms that "when a person baptizes, it is really Christ himself who baptizes." He is present in the proclamation of the word and "when the Church prays and sings." All

[2] *AAS* 39 (1947) 528–9; see A. Adam, *Foundations of Liturgy*, 3–11; A. Vagaggini, *Theological Dimensions of the Liturgy*, 21–34.

4

these affirmations underline the active role played by Christ in the exercise of his priestly office, an office which he performed as he preached the good news, healed the sick, freed those in bondage, and culminated by his death on the cross, resurrection from the dead, and bestowal of the Holy Spirit.

Another element of the definition is the role of the Church which Christ associates with himself in a capacity of minister. The phrases "through the hands of the priests," "when a person baptizes," "when the holy Scriptures are read," and "when the Church prays and sings" indicate the Church's ministerial role in the liturgy. Being an action of Christ and the Church, the liturgy "is a sacred action surpassing all others: no other action of the Church can equal its effectiveness by the same title and to the same degree."

An essential component of the liturgy is the Sacred Scripture. SC 24 states that "it is from Scripture that the readings are given and explained in the homily and that psalms are sung; the prayers, collects, and liturgical songs are scriptural in their inspiration; it is from the Scriptures that actions and signs derive their meaning." In consequence the celebration of the liturgy, whether of the Mass, sacraments, sacramentals, or the liturgy of the hours, always includes the proclamation of God's word.

According to SC 7, the ultimate aim of the liturgy is the perfect glorification of God and the sanctification of those who celebrate it. These are signified and brought about "by means of signs perceptible to the senses." Signs or symbols give to the liturgy a sacramental dimension, that is, they contain and reveal the presence of Christ and of the mystery which the Church celebrates. In the liturgy signs or symbols consist of words like sacramental formularies, gestures like handlaying, and material elements like water, bread, wine, and oil. The difference that exists among signs gives rise to the different forms of liturgical celebrations and thus to the various ways whereby sanctification is realized in the liturgy.[3]

To complete the definition of the liturgy it is useful to refer to the other articles of SC. A. Bugnini lists them as fundamental principles.[4] SC 10, inspired by *Mediator Dei*, calls the liturgy *culmen et fons*: "the liturgy is the summit toward which the activity of the Church is

---

[3] C. Vagaggini, 32–124; A. Verheul, *Introduction to the Liturgy*, 102–16.
[4] *The Reform of the Liturgy 1948–1975* (Collegeville, 1990) 39–48.

directed; at the same time it is the fount from which all the Church's power flows." SC 14, on the other hand, considers full, conscious, and active participation as the aim of the conciliar reform and promotion of the liturgy. Active participation is the right and duty of the faithful "by reason of their baptism." This brings us to SC 26 which declares that "liturgical services are not private functions, but are celebrations belonging to the Church." They manifest the whole Body of Christ, though "they concern the individual members in different ways, according to their different orders, offices, and actual participation."

Two other notions complete the conciliar definition of the liturgy. SC 38 speaks of "substantial unity" of the liturgy in opposition to "rigid uniformity." The liturgy is celebrated in the concrete situation of the worshiping community and hence takes into consideration their culture and traditions. This explains the need to adapt or inculturate the liturgy. SC 63b calls for the preparation of particular rituals based on the typical edition of liturgical books; "these rituals are to be adapted, even in regard to the language employed, to the needs of the different regions." In this connection SC 23 issues the reminder that a careful theological, historical, and pastoral investigation should always be made into each part of the liturgy to be revised, in order "that sound tradition may be retained and yet the way remain open to legitimate progress."

LITURGY AS ENCOUNTER WITH GOD

The liturgy can be defined also from the angle of encounter between the faithful and God.[5] This implies that through the Church's worship the faithful both as a body and as individual members enter into the presence of the triune God. Such encounter is personal on the part of the faithful as well as on the part of God. In the liturgy the Church offers worship to the Father, through Jesus Christ, in the unity of the Holy Spirit. The ancient doxological formulary expresses this succinctly: *Ad Patrem, per Filium, in Spiritu Sancto*. The formulary is patterned after the trinitarian activity in the history of salvation. The Father is the origin and hence the end of all creation and salvation; Jesus Christ is the sacrament who reveals the Father and the mediator who reconciles humankind with God; the Holy Spirit is the

[5] A. Verheul, 21–34.

power whereby Christ lifts up the fallen and leads them to the Father.

For this reason in the liturgy the Church normally addresses the Father, through Christ, in the unity of the Holy Spirit. The central prayers, like the Eucharistic Prayer, are directed to the person of the Father. Prayers are concluded invoking the mediation of Christ. The power of the Holy Spirit is called upon the people and sacramental elements.

The liturgy is personal encounter in the sense that human persons meet the three divine persons according to the particular role each of these plays in the history of salvation. The liturgy thus perpetuates God's actions and interventions in human history. In this sense S. Marsili calls the liturgy "the final moment in the history of salvation," in as much as it continues in our time what Christ in his time accomplished by his paschal mystery.[6]

The trinitarian dimension of the liturgy has given rise to such basic liturgical concepts as *anamnesis* and *epiclesis*. In the rites composed of words, gestures, and sometimes material elements the Church recalls or makes an *anamnesis* of what the Father has completed through Christ in human salvation. The act of recalling, of calling to mind, of making present is basic to the definition of the liturgy. It is through *anamnesis* that God's marvellous deeds, the *magnalia Dei*, are recalled by the liturgical assembly and are made present in their midst. Through *anamnesis* the worshipers are enabled to experience in their lives God's work of salvation. The celebration of the Mass and sacraments is thus always an *anamnesis* of God's saving work, a presence in ritual form, and an experience of faith.

Epiclesis, on the other hand, completes the action of *anamnesis*. The two concepts are related to each other in much the same way as the paschal mystery and the mystery of Pentecost. Just as the bestowal of the Holy Spirit on the Church on the day of Pentecost culminates Christ's saving work in his death and resurrection, so does the prayer of *epiclesis* culminate the action of *anamnesis*. When the Church recalls God's marvellous deeds in Christ, it also prays for the bestowal of the Holy Spirit who will consecrate or make holy the people and the sacramental elements used in worship. *Anamnesis* leads to *epiclesis*, just as the paschal mystery led to Pentecost. In the liturgy we not

[6] S. Marsili, "La liturgia della Liturgia nel Vaticano II," *Anamnesis* I, 91–2.

only recall the paschal mystery of Christ, we also receive the Holy Spirit.

Thus the definition of the liturgy as encounter with God involves the *ad extra* working of the Trinity in salvation history. This trinitarian dimension is expressed by the liturgy through its basic components of *anamnesis* and *epiclesis,* whereby the different roles of the three persons are recalled and their saving presence is invoked.

THE VARIOUS LITURGICAL ACTIONS

The conciliar Constitution on the Liturgy makes it clear that liturgical actions are those which the Church recognizes as part of its public worship. Thus it dedicates chapters and articles on the Mass, the sacraments, sacramentals and blessings, the liturgy of the hours, and the feasts in the course of the liturgical year. All these are considered liturgical and the Church claims them as its official form of worship.[7] The definition of the liturgy given above applies to each one, though in different ways. Christ is present in each celebration, because the liturgy is always the exercise of his priestly office. The Holy Spirit is bestowed in every liturgical celebration. Every liturgy is *anamnesis* of the paschal mystery and a pentecostal *epiclesis.*

The constitution reminds us, however, that "the liturgy does not exhaust the entire activity of the Church" (*SC* 9) and that "the spiritual life is not limited to participation in the liturgy" (*SC* 12). For this reason the Church highly endorses the popular devotions of the Christian people, which should be so fashioned "that they harmonize with the liturgical seasons, accord with the sacred liturgy, are in some way derived from it, and lead the people to it" (*SC* 13).

The distinction between what is liturgical and what is non-liturgical depends on what the Church claims as its official form of worship. S. Marsili's distinction between the cult *of* the Church (liturgy) and the cult *in* the Church (private devotions) is helpful.[8] This is so, because the Church has approved certain devotions, like the rosary, stations of the cross, and several novena prayers, for public use without granting them the status of liturgical worship.

---

[7] For the liturgical actions in the Oriental Churches, see A. Schmemann, *Introduction to Liturgical Theology,* 150–220.

[8] S. Marsili, "Liturgia e non-liturgia," *Anamnesis* I, 137–56.

The Constitution on the Liturgy limits itself to popular devotions. Today we speak more broadly of popular religiosity which includes also such acts as pilgrimages, religious drama and dance, and processions. Several of these forms of religiosity have their roots in the liturgy. In places where popular religiosity is vibrantly practiced it is important to balance it with the liturgy. It is also useful to examine ways whereby they can mutually enrich each other, in order that popular religiosity can share the doctrinal content of the liturgy, while the liturgy itself can acquire a more popular character.[9]

MUSIC, ART, AND FURNISHINGS

The definition of the liturgy is incomplete without music, art, and furnishings. For these are integral parts of the liturgical celebration. Although the liturgy can, strictly speaking, be celebrated without music, it is in the interest of active participation and the solemn form of divine worship to sing parts of the liturgy. Although the liturgy can make use of any decent and suitable space, it is fitting to celebrate it in the ambience of beauty, nobility, and dignity.

SC 112 requires that song be closely bound to the liturgical text and to the rite, in order to "add delight to prayer, foster oneness of spirit, or invest the rites with greater solemnity."[10] The arts, too, have an important function in divine worship.[11] SC 122 asks that fine arts set apart for the liturgy should be "truly worthy, becoming, and beautiful, signs and symbols of the supernatural world." In this connection the same article of the Constitution declares that "the Church has been particularly careful to see that sacred furnishings worthily and beautifully serve the dignity of worship."

From these conciliar statements it appears that music, art, and furnishings are more than cosmetic elements of the liturgy. Each has a ministerial role to play; each possesses a sacramental and symbolic character.

CONCLUSION

The liturgy can be defined in many ways, depending on what one wishes to stress: the priestly office of Christ, its ecclesial dimension,

---

[9] A. Chupungco, *Liturgical Inculturation. Sacramentals, Religiosity, and Catechesis* (Collegeville, 1992) 95–133.

[10] J. Gelineau, *Voices and Instruments in Christian Worship* (Collegeville, 1964).

[11] C. Valenziano, *Architetti di Chiese* (Palermo, 1995).

its symbolic nature, its component elements. In a sense there is no single definition of the liturgy that encompasses all its various aspects. Often one should be satisfied with a description of its components and with a general notion that emerges therefrom.

This and the other volumes of the handbook aim to unfold the richness and beauty of the liturgy as seen from its various angles.

Bibliography

Adam, A. *Foundations of Liturgy: An Introduction to Its History and Practice.* Trans. M. J. O'Connell. Collegeville, Minn., 1992.

Kavanagh, A. *On Liturgical Theology.* New York, 1984.

Lathrop, G. *Holy Things: A Liturgical Theology.* Minneapolis, 1993.

Marsili, S. "Liturgia." *Anàmnesis* 1:33-45. Turin, 1974.

Schmemann, A. *Introduction to Liturgical Theology.* New York, 1986.

Vagaggini, C. *Theological Dimensions of the Liturgy.* Collegeville, Minn., 1976. Trans. L. J. Doyle and W. A. Jurgens. Collegeville, Minn., 1976.

Verheul, A. *Introduction to the Liturgy: Towards a Theology of Worship.* Trans. M. Clarke. Collegeville, Minn., 1968.

Wainwright, G. *Doxology: A Systematic Theology.* New York, 1980.

Ephrem Carr, O.S.B.

2

Liturgical Families in the East

INTRODUCTION

This introductory description of the different liturgical families in the East necessarily touches on the basic elements of each family, namely history, liturgical books and languages, and particular theological and ritual features. Although elsewhere in the handbook these elements are treated at greater length, a certain amount of repetition is unavoidable at this point.

The liturgical families in the East are the descendants of the liturgies that developed and became standard either in the major cities which were centers of civil administration and subsequently of ecclesiastical jurisdiction within the Roman Empire or in the first churches founded outside the confines of that empire. The ecumenical council of Nicea (325) already acknowledged a pre-eminent status in the East for the churches of Alexandria, of Antioch, and of the "other provinces" (canon 6). It also grants a position of honor to Aelia (Capitolina), i.e., Jerusalem (canon 7). The "other provinces" were specified by the second canon of the ecumenical council of Constantinople (381) as the Asian diocese (capital: Ephesus), the Pontic diocese (capital: Caesarea in Cappodocia) and Thrace (capital: Heraclea).

The same council (canon 3) conferred a primacy of honor in the East on Constantinople, the new imperial capital, which Constantine officially inaugurated on May 11, 330. Later the Pontic, Asian, and Thracian dioceses were made dependent on Constantinople, New Rome, and it was named equal in privileges with the elder Rome at the ecumenical council of Chalcedon (451) in its canon 28. Thus by the mid-fifth century the principal ecclesiastical and eminent liturgical centers in the Eastern Roman Empire were Alexandria, Antioch, Constantinople, and Jerusalem. Outside this empire during the epoch of the formation of the above patriarchates, the church in Persia, with its center at Seleucia-Ctesiphon, the Armenian church, and the church in the Ethiopian Kingdom of Axum were likewise developing their own ecclesial and liturgical structures. The liturgical families in the East, the Alexandrian, the Antiochene or West Syrian, the Byzantine, the Armenian, and the Persian or East Syrian, correspond basically with the territorial organization of the Church in the fifth century. Due to the vicissitudes of history no separate Jerusalem rite has survived and the Ethiopians were subject to Alexandria until recently.

I. THE ALEXANDRIAN FAMILY

1. *The Coptic Rite*
The basis of the Coptic rite is the ancient liturgical observance of Alexandria, capital city of Roman Egypt. The name Coptic comes from the Greek αἰγύπτιος ("Egyptian") by way of Arabic (*qipt* or *qubt*). Although the liturgy was celebrated in Greek in the Hellenized cities, the rural areas began using some Coptic as early as the fourth century. In the fifth century the church in Egypt was split into two opposing factions by the theological decisions of Chalcedon, i.e. the Melkites ("partisans of the King"), the mainly Greek-speaking population which accepted the council, and the Copts who spurned the council and defended monophysite christology. The division became permanent in the sixth century. The Melkites gradually embraced the Byzantine rite like their counterparts in the patriarchates of Jerusalem and Antioch. Among the Copts the old Alexandrian liturgy underwent marked Antiochene influence when it was reorganized in the sixth century in the monasteries of Scetis with their contingent of Syrian monks. The exclusive use of Sahidic Coptic with a few short formulas left in Greek was legislated by Patriarch Benjamin (626–665). In a period of liturgical renewal sponsored by patriarchal authority in the eleventh and twelfth centuries, some Byzantine elements were introduced into the sacraments. Bohairic replaced Sahidic as the liturgical language by the twelfth century although Arabic was

already being used and prevailed after the fourteenth century. The Coptic liturgy takes its final shape from the canonical-liturgical legislation of Abuʿl Barakat († 1327) and the liturgical regulations of Patriarch Gabriel V (1409–1427).

Patriarch Gabriel II (1130–1144) restricted the number of anaphoras to three. Although the ancient Alexandrian anaphora of St. Mark is still used in its Coptic recension under the name of St. Cyril of Alexandria, the normal anaphora is now St. Basil in a shorter recension than its Byzantine namesake. The anaphora of St. Gregory Nazianzen is employed for the solemn feasts of the Lord. The latter two eucharistic prayers had their origin in Cappadocia.

Proper to the Coptic eucharistic celebration is the use of four New Testament readings (Paul, Catholic Epistles, Acts, Gospel) and the prayers of the faithful in the form of solemn intercessions similar to the Roman rite of Good Friday. Within the service there are two rituals of reconciliation with the solemn formulas of absolution addressed respectively to the Son and to the Father as in the sacrament of Penance. Another form of reconciliation is found in the cathedral evening and the morning Offices of Incense whereby the incense offering becomes a rite of reconciliation with absolution.

2. The Ethiopian Rite

The Ethiopian rite also derives from the ancient Alexandrian liturgy. The establishment of the church in the Ethiopian Kingdom of Axum is traced to the evangelizing zeal of two brothers of Syrian origin, Frumentius and Edesius. The former was consecrated bishop about 340 by Athanasius of Alexandria and the Ethiopian church remained hierarchically dependent on the Egyptian church until 1951. In the course of time the liturgical books brought from Egypt were translated from Greek, then from Coptic or Arabic into Geʿez and enriched by elements gathered from other sources. It was a work carried out largely in the monasteries, the intellectual centers of Ethiopian Christianity from the sixth century onwards. Because the bishops were foreigners who seldom spoke the language, the evolution of the Ethiopic rite went on without any central direction that could create a unified liturgical observance.

Among the materials that influenced the developing Ethiopian liturgy in its rites and euchology are three early Church Orders: the

Testament of our Lord Jesus Christ, which was translated into Geᶜez at an early stage and has supplied, among other things, the anaphora of our Lord Jesus Christ; the *Apostolic Tradition*, put into Geᶜez in the fourteenth century from the Arabic version of the Coptic *Sinodos* and the origin of the anaphora of our Holy Fathers, the Apostles; and the so-called Ethiopic *Didascalia*, which is actually a version via the Arabic of the first six books of the *Apostolic Constitutions*.

Waves of liturgical renewal came in the fifteenth and seventeenth centuries. Abba George Saglawi († 1426 ca.) composed a new Liturgy of the Hours that has come into general use in monasteries and parish churches. Reform of the liturgy formed part of the program of Emperor Zarᶜa Yaqob (1434–1468) after he reestablished the unity of the Ethiopian church. Under his patronage the feasts of the calendar were reorganized and canonical-rubrical instructions were issued for the administration of the sacraments and the celebration of the Eucharist. Further revisions in the eucharistic liturgy and in the sacraments of penance, anointing of the sick, and matrimony came two hundred years later.

The order of the eucharistic celebration corresponds largely to the Coptic usage, but the Creed has a form proper to the Ethiopic church and the use of drums, sistra, proper music and hymns gives the celebration its particular Ethiopian character. The Ethiopian rite has a rich collection of twenty anaphoras, some from the Alexandrian or Coptic tradition, two adapted from ancient Church Orders, others of Antiochene origins, and some indigenous Ethiopian compositions. In the Eucharist as well as in other liturgical services there is an abundant hymnography that is the product of generations of *dabtara*, the traditional singers-teachers of the Ethiopian church.

II. THE ANTIOCHENE OR WEST SYRIAN FAMILY

1. *The Syrian or Syro-Antiochene Rite*
The Syrian rite is the liturgy used by the present Syrian Orthodox and Syrian Catholic churches. Its base is the ancient liturgy of Antioch, capital of Roman Syria. The shape of the rite in the late fourth century can be gathered from the *Apostolic Constitutions*, the writings of John Chrysostom as presbyter at Antioch (386–398), and the *Baptismal Catecheses* of Theodore of Mopsuestia († 428). The liturgy of Jerusalem, part of the same imperial diocese, had an influ-

ence on the further evolution of the rite. It witnessed the assimilation of the liturgy of St. James whose anaphora became a model for the composition of later texts. The liturgical celebrations were in Greek in the cities, but they gradually took on a Syriac form in the countryside where the Syriac language and culture predominated.

As in Egypt, Syrian Christians became divided by reason of the council of Chalcedon into Melkites, who were loyal to the council and the emperor (*malko* = "ruler" or "king"), and the anti-chalcedonians. The Melkites gradually accepted also the liturgy of the imperial capital and became by the twelfth century part of the Byzantine rite. The Syrian faithful who rejected the council slowly formed their own church, a move fostered by Jacob Baradai († 578) and his establishment of an independent hierarchy from 543 onward. Thus the Asyrian church came to be called Jacobite. During the upheavals over christology in the fifth and sixth centuries the Antiochene liturgy was revised and augmented. An important role was played by Patriarch Severus (512–518, † 538), who reformed the ritual of baptism and composed a Hymn Book (ὀκτώηχος) with some of his own liturgical poetry.

The rite of the Syrian patriarchate of Antioch took on a different character with the predominant use of Syriac as the liturgical language by way of translations and adaptations realized mostly in the monasteries. One prominent translator and reformer of the liturgy was Jacob of Edessa († 708). The result was a melding of original Syriac material, especially poetic compositions of Ephrem († 373), Jacob of Serug († 521), his contemporary Simeon Quqoyo ("the potter") and others, with texts translated or adapted from the Greek. The Syrian rite reached its classic shape with Patriarch Michael the Great (1166–1199). With the aid of Bishop Dionysius bar Salibi († 1171) he compiled the Pontifical and oversaw the revision of some sacramental rites, e.g., penance and orders.

For the eucharistic liturgy the Syrian church has produced up to eighty anaphoras,[1] some as recent as the sixteenth century. Among the most ancient are the Antiochene anaphora of the Twelve Apostles, which is related to the Byzantine anaphora of St. John

---

[1] An incomplete list of seventy anaphoras with their manuscript sources and editions is provided by Alphonse Raes in *Anaphorae syriacae*, vol. 1 (Rome, 1939) xxxix–xlvi.

Chrysostom, and the anaphora of St. James from the Jerusalem tradition. As in the *Apostolic Constitutions*, the liturgy of the Word has six readings (Law, Wisdom, Prophets, Acts or Catholic Epistles, Paul, Gospel). An original Syrian ritual form in the Eucharist and other liturgical services is the incense rite with the priestly *sedro* ("order") prayer which consists in an introduction (*Prooemion*), the *sedro* prayer proper, burning incense with the hymn (*qolo*) of incense, and the prayer for acceptance of the incense offering (*etro*). The rich and varied poetic compositions that have accumulated in the Liturgy of the Hours have in large measure supplanted the psalms.

2. *The Maronite Rite*

The Maronite Rite stems from the liturgical observance of the monasteries and Christian communities within the sphere of influence of the monastery of St. Maron († 410) near Apamea in Syria. The Syriac Christians there were firm supporters of Chalcedon and thus targets of anti-Chalcedonian neighbors. They also came into conflict with local Melkites because of their disavowal of the dyothelite ("two wills") formulas of the Third Council of Constantinople (680–681). Faced with the hostility of Moslems on the one side and of Jacobites and Melkites on the other, the Maronite nation migrated to the mountains of Lebanon in the eighth century and there formed an autonomous church. The Maronite liturgy, formed within a monastic environment, maintained many ancient Syriac usages and thus has features in common with both East Syrian and West Syrian traditions. Some euchological texts derive from the ancient rite of Jerusalem.

After centuries of virtual isolation, the Maronites came under Latin influence with the Crusades. In 1182 the Maronite nation confirmed its unbroken communion with Rome. A progressive Latinization of liturgical observances began in the thirteenth century. With the Ottoman conquest of the region in the sixteenth century, increased dependence on Rome accentuated the process. New Latinisms were introduced into the two missals printed in Rome in 1592–1594 and 1716. The latter included for the first time the anaphora of the Holy Roman Church, broadly based on the Roman Canon, which became the anaphora ordinarily used until recently. The high point of Latinization came in the provisions of the Synod of Mount Lebanon (1736). The different forms of consecration in the various anaphoras were replaced by one standard text for all in 1755. The twentieth century has brought a movement of liturgical renewal among the Maronites. A restored ritual was published in 1942 and a missal in 1992 as part of a liturgical reform still in progress.

The Maronite eucharistic liturgy is basically a version of the Syriac liturgy of St. James. Today the liturgical language is Arabic with some parts, e.g., the consecration, in Syriac, but the monasteries maintain the use of Syriac. In contrast with the Syro-Antiochene Rite, the Maronite Eucharist has only two readings: Paul and the Gospel. Of the twenty-two anaphoras in Maronite manuscripts, only six are included in the newest missal. Together with the texts of many anaphoras, the Maronite rite shares with the Syrian tradition the basic structure of the sacraments, though it uses a formula in the first person for baptism and absolution. The organization of the liturgical hours is similar in both, but the Maronite version is simpler with fewer variable texts.

3. The Malankara Rite

The Malankara Rite is the liturgy shared by the Malankara Orthodox and Catholic churches in India. The Antiochene liturgy reached South India with the Syrian Orthodox bishops sent in the seventeenth and eighteenth centuries in response to the request of the Thomas Christians who repudiated the juridical and liturgical Latinization imposed on the Malabar Rite. The Malankara liturgical usages follow the Syrian Rite with local variations that sometimes represent an earlier stage of the Syrian tradition, e.g., the Liturgy of the Presanctified Gifts on Lenten weekdays and Friday of Passion week. Malayalam has largely replaced Syriac as the liturgical language.

III. THE BYZANTINE FAMILY

The liturgy of the Byzantine Rite is used with some local variations in the world-wide communion of autonomous Eastern Orthodox churches which accept the pre-eminence of the patriarch of Constantinople and the authority of Byzantine canonical, theological, and liturgical sources. Since the new imperial capital, Constantinople, was only founded in the fourth century by Constantine on the site of Byzantium, it had no ancient liturgical tradition of its own. At the beginning it presumably followed the liturgical usages of the metropolitan see, Heraclea.

Quickly, however, the consciousness of its role as imperial city and the presence of the court with its solemn ceremonial led the church of Constantinople to begin to create an independent liturgy of equal splendor and majesty by assimilation and elaboration of elements of court ceremony and of liturgical observances of the major centers along the axis from Constantinople to Jerusalem, i.e., Caesarea in Cappadocia, Antioch, and Jerusalem. From Cappadocia came the oldest Eucharistic liturgy, attributed to St. Basil, elements of the prayer of the Hours, e.g., Φῶς ἱλαρόν, and other observances in common with the old Armenian liturgy. The influence of Antioch, the great center of Syrian and Palestinian Christianity, was reinforced by the bishops who came from that district, Nectarius of Tarsus (381–397), John Chrysostom (398–407), and Nestorius (428–431). The elements from the Antiochene tradition in the structure of the Office and the administration of the sacraments and the adoption of the anaphora attributed to St. John Chrysostom are the reason why the Byzantine rite is often considered a branch of the Antiochene family. The contribution of Jerusalem can be noted especially in the Liturgy of the Hours, in the rituals of the Great Week, and in hymnody. The Byzantine liturgy took its classic shape between the sixth and the ninth century in the Cathedral of Hagia Sophia and in the Stoudion monastery at Constantinople. The oldest extant witness is the *Barberini Euchologion*, copied in the late eighth century in Magna Graecia (Southern Italy).

From the end of the eighth century and especially through the mission of Cyril († 869) and Methodius († 885), Apostles of the Slavs, the Byzantine liturgy was diffused among the Slavic peoples in the Balkan Peninsula, then among the Romanians, and finally among the Russians with the conversion of Vladimir in 988. The older Byzantine Rite of the tenth to twelfth centuries was maintained in the Old Slavonic books until the reforms of the Russian Patriarch Nikon (1652–1666) to correspond to the liturgical usages of the contemporary patriarchate of Constantinople in the standard printed editions. The Old Believers who went into schism under Nikon still preserve the older forms.

After the radical disruption of normal liturgical and ecclesial life at Constantinople with the Fourth Crusade (1204), the restoration of the Paleologue emperors (1261) also brought a renovation of the liturgy.

The destruction of numerous liturgical books by the Latins necessitated a reconstitution of many rites. The τυπικόν (Ceremonial and Ordo-Calendar) of the Palestinian monastery of St. Saba and its form of the Liturgy of the Hours became standard. The definitive shape of the Byzantine liturgy was fixed by the Greek liturgical books printed in the sixteenth and seventeenth centuries.

The Byzantine eucharistic celebration is particularly solemn in its sumptuous vesture and stately ceremonial with frequent use of incense and two entrance processions. The element of mystery in the celebration is reinforced by the iconostasis adorned with splendid icons between nave and sanctuary. Of the two traditional eucharistic liturgies that of St. John Chrysostom has superseded the more elaborate one of St. Basil as the ordinary celebration since the eleventh century. The Greek liturgy of St. James is also used in some Byzantine traditions on the feast of St. James (October 23). In all the anaphoras there is an emphasis on the solemn epiclesis. The participation of the faithful in the Eucharist is promoted by the frequent litanies (10) throughout the celebration. Hymnody has a minor part in the eucharistic rite, but in the Office it plays a predominant role even to replacing the Biblical psalms and canticles.

IV. THE ARMENIAN FAMILY

The Armenian liturgy was formed and flourished in the Armenian nation in the region around Lake Van. The first missionaries came from northern Mesopotamia in the second and third centuries and brought along their Syriac variety of the Antiochene Rite that originated in Edessa. But it was the mission of Gregory the Illuminator († 325) connected with the church of Caesarea that effected the conversion of King Tiridates III and of the Armenian nation in 301 and that carried the Cappadocian liturgy to Armenia.

The increasing drive for an independent and indigenous Christianity was advanced by the creation of the Armenian alphabet by Mesrob Mashtocᶜ († 439) in 405–406. With the backing of Catholicos Sahak the Great († 438), Mesrob and his schools of scholar-translators turned the Scriptures and the liturgical texts in current use into Armenian. In the fifth and sixth centuries this liturgy was enriched and to an extent modified significantly by the introduction of extensive materials translated from the Jerusalem tradition, e.g., the *Jerusalem Lectionary* in Armenian (ca. 417–439). Between the seventh and the eleventh century the Armenian Rite also underwent several stages of Byzantine influence. Some ceremonies and euchology thus repeat or imitate the usages of Constantinople, e.g., in the Eucharist and some of the sacraments. This melding of various traditions often led to the reduplication or multiplication of prayers and rituals. Liturgical celebrations were enhanced by the hymns composed by Gregory of Narek († 1010) and Catholicos Nerses IV Shnorhali († 1173). During the period of Latin influence in Little Armenia (Cilicia) in the twelfth to the fourteenth century, some secondary Latinization in external forms, e.g., bishop's miter, and rituals, e.g. prayers at the foot of the altar with *Confiteor* and Psalm 42(43), became part of the Armenian Rite.

For the Eucharist unleavened bread is used and the Orthodox Armenians do not mix water with the wine. Communion is given under one species only. The Liturgy of the Word has three readings (Old Testament, Epistle, and Gospel) and the Creed follows immediately after the Gospel as was the Latin usage. Of the eight anaphoras of the Armenian tradition, the most ancient is the early form of the Cappadocian anaphora of St. Basil, known in Armenian under the name of St. Gregory the Illuminator. Only one anaphora, St. Athanasius, is employed today. In the Eucharistic Prayer there is a hymn to the Father after the anamnesis and a hymn to the Holy Spirit after the epiclesis. The Armenian calendar celebrates the Nativity and the Epiphany as one feast on January 6; it never incorporated the western feast of Christmas.

V. THE PERSIAN OR EAST SYRIAN FAMILY

1. *The Assyrian or Chaldean Rite*

The liturgy of the Church in the Persian Empire (which included areas of ancient Assyria and Chaldea) evolved from the liturgy developed in Edessa, the cradle of Syriac Christian culture and center of missionary endeavors in the Fertile Crescent. Edessa was within the Roman diocese of the East (*Oriens*), which had its headquarters in Antioch. Because of the animosity between the two empires, the Christian church, to which the Roman emperors belonged, underwent in Persia a lengthy period of persecution (344/345–399) which left it in complete disarray. Under the King of Kings Yezdegerd I

(399–420), it was able to elect a new Catholicos, Isaac, and hold a national synod at Seleucia-Ctesiphon (410) to reorganize its ecclesial and liturgical life. With the aid and counsel of Bishop Marutha of Maipherqat, ambassador of the Syrian church, the renewal was done in accordance with the usages of the "Western Fathers," i.e., of the patriarchate of Antioch. Shortly thereafter, however, for political expediency the church in Persia declared itself independent of the western patriarchs at the Synod of Markabta (424) under Catholicos Dadishoᶜ and underlined its difference theologically at the Synod of Seleucia-Ctesiphon (486) under Catholicos Acacius by adopting the christology of Nestorius, who had been condemned at the imperial council of Ephesus (431).

The present Assyrian or Chaldean liturgy is basically the rite as codified under the direction of Catholicos Isho ᶜyahb III (647–648 ca.–657–658) after the Arab conquest. The extensive ritual reforms credited to him included the standardization of the pre-anaphoral prayers, the approval of only the anaphoras of the Holy Apostles Addai and Mari, of Mar Theodore and of Mar Nestorius, the adaptation of the rites of Christian initiation for the baptism of children, the compilation of the *Hudra* with offices for Sundays, feasts and fasts, the rearrangement of the liturgical year and calendar, the systematization of the cathedral Offices of Vespers, Matins, dominical, and festal Vigils, and the establishment of norms for the lectionary system on the basis of which a lectionary was produced shortly thereafter at the Upper Monastery near Mosul.

In the Middle Ages additions were made to the Liturgy of the Hours. Psalm prayers for Vigils and Matins were inserted by Catholicos Elias III Abu Halim (1176–1190) and his successor Yahballaha (1190–1222) compiled the *Gazza* ("Treasure"), a liturgical book of poetic hymns and antiphons for festal Nocturns. The *Warda* ("Rose") collects the poetical antiphons of George Warda († 1300) for liturgical use. From the sixteenth century sections of the Assyrian Church of the East have established union with Rome. These Chaldean Catholics use rituals translated from the Latin for confirmation, auricular confession, and the anointing of the sick.

The Syriac liturgy of the Assyrian and Chaldean churches exhibits a sober simplicity that maintains many archaic features and ancient structures in the Eucharist, the celebration of the sacraments, and the semitic pentecostade form (fifty-day period of seven weeks and one day) of the liturgical year.[2] The normal anaphora, Addai and Mari, which in its earliest form — without the *cushapa* prayers — may go back to the third century, is unusual in that it does not include the words of institution in any of the ancient manuscripts or in present Assyrian usage. The archaic Syriac hymn *Lakhumara* ("To you, O Lord") is a characteristic feature of the eucharistic celebration and the Offices of Vespers and ferial Matins. Although Syriac remains the liturgical language, Arabic is sometimes used in the liturgy of the Word for the prayers and the four readings (Law, Prophets, Apostle, Gospel). The liturgical use of the hymns of Ephrem († 373) is shared with the West Syrian family.

2. *The Malabar Rite*

The Malabar Rite takes its name from the southwest coast of India in Kerala State. Christianity is held to have come to the region with the evangelizing mission of St. Thomas the Apostle. Whatever the liturgical usages of the earliest generations of Thomas Christians may have been, the Christian communities in South India were linked to the Persian church from the fourth century until the arrival of the Portuguese in the sixteenth century. The liturgy that the Latin missionaries found there was a form of the East Syrian Rite with some Christianized Hindu practices, e.g., the use of the *thali*, a braided cord, in the ritual of marriage.

The effort to purge the Malabar liturgy of any trace of Nestorianism eventually led the archbishop of Goa with the aid of the Jesuit missionaries to convoke the Synod of Diamper (1599) which resulted in a wholesale imposition of Latin usages on the Thomas Christians. About all that remained of the original rite was the Syriac language, the Divine Office, and the fundamental shape of the eucharistic liturgy into which many Latinisms were introduced. Only one anaphora, Addai and Mari, was approved with any possible heterodoxy eliminated and with the words of consecration added at the end. Unleavened bread was prescribed for the Eucharist and communion under only one species. For use in the celebration of

---

[2] For the pentecostade calendar see E. Carr, "The Liturgical Year in the Syriac Churches: Adaptation to Different Ecclesial-Liturgical Ambients," in *L'adattamento culturale della liturgia: Metodi e modelli. SA* 113 (Rome, 1993) 47–59.

the sacraments a sixteenth-century Portuguese *Rituale* was translated into Syriac. A Syriac version of the *Pontificale Romanum* was also produced. The manuscripts of the old liturgical books were destroyed to prevent their use. A new calendar was issued to remove any and all Nestorian saints. Although the Synod was not officially approved by Rome, its regulations were enforced in India.

Opposition to the synodal decisions reached a peak with the solemn oath at the Kunan Cross in 1653, but many of the rebels were gradually persuaded to change their mind. The Thomas Christians who refused to yield to the Latinization eventually succeeded in contacting the patriarch of the Syrian Orthodox church who agreed to receive them under his jurisdiction and to give them a bishop provided that they accepted the theology and liturgy of his church. This gave rise to the Malankara Rite in India.

Liturgical reform to restore the oriental character of the Malabar Rite began with Pope Pius XI in 1934. The restored Syriac *Qurbana* ("Offering" = Eucharist) approved by Pope Pius XII in 1957 was introduced in 1962. The eucharistic liturgy has undergone further revisions since then, but the reformed liturgy has met continued resistance in some sectors of the Malabar church. Since the 1960s Malayalam has supplanted Syriac as the liturgical language.

Bibliography

Dalmais, I.-H. "The Eastern Liturgical Families." In *The Church at Prayer: An Introduction to the Liturgy*. Ed. A.-G. Martimort and others. Vol. 1, *Principles of the Liturgy*, 27–43. Collegeville, Minn., 1987.

———. *Les liturgies d'Orient*. 2nd ed. Rites et symboles 10. Paris, 1980.

Federici, T. "Le liturgie dell'area orientale." *Anàmnesis* 2:110–128.

Gelsi, D. "Orientali, liturgie." *NDL* 983–1007.

Janin, R. *Les églises orientales et les rites orientaux*. 4th ed. Paris, 1955.

King, A. A. *The Rites of the Eastern Churches*. 2 vols. Rome, 1947–1948. Reprinted under the title *The Rites of Eastern Christendom*, London, 1950.

Macomber, W. F. "A Theory on the Origins of the Syrian, Maronite and Chaldean Rites." *OCP* 39 (1973) 235–242.

Madey, J., ed. *The Eucharistic Liturgy in the Christian East.* Kottayam, 1982.

Raes, A. *Introductio in liturgiam orientalem.* Rome, 1962.

Salaville, S. *An Introduction to the Study of Eastern Liturgies.* Trans. J.M.T. Barton. London, 1938.

Gabriel Ramis

3

Liturgical Families in the West

The liturgies that were formed in the West are the Roman, the Ambrosian, the Hispanic, the Gallican, and the Celtic. Of these liturgies, the only ones that have survived until our time are the Roman and the Ambrosian. The Roman is celebrated in all of the West and in Africa, Latin America, and the Far East; the Ambrosian is limited to the Archdiocese of Milan.

The Hispanic, although it has survived until our day, is only celebrated in the Chapel of the Corpus Christi in the cathedral of Toledo and in some parishes of that city. It is also occasionally celebrated in other dioceses of Spain.

The Gallican liturgy and the Celtic liturgy, however, have stopped being used completely. But even though they are not celebrated, they have left us with a considerable liturgical documentation that describes their development.

Besides these liturgies that either have survived until today or have already fallen into disuse, we should mention some other liturgies whose documentation we do not possess. There are some that did not reach a high degree of development, and thus we are not able to call them "liturgies," nor distinguish them from the other Western liturgies already mentioned.

Among these liturgies we should name the African, a liturgy that, in spite of having evolved and having acquired a great development as well as a high level of consolidation, has not left us any document of its liturgical life. This is due in great part to the fact that with the invasion of the Vandals and Moslems, the churches of northern Africa disappeared.

We also must mention the Italian liturgies: the *beneventana* and *campana*, and those celebrated in the exarchy of Ravenna and in Aquileia. In Portugal the liturgy of Braga was practiced.

All of these are incorrectly called liturgies because they do not have the kind of structure that enables them to be differentiated from the other Western liturgies. They are rites that either were created as Roman or that have romanized themselves completely, conserving some characteristics of their own respective churches.

THE ROMAN LITURGY

There is no doubt that Rome by being the see of Peter had major importance among all the churches. Consequently the liturgy that was formed in Rome, starting in the eighth century, slowly became important throughout the West. Its importance grew until it came to be almost the only liturgy that was celebrated in all the Church, except for the Eastern Churches and the Church of Milan.[1]

The Roman liturgy refers to the liturgy that began and developed itself in the city of Rome, in the environment of the pope and of the *tituli*, which were the churches governed by a priest.

After the fourth century, with the definitive adoption of Latin in the Roman liturgy, began a great production period of Office books, and of later codification of the Sacramentaries. It is above all the age that passes from Leo the Great (440–461) to Gregory the Great (590–604), the fifth and sixth centuries. The production of these centuries is crystallized in the Veronese Sacramentary, and in other Sacramentaries, particularly, the Gelasian and the Gregorian.

Besides Sacramentaries there are also Lectionaries, the books that contain the readings of the Mass taken from the Bible, with directives as to which readings are to be read.

This liturgy also spread outside Rome: For example, Charlemagne accepted the Roman books in his kingdom and introduced this liturgy in his empire.

Outside of Rome the sacramentaries and the liturgy in general assumed formulas and rites that were not exactly Roman. Thus began the Romano-Frankish liturgies or the Romano-Germanic liturgies,

[1] E. Cattaneo, *Il culto cristiano in Occidente. Note storiche* = BEL. Subsidia 13 (Rome, 1992); C. Vogel, *Introduction au sources de l 'histoire de culte chrétien au Moyen Age* = Biblioteca degli Studi Medievali 1 (Spoleto, 1966).

which were basically Roman liturgies that had assimilated some elements of the countries and cultures in which they were being used.

This liturgy slowly started imposing itself on other Western liturgies, except for the Ambrosian. It was with Gregory VII (1073–1085) that the liturgical unification of all the West was reached. The discovery of America at the end of the fifteenth century (1492) brought this liturgy to the new world. The missionaries that preached the Gospel in both North and South America also introduced the Roman liturgy to the continent.

The missionary work of the sixteenth century and after brought the Roman liturgy to the Far East (the Philippines, Japan, and China) and to the African continent (black Africa).

In the sixteenth century the Council of Trent promoted liturgical reform. A product of this reform was the edition of the missal and breviary, which were widely accepted. With the tridentine reform the Roman liturgy consolidated itself in most of the Catholic world.

After the tridentine reform followed a period of liturgical stability until the reforms of Pius X, Pius XII, and John XXIII, and these were followed by the liturgical reform of the Vatican Council II.

AFRICAN LITURGY

By African liturgy we understand the liturgy celebrated in Northwest Africa, from the time that Christianity was preached in this area until its disappearance due to the invasions of the Vandals and the Moslems.[2] This liturgy developed in Northwest Africa in the area of the three, and later four, Roman provinces that existed in Africa in the fourth century.

This phenomenon of the restriction of Christianity in Roman Africa to only the Romans or the Afro-Romans without reaching to the lower levels of society, the actual "African" levels, explains the disappearance of the church of Africa. Once the Roman Empire disappeared, the Church vanished as well.

Although we do not have any direct liturgical documentation of this church, from the information that the Fathers of the African church have given us, we can deduce that in Africa a liturgy of great

[2] B. Botte, "Liturgie dell 'Occidente," in A-G. Martimort, *La Chiesa in preghiera* (Rome, 1963) 28–36; J. B. Thibaut, "La liturgie romano-africaine," in AA.VV. *La liturgie romaine* (Paris 1924) 81–96.

personality was developed and structured. This liturgy probably exercised its influence in other Western liturgies, such as the Hispanic and the Gallican.

This liturgy was celebrated in Latin, whereas in Rome the liturgy was still celebrated in Greek. It also had the entire sacramental celebration clearly structured: Mass, sacraments, liturgical year, and Divine Office.

AMBROSIAN LITURGY

Although this liturgy is called the Ambrosian, this name does not imply that the liturgy was all the work of Ambrose, nor does it even mean that he began it. Without a doubt Ambrose had influence in the development of this liturgy, and due to the fame of this bishop of Milan, the liturgy adopted his name.[3]

Scholars have different opinions regarding the origin of the Ambrosian liturgy: some advocate an Eastern origin, while others argue for a Roman origin. Although the Roman liturgy has exercised a great influence over the liturgy of Milan, its Eastern influences cannot be ignored.

Throughout its history this liturgy, which still is used today, has passed through diverse stages: assimilation of elements of other liturgies, shedding elements inappropriate to the character of this liturgy, self-conservation before Charlemagne's attempts of Romanization, adjustment to the norms of the tridentine liturgical reforms, and those of Vatican II, and the revision and edition of the *Missale Ambrosianum*, which has, with limitations, reevaluated the authenticity of the rite.

GALLICAN LITURGY

The liturgy that was formed in the southern half of Gaul, or medieval France, is what we call the Gallican liturgy. This liturgy's time of greatest creativity and fruitfulness was the sixth century, but after-

---

[3] P. Borella, *Il rito ambrosiano* (Brescia, 1964); A. Paredi, *Storia del rito ambrosiano* (Milan, 1990); A. M. Triacca, "La liturgia ambrosiana," in AA.VV. *Anamnesis 2*, 88–110.

wards it faded away with the adoption of the Roman rite through the reform of Charlemagne.[4]

The Gallican liturgy, although being more important, did not develop completely as the Ambrosian and the Hispanic liturgies did. The time of splendor for the Gallican liturgy is the sixth century with Cesarius of Arles.

The Hispanic rite probably began at the same time as the Gallican and was established with the same foundations and from the same historical time frame as well.

In the churches of Gaul and Spain there was a heritage of liturgical traditions proceeding from the East and Italy, but above all from Latin Africa. With these liturgical materials the Gallican and Hispanic rites were formed, and they tried to do in their own churches and by their own means something similar to what occurred in Rome in the fifth century. In other words, they tried to organize their own rite.

The Gallican rite disappeared at the end of the eighth century because Charlemagne adopted for his kingdom the liturgical books brought from Rome.

HISPANIC LITURGY

The Hispanic liturgy was created and developed in the Iberian peninsula from the beginning of Christian preaching until its suppression by Pope Gregory VII in the year 1080.[5] This liturgy has three different names: the Hispanic, the Visigothic, and the Mozarabic. Since the time of Cisneros, the third qualifier has normally been used. In fact, these three qualifiers correspond to three historical periods in which the liturgy has lived and developed. The Hispanic corresponds to the Roman period; the Visigothic to the time of the Visigoth kingdom; the Mozarabic to the period of Moslem domination.

The most appropriate name is the Hispanic, the simple reason being that this liturgy already existed in the Roman period. To call it only Visigothic or Mozarabic is to deny a period, the first one of its

---

[4] F. Cabrol, *Les origines de la liturgie gallicane*, RHE 26 (1930), 951–62; H. Leclerq, *Liturgie Gallicane*, DACL VI/1 (Paris, 1924) 473–596; J. B. Thibaut, *L'ancienne liturgie gallicane. Son origine et sa formation en Provnce aux Ve et VIe. siècles sous l'influence de Cassian et saint Cesaire d'Arles* (Paris, 1929).

[5] J. Pinell, "Liturgia Hispánica," in *Liturgia: Diccionario de Historia Ecclesiástica de España II* (Madrid, 1972) 1303–20; id., "La liturgia ispanica," in AA.VV. *Anamnesis* 2, 70–88.

existence. It is also true that for historical reasons we cannot deny the other two names that this liturgy has been called.

There is no common agreement among scholars regarding the origin of the Hispanic liturgy. At times their opinions contrast greatly. Surely the most plausible opinion is that of Pinell, who affirms that the Hispanic liturgy, as with the Gallican, could have been formed from a common liturgical patrimony proceeding from Latin Africa.

This liturgy, in spite of the suppression by Gregory VII in 1080, continues to be celebrated even today in the Chapel of the Corpus Christi in the cathedral of Toledo and in some parishes of that city. It is celebrated above all for those who are descendants of the old Mozarabs.

The euchological schools of Tarragon, Seville, and Toledo were very important to the formation of this liturgy. It is also possible that Cartagena and Mérida have contributed more than a little to the publishing of office books. The names of Leander, Isidore, Eugenius, Ildefonse, and Julian are associated with these schools.

Following the decisions of Vatican II, this liturgy has been revised and reformed. Between 1991 and 1995 the *Missale Hispano-Mozarabicum* and the *Liber Commicus* were published.

CELTIC LITURGY

The Celtic liturgy developed in Ireland, and it is represented through the sources that have survived until our time. There are few existing sources and those we have are very old, dating back to the seventh century.[6] We cannot call this a liturgy in a strict sense, as we have referred to the other western liturgies. The Celtic liturgy never reached a full development. It is fundamentally a Roman liturgy with influences of the Gallican, Ambrosian, and Hispanic liturgies. The sources of this liturgy give us an outline of *ordo missae* and of the monastic Office.

OTHER WESTERN LITURGIES

Some other liturgies also existed in the West, although they did not acquire a full structure and little documentation regarding them remains.

---

[6] F. E. Warren, *The Liturgy and Ritual of the Celtic Church* (Oxford, 1881).

The most important of these is the liturgy of Aquileia, for which we have some proof of its existence. Scholars do not agree on its origin. Some say that it simply came from Rome, others from Constantinople or from Alexandria, still others say it is from Milan.

From this liturgy the *Capitularia Evangeliorum* of the manuscripts *Forojuliensis* and *Rehdigeranus* developed, the first from the end of the seventh century or beginning of the eighth, the second from the eighth century. In addition to these *capitularia*, we know that Paulinus of Aquileia (✝ 802) wrote hymns, but documentation of this fact is very vague. The Synods of Aquileia and Como of the sixteenth century tell us of the Aquileian missal and breviary.

There is no doubt that the church of Ravenna had its importance, but we do not have any documents showing that this church fully developed its liturgy. There is no doubt that Ravenna, as an imperial capital (fifth century) and as the Byzantine provincial capital (sixth–seventh centuries), had its influence, whether it was through the Arianism introduced with the conquest of Theodoric, or through the influences of the Byzantine Empire after being reconquested by Belisarion the Byzantine until it fell to the Lombards in 751.

Regarding the area of Naples, we have some fragments of Pauline readings from the church of Capua in the sixth century, as well as some *capitularia evangeliorum*, the oldest of these probably being from the second half of the sixth century, while the others are from the eighth.

Bibliography

Baumstark, A. *Comparative Liturgy.* Rev. B. Botte. Trans. F. L. Cross. Westminster, Md., 1958.

Bishop, W. C. "The African Rite." *JThS*, o.s. 13 (1912) 250–277.

Borella, P. *Il rito ambrosiano.* Brescia, 1964.

Botte, B. "Liturgie dell'Occidente." In *La Chiesa in preghiera.* Ed. A.-G. Martimort, 28–36. Rome, 1963.

Cabrol, F. "Afrique." *DACL* 1 (1907) 576–657.

_____. "Les origines de la liturgie gallicane." *RHE* 30 (1930) 951–962.

_____. "Mozarabe (La Liturgie)." *DACL* 12/2 (1935) 390–491.

Cattaneo, E. *Il culto cristiano in Occidente: Note storiche.* 3rd ed. BELS 13 Rome, 1984.

Goagoud, L. "Celtiques (Liturgies)." *DACL* 2/2 (1907) 2969–3032.

King, A. A. *Liturgies of the Primatial Sees.* London, 1957.

Leclerq, H. "Liturgie gallicane." *DACL* 6/1 (1924) 473–596.

Lejay, P. "Ambrosienne (Liturgie)." *DACL* 1 (1907) 1373–1442.

Martimort, A.-G., ed. *The Church at Prayer.* Vol. 1, *Principles of the Liturgy.* Collegeville, Minn., 1987.

Metzger, M. *Histoire de la liturgie: Les grandes étapes.* Paris, 1944.

Paredi, A. *Storia del rito ambrosiano.* Milan, 1990.

Pinell i Pons, J. "Liturgia Hispánica." In *Liturgia:* Diccionario de historia eclesiástica de España 2:1303–1320. Madrid, 1972.

_____. "La liturgia ispanica." In *Anàmnesis* 2:70–88.

_____. "La liturgia gallicana." In *Anàmnesis* 2:62-67.

_____. "La liturgia celtica." In *Anàmnesis* 2:67–70.

_____. "Liturgie locali antiche (origine e sviluppo)." *NDL* 776–783.

Thibaut, J.-B. "La liturgie romano-africaine." In *La liturgie romaine*, 81–96. Paris, 1924.

_____. *L'ancienne liturgie gallicane, son origine et sa formation en Provence aux Ve et VIe siècles sous l'influence de Cassien et de saint Cèsaire d'Arles.* Paris, 1929.

Triacca, A.-M. "La liturgia ambrosiana." In *Anàmnesis* 2:88–110.

_____. "Le liturgie occidentali." *DPAC* 2:1985-1990.

Vogel, C. *Medieval Liturgy: An Introduction to the Sources.* Trans. and rev. W. Storey and N. Rasmussen. Washington, 1986.

Warren, F.-E. *The Liturgy and Ritual of the Celtic Church.* Oxford, 1881.

Renato De Zan

4

Bible and Liturgy

I. INTRODUCTION

The link between Bible and liturgy is a complete and natural relationship, unfortunately not always correctly appreciated.[1] Granted, there is a relationship between Bible and liturgy based on use, in which "the liturgy . . . is the perfect actualization of the biblical texts, for it places the proclamation in the midst of the community of believers, gathered around Christ so as to draw near to God."[2] In other words, the two terms Bible/liturgy emphasize the presence of the Bible in the liturgy. Not stressed is the fact that these two terms also imply other relationships. The sacred text bears witness, with various nuances, to the cultic experience of the Jews and the Christian community. The biblical witness not only preserves detailed descriptions of ritual practices; it also preserves accounts of how these practices developed and at times even gives prayer texts (unfortunately these are usually separated from the ritual practices). In this case the relationship between Bible and liturgy is taken to be the same as the presence of the liturgy in the Bible. It seems, then, the two terms

---

[1] An important place is given to the liturgy in the document of the Pontifical Biblical Commission, *The Interpretation of the Bible in the Church* (Vatican City, 1993). After presenting the methods, approaches, various hermeneutic questions and characteristic aspects of Catholic interpretation, the document deals with the interpretation of the Bible in the life of the Church. The paragraph is divided into two parts: actualization and use of the Bible. In the second part there is a short section on the use of the Bible in the liturgy, immediately followed by a section on the use of the Bible in *lectio divina*, pastoral ministry and ecumenism.

[2] Pontifical Biblical Commission, *The Interpretation*, n. 110–1.

Bible/liturgy can be explained in two phases, neither of which is exhaustive: the liturgy in the Bible and the Bible in the liturgy.

This view of the subject presents certain weaknesses. The first is the difference of reciprocity. Studying Jewish and Christian liturgical data is not the same as studying how much Scripture there is in the liturgy. In the first case (liturgy in the Bible) the biblical text preserves, as a memory, information[3] about the Jewish and Christian liturgy in the same way it preserves much other information about the various Jewish institutions and the newborn community.[4] In the second case (Bible in the liturgy) the relationship between the two elements is completely different. The Bible is not one of many elements that make up the liturgy; rather it is the essential and sustaining element.[5] The liturgy is the Bible transformed into Word proclaimed, prayed, and actualized: the liturgy is Word that is celebrated. Thus the link between Bible and liturgy, when the latter is seen as present in the former, is not the link between Bible and liturgy when the former is seen as present in the latter. This leads to a second observation. The link between Bible and liturgy is present not only in our celebrations today. It is present in its own way at the beginning of salvation where the foundational saving Event took place. In the Old Testament as in the New, both the primitive celebration and the Word are situated in the foundational saving Event, for the foundational saving Event is at the same time a primitive (original) celebration and Word. The primitive celebration presents itself as a model to be repeated in later celebrations and as guardian of the Word. The Word presents itself, on the one hand, as an interpretation and memory of the founding event, and on the other as a memory and ritual practice providing a norm for later celebrations. Thus the

[3] The information about the Jewish and Christian liturgy preserved in the Bible is incomplete. Missing is a whole series of data that can be only partially reconstructed from rabbinic and patristic writings.

[4] See R. de Vaux, *Le istituzioni dell'Antico Testamento* (Turin, 1973); Maier, *Il giudaismo del secondo tempio* (Brescia, 1991); E. Schürer, *Storia del popolo giudaico al tempo di Gesù*, vols. I–II (Brescia, 1987).

[5] "Sacred scripture is of the greatest importance in the celebration of the liturgy. For from it are drawn the lessons which are read and which are explained in the homily; from it too come the psalms which are sung. It is from Scripture that the petitions, prayers and hymns draw their inspiration and their force, and that actions and signs derive their meaning" (*SC* 24).

two terms Bible/liturgy can be linked in three ways: (1) the liturgy in the Bible, (2) the intratextual continuum "Bible and liturgy"[6] (foundational saving Event) and (3) the extratextual continuum "Bible and liturgy" (the Bible in the liturgy).

In these pages, necessarily brief, it is impossible to spend time examining the biblical text to show how many liturgical elements it preserves.[7] Instead, more by way of statements than explanations, we shall touch upon the main themes linked to the other two relationships: the intratextual continuum "Bible and liturgy" (foundational saving Event) and the extratextual continuum "Bible and liturgy" (the Bible in the liturgy).

II. BIBLE AND LITURGY AS INTRATEXTUAL CONTINUUM (FOUNDATIONAL SAVING EVENT)

To examine this theme means to undertake a study that is rich and complex by reason of its various unexplored aspects. This is because the Bible and the liturgy are not approached — as is often the case — as two autonomous realities, alike in some ways and opposite in oth-

---

[6] The adjective "intratextual" is used to indicate that the elements of the subject are all found in Scripture. The adjective "extratextual" is used to indicate that the elements are found outside the biblical text and within the liturgical ritual practice, and later in the celebration.

[7] Biblical studies dealing with the liturgy in the Bible are numerous. But it should be noted that equal sensitivity is not always found in the Bibliography. In Nober's *Elenchus Bibliographicus Biblicus* some paragraphs in chapter 15 ("Biblical Theology") are devoted to liturgical aspects of Bible. This sensitivity has been gradually lost under North's new editorship (see general index in R. North, *Elenchus of Biblica 1988* [Rome 1991], and R. North, *Elenchus of Biblica 1991* [Rome, 1994]). We find a completely different mentality in the volumes of the *Internationale Zeitschriftenschau für Bibelwissenschaft und Grenzgebiete*, Düsseldorf. Langevin's extensive biblical bibliography is equally sensitive: P. E. Langevin, *Bibliographie Biblique 1930–1970*, (Québec, 1972); P. E. Langevin, *Bibliographie Biblique 1930–1975* (Québec, 1978); P. E. Langevin, *Bibliographie Biblique 1930–1983*, (Québec, 1985). In its index of principal topics (Rubrical Index) we find many entries and bibliographical references of liturgical interest: new Adam, adoption, advent, agape, agony, altar, ark of the covenant, ascension, assembly, baptism, blessing, circumcision, community, contrition, covenant, conversion, cult, Day of Yahweh, diaconate, episcopate, Eucharist, expiation, extreme unction, fasting, feast, goat, Holy Thursday, horn, incubation, jubilee, lamb, Levites, liturgy, mediation, Mass, sacred places, Sunday, water etc.

ers, but rather as a single reality in which, in the order of salvation, the liturgy complements the Bible and vice versa.

Scripture preserves the memory of the foundational saving Event.[8] This Event is essentially Word. The author of the Letter to the Hebrews[9] begins his work with a summary that makes our present statement of the theme easier: "In times past God spoke (λαλήσας) in partial and various ways (πολυμερῶς καὶ πολυτρόπος) to our ancestors through the prophets; in these last days (ἐπ᾽ ἐσχάτου), he spoke (ἐλάλησεν) to us through the son" (Heb 1:1-2a). The entire Letter to the Hebrews shows what Jesus accomplished. The offering he made by his death and resurrection is presented in a special way, for these are the events by which he is made High Priest. God speaks through what the person of the Son is, does, and says (person as Word-event). Since there is a parallel between the Word of God "in these last days" and the Word of God "in times past" and "in various ways," it becomes clear that in the Old Testament world the divine Word, before it was spoken, was an event.[10] The Bible is an inspired guarantee that God wished to communicate himself in a manner and in a history that are distinctive and unique — yesterday, today, and in the future. They are at the same time a "measure" and a "locus" of salvation for all believers of all times; a "measure" and a "locus" of salvation that bind, commit, and determine the Church.

Proceeding in summary fashion, we can find in the two experiences of the Old and New Testament (in the unity provided by the category of promise-fulfillment and in the difference provided by the category of "transcendence") certain common elements that show the continuum to which Scripture testifies (intratextual continuum).

A. Scripture presents at the beginning the primordial-original saving Event, already experienced as celebration by a group of people.[11]

[8] For the Jews this was the Passover, for Christians the paschal mystery of Jesus.

[9] See H. Luz, *Der alte und der neue Bund bei Paulus und Hebräerbrief*, in "Evangel. Theol." 27 (1967) 318–6; A. Vanhoye, *La structure littéraire de l'Epître aux Hébreux* (Paris, 1963); H. Zimmermann, *Das Bekenntnis der Hoffnung. Tradition und Redaktion im Hebräerbrief* (Cologne, 1977).

[10] For a summary, see G. Gerleman, *Dabar-parola*, in Jenni-Westermann, *Dizionario Teologico dell'Antico Testamento*, vol. I (Turin, 1978) coll. 375–83.

[11] For the OT, see Exod 12:1-13, 16; for the NT see 1 Cor 11:23 (Matt 26:26-28; Mark 14:22-24; Luke 22:19-20) in connection with the accounts of the Lord's passion, death, and resurrection.

B. There is a profound relationship between the foundational saving Event, experienced by a group of people that have become a primitive assembly, and subsequent celebrations by the same people, no longer as primitive but as a subsequent assembly. This relationship has two dimensions. The first links the primitive celebration (foundational saving Event) to the assembly that is celebrant and protagonist of the Event, the assembly that in time celebrates no longer as mere witness, but as custodian and first interpreter of the Event. The second dimension links the primitive celebration (foundational saving Event), through the celebrating assembly, to subsequent celebrations, all of which are linked to the definitive and eschatological fulfillment of the salvation begun in the foundational saving Event itself.

C. There is also a profound link between the first assembly, historical protagonist of the foundational saving Event, and subsequent assemblies, separated from the first by time and space. These subsequent assemblies, sprung from the first assembly, faithfully receive the memory of the Event, its first interpretation and the laws for celebration. Moreover, as its custodians, they transcend and enrich the first interpretation, and by reason of the dynamics inherent in human celebrations (anthropology) they add to the laws for celebration, respecting their original spirit.

D. The first assembly, while it fulfills subsequent celebrations, recalls and interprets the foundational saving Event. This is the oral phase of the memory-interpretation that will later be written down. The written text will contain the memory of the foundational saving Event, its primitive interpretation, its fundamental laws for celebration, an essential explanation of the various links (identity between the protagonist group and the first celebrating assembly; succession-belonging between the first celebrating assembly and subsequent celebrating assemblies; tension between the foundational saving Event and subsequent celebrations) the reinterpretations and subsequent changes in celebration.

E. There is also the biblical text, a memory and interpretation of the event, filled with a divine, saving power that transcends pure memory and interpretation. Indeed, the text is a bearer of salvation, and for the Christian liturgy it forms an essential part of post-biblical celebrations.

F. Finally, there is a celebration that cannot be autonomous with respect to the text that produced it. The liturgy is born from the Word and is shaped by it, even though a contributing part is also played by the theological and cultural understanding of different times and places where the celebrating community lives. But at the same time the liturgy takes the Bible from a situation of Word as memory to a situation of Word as agent of salvation, a maximum expression of identity for the Word itself. Indeed, we may recall the words of Deutero-Isaiah (Isa 55:10-11).

At the end of this summary showing the intratextual continuum between liturgy and Bible, two brief additions are still necessary: (1) there is an intimate relationship between belief, celebration, and transmission, and (2) there is integral relationship between the liturgy and the birth of the Bible.

In light of what we have said, there is obviously an inseparable link between belief, celebration, and transmission. The pair of terms "believe/celebrate" are especially evident in the Gospel of John, where the expression "so that through believing you may have life in his name"[12] links faith and celebration inseparably. The short series of Johannine texts that contain the expression (John 3:15, 16; 6:40) belong to texts that are typically liturgical. The first two quotations are from Jesus' discourse with Nicodemus (John 3:1-21) whose basic theme is "rebirth from above," clearly baptismal in nature (see v. 5). The third is part of Jesus' so-called discourse on the Eucharist in the synagogue at Capernaum (John 6:22-58), where eternal life is expressly linked to the experience of eating Christ's flesh and drinking his blood (see vv. 53-54). The pair of terms "believe/celebrate" are inseparably linked to the statement: "For as often as you eat this bread and drink the cup, you proclaim the death of the Lord until he comes" (1 Cor 11:26).[13]

Many biblical texts originated in the liturgy, but many others originated in other contexts such as catechesis, law, prophecy, etc.[14] They

[12] The paradigm of this expression is made up of the verb πιστεύω + the verb ἔχω + the noun ζωή. This paradigm is found in John 3:15, 16; 6:40.

[13] In the OT, the pair of terms "believe/celebrate" were also linked to tradition. See, for example, the literary genre of "Kinderfrage" in Exod 12:26; 13:18; compare 12:14 (as a perpetual institution), 12:17 (as a perpetual institution) and 12:24 (for yourselves and your descendants).

[14] See A. Lamaire, *Le scuole e la formazione della Bibbia nell'Israele antico* (Brescia, 1981).

continued to be transmitted in these contexts. But when it came to editing the text, we can almost say that at the editorial level the Bible was intended for the liturgy. While we cannot prove conclusively that it was intended *solely* for the liturgy, we have enough evidence at present based on the data to say that it was intended *also* for the liturgy.[15] Scripture is for faith that celebrates. Only in faith that celebrates does the Bible reach its highest level of expression. This fact was immediately seen by the ancients: among the requisites for acceptance into the biblical canon, a writing had to display not only apostolic origin, but it also had to be read at liturgical celebrations.

III. BIBLE AND LITURGY AS EXTRATEXTUAL CONTINUUM (THE BIBLE IN THE LITURGY)

Leaving the biblical text and turning our attention to the celebration, we may note that the continuum between Bible and liturgy assumes two different forms. The first pertains to the underlying structure of the Celebration;[16] the second consists in the reformulation of Scripture in the celebration.

A. The Underlying Structure of the Celebration

When *Sacrosanctum Concilium* says that the prayers draw their inspiration and their force from Scripture, there is much more to this statement than might appear at first glance. The texts, after all, are made up not only of expressions, sentences, and pericopes. They also have a consequentiality that follows certain logical patterns or structural schemes. Beneath the succession of texts lies a recurring "model," an "archetypye," a "plan," an "example to imitate" that transforms and orders both the individual prayers and the entire celebration. Indeed,

---

[15] See Sanders, *Identité de la Bible, Torah et Canon* (Paris, 1975); Ph. Bêguerie, *La Bible née de la liturgie*, in *MD* 126 (1976) 10–116; K. P. Jörns, *Liturgie: berceau de l'Écriture*, in *MD* 189 (1992) 55–78.

[16] See the studies that have looked for the roots of Christian liturgy in the Jewish expression of the biblical data. Among the many classic works, we may recall the following: W.O.E. Oesterley, *The Jewish Background of the Christian Liturgy* (Oxford, 1925); H. Lietzman, *Messe und Herrenmahl* (Bonn, 1926); F. Gavin, *The Jewish antecedents of the christian sacraments* (London, 1928); G. Dix, *The Shape of the Liturgy* (London, 1945); L. Ligier, *Autour du sacrifice eucharistique. Anaphores orientales et anamnèse juive de Kippur*, in *NRT* 82 (1960); J. P. Audet *Esquisse historique du genre littéraire de la "bénédiction" juive et de l' "eucharistie" chrétienne*, in *RB* 65 (1958) 371–99.

the structure for celebration and the structuring of liturgical texts are derived from certain prayer and celebration schemes that are biblical in nature.

The fundamental structure linking the foundational saving Event to Celebration, Scripture, and Fulfillment, is an overall framework within which every subsequent celebration is inserted and from which it derives meaning. Various elements make up this fundamental structure, the most important being the covenant, the passover meal, and blessings.

1. The covenant is the legal structure that regulated the life of the ancient Semites. It is also the theological structure employed by Scripture to signify the relationship between God and his people. Jesus himself points to the new covenant as the basic structure for celebration: "This cup is the new covenant in my blood" (Luke 22:20; 1 Cor 11:25; see also Matt 26:28; Mark 14:24). The allusion to OT biblical texts (compare Exod 24:8 and Zech 9:11 with Matt and Mark; Jer 31:31 with Luke and 1 Cor) shows that Jesus is using the term "covenant" in the theological sense of pact, which is the meaning the term *bᵉrîth* assumed in the Bible.[17] In the celebration of the biblical covenant we find two ritual moments, distinct yet closely related: the sacrificial rite and the proclamation of the covenant document. Structurally speaking, the Christian Celebraton is built upon the two inseparable moments of Word and Sign. This twofold division is found above all in the celebration of the Mass (see *Praenotanda Ordo Lectionum Missae* 1981, n. 10).

2. The Passover meal[18] began as a family celebration (Egyptian Pasch) and became a feast of the people, taking on a national character (feast of the temple). By the time of Jesus the feast had assumed an ambivalent character: the lamb was slaughtered in the temple but consumed liturgically during a family meal (late Jewish feast). The Passover meal is another biblical element that becomes a structure for the Christian Celebration.

---

[17] See V. Korosec, *Hethitische Staatsverträge. Leipziger rechtswissenschaftliche Studien* (Leipzig, 1931); G. Mendenhall, *Law and Covenant in Israel and the Ancient Near East* (Pittsburgh, 1955); K. Baltzer, *Das Bundesformular* (Neukirchen, 1960); D. McCarthy, *Treaty and Covenant* (Rome, 1963); P. Buis, *La notion d'alliance dans l'AT* (Paris, 1976).

[18] See N. Füglister, *Die Heilsbedeutung des Pascha* (Munich, 1963).

3. The Jewish blessing is another religious structure that is biblical in origin.[19] Despite the need for certain qualifications,[20] we can say in general that the Jewish cultic blessing[21] is subdivided into three phases (invitation to bless, anamnesis of the *mirabilia Dei*, concluding doxology) and has a threefold importance: as anamnesis, as thanksgiving, and as prayer. Thus we have the link between *berakah* (blessing) and Eucharist, which is by no means exhaustive, still less identical,[22] since there is no sacrifice associated with blessing.[23]

Within these divisions there is another group of fundamental realities that play an important structuring role, for example sacrifice and anamnesis.

4. Sacrifice is one of the centers of OT worship that becomes a paradigm for understanding the saving death of Jesus within the category of cultic sacrifice. Together with his saving resurrection, it becomes the center, cause, model, and content of every Celebration.[24]

5. Jesus expressly commanded his disciples to make anamnesis[25] (see 1 Cor 11:24, 25). Although it is difficult to understand fully the meaning of this expression, we can say that anamnesis is a biblical structure for celebration that has passed over into the Celebration. Through the anamnesis the action of the Spirit "makes Christ's saving act present in an effective and dynamic manner."

---

[19] J. P. Audet, *Genre littéraire et formes cultuelles de l'Eucharistie. "Nova et vetera,"* in *Eph.Lit.* 80 (1966) 353–85. This is a mature and expanded version of an article that appeard in *RB* 65 (1958) 371-99, which in turn was an expanded version of a paper given in 1957 at the International Congress on the Four Gospels held in Oxford.

[20] See T. J. Talley, *De la "Berakah" à l'Eucharistie. Une question à reéxaminer,* in *MD* 125 (1976) 1–39.

[21] There is a second type of short blessing called "spontaneous" which consists of two parts: the invocation with the epithet "blessed" addressed to God, and the explanation of the reason for this "blessing."

[22] See R. J. Ledogar, *Acknowledgment: Praise Verbs in the Early Greek Anaphoras.* (Rome, 1968).

[23] See H. Caselles, *Eucharistie, bénédiction et sacrifice dans l'Ancien Testament,* in *MD* 123 (1975) 7–28.

[24] See B. Neunheuser, *Sacrificio,* in *NDL,* 1285–1303.

[25] F. Chanderlin, *Do This as My Memorial,* (Rome, 1982). See especially the excellent article by B. Neunheuser, *Memoriale,* in *NDL,* 820–38, with ample bibliography.

Finally there are other structuring elements whose influence is felt in various ways in the Celebration. Among them are the *rîb* and the *todah*.

6. The *rîb*[26] is a Semitic legal structure used by the prophets to make the experience of pardon come alive for the people of God. Its form is very simple: first God accuses with his Word,[27] and then the people, in light of the Word, acknowledge their sin. The *rîb* normally ends with full pardon on the part of God. The Word precedes conversion, reproving and enlightening, guiding it and granting pardon.

7. The *todah*[28] is a prayer that arose after the exile in a fundamentally penitential context. Through it the people confessed their own unfaithfulness and at the same time the superiority of their ever-faithful partner (God). Confession of sin was part of the confession of faith: the Word-Event was "remembered" in order to confess God's goodness and faithfulness and to acknowledge the people's negative response.[29]

B. *The Reformulation of Scripture in the Celebration*

Scripture is present in the Celebration not only at the level of underlying structure but also at a more immediate level. There are signs-symbols and gestures in the Celebration that are derived directly from Scripture. But we must show in particular how the Celebration prays Scripture, reformulates it in its prayer texts, and proclaims it in

[26] See J. Vella, *La giustizia forense di Dio*, (Brescia, 1964); J. Harvey, *Le Plaidoyer prophétique contre Israël après la rupture de l'Alliance*, (Montréal, 1967); K. Nielsen, *Yahweh as Prosecutor and Judge. An Investigation of the Prophetic Lawsuit (Rîb-Pattern)*, (Sheffield, 1978).

[27] Usually it is a question of some negative event, reinterpreted by the prophets as a divine and accusing word.

[28] See H. Grimme, *Der Begriff von hebräischem hôdâ und tôdâ*, in ZAW 17 (1940–1941) 234–40; C. Westermann, *jdh - esaltare*, in Jenni-Westermann, *Dizionario Teologico dell'Antico Testamento*, vol. I, (Turni, 1978), coll. 584–91.

[29] Giraudo has advanced the thesis that some anaphoras would have originated from the *todâh* (C. Giraudo, *La struttura letteraria della preghiera eucaristica. Saggio sulla genesi letteraria di una forma*, [Rome 1981]). This thesis has been partly challenged by Mazza, who has shown that Giraudo's study, although well documented and stimulating, does not take into account the fact that the Eucharist is situated within a Passover meal and is linked to the *Birkat ha-mazon* (E. Mazza, *L'anafora eucaristica. Studi sulle origini*, [Rome 1992]). This prayer has a threefold structure: blessing, narrative, and intercession. This structure is found in the Christian anaphoras.

the Liturgy of the Word. In these few pages we shall emphasize especially reformulation and proclamation.

1. *The reformulation of Scripture.* Twofold attention to Scripture and the celebrating assembly immediately gave rise in the Church's liturgy to a special language: prayer from the biblical text. This characteristic has always been a feature of the prayers of the liturgy of the Church. Scripture is present in prayer either as a citation or as an allusion.

As an example of citation we can consider text 1333 of the *Sacramentarium Veronense.* It amplifies a seemingly very poetic expression *(splendor gloriae tuae)* in order to refer to the person of the Savior and the event of the incarnation. Taking as its point of departure the words *splendor gloriae* understood as a person, this expression is a literal citation of Hebrews 1:3: ". . . *qui [Filius] cum sit splendor gloriae et figura substantiae eius, portansque omnia verbo virtutis suae, purgationem peccatorum faciens sedet ad dexteram maiestatis in excelsis. . . .*" By using the expression *splendor gloriae,* the biblical passage intends to prove the divinity of Jesus by showing the strict unity between Father and Son. The Greek term underlying the word *splendor* means emanation and image in the book of Wisdom (Wis 7:25-26). This theme (unity of Father and Son: the Son as "revealer" of the Father) is typically Johannine, but for the author of the liturgical text there is no succinct expression in John like this one from the Letter to the Hebrews *(splendor gloriae)* to express such a rich and complex reality. On the other hand, if the expression *splendor gloriae* is understood as an event, it is a literal citation of Ezekiel 10:4: *Et levata est gloria Domini desuper cherub ad limen domus, et repleta est domus nube, et atrium repletum est splendore gloriae Domini.* This text from Ezekiel depicts the final moments of God's presence in the temple in Jerusalem. He is withdrawing his presence, *splendor gloriae,* from the temple in order to punish the people for their sins. Since the incarnation of the Son means the return of the *splendor gloriae* among the people, it means that God is newly present among his creatures and that punishment is removed. Salvation is no longer a reality to be hoped for; being present, it needs only to be accepted.[30]

[30] This mention of the divine glory as the concrete presence of God among his people leads us to consider the desperate plea of Moses, who asked God to show him the divine glory (Exod 33:18-23). But here it is no longer a question of a biblical citation in a liturgical text, but rather of a biblical allusion in a liturgical text.

As an example of allusion[31] we can consider the text of the Opening Prayer[32] for the Second Sunday of Lent in the *Missal of Paul VI*. It is easy to see that the elaboration *(nobis dilectum filium tuum audire praecepisti)* contains a clear reference to the words spoken by the Father at the transfiguration of Jesus as recorded by Matthew and Mark (Matt 17:5; Mark 9:7; see also Deut 18:15 and Ps 2:7). There is also a clear reference to the theme of God as shepherd in the petition of the same prayer *(verbo tuo interius nos pascere digneris)* with an obvious reference to Psalm 23; Sirach 18:13; Isaiah 40:11 (see also Eccl 12:11; Jer 31:10, Ezek 34; Zech 9:16; 10:3; John 10:1-21; Heb 13:20; etc.). Much more interesting is the petition's conclusion *(ut, spiritali purificato intuitu, gloriae tuae laetemur aspectu)*. The vocabulary is typically patristic-liturgical, and at first glance the liturgical text seems to have no connection at all with the biblical text and its respective theology. The verb *laetor* expresses joy at the experience in time of the world to come. Moreover, the ablative absolute *(spiritali purificato intuitu)* and the complementary ablative at the end of the petition *(aspectu)* emphasize the experience of seeing. The text of the final part of the petition explicitly says several things: our interior world is called upon to purify itself so as to enjoy — in time — the vision (neither total nor exhaustive) of something that pertains to the world of God. If, among the many possibilities, we turn our attention to the link between the themes of "glory" and "seeing," we find that they are linked by two underlying OT texts: Psalm 69 (68):33 *(Videant pauperes et laetentur . . .)* and Psalm 107 (106):42 *(Videbunt recti et laetabuntur . . .)*. Those who "see" and "rejoice" are the *pauperes* and the *recti*, inasmuch as they are the only ones according to biblical tradition who are able to detect God's work in history. We also find these two traits in the apostles, who socially speaking were nobodies, yet were justified by Jesus. Scripture says of the apostles: *"Gavisi sunt ergo discipuli, viso*

---

[31] Our task is one of onomasiology (which means that a biblical concept may be expressed by various prayer terms). An example of such work can be found in A. Blaise and A. Dumas, *Le vocabulaire latin des principaux thèmes liturgiques*, (Turnhout, 1966).

[32] The source is the *Liber Mozarabicus Sacramentorum*, n. 385 (M. Ferotin, *Liber Mozarabicus Sacramentorum* [Paris, 1912]). The text may be even older than the *Liber* if the expression *spiritali purificato intuitu* goes back to St. Leo the Great (*Sermones*, 26, 1).

Domino . . ." (John 20:20). The disciples, who embody the image of the humble and the just, are protagonists of eschatological joy because they saw the risen Lord. The praying assembly, like the apostles, begs for a foretaste — in time — of the encounter with the glorious and transfigured Christ. This can take place only through inner purification *(spiritali purificato intuitu)* since today the assembly can experience heavenly realities only *per speculum in aenigmate*. Only in the *eschaton* will it see God face to face and know him perfectly (see 1 Cor 13:12). What does the phrase "with our inner eyes purified" mean? The liturgical text recalls Ezekiel 8:2 *(Et vidit: et ecce similitudo quasi aspectus ignis, ab aspectu lumborum eius et deorsum igni, et a lumbis eius et sursum quasi aspectus splendoris, ut visio electri . . .).* The prophet suggests that inner contemplation is to be identified with a "luminous" inner experience. But this luminous inner experience is already somehow recalled in the petition of the Opening Prayer itself, which reads: *verbo tuo interius nos pascere digneris* . . . . In the Word that purifies interiorly the assembly is prepared to receive what the Word reveals in our hearts: the face of the transfigured Christ.

These two brief examples do justice to the words of *SC* 24: "It is from scripture that the petitions, prayers and hymns draw their inspiration and their force." But we have seen how Scripture is not only reformulated in the prayer texts; it is also proclaimed in the Liturgy of the Word.

2. *The proclamation of Scripture.*[33] Scripture is fully actualized in the Liturgy of the Word. "In principle, the liturgy, and especially the sacramental liturgy, the high point of which is the Eucharistic celebration, brings about the most perfect actualization of the biblical texts, for the liturgy places the proclamation in the midst of the community of believers, gathered around Christ so as to draw near to God. Christ is then 'present in his word, because it is he himself who speaks when sacred Scripture is read in the church' (*SC* 7). Thus the written text becomes again a living word."[34] If this is the theological

---

[33] There are numerous studies on this topic. See *La Parole dans la Liturgie,* (Paris, 1970); M. Lessi-Ariosto, *Parola di Dio, pane di vita. Ordinamento delle Letture della Messa,* (Cinisello Balsamo, 1986); A. Milano, *La Parola nella Eucaristia. Un approccio storico-teologico,* (Rome, 1990).

[34] Pontifical Biblical Commission, *The Interpretation of the Bible in the Church,* (Vatican City, 1993), 110–1.

dimension of the proclaimed biblical text, it remains a matter of some complexity to understand the biblical-liturgical reading as proclaimed in the celebration. Since a full discussion is impossible in a few lines, in order to provide a discussion that is sufficiently complete although necessarily brief, it is better if we limit ourselves to a few important considerations on the Lectionary for Sundays and feasts.

Our first observation on the proclamation of Scripture in the Liturgy of the Word concerns the outward appearance of the pericope. The biblical passage is lifted from its original context in the Bible and placed within a new context, that of celebration. In some ways this change of context changes the text's meaning. Therefore, an exegetical interpretation[35] of the passage is no longer enough when that same passage is placed in the context of a celebration made up of specific biblical and prayer texts. *The Praenotanda Ordo Lectionum Missae* of 1981 (note 7 to number 3) says: "The same text may be read or used for diverse reasons on diverse occasions and celebrations of the liturgical year; this has to be remembered in the homily, pastoral exegesis, and catechesis. The indexes of this volume will show, for example, that Romans 6 or 8 is used in various liturgical seasons and celebrations of the sacraments and sacramentals."

The change, then, is not merely a change of context. Very often it extends to other changes that are smaller, yet not without consequences. Biblical texts in the Lectionary are frequently modified in three distinct ways.

a. Opening Words. In the Lectionary, the gospel for the Thirtieth Sunday of the Year, Cycle B, (Mark 10:46-52) begins with these words: "As Jesus was leaving Jericho . . . ." But in the original biblical text this passage begins as follows: "They came to Jericho. And as he [Jesus] was leaving Jericho . . . ." In the original context the account is situated within Jesus' great journey to Jerusalem, where the paschal mystery is to be accomplished. But cutting the opening words serves to isolate the episode and make it important in its own right. The result is clear. The concluding verse ("Immediately he received his sight and followed him on the way") loses all its meaning of imitat-

---

[35] Exegetical interpretation of a passage means the way a scripture scholar would normally interpret the passage in its original biblical context.

ing Jesus by following him to Calvary and the resurrection. Instead it becomes a following based on attraction and gratitude.

b. Closing Words. In the Lectionary, the gospel for the Twenty-Sixth Sunday of the Year, Cycle B, (Mark 9:38-48) begins with an inexplicable change: "John said to Jesus . . ." (the original biblical text has "John said to him . . ."). John is raising the question of the exorcist who is not one of the Twelve (original biblical text), not responding to Jesus (biblical-liturgical text). In fact we do not know to which words of Jesus John is reacting. But what limits the meaning of the text is the final cut made by the Lectionary, dubious from a literary point of view. Instead of continuing all the way to Mark 9:50, it breaks off immediately after Mark 9:48. In this way the biblical-liturgical passage joins the theme of the outsider (Mark 9:38-41) to that of scandal (Mark 9:42-48), removes the exegetical problem of the last two verses (vv. 49-50), and points up the contrast between Jesus and John.

c. Omission of Certain Verses. In the Lectionary, the text of the first reading for the Fourth Sunday of Easter, Cycle C, (Acts 13:14, 43-52) is missing the passage that contains Paul's address in the synagogue at Antioch in Pisidia (vv. 15-42). In his homily, beginning with the Law and the Prophets, Paul proclaims the kerygma of Jesus. Only in the light of this can v. 43 (where the biblical-liturgical text resumes) be understood: "Many Jews and worshipers who were converts to Judaism followed Paul and Barnabas, who spoke to them and urged them to remain faithful to the grace of God." No doubt the biblical-liturgical text is a bit problematic: "[In those days, Paul and Barnabas] continued on from Perga and reached Antioch in Pisidia. On the sabbath they entered the synagogue and took their seats. Many Jews and worshipers who were converts to Judaism followed Paul and Barnabas, who spoke to them and urged them to remain faithful to the grace of God." Exegetically speaking, we cannot understand precisely why many Jews followed Paul and Barnabas. Liturgically speaking, even though the text is awkwardly stitched together, we understand that the reason many Jews followed the apostles is linked to the authority of their exhortation to perseverance.

Besides the new context and modifications, other factors lead to an understanding of the biblical-liturgical text that is much different from one based on an exegetical reading. We are speaking basically of four elements.

a. There is a hierarch among the biblical-liturgical texts. "The reading of the gospel is the high point of the Liturgy of the Word. For this the other readings, in their established sequence from the Old and New Testament, prepare the assembly."[36] Every gospel passage provides an explanation and viewpoint from which to reinterpret and understand the paschal mystery of Jesus celebrated in that liturgical moment. If the other texts are fundamentally oriented toward the gospel, clearly their understanding depends on their link with the gospel and on the basic christological interpretation of the readings.

b. The Christological interpretation[37] of the OT reading.[38] The words of *DV* 15 and 16 are clear: "The primary objective of the plan and lay-out of the Old Testament was that it should prepare for and declare in prophecy the coming of Christ, universal redeemer, and of the messianic kingdom (see Luke 24:44; John 5:39; 1 Pet 1:10), and should indicate it by means of various foreshadowing signs and symbols (see 1 Cor 10:11). . . . For although Christ founded the new Covenant in his blood (see Luke 22:20; 1 Cor 11:25), nevertheless the books of the Old Testament, all of them given a place in the preaching of the Gospel, attain and display their full meaning in the New Testament (see Matt 5:17; Luke 24-27; Rom 16:25-26; 2 Cor 3:14-16) and, in their turn shed light on it and explain it." The logical consequence of these statements is clear: "Christ himself is the center and fulness of all of Scripture, as he is of the entire liturgy."[39] The liturgy, then, remains faithful to the tradition of the Christological reading of the OT, despite certain attempts that tend to go in other directions.[40]

c. The relationship between the first reading and the gospel. The link between the first reading and the gospel is normally thematic: "The best instance of harmony between the Old and New Testament readings occurs when it is one the Scripture itself suggests. This is

---

[36] *Praenotanda Ordo Lectionum Missae*, n. 13.

[37] This follows immediately from this statement: "Christ himself is the center and fulness of all of Scripture, as he is of the entire liturgy" (*Praenotanda Ordo Lectionum Missae*, n. 5), a statement that fully respects *DV* 15.

[38] On the Sundays of Easter the first reading is taken from the Acts of the Apostles and not from the OT (*Praenotanda Ordo Lectionum Missae*, n. 100).

[39] *Praenotanda Ordo Lectionum Missae*, n. 5.

[40] See J. L. McKenzie, *A Theology of the Old Testament* (New York, 1974).

the case when the teaching and events recounted in the texts of the New Testament bear a more or less explicit relationship to the teaching and events of the Old Testament."[41] But it can also be prophetic (promise-fulfillment), typological (anticipation-fulness), or pedagogical (mentality, wisdom, etc.): "The primary objective of the plan and lay-out of the Old Testament was that it should prepare for and declare in prophecy the coming of Christ, universal redeemer, and of the messianic kingdom (see Luke 24:44; John 5:39; 1 Pet 1:10), and should indicate it by means of various foreshadowing signs and symbols (see 1 Cor 10:11). For in the context of the human situation before the era of salvation established by Christ, the books of the Old Testament provide an understanding of God and humanity and make clear to all how a just and merciful God deals with humankind. These books, even though they contain matters which are imperfect and provisional, nevertheless contain authentic divine teaching" (*DV* 15). Finally, there is the most elementary kind of relationship, that which is suggested directly by the headings prefixed to the individual readings of the *Ordo Lectionum*.[42]

d. The interpretation of the second reading during the major liturgical seasons. We know that in ordinary time the second reading follows the rule of *lectio semicontinua*,[43] a rule that was followed during most of the liturgical year in the early Church.[44] For the major liturgical seasons, certain indications[45] lead us to regard the second reading

[41] *Praenotanda Ordo Lectionum Missae*, n. 67.

[42] Ibid., n. 106.

[43] Ibid., n. 107.

[44] T. Federici, *La Bibbia diventa Lezionario. Storia e criteri attuali*, in R. Cecolin (ed.), *Dall'esegesi all'ermeneutica attraverso la celebrazione. Bibbia e Liturgia I* (Padua, 1991) 192–222.

[45] The *Praenotanda Ordo Lectionum Missae* contains suggestions for each major liturgical season. For Advent "the readings from an apostle serve as exhortations and proclamations, in keeping with the different themes of Advent" (n. 93). For Christmas the second readings have been chosen from the Roman tradition and have special connotations for the feast of the Holy Family — the virtues of family life — and for Epiphany — the call of all people to salvation (see n. 95). For Lent "the readings from the letters of the apostles have been selected to fit the gospel and the Old Testament readings and, to the extent possible, to provide a connection between them" (n. 97). Finally, for the Easter season "the [second] reading from St. Paul concerns the living out of the paschal mystery in the Church" (n. 99).

as an element suggesting "witness." The texts tend to suggest values and behaviors that fit in with the point of view from which the paschal mystery is being celebrated.

We have finished our excursion into hermeneutics by attending to the biblical-liturgical passages and their relationships. Full discussion calls for a final observation: the biblical-liturgical texts of the Lectionary are situated within a celebration of which they form an integral part. Therefore, the biblical texts of the Lectionary must be understood in light of the celebration. In other words, all the biblical themes that have emerged from our attempt at understanding need to be clarified through thematic dialogue with the prayer texts of the celebration itself.

IV. EPILOGUE

The two terms Bible/liturgy reveal all their wealth if we understand them as a continuum. This statement, still not fully investigated, transcends the statement "liturgy in the Bible" and "Bible in the liturgy" because it enables us to uncover and confront themes that in different ways would remain hidden. Moreover, it gives us the opportunity to articulate them in a way that is new and more pertinent to the Celebration. The brief discussion just finished did not intend to be complete, given the natural limitations of a handbook. However, the more important data and major emphases have been presented so that the underlying link between Bible and liturgy might become clearer. While this process helps us approach the Mystery respectfully, at the same time it could initiate a deeper dialogue: between liturgical scholars and the Mystery of Scripture, between biblical scholars and the Mystery of the Celebration. What originated as a continuum should be experienced and understood as such.

Bibliography

Cecolin, R., ed. *Dall'esegesi all'ermeneutica attraverso la celebrazione.* Bibbia e liturgia 1. Padua, 1991.

Daniélou, J. *The Bible and the Liturgy.* Notre Dame, Ind., 1956.

De Zan, R., ed. *Dove rinasce la Parola.* Bibbia e liturgia 3. Padua, 1993.

Gavin, F. *The Jewish Antecedents of the Christian Sacraments*. London, 1928. Reprint New York, 1969.

Grelot, P. *L'Introduction à la Bible: Le Nouveau Testament*. Vol. 8, *Homélies sur l'Ecriture à l'époque apostolique*. Paris, 1989. Vol. 9, *La liturgie dans le Nouveau Testament*. Paris, 1991.

Hahn, F. *The Worship of the Early Church*. Philadelphia, 1973.

Jörns, K. P. "Liturgie: Berceau de l'Ecriture." *MD* 189 (1992).

Le Déaut, R. *Liturgie juive et Nouveau Testament: le témoignage des versions araméenes*. Scripta Pontificii Instituti Biblici 115. Rome, 1965.

Moule, C.F.D. *Worship in the New Testament*. 3rd ed. London, 1964.

Oesterly, W.O.E. *The Jewish Background of the Christian Liturgy*. Oxford, 1925.

Terrin, A. N. *Scriptura crescit cum orante*. Bibbia e liturgia 2. Padua, 1993.

Vezzoli, O. "Bibbia e liturgia." In *La Bibbia*, 3223–3242. Casale Monferrato, 1995.

Basil Studer, O.S.B.

5

Liturgy and the Fathers

In their discussions and acceptance of the faith of Nicaea (325), fourth-century bishops and theologians began to appeal not only to Sacred Scripture, but also to the Fathers.[1] At first this name was used with reference to those who had taken part in the first ecumenical council. Later it was extended to all who had joined their colleagues in testifying to and defending the Catholic faith defined by that council. From the fifth century on, the name "Fathers" was also given to all ecclesiastical writers, whether bishops or not, who had been acknowledged as witnesses of the true faith. Following in the wake of Augustine, Vincent of Lérins referred to the holy Fathers "who in their times and places persevered in the unity of communion and faith and were regarded as approved teachers."[2] Today when scholars speak of the "Fathers of the Church," they no longer mean only those writers who were conspicuous for their antiquity, orthodoxy, holiness of life, and approval by the Church — as was said in Catholic circles after the Council of Trent. Instead they include in this name all Christian writers of the first five or eight centuries. It is in this broad sense that we speak here of the Fathers, patristic theology, and the patristic age. Those writers who lived more or less outside the Great Church or were considered — rightly or wrongly — as marginal by later writers, testified in their own way to the acceptance of the Gospel of Jesus Christ. Even though they were dissenters, they can often help us understand better the testimony of those who are

[1] See *DPAC*, s.vv. "Argomentazione patristica," "Padre" and "Padri della Chiesa."

[2] Vincent of Lérins, *Common* 29, 1.

usually acknowledged as authentic witnesses of the faith and
Christian life.[3]

1. PRIVILEGED TESTIMONY

No doubt the existence of post-apostolic communities and their conditions can be known by people today chiefly through the written
documents left by early Christian writers. It was they who bore witness to the faith and life of the first generations of believers. Following
Augustine, who distinguishes between *fides historica* and *fides
religiosa*,[4] their testimony can be considered as historical or theological.

On the one hand, early Christian writers furnish a wealth of information on the spread of Christianity in the area around the
Mediterranean, on the history of the growing number of communities, and on the gradual Christianization of the Roman provinces and
even the surrounding regions. Thus it is not surprising that the origin
and evolution of liturgical life are known primarily through their
writings, handed down from age to age even to the present. Thanks
to this evidence, which is certainly abundant, modern readers can get
an idea of the organization of liturgical celebrations, especially
Christian initiation, study the origin of sacred times, especially the
feast of Easter, learn about the evolution of ecclesial ministries, and
understand the symbolic meaning Christians attached to their acts of
worship.

But believers today are not satisfied with a purely historical study
of the Church's liturgy. They are trying to grasp the deeper meaning
of Christian worship. Thus they look at the early liturgy within the
framework of the secular dialogue about belief in God. They see that
it is at the heart of the ongoing conversation between the first
Christians and their God. People who believe in Christ are convinced
that their dialogue with God must be apostolic, that is, based on apostolic tradition as handed down especially in Sacred Scripture. They
are also convinced that their dialogue of faith is truly apostolic only
to the extent that it takes place within the wake of the tradition of the
post-apostolic Churches — especially those closer to the origins of

---

[3] For criteria to ascertain the degree of trustworthiness of Christian writers, see
B. Studer, in J. Feiner and M. Löhrer (ed.), *Mysterium Salutis* I (Einsiedeln, 1965)
588–99.

[4] Augustine, *De Civit.* 15, 9; 18, 38.

Christianity. With these two premises in mind, Christians today also know that their liturgical dialogue with God will be apostolic only if it recovers the voice of those who in the beginning celebrated the liturgy of the Church of God. More concretely, the faithful and especially liturgical theologians who wish to be nourished by the faith of their fathers and mothers and share the faith of the early liturgical assemblies, need the theological witness of the early Church's writers. Only by knowing these writings and recognizing their theological value, will they be guaranteed a share in the spirit that inspired the liturgy of the patristic age, itself based on the liturgy of the apostolic communities.[5]

This twofold witness, historical and theological, is found first of all in the Church Orders that date back to the first four centuries.[6] These documents were written by private individuals whose names are unknown. But since they were issued under apostolic authority, they were accepted by most of the patristic Churches. They include the Teaching of the Twelve Apostles, called simply the *Didache* (late 1st century), the *Traditio Apostolica*, once attributed to Hippolytus of Rome (early 3rd century), the *Didascala* (3rd century), and the *Apostolic Constitutions* (late 4th century).[7] Since they contain not only information about the development of the sacramental rites, but also models of liturgical prayer, they enable us to reconstruct to a large extent the origin and historical development of the various liturgical traditions.

In order to reconstruct the history of Christian initiation, we must also turn to the mystagogical catecheses. These include explanations of baptism and the Eucharist given to the newly baptized at Easter and during the following week. Most of them are from very famous bishops of the fourth and fifth century: Cyril of Jerusalem, John Chrysostom, Theodore of Mopsuestia, Ambrose of Milan, and

---

[5] The earliest documentary evidence for the history of the liturgy will be presented, along with pertinent bibliography, in the chapter entitled "Liturgical Books in the First Four Centuries."

[6] G. Schöllgen, *Zur Entstehung und Entwicklung der frühchristlichen Kirchenordnungen:* FCh 1 (1991) 13–21; A. Faivre, *Ordonner la fraternité: pouvoir d'innover et retour à l'ordre dans l'Église ancienne* (Paris, 1992).

[7] See the edition of the *Apostolic Constitutions* edited by M. Metzger in SCh and also *DPAC*, s.vv. The individual documents will be treated in part IIIA, chapter 1.

Augustine. Since they were given in Jerusalem, Antioch, and Milan, they reflect traditions that are of prime importance for the history of liturgy. Although Hippo did not give birth to a liturgical family, the catecheses of Augustine greatly influenced Latin sacramental theology, thanks to their extraordinary spread.

With regard to the liturgical year, most of our information comes from the preaching that took place on the various feasts. First of all, we should mention the 2nd-century Easter homilies of Melito of Sardis, Pseudo-Hippolytus, and others. They clarify the meaning of the most important Christian feast.[8] They are also the most important witness to the first developments of Christian exegesis, based on liturgical theology. Later developments in the sacred times are known chiefly from the feast day sermons of the great bishops of the imperial Church. The discourses of Gregory of Nyssa are worth special mention for they enable us, perhaps better than others, to understand the meaning of the Christian feast.[9] Also interesting are the sermons of Leo I, which emphasize the sense of *hodie*, that is to say, the presence of the mysteries of Jesus in the celebrations of Christmas, Epiphany, Easter, Ascension, and Pentecost.[10]

The last thing to be considered as primary evidence in the history of liturgy is church history. In this area Eusebius of Caesarea obviously holds first place. His *Historia Ecclesiastica* is our chief source for the history of Christianity during the first three centuries, including the liturgical life of the early Christian communities. It contains information on the cult of the martyrs, the Easter controversy and the first buildings for worship, along with details on the history of baptism and the Eucharist, as well as the meaning of the Christian feast and the Christian use of mystery language. This priceless information can be supplemented by the historical writings of Eusebius's successors, as well as by the hagiographic literature, for example, the martyrdom of Polycarp.

---

[8] R. Cantalamessa, *La Pasqua nella Chiesa antica* = Traditio christiana 4 (Turin, 1978).

[9] B. Studer, "Das christliche Fest, ein Tag der gläubigen Hoffnung," *SA* 95 (Rome, 1988) 517–29.

[10] B. de Soos, *Le mystère liturgique d'après saint Léon le Grand* (Münster i.W., 1958) 22–7.

In addition to these major sources for liturgical history, almost all of early Christian literature contains more or less important evidence about the development and meaning of Christian worship in the patristic age. We should mention especially the theological treatises on baptism,[11] the Eucharist,[12] and prayer.[13] Also of interest are the biblical commentaries. In them great early Christian exegetes such as Origen, Chrysostom, Theodoret, Augustine, and many others, often comment on biblical texts related to the Christian rites (John 3; Matt 28:19f; Rom 6; 1 Cor 11, etc.). But that is not all. They also develop some of the basic concepts of patristic liturgical theology, such as μυστήριον, *sacramentum*, salvation history, the unity of the Old and New Testaments, etc. Then we should add the synodal documents insofar as they have to do with worship[14]. In addition, there are the collections of letters of bishops, popes, and even emperors, such as the letters of Constantine the Great.[15] Finally, there are the poetic works of Ambrose, Prudentius, and Paulinus of Nola.[16]

All of this rich and varied evidence allows us to see how the Christian liturgy, beginning with the worship of the apostolic communities, took shape in a quasi-definitive manner during the first centuries. In particular we can understand the factors in its historical development: its Jewish matrix, the positive and negative influences of Greco-Roman cults, the philosophy of the Logos, the Roman legal mentality. We can also sense the deeper meaning the Fathers gave to the liturgy of their communities and consider the *pro nobis* aspect of early Christian worship, that is, the perennial timeliness of the faith that inspired it.

[11] Tertullian, *De baptismo*; Cyprian, *Epist.* 69–75; Augustine, *Opere antidonatiste*: BA 28–32.

[12] Cyprian, *Epist.* 63.

[13] Tertullian, *De oratione*; Origen, *De oratione*; Cyprian, *De oratione*. See A. Hamman, *La prière. Les trois premiers siècles*; for Augustine, see M. Vincent, *Augustin, maître de prière d'après les Enarrationes in Psalmos* = Théologie historique 84 (Paris, 1990).

[14] C. Munier, *Collezioni Canoniche: DPAC* 729–34.

[15] A. di Berardino, *L'imperatore Costantino e la celebrazione della Pasqua*: G. Bonamente and F. Fuso (eds.) *Costantino il Grande* (Macerata, 1992) 362–84.

[16] J. Fontaine, *Naissance de la poésie dans l'Occident chrétien*, (Paris, 1981).

2. LITURGY, A SOURCE OF THE CHRISTIAN LIFE

We know that all the Fathers' theological activity was strongly influenced by practical concerns. They were pastors and heads of Christian communities. Above all they were anxious to arouse and nourish the faith of the souls entrusted to them. They never ceased to exhort and encourage their faithful. They constantly tried to make Sacred Scripture real for them, to make the gospel of Christ part of their daily lives. They were committed to orthodoxy and the freedom of the Church; in these cases their arguments were always *ad hominem*, respecting the positions of their interlocutors. This statement is true especially, though not exclusively, of their preaching and letter writing — indeed of most of their writings. Very few works are "unconcerned." Perhaps Augustine's *De Trinitate* is such a work, although it was meant to be used for the *exercitatio mentis*.[17] The extent to which the Fathers were always pastorally concerned is perhaps clearer in the literary works of Ambrose of Milan. In fact, most of his dogmatic, exegetical, and spiritual writings are discourses and homilies.[18]

If we carefully consider this pastoral orientation found in all patristic writings, we see that the testimony of the Fathers confirms one of the most conspicuous features of the early liturgy: its connection with the daily life of Christians. Liturgical celebrations at that time went well beyond mere cult. They were not only a proclamation of the *magnalia Dei*, a commemoration of the mysteries of Jesus Christ, or the adoration and thanksgiving due to the three Persons in one God. They were also inspired by an interest in asceticism and spirituality. They flowed into a life of faith, hope, and love. It is precisely this existential dimension of the early Christian liturgy that is revealed to one who reads the writings of the Fathers, which are mostly homilies or at least parts of sermons given in liturgical assemblies. The following facts should convince us of this.

From the beginning — as the *Didache* (ch. 7) already attests — the catechumens, with the help of the entire community, were supposed to prepare themselves for baptism by prayer and fasting. This was the meaning of conversion (μετάνοια, *paenitentia*), as the *Didache*

---

[17] B. Studer, *Gratia Christi - Gratia Dei bei Augustinus von Hippo* (1993) 187-96.

[18] See the introduction to Ambrose in the Patrologies, especially T. Graumann, *Christus interpres. Die Einheit von Auslegung und Verkündigung in der Lukaserklärung des Ambrosius von Mailand* (Berlin, 1994).

would have us understand it.[19] How serious these moral demands were is shown by the origin and evolution of Lent, which was seen primarily as the end of the catechumenate, that is, of the preparation for baptism which was to be administered at the Easter vigil.[20] During this "propaedeutic" period, preachers not only explained the Creed and the Lord's Prayer; they also insisted in a special way on the moral demands of the Christian life.[21]

Catechesis of the newly baptized moved along the same lines. Unlike Cyril (John?) of Jerusalem and others, Chrysostom did not spend much time explaining the "mysteries" during Easter Week. Following the apostle Paul, whom he greatly admired, he emphasized instead that "baptism marks the entrance into a new life and is a new creation that must show itself in new ways of behavior."[22] Augustine, on the other hand, when initiating the neophytes into the Eucharistic celebration, refers to its rites. But he is more concerned with teaching them that Christians must identify themselves with the sacrifice of Christ.[23] It is they who are the body that is placed on the altar.[24] Together with Christ the Head and united with their brothers and sisters, they make up the *Christus totus*, the entire body of Christ.[25] It is in this sense that their prayer becomes constant and logically translates itself into works. All of this is expressed by Leo the Great in his usual concise manner. In one of his Easter sermons he reminds his faithful that in baptism Christians become a new thing, a *caro crucifixi*, and that this union with Christ crucified is deepened in the Eucharist and in all daily life.[26]

The link between liturgical celebration and daily life is also seen in the feast-day sermons. The Fathers, when extolling the mystery which is celebrated on a feast of the Lord, or the greatness of a saint which is commemorated on his or her *dies natalis*, never fail to end their eulogies with an exhortation. Indeed, following the practices of

---

[19] *Didache*, 1–6: the Two Ways. See also Tertullian, *De paenitentia*.

[20] DPAC 627ff.

[21] J. Daniélou, *La catechesi nei primi secoli* (Turin, 1982) 135–44.

[22] J. Daniélou, *La catechesi*, 144–47, especially 145.

[23] See Augustine, *Sermo* 227.

[24] See Augustine, *Sermo* 272.

[25] See Augustine, *Sermo* 227; *Sermo* 228B, 2ff.

[26] Leo, *Tract*. 63, 6f.

ancient rhetoric, they employ a more solemn language for these *exordia*. Here we need only look at the sermons of Leo the Great. In his sermons for Lent and Holy Week, he invites the faithful to prepare themselves for the feast of Easter and to live the mystery of the Lord's resurrection.[27] On the feast of the Ascension, he not only invites them to joy and thanksgiving but also exhorts them to make their life a pilgrimage toward heaven.[28] The *natale apostolorum* and the feast of St. Lawrence give him a chance to speak to the Roman faithful about the *praesidium* and *exemplum* of all the saints, even as he recommends in a special way the *excellentia* of Rome's patrons.[29]

These few examples — which could easily be multiplied — show that, according to the Fathers of the Church, liturgical prayer must be prolonged through daily good works; that the reason Christian communities celebrate rites and feasts is to direct and sustain their members on their earthly pilgrimage toward the heavenly homeland; in a word, that the liturgy is the principal source of the life of faith, the clothing without which faith would remain naked, as Tertullian says of baptism.[30]

3. LITURGY, AN EXPRESSION
AND NORM OF RIGHT BELIEF

The link between the liturgy and the daily life of the Christian also includes faith. This aspect deserves special attention. When the Fathers spoke of faith, they meant by this term not only an attitude of trust in God, a continuous orientation to eternal life. For them, as for the authors of the New Testament, belief also meant acceptance of the Word of God. There was a content to faith; it had to be correct and sound.

This basic given of Christianity can be seen above all in the context of baptism.[31] It is not without reason that baptism was called the *sacramentum fidei*.[32] We know that from the very beginning the bap-

[27] See Leo, *Tract.* 47, 3; 50, 3; 65, 5 etc.

[28] Leo, *Tract.* 74, 5.

[29] Leo, *Tract.* 82, 7; 85, 4.

[30] Tertullian, *De baptismo* 13, 2.

[31] L. Villette, *Foi et sacrements. I. Du Nouveau Testament à s. Augustin* (Paris, 1959).

[32] Augustine, *Epist.* 98, 10; *Epist.* 157, 4, 34; *Bapt.* I 8, 11; Fulgentius, *De fide ad Petrum* 73; Hilary, *Trin.* XI, 1; see also Y. Congar, in *Mysterium Salutis* IV/1 (Einsiedeln, 1972) 479, with the indicative studies.

tismal washing was preceded by a profession of faith.[33] Along with the renunciation, this profession of faith very soon became an integral part of the baptismal rite.[34] Christian writers never ceased to stress the basic demand for conversion to the Christian religion. They did this first in their baptismal instructions, either in the initial catechesis or in the sermons on the Creed.[35] Dealing with various aspects of baptism during the baptismal controversies, they insisted on the need to profess the faith. Augustine stressed the importance of baptismal faith when discussing the case of children who could not make a profession of faith.[36] Obviously the Fathers did not accept any faith but always demanded the orthodox faith. We see this in their discussions on the validity of baptism. Even those who were opposed to repeating the baptism administered by heretics did not consider any baptism whatsoever as valid. For them, the legitimacy of the baptismal rite depended upon profession of faith in the Holy Trinity.[37] It is significant in this regard that Cassian reminded Nestorius of the profession of faith he had once made in the Church of his birth. Leo did the same in his polemic against Eutyches.[38]

There is a second aspect worth considering. The profession of faith, according to the Fathers, was more than just a necessary condition for admission to the ecclesial community. For them the baptismal profession of faith, as well as other rites or liturgical prayers, constituted a theological criterion. In other words, they were applying the saying, *lex orandi-lex credendi*, more or less explicitly. This principle was enunciated by Prosper of Aquitane, a disciple of Augustine. In order to prove to the so-called semi-Pelagians the need for the initial grace of faith, he stated unequivocally: *Praeter has autem beatissimae et apostolicae Sedis inviolabiles sanctiones . . ., obsecrationum quoque sacerdotalium sacramenta respiciamus, quae ab Apostolis tradita in toto mundo*

[33] Acts 8:37; Justin, *Apol.* I, 61.

[34] *Trad. Apost.* 21.

[35] J.N.D. Kelly, *Early Christian Creeds*, and especially C. Eichenseer, *Das Symbolum Apostolicum beim Heiligen Augustinus* (St. Ottilien, 1960).

[36] Augustine, *Epist.* 98, 6.

[37] Augustine, *Bapt.* VI, 25, 47; VI 36, 70. See also J. Finkenzeller, *Ketzertaufe: LThk* 6 (1961) 131ff, with reference to canons 8 and 19 of Nicaea.

[38] Leo, *Tomus ad Flavianum: Epist.* 28, 1. See also J. P. Jossua, *La salut. Incarnation ou mystère pascal chez les Pères de l'Église de s. Irénée à s. Léon le Grand* (Paris, 1968) 269ff, which emphasizes the importance of the Creed in Leo's preaching.

atque in omni Ecclesia catholica uniformiter celebrantur, ut legem credendi lex statuat supplicandi.[39] In reality the principle had been in effect long before the fifth century. Irenaeus had criticized the Gnostics for celebrating the Eucharist without believing in the salvation of the entire human being (*salus carnis*).[40] Tertullian had likewise criticized the Marcionites, for although they used the sign of the cross, the sacraments of the Church, and the purifying of sacrifices, they were unwilling to recognize that the Spirit of the Creator was speaking for Christ through them.[41] Origen had shown the real distinction between the divine Persons by appealing to the Eucharistic Prayer in which the community called upon God the Father through his Son.[42] The baptismal order attributed by Matthew to the risen Christ (Matt 28:19) had become one of the chief arguments in favor of the true divinity of the Son and Holy Spirit during the Arian controversy.[43] This argument had acquired even greater force in Basil of Caesarea's *De Spiritu Sancto.*[44] The great defender of the divinity of the Holy Spirit had not only considered the Trinitarian doxologies;[45] he had also stressed the baptismal experience, which involved not only obedience to the Lord's command and recitation of the gospel formula, but was above all an expression of faith in the Father, Son, and Holy Spirit.[46] Augustine himself (from whom Prosper obviously drew inspiration) had concluded to the general existence of original sin from the exorcisms said over children.[47] In reply to various questions raised by his friend Januarius, the bishop of Hippo had already de-

[39] Prosper, *Capitula* 8: DS 246, with reference to *De vocatione gentium* I, 12 (*ML* 51, 664Cs). See also *Capitula* 9: DS 247, where Prosper also refers to the baptismal exorcisms, which were said over children.

[40] Irenaeus, *Adv. Haer.* V 2, 2.

[41] Tertullian, *Adv. Marcionem* III 21, 7, with the entire context.

[42] Origen, *Dial. Heracl.* 4: SCh 67, 62ff. See P. Nautin, *Origène* (Paris, 1977) 115–8.

[43] B. Studer, *Dio Salvatore*, 334f; J. Pelikan, *The Emergence of the Catholic Tradition* (Chicago, 1971).

[44] B. Studer, *Dio Salvatore*, 211–6; B. Pruche (ed.), *Basile de Césarée, Sur le Saint Esprit:* SCh 17bis (Paris, 1968).

[45] Basil, *Spir. Sanct.* 19–24.

[46] Ibid. 27 and 29. See J. Verhees, *Pneuma. Erfahrung und Erleuchtung in der Theologie des Basilius des Grossen:* Ostk. Studien 25 (1976) 43–59.

[47] Augustine, *Pecc. mer. rem.* I 34, 63. See A. Trapé (ed.), *Agostino, Natura e grazia, introduzione generale:* NBA 17/1, XCII–CIII.

veloped a significant liturgical methodology by the year 400. According to his theory, liturgical practices are to be judged by the following criteria: biblical origin, apostolic tradition, authority of plenary councils, observance by all the Churches in the case of feasts and universal rites,[48] and observance by a local Church, simplicity, and conformity with faith and good morals in the case of particular rites.[49] But if we stop to think of it, this last rule overturns the principle *lex orandi-lex credendi*. It makes right belief precede correct liturgical practice. But in any case it confirms the close link between faith and liturgy. Thus there is no question that for the Fathers of the Church the liturgy is not only an expression, but also a norm of authentic Christian belief.

4. LITURGY AND PATRISTIC EXEGESIS

The Christian liturgy took shape in the apostolic communities upon the matrix of Jewish worship. Thus its foundation is essentially biblical. But its later development, like its origins, cannot be considered apart from Sacred Scripture. Liturgical celebrations included the reading of biblical texts; moreover, they came to be in light of the passages that were chosen for them. The language of prayer reflected that of the sacred writers. The χάρις or *sacramentum* of the feast being celebrated coincided with what the *historia sacra* (as Augustine calls the Bible)[50] tells of the saving deeds of Israel's God, fulfilled through Jesus Christ, Son of God, in the power of their Spirit.

For a better understanding of this close link between Bible and liturgy, we must consider some of the more typical features of the exegesis of the Fathers. The distinctive note of patristic interpretation of Scripture can be summarized by the word "actualization." The major concern of early Christian exegetes was to actualize the sacred texts by bringing them into the daily lives of their hearers and readers. They were attempting to make the biblical narratives a vision of faith, as St. Leo says.[51] They wanted, as Basil tells us, to lead the faithful to admire the beauties of creation as described in the Bible, so

---

[48] Augustine, *Epist.* 54, 1, 1.

[49] Augustine, *Epist.* 54, 1, 1–2, 2.

[50] Augustine, *De Civit.* XV 12, 2, as well as other texts in *De Civit.* XV and XVI.

[51] Leo, *Tract.* 66, 1; 70, 1. See B. Studer, *Die Einflüsse der Exegese Augustins auf die Predigten Leos des Grossen*, Miscell. M. Pellegrino (Turin, 1975) 915–30.

as to make alive in them the memory of God.[52] They were convinced, as Athanasius says in his letter to Marcellinus, that Christians must appropriate the prayers of the Bible, especially the psalms, as their own.[53] As Augustine put it, they were guided by the idea that Bible reading must be useful, in other words, it must serve to promote love of God and neighbor.[54]

In actualizing the sacred texts, Christian exegetes did not spend much time on passages that were clear. Often they were content to paraphrase what seemed obvious. Instead they devoted themselves with great diligence (ἀκρίβεια, *diligentia*) to ambiguous or difficult texts. To clarify the *obscura*, they turned to parallel texts they thought were evident. If this was impossible, they attributed a figurative sense to the biblical words. But we must not think that the allegorical or typological meaning, as we say today, was the most important. On the contrary, what mattered was the literal sense. The figurative sense was called for only when the obvious meaning created problems for a Christian reader. The first commandment was taken literally, even though it may have been seen in the light of Jesus's love, the model of all Christian love. On the other hand, circumcision or other Jewish rites no longer practiced by Christians, were objects of a more pro-found interpretation, as the Fathers often said. But we should note that Origen, considered an allegorist and often looked down upon as such, regarded even the text's literal sense as a *sensus interior*.[55] Two things need to be stressed. On the one hand, the Fathers often ex-plained biblical texts without giving them a figurative meaning. For example, commenting on the creation of the fish, Basil presented a whole chapter of natural science, with obvious references to profane sources.[56] On the other hand, so-called typological exegesis — in which a person (Moses) or event (the Exodus) in Israel's history is seen as prefiguring a person (Jesus/Peter) or event (baptism) in Christianity — should not be reduced to a kind of figurative sense. Also emphasized were examples from *historia magistra*, models of life.

[52] Basil, *Hexaem.* V, 2; PG 29, 97C. See I, 1: PG 29, 5C; PG 29, 117BC.

[53] Athanasius, *Epist. Ad Marcellinum*, 11–26.

[54] Augustine, *Doct. chr.*, I 36, 40–37, 41.

[55] Origen, *Com. Rom.* 5, 1: FCh 2/III, 40–82, especially 40, 13; 2, 5: FCh 2/I, 190–4. See T. Heither, in FCh 2/I, 21ff.

[56] Basil, *Hexaem.* VII, 1f: SCh 26, 390–402.

Moreover, Christians compared the realities of the Old Testament with those of the New because they assumed a similarity between two religious experiences, two prophetic roles,[57] two ways of encountering God.[58]

The importance of these statements becomes even clearer in light of what we might call double exegesis.[59] Quite soon, in fact, Christian writers were interpreting the words of the Bible and liturgical data in the same manner. Origen understood the temple, altar, and statues — realities which did not exist for the faithful at that time — in a purely figurative or "moral" sense.[60] On the other hand, he explained religious gestures that were in use — such as genuflecting or turning toward the East to pray, along with the sacred times, especially the feast of Easter — either literally or in a figurative ("moral" and "mystical") sense.[61] Augustine perfected this type of double exegesis.[62] He applied the concept of *sacramentum* to the words of Scripture as well as to liturgical realities. He noted that in both cases there is no *sacramentum* unless there is a *similitudo*.[63] Two other considerations should be added. On the one hand, a comparison between biblical exegesis and liturgical interpretation helps us to understand better the symbolism dominating all Christian liturgy. The words of Scripture were understood as signs of eternal realities, of the "Word" revealed by God; similarly, liturgical rites and feasts were celebrated as sacred signs that allowed a person to encounter Christ. Even though all Christian exegetes did not share Origen's thinking, nevertheless his Logos Christology expressed the basic conviction of all, namely, that believers encounter Christ in the reading of the Bible and in the liturgy. Both contain the mystery of the Logos. If Jerome could say that *ignoratio scripturarum ignoratio Christi est*,[64] surely this well-known programmatic expression could be completed with another: *ignoratio liturgiae ignoratio Christi est*. On the other hand, based on a

[57] See the themes of Elijah/John, Jeremiah/Jesus, Moses/Peter.

[58] For example, Gregory of Nyssa, *De vita Moysis* (CPG 3159), who presents the religious experience of Moses as a model of the search for God.

[59] B. Studer, *L'esegesi doppia in Origene: ASE* 10 (1993) 427–37.

[60] Origen, *C. Celsum* VIII, 17–20.

[61] Origen, *Orat.* 31f; *C. Celsum* 8, 21ff; *Com. Io.* XIII 18, 111f.

[62] Augustine, *Epist.* 55, especially 55, 7, 13.

[63] See Augustine, *Epist.* 98, 9.

[64] Jerome, *Com. Is.* I, 1.

careful study of double exegesis, we can conclude that the liturgical use of mystery language — which was so important beginning with Eusebius of Caesarea — did not originate from contact with the so-called mysteries. Its beginnings, already seen in Origen, and its growing importance are due instead to the decisive influence of the exegesis into which such language had already been introduced by Philo of Alexandria, who was not at all interested in the "mysteries."[65]

Moreover, proper evaluation of patristic exegesis demands that we recognize its apostolic origin. It is true, of course, that biblical hermeneutics underwent further development in a Hellenistic environment, especially in Alexandria.[66] This result of modern research is beyond question. But in essence patristic exegesis goes back, as the apostle Paul attests in his letters, to the beginnings of Christianity. Although it would be difficult to prove historically, we might even say it was Jesus himself who initiated Christian exegesis. While his Qumran contemporaries were applying biblical prophecies to their own community, using the method of *pesher*, Jesus went even further. He identified the coming of the kingdom of God with his own person. He presented himself as one sent from heaven, as a representative of the God of Israel. Thus he gave a new meaning to all of Scripture. If Paul, borrowing the principles of rabbinic exegesis, would later maintain that everything the Bible has to say about the people of God is useful for Christians, he did not stop there. Like the other New Testament authors — and certainly under the decisive influence of Jesus himself — he viewed all these accounts in the light of Christ. But this statement involves a unique paradox. According to modern exegesis, the fact that the Christian interpretation of the Bible goes back to Jesus seems more certainly proven than the origins of Christian worship. The role of the post-Easter community appears to have been more important in the formation of the baptismal rite and the commemoration of the Lord's passion than in the Christian use of Sacred Scripture. But for the Fathers, who did not distinguish between the historical Jesus and the risen Christ, it was obvious that

---

[65] B. Studer, *Der christliche Gottesdienst, eine Mysterienfeier:* SA 113 (Rome, 1993) 27–45, especially 39–43.

[66] B. Neuschäfer, *Origenes als Philologe*, (Basilea, 1987); C. Schäublin, *Zur paganen Prägung der christlichen Exegese:* J. van Oort and U. Wickert (eds.), *Christliche Exegese zwischen Nicäa und Chalcedon* (Kampen, 1992) 148–73.

Christ was the *auctor sacramentorum*.[67] Justin strongly insists on the institution of the Eucharist by Jesus.[68] Tertullian loves to speak in this context about the *forma* prescribed by the Lord.[69] For Cyprian, institution by Jesus is the basis of a proper understanding of the Eucharistic sacrifice.[70] Ambrose and Augustine after him would speak of the *auctor sacramentorum*.[71] Moreover, the common exegesis of John 19, according to which the blood and water that flowed from the pierced side of Christ symbolized baptism and the Eucharist, is simply one more proof of this conviction shared by the Fathers. But it is far less certain that Christian exegetes believed their interpetation of the Bible went back to Jesus himself. Surely they were referring to the exegesis of Paul. It seems they did not pay much attention to the rabbi of Nazareth. They saw Christ not so much as an interpreter of the Bible but as its author.[72] In the wake of the Letter to the Hebrews and the Johannine prologue, they extolled the Logos through whom God spoke in the writings of the Old Testament, then in the words and deeds of Jesus, and who continues to speak in the reading of Scripture and in the liturgy.[73]

As mentioned before, patristic actualization of the Bible through exegesis took place primarily in the liturgical assembly. Origen himself, who used to explain the Scriptures to his hearers each day, is apparently no exception. He often ended his homilies with a prayer; indeed it is clear that he delivered them in a spirit of prayer.[74] This

[67] The expression *auctor sacramentorum* goes back to Ambrose. See Ambrose, *De sacram.* IV 4, 13.

[68] Justin, *Apol.* I, 66, 3.

[69] Tertullian, *Bapt.* 13, 3: *Lex enim tinguendi imposita est, et forma praescripta: Ite, inquit, docete . . .* (Matt 28:19); *Orat.* 1; 4; 29 (it should be noted that prayer also includes the Eucharist).

[70] Cyprian, *Epist.* 63, especially 63, 1 and 14.

[71] Ambrose, *De sacram.* IV 4, 13; Augustine, *Contra Litt. Petriliani* II 34, 57. See BA 28.88.

[72] Ambrose, *Exp. Lc.*VII, 50, has certainly created the most beautiful expression: *scripturae verus interpres Christus.* However, he understands this formula to mean the orthodox exegesis of the defenders of Nicaea. See T. Graumann, *Christus interpres*, 200ff.

[73] B. Studer, in *Storia della Teologia*, 438–41: "Auctoritas Dei Verbi in Ecclesia."

[74] W. Schültz, *Der christliche Gottesdienst bei Origenes* (Stuttgart, 1984) 73–119, and especially H. Crouzel, *Les doxologies finales des homélies d'Origène, selon le texte grec et les versions latines: Augustinianum* 20 (1980) 95–107.

fact is perhaps more important for understanding patristic exegesis than for understanding the liturgy. In the context of the liturgy, actualization of the sacred texts became, so to speak, even more actualizing. To celebrate the mysteries of salvation as recounted in the Bible meant to experience the saving presence of God. The exhortations and scriptural words of encouragement, emphasized by the preacher, were even more convincing in a liturgy celebrated with full participation. Melito who proclaims the paschal mystery,[75] Gregory of Nyssa who speaks of each feast's χάρις,[76] Augustine who on the feast of Christmas extols the *dies*,[77] Leo who from time to time develops the *hodie*[78] — all these merely confirm how much Christians of the patristic age perceived in the liturgy the ever-provocative timeliness of the Bible. Although the liturgy illustrates better the chief goal of patristic exegesis, which is to edify the community, the link uniting liturgy and patristic exegesis is nonetheless evident.

Lastly, anyone who wishes to grasp the full meaning of patristic exegesis must never forget that Christians interpreted the Bible according to the scholastic practices of the time.[79] Without wishing to take back what we have said about the apocalyptic and rabbinical origins of Christian exegesis, we would admit that at least from the second century — and in a certain sense even before — interpreters of the Bible approached it as they had learned in school. Recent patristic research has stressed this basic fact by referring to the works of the most famous exegetes. There is an important study on Origen as a philologist.[80] Acceptance of the ancient literary genre of *quaestiones et responsiones* has been particularly studied.[81] Much attention has been paid to cultural background in the exegesis of Jerome and

---

[75] Melito of Sardis, *Sur la Pâque*: SCh 123.

[76] B. Studer, *Das christliche Fest, ein Tag der gläubigen Hoffnung*, 517–29.

[77] Augustine, *Sermo* 189, 3; 190, 1, 1; 226, 1. See M. Pellegrino, *L'influsso di s. Agostino su s. Leone nei sermoni sul Natale e sull'Epifania*: Annali del P. Istituto "S. Chiara" 11 (Naples, 1961) 101–32.

[78] M. B. de Soos, *Le mystère liturgique d'après s. Léon le Grand* (Münster, W., 1958) 22–27; 133–34, with texts.

[79] B. Studer, *Eruditio veterum*, in *Storia della Teologia* I, 333–71.

[80] B. Neuschäfer, *Origenes als Philologe* (Basel, 1987).

[81] See the various studies in *ASE* 9/2 (Bologna, 1992).

Theodoret, to give just two examples.[82] Monographs have shown special concern for the hermeneutic theories developed in the prologues to the commentaries.[83] In this regard we need only recall the many important studies published on Augustine's *De doctrina christiana*.[84] The link between patristic exegesis — at least as it developed in the imperial Church — and Greco-Roman literary culture is perhaps more clearly seen in what we might call the *schola Christi*. This idea was first developed by Augustine, professor of rhetoric and the greatest expert on the *tractatores catholici* or traditional exegesis. According to him, reading of the classics was replaced in Christian schools by reading of the Bible. Just as students in contemporary secular schools drilled themselves on the famous writings of the past — reading them, interpreting them, meditating on them, memorizing them so as to enjoy their beauty and imitate their ideals — so Christians did the same when they read or listened to the texts of Scripture together. Augustine stresses that these new interpretations of the texts took place especially in liturgical assemblies.[85] Of course we must not over-generalize the Augustinian ideal of the *schola Christi*. However, it is significant that the idea of the Christian δι-δασκαλέιον is also found in Basil.[86] In the West, this Augustinian theme was already suggested in Tertullian[87] and was later taken up by some of Augustine's disciples: Quodvultdeus, Facundus of Hermiane, and Cassiodorus.[88]

---

[82] P. Jay, *L'exégèse de saint Jérôme* (Paris, 1985), and J. N. Guinot, *L'exégèse de Théodoret de Cyr* (Paris, 1995).

[83] T. Graumann, *Christus interpres*, 29–96, especially 33–36; I. Hadot, *Les introductions aux commentaires exégétiques chez les auteurs néoplatoniciens et les auteurs chrétiens*: M. Tardieu (ed.), *Les règles de l'interprétation* (Paris, 1987) 99–122.

[84] C. Ceriotti (ed.), *De doctrina christiana* = Lectio Augustini (Rome, 1995), K. Pollmann, *De doctrina christiana*, Diss. habil. (Constance, 1995).

[85] Augustine, *Disc. chr.* 5, 5.

[86] Basil, *Hexaem.* V 5, 4; II 1, 2.

[87] Tertullian, *Scorpiace* 9, 1; CCL 2, 1084: *alia in Christo et divinitas et voluntas et schola*. In a context that is clearly anti-philosophical we have the question of *pracepta et exempla* as well as *disciplina*.

[88] Quodvultdeus, *Sermo* 11, 1, 6: CCL 60, 441: *Haec est schola, ad quam parvuli spiritu deducuntur, ut discant a caelesti magistro non alta sapere, sed humilibus consentire* (compared to grammar and rhetoric); s. 2, 7, 27: CCL 60, 297; s. 13, 4, 1: CCL 60, 475. Facundus of Hermiane, *Pro defensione* XII 1, 4 CCL 90A, 365 (anti-heretical

5. LITURGY, AN ACTION OF THE COMMUNITY

"The Church makes the Eucharist and the Eucharist makes the Church." This well-known axiom might be expanded to say: "The Church makes the liturgy and the liturgy makes the Church." At any rate, this statement appears in an even clearer light when examined in the context of patristic theology. The following facts show this.

When they refer at different times to Christian initiation, either in catechesis or in theological treatises, the Fathers of the Church stress its community significance. They not only emphasize that baptism means admission to the community. They also point out the community aspects of the celebration, the common prayer and fasting that were part of the preparation for baptism,[89] the profession of faith in the presence of all, the kiss of peace shared by all,[90] and in particular the responsibility of the sponsors before the community.[91] A sense of community is also found in texts that discuss second penance. Penitents, it was said, should not be ashamed in the presence of the others but rather trust in their prayers.[92] As for the Eucharist, it is helpful to recall how Christian writers described the Sunday assembly. See, for example, the description found in Justin's *Apology*,[93] or that provided by the *Apostolic Constitutions*.[94] Gregory of Nyssa also has a beautiful description of the crowd that had gathered to celebrate the feast of Theodore the Martyr.[95] Van der Meer's chapter, "A Sunday in Hippo," which is a mosaic of many pieces from the writings of Augustine, is also instructive.[96] Nor should we forget liturgical forms expressing the communion of all the Churches, such as the collegial ordination of bishops, prescribed by the Council of Nicaea

---

context). Cassiodorus, *De anima* 17: CCL 96, 572 ("scholastic" context); *Exp. Ps* 15, 11: CCL 97, 142: *Schola caelestis, eruditio vitalis, auditorium veritatis, disciplina certissime singularis. . . .*

[89] *Didache* 7, 4; Justin, *Apol.* I 61, 2.

[90] Justin, *Apol.* I 65, 2; Augustine, *Conf.* VIII 2, 3. For other texts, see A. di Berardino, "Bacio": *DPAC* I, 466f.

[91] *Trad. Apost.* 20; Tertullian, *Bapt.* 18, 4. See H. Erharter: *LThk* 8 (1963) 166.

[92] Tertullian, *Paenit.* 10.

[93] Justin, *Apol.* I 67, 3–8.

[94] *Apostolic Constitutions* II, 57, especially n. 10–13: SCh 320, 314ff. See SCh 329, 42, with other studies on the liturgical assembly.

[95] Gregory of Nyssa, *De s. Theodoro* (CPG 3183).

[96] F. van der Meer, *Augustinus der Seelsorger* (Cologne, 1951) 454–70.

(can. 4). The following facts are also worth noting: election by the clergy and people of the bishop who is to be ordained, concelebration by the local bishop with visiting bishops, and the exchange of diptychs.

But it is not enough to mention these external facts. We also need to take into account the ecclesiologies underlying the community liturgy. During the patristic era, we find a whole range of models of community or Church, depending on the various times and places. The idea of fraternity prevailed at first. Quite soon we find the concept of the *Ecclesia, Domina et Mater*.[97] Beginning in the fourth century, influenced by Athanasius and Ambrose, this ecclesiological ideal was combined with that of Mary, *virgo et mater*.[98] The Church is also presented as a body. This is important because it not only took up the Pauline theology of the body of Christ, but also — at least in the context of the imperial Church — the socio-political concept of the *corpus christianorum*.[99] The ecclesiology of the City of God is at the same time biblical and political. As mentioned before, Basil, and especially Augustine and his followers presented the Church as a school. The image of a house is also interesting. This was developed above all by Augustine, but it is already found in Origen and others. Finally, the theme of the *communio sanctorum* deserves mention. At first this expression referred to participation in the holy things, the "sacraments." But around the year 400 it began to mean the communion of saints, both living and dead. This idea was not entirely new. Origen had already explained the holiness of the place of prayer, referring to the presence of Christ, the angels, and the departed.[100] Beginning with the Revelation of John, the entire patristic concept of the Church was dominated by the presence of the angels, in other words, communion with the Church in heaven, realized above all in the liturgical assembly. Perhaps its most magnificent expression is found in Augustine's *De Civitate Dei*.

---

[97] K. Delahaye, *Ecclesia Mater. Chez les Pères des trois premiers siècles* (Paris, 1964).

[98] A. Müller, *Ecclesia - Maria. Die Einheit Marias und der Kirche* (Fribourg, 1955).

[99] A. Hamman, *Corpo mistico: DPAC* I, 788f (theological concept); E. Herrmann, *Ecclesia in Re Publica* (Frankfurt, 1980), especially 201f and 183f; A. Ehrhardt, *Das Corpus Christi und die Korporationen im spätrömischen Reich:* ZRG RA 70 (1953) 299–347.

[100] Origen, *De oratione*, 31, 4–7.

Clearly these ways of conceiving the Church reflected an ideal more or less charismatic, more or less institutional. The fraternal community of the early days must not be confused with Cyprian's *institutum salutare*.[101] But it is equally clear that the different ways of picturing the ecclesial community were reflected in the different ways of celebrating the liturgy. People would gather with the brothers and sisters to offer together the sacrifice of praise, or they would enter a building set aside for worship to attend a liturgy celebrated by the clergy and to receive the gifts of Mother Church. To say *gratias tibi agentes quia nos dignos habuisti adstare coram te et tibi ministrare*,[102] is not the same as to say *gratias agentes tibi quia nos dignos habuisti coram te et tibi sacerdotium exhibere*.[103]

To understand fully the community liturgy of the Fathers, we must add a thought on one consequence of this community approach — what some refer to as "objective piety." What mattered in the liturgy of an early Christian community was not the individual believer's feelings or affections of the heart, but rather the common expression of faith. Those who attended the liturgical celebration shared the same experience. Together they repented; together they felt the joy of the whole community. Personal feelings, of course, were not absent. Augustine wept when he heard the psalms and hymns sung in the basilicas of Milan; but what impressed him most was the singing of the entire community.[104] This was just how Athanasius had first recommended that the psalms be sung, as long as the cantor was able to edify the faithful.[105] Personal prayer was certainly not absent. There is abundant evidence of the intimate conversations that more fervent Christians held with their God, or with Jesus, their master. But as Benedict admonishes his monks, personal prayer should be brief.[106] The "objectivity" of the patristic liturgy is also due to the fact that Christians celebrated on the same occasions. The feasts, or rather the festive times with their ascetical and spiritual preparation and the weeks that followed, involved everyone together. The sermons for

[101] B. Studer, *Soteriologie der Kirchenväter*, 99f.
[102] *Trad. Apost.* 4 (Version L): FCh 1, 226.
[103] *Trad. Apost.* 4 (Version E): FCh 1, 226.
[104] Augustine, *Conf.* X 33, 50. See *Conf.* IX 7, 15.
[105] Athanasius, *Epist. ad Marcellinum*, 27ff.
[106] Benedict, *Regula Monasteriorum* 20, 4f.

Eastertime attest to this, for example, Augustine's discourses on the singing of the *alleluia*[107] or the Lenten sermons of Leo the Great.[108] Finally we must note the importance of the word.

Here it is not enough to point out that liturgical celebrations involved common listening to the Scriptures, that all the members of a community were nourished by the same spiritual food. We must also remember that the early liturgy was celebrated in a culture of the Word. People did not read silently but aloud, and as a result they could always hear the words read. They were also attentive to the meaning of the word. They loved wordplays. The preachers' comments on the readings they had heard together reminded them of the public *declamationes* of great orators. These statements are certainly true above all for the golden age of patristics. But we should not forget that this period was decisive for the literary creation of liturgical prayer. Moreover, we cannot underestimate the culture of the word operative in the imperial Church. In fact, the beauty of the liturgical language, still admired today by people who are sensitive to the esthetic values of human communication, goes back to it.

Perhaps not everyone understood it as did Augustine. In his *Confessions,* inspired by the psalms he heard read in common, his language reaches heights that are indeed worthy of God, although it is too bold to speak of praise worthy of the unspeakable God. Moreover, in his hermeneutic work *De doctrina christiana,* he dealt especially with *elocutio,* showing its limits but also its value. J. Fontaine, concluding his reflection on these writings of Augustine, did not hesitate to say: "In other words, literary beauty retains a higher usefulness in the service of the Christian mission."[109] Although not everyone was as open to ancient esthetics as the bishop of Hippo, who was a former professor of rhetoric, there were many who spoke of the sweetness of the psalms as sung and heard during the celebration of the mysteries of Christ, the incarnate Word of God.[110]

[107] Augustine, *Sermo* 210, 8, with S. Poque, in SCh 116, 50f.

[108] Leo, *Tract.* 39–50, with R. Dolle, *L'entrée dans le Carême avec saint Léon le Grand: Assemblées du Seigneur* 26 (1962) 69–80.

[109] J. Fontaine, *Des écrivains à part entière: Présence des Sources Chrétiennes = Connaissance des Pères de l'Église,* 51 (1995) 12f.

[110] Basil, *Hom. Ps.* 1: PG 29, 209A - 213C; Theodoret, *Com. Ps.* preface: PG 80, 857A–865 B. See also J. Fontaine, *Naissance de la poésie dans l'Occident chrétien* (Paris, 1981) on the liturgical poetry of Ambrose, Prudentius, and others.

6. LITURGY AND PATRISTIC PIETY

The Gospel of Jesus Christ, Son of God, can never be exhausted — by no generation, culture, or time. It is too rich, too varied, too profound. On the other hand, the men and women who hear the good news proclaimed are too dissimilar in mentality, culture, and sensibility to understand it in the same way. This statement, perhaps too summary, is also true of the liturgy of the patristic age. The very fact that different liturgical traditions began to take shape quite soon proves it. Based on the evolution we observe beginning in the fourth century, we can speak of liturgical families, that is, liturgies that took shape around the major episcopal sees of Antioch, Alexandria, Rome, Milan, etc.

As a first explanation of this basic fact, we would point out that the bishops and theologians who were the driving force behind the development of the various liturgical traditions were of different cultures and experienced Christian realities in different ways. Cyril of Jerusalem could not help being deeply impressed by the holy places in the life of Jesus. Chrysostom, bishop of the imperial capital, was always open to the life of his city. Ambrose of Milan could not forget his past as a magistrate or the obligations of an ecclesiastical organizer. Leo the Great always felt that he was bishop of the Eternal City, center of the *orbis terrarum*. But explaining the variety of liturgical traditions by the characteristics of place or the talents of individuals does not yet lead us to the heart of the matter. We must also keep in mind the richness of the gospel, mentioned at the beginning of this section. Let us consider the piety of the Fathers and its diversity.

It is no exaggeration to say the piety of Paul and John is clearly trinitarian. For Paul we need only refer to chapters 6–8 of the Letter to the Romans, and for John to the so-called farewell discourse (John 14–17). It is no surpise, then, that as soon as the Pauline Letters and Fourth Gospel were accepted as authoritative, theological reflection was at once dominated by a trinitarian thrust. This is attested, first of all, by Irenaeus of Lyons. According to him, salvation comes to us from the Father through the Son and Holy Spirit, and we return in the Spirit through Christ to the Father. In Origen this trinitarian vision took on a coloring that was perhaps too philosophical, but it is still basic.[111] The theology of the image, developed by Athanasius and

[111] B. Studer, *Dio Salvatore*, 94–1–1, 116–30.

then by the Cappadocians, continued largely along these lines. A Christian's dignity is to be, in the grace of the Spirit, the image of the image of God. Although Augustine was fond of the saying *Per Christum hominem ad Christum Deum*, he remained faithful to the Pauline ideal of *Per Christum in Spiritu Sancto ad Patrem*. The persistence of these trinitarian themes is by no means unimportant for an understanding of the liturgy. Without it, we cannot fully understand why the Eucharistic Prayers are addressed to the Father. Consciousness of the Trinity perhaps did not gain the same place in the minds of Christians. But the use of trinitarian doxologies is familiar to all who attend the liturgy, to say nothing of the fact that believers continue to make the sign of the cross with which they were baptized: in the name of the Father, and of the Son, and of the Holy Spirit.

Still we cannot deny that trinitarian piety, influenced by the cosmological formulation of trinitarian theology, which took place during the second century and became problematic at Nicaea and in the ensuing debates, gave way to a certain Christocentrism. We see this in the *Christus omnia* of Ambrose, in the spirituality of Evagrius, and in the importance given to Christ in the Rule of St. Benedict. It is also confirmed by iconography, where in the basilicas Christ is portrayed as Pantocrator and at the same time president of the liturgical assembly.[112] J.A. Jungmann, in his famous work, has thoroughly studied the degree to which this Christological reduction also influenced liturgical prayer.[113] It is true that the official prayer remained Trinitarian, as has been said. But the Christocentric background left its mark on the liturgy. Christological exegesis of the Bible, as we see in the explanation of 2 Corinthians 5:19 ("God in Christ was reconciling the world to himself"), is found in the interpretation of Christ's presence in the liturgy. Just as Christ our God reconciled the world to himself in Christ the man, so the *virtus divina* which was once responsible for the miracles of Jesus is still at work in the sacraments of the Church.[114] This unequivocal statement by Leo the Great was not new. It was suggested in the sacramental theology of Ambrose and greatly

[112] C. Ihm, *Die Programme der christlichen Apsismalerei vom vierten Jahrhundert bis zur Mitte des achten Jahrhunderts* (Wiesbaden 1960) 12–28; A. S. Effenberger, *Frühchristliche Kunst und Kultur* (Munich, 1986) 140–43.

[113] J. A. Jungmann, *Die Stellung Christi im liturgischen Gebet* (Münster, 1962).

[114] Leo, *Tract.* 63, 6; 66, 4.

developed by Augustine. Ambrose had insisted on the *verba caelestia* of the *auctor sacramentorum* — words by which the transubstantiation of the bread and wine takes place in the Eucharistic consecration.[115] On the other hand, Augustine had defended against the Donatists the validity of baptism administered by heretics with his *Christus baptizat*, where he obviously means Christ as God. Still, this insistence on the divine action of Christ, which must be seen in the context of the trinitarian adage *omnia opera ad extra communia sunt*, was mitigated to some extent by these writers insofar as they also continued to speak of the heavenly intercession of the risen Christ. However, the tension between faith in the *virtus divina* at work in the sacraments and faith in the risen Christ who intercedes at the right hand of the Father remains even today. Many people repeat every day formulas such as *Kyrie eleison* or *Exaudi Domine*, without thinking much about the heavenly priesthood of Jesus Christ (Heb 7:26ff), the flesh that is eaten and the blood that is drunk for eternal life (John 6:54), the Lamb standing as if slain (Rev 5:6), or the fact that they will reign with Christ forever (see Rev 11:15).

We must end this consideration by emphasizing a theme that is closely connected with the Christocentrism of the Fathers. During the first centuries a priestly spirituality was formed that would later be summarized in the expression *alter Christus*.[116] As we know, earlier Christian writings paid little attention to the liturgical functions of the community's ministers, and when they did emphasize their liturgical role, they did not call them "priests," a dignity they reserved for Christ. But ecclesiastical writers gradually became more interested in the priestly ministry and praised its dignity. Eventually they more or less identified the ordained priest with Christ the priest. Cyprian, in his letter on the Eucharist, explains that through him the bishop-priest takes the place of Christ; by imitating the gestures of Jesus, he represents Christ himself.[117] Ambrose of Milan expressed himself similarly, saying: . . . *etsi nunc Christus non videtur offerre, tamen ipse of-*

---

[115] Ambrose, *Sacr.* IV 4, 14f; *Myster.* 52ff.

[116] J.M.R. Tillard, *Sacerdoce: DSp* 14 (1990) 1–37, especially 12f; also P. Fonk, *Alter Christus: LThk* 1 (1993) 453f (bibliography).

[117] Cyprian, *Epist.* 63. See O. Perler, *L'évêque, représentant du Christ selon les documents des premiers siècles: L'Épiscopat et l'Église universelle = Unam Sanctam* 39 (Paris, 1962) 31–66.

fertur in terris, quia Christi corpus offertur, immo ipse offerre manifestatur in nobis, cuius sermo sanctificat sacrificium quod offertur.[118] In his work on the priesthood which became very famous, John Chrysostom does not present the bishop as an image of Christ, but he does place him above the heavenly powers.[119]

This emphasis on the dignity of the priest can be explained by various factors. First, there was the influence of the biblical vision of the Levitical priesthood which appears already in the *Prima Clementis.*[120] Then there was the change from the Eucharist as a spiritual sacrifice to the Eucharist as the sacrifice of the cross. Finally, there was the formation of the presbyterate, centered on one altar in the Christian basilicas, along with the ever growing social prestige of the priest in the imperial Church. This relatively late concept of Christian ministry was bound to influence the structure of liturgical celebrations, especially the dispositions with which the clergy performed them and the faithful attended them. In the patristic age the "clericalization" of the liturgy did not yet reach the point it did in the Byzantine and medieval Churches. But the evolution in that direction is already clear.

In a certain sense we can even speak of an imperial spirituality. To the extent that Christians identified themselves with the Roman Empire, they borrowed ideas and terms from the political matrix to express their faith in Christ. Almost from the beginning the concepts of salvation and savior entered the Christian vocabulary. But it displayed the marks of Roman soteriology much more in the third century, as Cyprian attests.[121] During the age of Constantine this Roman reinterpretation of the Gospel of Christ finally gained the upper hand. More than ever, Jesus Christ was honored with imperial titles or biblical titles reinterpreted. We see this especially in the spread of the title *Dominus Salvator.* His work was described in triumphal terms. Christians had almost unanimously accepted the idea that unity of belief was the basis for the political unity of the empire. The fact that they were rooted in such a mentality had its natural repercussions in the area of liturgy. Rituals for major solemnities were

[118] Ambrose, *Expl. Ps.* 38, 25f.

[119] A. Wenger, *Jean Chrysostome: DSp* 8 (1974) 843ff: *Le sacerdoce*, with *De sacerd.* III, 4: PL 48, 642.

[120] *1 Clem* 40. See A. Jaubert, SCh 167, 48ff.

[121] See B. Studer, *Soteriologie der Kirchenväter*, 99f.

adapted to the ceremonial of the court. Political vocabulary found its way into liturgical language.[122] The clearest proof of this is the manner of celebrating feasts introduced in the fourth century. We need only recall the acceptance of the idea of the *adventus salvatoris*.[123] Moreover, it is clear that if this phenomenon of the imperial Church changed the *sentire cum Ecclesia*, it also favored the Christocentrism mentioned above. The fourth-century Christians' manner of celebrating the liturgy was determined not only by a new concept of the Christian community, but also by a renewed reverence for Jesus Christ, the true emperor and king of glory.[124] It is obvious that this "imperial" inculturation of the liturgy is understood first of all through Christian literature, especially the feastday sermons of the great bishops such as Chrysostom, Ambrose, Augustine, and Leo.[125]

CONCLUSION

Anyone ignorant of the wealth of evidence left by the Fathers of the Church to later generations of Christians, cannot discern the Judaeo-Christian origins and subsequent development of the Christian liturgy, cannot fully understand its essential structures, cannot accurately measure its faith foundations, cannot appreciate its biblical and Greco-Roman forms of expression, cannot grasp the expressive richness of its symbols, cannot admire all its beauties. Only those who get in touch with the first fathers and mothers of the Christian faith can be fully assured of the apostolic authenticity of their dialogue

[122] W. Dürig, *Pietas liturgica* (Regensburg, 1958); H. Büsse, *"Salus" in der römischen Liturgie. Ein Beitrag zur Sprache und Theologie liturgischer Gebetstexte* (Rome, 1959).

[123] G. Hellemo, *Adventus Domini. Eschatological Thought in the 4th Century Apses and Catechesis = Suppl.Vig.Chr. 5* (Leiden, Brill, 1989); P. Dufraigne, *Adventus Augusti, Adventus Christi. Recherches su l'exploitation idéologique d'un cérémoniel dans l'antiquité tardive* (Paris, 1994).

[124] P. Beskow, *Rex gloriae. The Kingship of Christ in the Early Church* (Uppsala, 1962); P. Stockmeier, *Theologie und Kult des Kreuzes bei Johannes Chrysostomus. Ein Beitrag zum Verständnis des Kreuzes im 4. Jahrhundert* (Trier, 1966); B. Studer, *Die anti-arianische Auslegung von Psalm 23, 7–10 in De Fide IV, 1–2 des Ambrosius von Mailand*: Y. Duval (ed.), *Ambroise de Milan* (Paris, 1974) 245–66; F. Heim, *Victoire*, 135–98; Idem, *Gratia Christi - Gratia Dei*, 272f, and especially S. Poque, *Le langage symbolique dans la prédication d'Augustin d'Hippone* (Paris, 1984) 99–111: "Victoire."

[125] P. A. McShane, *La Romanitas et le Pape Léon le Grand. L'apport culturel des institutions impériales à la formation des structures ecclésiastiques* (Paris, 1979).

with the God of Israel, the Father of Jesus Christ and source of the spiritual life.

Bibliography

Brovelli, F. "Fede e liturgia." *NDL* 543–555 (bibliography).

Carroll, T. K. *Liturgical Practices in the Fathers.* Wilmington, Del., 1988.

Di Berardino, A., and B. Studer, eds. *History of Theology.* Vol. 1, *The Patristic Period.* Trans. M. J. O'Connell. Collegeville, Minn., 1997.

Orazzo, A., ed. *I padri della Chiesa e la teologia. In dialogo con Basil Studer.* Turin, 1995.

Pellegrino, M. "Liturgia e padri." *DPAC* 1:1976–1979. Casale, 1983.

____. "Padri e liturgia." *NDL* 1008–1015.

Triacca, A. M. "Liturgia e padri della Chiesa: Ruoli reciproci." *Seminarium*, n.s. 30 (1990) 508–530.

Patrick Lyons, O.S.B.

6

Liturgy and Ecumenism

INTRODUCTION

To speak of the ecumenical aspect of the liturgy is to draw attention to the fact that liturgy, both as a science and as a lived experience, influences the modern ecumenical movement, and to hint too that the relation is in some way reciprocal, that ecumenism has implications for liturgy. The ecumenical aspect of the liturgy is exemplified in a special way when liturgical prayer is celebrated in common by Christians of the divided Churches and when liturgical studies undertaken with ecumenical awareness play a rôle in the renewal of the liturgy of the separated Churches. Both of these situations are in evidence today.

The ecumenical significance of liturgy emerged in modern times as a result of the growth, in the West more especially, of two aspects of renewal of church life which at first appeared unrelated, the liturgical and ecumenical movements. In the later decades of this century an inter-relationship has become both clearer and more extensive. The various Christian traditions in the West have experienced a process of convergence in liturgical practice which has proved of value in paving the way towards mutual recognition and reconciliation on the part of the Churches. Insofar as Christians of different traditions can celebrate liturgical prayer in common — for the most part, non-sacramental liturgy — there is already an anticipation of this reconciliation. Liturgy has thus come to be seen as of ecumenical importance, while conversely, the insights gained from theological dialogue between the Churches have had a formative influence on the renewal of liturgy within the individual traditions, with the result that ecumenism has for its part become significant for liturgy.

HISTORICAL LINKS

The two movements would appear to have arisen from different concerns — and in fact with different chronologies — within the Churches but they are nonetheless aspects of renewal in Christianity, and are really two members of a triad of related Christian concerns, the third of which is mission. This century has seen movements of renewal centred on each of these three concerns, with the early stages belonging in fact to the preceding century, and their essential relatedness has meant that renewal under one aspect in the end involves the others. The historical roots of the connection between them are to be found in the liturgical movement in the Catholic Church from the mid-nineteenth century. Its influence outside the Catholic Church was felt at first in Anglicanism when the second generation of the Tractarian (Oxford) movement sought to express liturgically the insights gained in ecclesiology, especially the central place of the sacraments.[1] Anglicanism in the United States (Episcopal Church) was in turn prominent in the ecumenical movement of the twentieth century, which from its earliest phase listed liturgical renewal among its concerns. This movement had received its initial stimulus from the pan-Protestant missionary movement of the late nineteenth century and in particular from the Edinburgh Missionary Conference of 1910.

SCRIPTURAL WARRANT

This historical connection illustrates a teaching already found in Scripture. There is the well-known scriptural warrant for the connection between the ecumenical and missionary concerns in the text of John 17:21: "Father, may they be one in us . . . so that the world may believe. . . ." But it is also scriptural teaching that the unity of the community is a pre-requisite for true worship. Along with Christ's admonition about the need to be reconciled before participating in the liturgy (Matt 5:24), there is Paul's exhortation to be united in mind and voice so that "you may give glory to the God and father of our Lord Jesus Christ" (Rom 15:6). "Thus ecumenism's goal becomes

[1] Cf. *The Renewal of Worship*, ed. R.C.D. Jaspers (London 1965) 4.

not only evangelisation but an acceptable doxology."[2] The existence of this triadic connection between liturgy, ecumenism, and mission is in fact fundamental for a true discussion of the connection between the first two and is being more frequently acknowledged today, especially in documents from the Faith and Order Commission of the World Council of Churches.

OFFICIAL DOCUMENTS

The ecumenical aspect of liturgy may be conveniently illustrated by referring to the documents which have emerged in modern times within the Churches and in agreements between them. Of significance here from the Catholic viewpoint are the documents of Vatican II which show a clear connection between liturgy and ecumenism. The Constitution on the Liturgy, in its programmatic first paragraph, saw cogent reasons for undertaking the reform and promotion of the liturgy because of its declared overall aim, which included among its components the fostering of "whatever can promote union among all who believe in Christ" (SC 1). The Decree on Ecumenism in its turn reckoned the liturgical movement, among other contemporary expressions of renewal in the church, one of the "promises and guarantees for the future progress of ecumenism" (UR 6). Since the same phenomenon of liturgical renewal was also in train in other Churches at that time, the statement, which referred principally to the Catholic Church, has in fact additional relevance. The decree did go on, in its practical norms, to issue a warning that worship in common (*communicatio in sacris*) was not to be considered as a means to be used indiscriminately for the restoration of unity among Christians (UR 8). While the value of prayer in common as a means of promoting unity was recognized (in the decree), the nature of liturgical prayer presupposed the unity of the praying community and therefore imposed constraints on worship shared by members of divided Churches. Hence the enigmatic pairing of principles which the council felt had to sum up its position at that point: "The expression of unity very generally forbids common worship. Grace to be obtained sometimes commends it" (UR 8).

---

[2] G. Wainwright, "Where liturgy and ecumenism embrace" in *Euntes Docete*, Analecta Wenceslao Swierzawski oblata (Kraków, 1993) 190.

These were principles concerning the connection between liturgy and ecumenism issued by Vatican II at the beginning of the Catholic Church's involvement in the ecumenical movement and they have not in essence changed. Subsequent directives, however, especially the second edition of the *Directory on Ecumenism* (1993), have taken account of the significant though far from complete convergence between the various Christian traditions, including the Orthodox world, since then and have established norms concerning even eucharistic sharing, in certain specified situations. The *Directory* encourages shared prayer, including the liturgical kind, as a means of fostering convergence of the traditions themselves: "Such prayers in common are certainly a very effective means of petitioning for the grace of unity, and they are a genuine expression of the ties which still bind Catholics to these other Christians. Shared prayer is in itself a way to spiritual reconciliation."[3] In the case of non-sacramental liturgical prayer, it declares that participation in such celebrations as Morning or Evening Prayer will enable people of different liturgical traditions — Catholic, Eastern, Anglican, and Protestant — to understand each other's community prayer better and to share more deeply in traditions which have often developed from common roots.[4] Here there is recognition that ecumenical sharing in liturgy brings not only better understanding but also some unspecified participation in the life of the other tradition.[5]

The regulations governing sharing in sacramental worship distinguish between the Eastern Churches and "Other Churches and Ecclesial Communities" — a reference to the traditions arising from the Reformation. The fact that the Eastern Churches are recognised (in *UR* 15) as having true sacraments, above all, the priesthood and the Eucharist, provides grounds for the Directory's "allowing or even encouraging some sharing in liturgical worship even of the eucharist,

[3] Pontifical Council for Christian Unity, *Directory for the Application of Principles and Norms on Ecumenism* (Vatican City, 1993) no. 108, 63.

[4] Ibid. no. 117, 65.

[5] The nature of this participation is becoming of interest in the ecumenical movement because of the prominence now being given to non-sacramental sharing, in the wake of reservations about the appropriateness of intercommunion. The term "sacrament of presence" has been used. Cf. *So We Believe, So We Pray. Towards Koinonia in Worship*, ed. T. F. Best and D. Heller, FOP 171 (Geneva, 1995) Report of the Consultation, no. 59 (e) 19.

with these churches. . . ."[6] The grounds for the decision are given as "ecclesiological and sacramental." This means in effect that the celebration of the liturgy brings to the fore an ecclesiology which at least in an episodic manner overcomes the division between the Catholic and the Eastern Churches. On the basis of the pre-conciliar institutional ecclesiology with its juridical requirements concerning unity in faith, the sacramental bond of baptism, and the acceptance of Catholic authority, such sharing would have been considered an aberration. The ecumenical import of liturgy is so powerful in this context that the sharing envisaged includes both sacramental "hospitality" extended to Christians belonging to the Eastern churches and the acceptance of such hospitality by Catholics, if it is offered.

The ecumenical potential of the liturgy is more restricted in the case of sharing sacramentally with the Reformation Churches because of the ecclesiological reservations set out in *Unitatis Redintegratio* on which the *Directory* relies. It is recognised that "by baptism members of other churches and ecclesial communions are brought into a real, even if imperfect communion with the Catholic church."[7] But the recognition of ecclesial reality in these communities of baptised is not the same as that accorded to the Eastern churches; they are considered to lack the fullness of the means of salvation belonging to Christ's Catholic church, especially "the proper reality of the eucharistic mystery in its fullness" (*UR* 22), and so liturgical sharing is more restricted and its effects less clear. The principle that "eucharistic communion is inseparably linked to full ecclesial communion and its visible expression" (*UR* 22), which logically applies in the case of sharing with the Eastern Churches also, here has the effect of excluding an ecclesial basis on which liturgical sharing can take place because of this lack of fullness of the means of salvation. Members of Reformation Churches are then in this context treated as individual Christians. Accordingly, the approach to sacramental hospitality is one-sided, when compared with the case of the Eastern Churches. Eucharistic hospitality may in some cases be offered to members of the Reformation Churches, but reciprocal gestures may not be accepted. Nevertheless, there is an interesting development in the *Directory* (compared with its predecessor of 1967) in that sacra-

---

[6] *Directory for the Application of Principles and Norms on Ecumenism*, no. 122, 66.

[7] Ibid. no. 129, 68. Cf. *UR* 3.

mental hospitality offered may now in certain circumstances include the sacraments of penance and anointing of the sick. As in the case of eucharistic hospitality granted to a member of the Eastern Churches, it may be asked what kind of communion with the Catholic Church does the eucharist effect in the case of a Western non-Catholic Christian and "episodic" would seem the only possible description. But since the sacrament of penance is in essence a rite of reconciliation — with God and with the church — the description clearly becomes problematic when applied to the conferring of this sacrament on someone not in communion with the Catholic Church. Here, as in all the cases mentioned of liturgical sharing with members of the other Churches, liturgy has important implications for ecumenical theology, in effect, for theology in general.

For its part, the ecumenical movement which had emerged earlier in the Protestant world, and found expression in the Faith and Order conferences of 1927 (Lausanne) and 1937 (Edinburgh), took account at an early stage of liturgy and included the study of it in its agenda. The 1937 conference set up an international commission to study patterns of worship (as the liturgy was usually called in those circles) and their importance in the various Churches.

The Report of this commission, "Ways of Worship," did not appear until 1951 and formed the basis for discussion of worship at the Faith and Order conference at Lund in 1952. This was a time when in the ecumenical movement studies of the traditions of the different Churches were of a comparative kind and liturgy was seen as the symbol of division, the occasion when disunity became most explicit and the sense of separation most acute. But discussion of the Report at Lund did bring the participating Churches to a new awareness of the importance of liturgy in the life of the Christian Church. It was recognised that "worship, no less than Faith and Order, is essential to the being of the church" and further that its setting is the mission of the church to the world.[8] This latter conviction was to be developed at subsequent ecumenical gatherings, helping to highlight the importance of the inculturation of liturgy.

After Lund a new international commission was established, the report of which was presented at the Fourth Faith and Order World

[8] *The Third World Conference on Faith and Order: Lund 1952*, ed. O. Tomkins (London, 1953) 39.

Conference at Montreal in 1963. At Montreal, worship was no longer discussed in descriptive and comparative terms but was seen as of fundamental ecclesiological importance. The Section IV Report, "Worship and the Oneness of the Church," described worship as the central and determinative act of the Church's life.[9] Its study was essential therefore in the quest for unity by the still divided Churches. "It is of crucial importance that we should investigate its forms and structures, its language and spirit, in the expectation that this process may throw new light upon various theological positions and affirmations, perhaps even lend new meaning to them, and thus open new possibilities in ecumenical dialogue."[10] The emphasis here is on how the study of liturgy might contribute to dialogue; liturgy as a factor promoting unity has not yet emerged in Faith and Order while it is acknowledged in the contemporaneous discussions at Vatican II as can be observed in the conciliar document. At this point Montreal does recognize, however, the link between liturgy and mission: "We heartily agree that mission is integral to worship."[11]

These discussions took place at the level of the Faith and Order Commission, the earlier movement of that name having become part of the formal structure of the World Council of Churches (WCC) when that body was created in 1948. In the WCC itself worship was also becoming an area of interest, especially because Orthodox churches were becoming members of that body, but by the time of the Fourth General Assembly of the WCC at Uppsala in 1968 a preoccupation with secularization caused worship to be treated as one of the six main topics but from a limited and somewhat pessimistic perspective, with the Orthodox fearing that worship was in fact being surrendered to secularization. But there was a certain value in the Uppsala approach in that it brought to the fore the relation between liturgy and life and recognized that however objective a thing liturgy is, it has to be related to the culture of the day. The inculturation of the liturgy remains a concern today and provides continuing evidence that linked with issues of liturgy and ecumenism there is always that of mission.

[9] *The Fourth World Conference on Faith and Order: Montreal 1963*, eds. P. C. Rodger & L. Vischer, FOP 42 (London) no. 106, 69.

[10] Ibid., no. 107, 70.

[11] Ibid. no. 126, 76.

A long-standing awareness of the connection between unity and mission in Protestant ecumenical circles brought with it a tendency to foster the missionary effort by promoting pragmatic forms of sharing, extending even to the Eucharist, between Churches which nonetheless remained fundamentally divided. The Eucharist became in this way a means of attaining, rather than the ultimate sign of, unity. In 1963, however, on the recommendation of the Montreal Faith and Order Conference,[12] the WCC arranged that future conferences should include both a celebration of the liturgy of a Church which could not conscientiously offer an invitation to members of other Churches to communicate and also a celebration where an invitation would be extended to all. Most Churches of the Reformation tradition have decided since then to allow access to the Eucharist to all the baptized, on the grounds that baptism itself provides the unity which is expressed by eucharistic sharing. But the increasing influence of the Catholic Church (which joined in 1968) and of the Orthodox Churches in the Faith and Order Commission has led to a more ecclesiological discussion of the question of eucharistic sharing and a more cautious attitude. In the course of the Commission's project on baptism, Eucharist, and ministry which came to fruition after many years of discussion, baptism was initially seen as the only requirement for eucharistic sharing, but by 1982 at Lima a paragraph on eucharistic sharing as one of the implications of baptism had been removed and replaced by a statement that the one baptism into Christ constitutes a call to the Churches to overcome their divisions and visibly manifest their fellowship.

The Faith and Order Commission has continued to show awareness that common prayer and reflection on the ecumenical significance of worship and spirituality are fundamental in all ecumenical efforts.[13] The Fifth Faith and Order World Conference at Compostela in 1993 was on the theme of *koinonia.* Its section devoted to the liturgical aspect of *koinonia* was concerned with the process of reception

[12] *Fourth World Conference on Faith And Order: Montreal 1963,* Report, no. 142 (b), (c) 79.

[13] Cf. G. Gassmann, "Montreal 1963-Santiago de Compostela 1993: Report of the Director," *On the Way to Fuller Koinonia, Report of the Fifth World Conference on Faith and Order: Compostela 1993,* ed. T. F. Best, G. Gassmann, FOP 166 (Geneva, 1994) 15.

by the Churches of the document issued by the Commission at Lima in 1982, *Baptism, Eucharist and Ministry.* The Lima agreement has attracted an attention hitherto unprecedented in the history of the ecumenical movement. It points to an emerging agreement which goes beyond the systematic theology of sacraments to the fundamental elements of liturgy and the pattern of its celebration. Thus an ecumenical liturgy becomes a real prospect and the Lima document actually includes a specially written anaphora, though it was accepted that its use on ecumenical occasions would be possible only for those Churches which already accepted intercommunion.

At Compostela it was felt that the interest focused on this liturgical-ecumenical document should stimulate reflection in a more explicit and direct way on the inter-relation between common worship and the theological efforts towards full communion, and on worship as impulse and source of strength on the way to *koinonia* in its fullness. This led to a Consultation on the theme "Towards *Koinonia* in Worship" held at Ditchingham, England, in 1994. The Report of the Consultation includes the statement: "Theological convergence, liturgical renewal, and the recognition of the indissoluble relationship between worship and mission in Christ's way, are all part of the momentum driving the churches towards koinonia in worship."[14]

ECUMENICAL LITURGICAL COLLABORATION
The Ditchingham Report noted that liturgical scholars have come closer to a common sense of how liturgy is ordered. "Working with these findings, the renewed liturgies of many churches have a common shape which creates a sense of common heritage of worship among the churches." [15] Liturgical renewal in the Churches has thus become an ecumenical enterprise and the network of relationships between liturgical texts used in the various Churches has become extremely complex. This very fact testifies to a shared sense both of the nature and the centrality of liturgy in the various Churches. There have been some landmark events in this progressive consensus. The post-conciliar liturgical reforms in the Catholic Church have been arguably the most important factor in liturgical renewal considered as

[14] *So We Believe, So We Pray. Towards Koinonia in Worship.* Report of the Consultation, no. 26, 11.
[15] Ibid. no. 30, 12.

a movement involving all the Churches. In a remarkable move, the Vatican Council (*SC* 36, §2) allowed the use of the vernacular in the liturgy, thus making a radical concession to popular participation. This had been a central demand of the sixteenth-century Reformers, and its refusal by the Council of Trent as a matter of principle, namely, that the Eucharist is first and foremost the act of Christ himself, had come to symbolize a fundamental difference of approach to liturgy, and in this important respect the difference between the Catholic and Protestant Churches since then. By allowing the vernacular, the Vatican II, and the *General Instruction of the Roman Missal* which followed[16] intended that through full active participation the eucharistic celebration should become the action of the whole people of God assembled around Christ. To this most ecumenically potent innovation was added the provision of new Eucharistic Prayers. This has multiplied the Catholic Church's ecumenical contribution to liturgy in that these prayers were based on the earliest anaphoras and so have been acceptable as models for the eucharistic prayers which other churches have been inspired in consequence to introduce.[17] It can be said that nowhere is the ecumenical aspect of the liturgy so evident today as in the chief expression of liturgical worship, the eucharistic prayer.

The influence of the 1969 Catholic Lectionary (*Ordo Lectionum Missae)* has also been extensive among the other Churches. In the United States an adaptation of it was introduced almost immediately by the Presbyterian Churches, and the Consensus on Church Union (COCU) — a group of nine Protestant Churches — published its version in 1974. Others followed with their own versions and in 1983 the Consultation on Common Texts (CTT)[18] produced the *Common Lectionary*, a harmonization of the variants of the *OLM* already in use. This is now in its second version. In England, the Joint Liturgical Group (established on an ecumenical basis on the suggestion of the

---

[16] Cf. *General Instruction of the Roman Missal*, nos. 11, 12.

[17] Cf. J.-M. R. Tillard, "La réforme liturgique et l'unité des Chrétiens," *Liturgia opera divina e umana*, ed. P. Jounel et al. BELS, 26, Rome, 1982, 232: "Plusieurs projets prévoient, par exemple, l'utilisation quasi littérale d'une des anaphores catholiques nouvelles."

[18] Begun in 1964 as a result of informal meetings between Catholic and Protestant liturgists in the U.S., its initial organization was considerably assisted by ICEL.

Archbishop of Canterbury in 1963) has produced independently of CL and *OLM* a lectionary characterized by a four-year cycle. Ecumenical cooperation in the production of liturgical texts in European languages other than English has been mainly concerned with the agreed versions of the texts of the *Gloria,* Creed, *Sanctus,* etc., but there has been some cooperation in relation to Scripture texts through the use of ecumenical translations of the Bible, though not in establishing the cycle of readings proper to a lectionary. Thus it is clear that a further international collaborative effort is needed to produce a truly ecumenical lectionary.

The collaboration in liturgical renewal and the increasing convergence noted above are directly relevant to the churches' search for visible unity. Convergence between the Churches must in the end be experienced within the context of the community gathered in prayer and in praise of God. Shared celebrations of a Liturgy of the Word or the Liturgy of the Hours offer notable opportunities in this regard, as a stage on the way to mutual recognition and reconciliation. They point the way to a fully ecumenical liturgy culminating in the celebration of the Eucharist but as yet their potential is insufficiently availed of in the Churches. This is sometimes due to a failure to discern the real though limited degree of theological accord which has entered into the life of the churches through texts developed in the liturgical renewal. These texts are themselves sometimes dependent on the agreements formulated by ecumenical theological commissions, international and local, and sometimes precede them, arising instead from ecumenical relationships of a more experiential nature. The connection between the *lex orandi* and the *lex credendi* is a complex one but it is rooted in a *lex vivendi:* each celebrating community is called to recognize and respond to grace offered in the liturgy. The grace and the challenge of reconciliation which lies at the heart of the liturgy is in the end the source of its ecumenical significance.

Bibliography

Allen, H. "The Ecumenical Import of Lectionary Reform." *Shaping the English Liturgy.* Ed. P. Finn and J. Schellman, 361–383. Washington, 1990.

Békés, G. J., and V. Vajta. *Unitatis redintegratio, 1964–1974: The Impact of the Decree on Ecumenism.* SA 71. Rome, 1977.

Best, T., and G. Gassmann. *On the Way to Fuller Koinonia: Report of the Fifth World Conference on Faith and Order: Compostela, 1993.* FOP 166. Geneva, 1994.

Best, T. F., and D. Heller, eds. *So We Believe, So We Pray: Towards Koinonia in Worship.* FOP 171. Geneva, 1995.

Jordahn, O. "The Ecumenical Significance of the New Eucharistic Prayers of the Roman Liturgy." *SL* 11 (1976) 101–117.

Jounel, P., and others, eds. *Liturgia, opera divina e umana.* BELS 26. Rome, 1982.

Lanne, E. "The Lima Text: A Contribution to the Unity of the Churches." *SL* (1986–1987) 108–127.

Losky, N., and others, eds. *Dictionary of the Ecumenical Movement.* Geneva, 1991.

Pontifical Council for Christian Unity. *Directory for the Application of Principles and Norms on Ecumenism.* Vatican City, 1993.

Rodger, P. C., and L. Vischer, eds. *The Fourth World Conference on Faith and Order: Montreal, 1963.* FOP 42. London, 1964.

Tomkins, O., ed. *The Third World Conference on Faith and Order: Lund, 1952.* London, 1953.

Part II

Historical Overview of the Liturgy

Anscar J. Chupungco, O.S.B.

7

History of the Liturgy
Until the Fourth Century

THEOLOGICAL AND HISTORICAL PREMISES
The Constitution *Gaudium et spes* of Vatican II, art. 58, declares that "the Church has existed through the centuries in varying circumstances and has utilized the resources of different cultures in its preaching to spread and explain the message of Christ, to examine and understand it more deeply, and to express it more perfectly in the liturgy and the various aspects of the life of the faithful." We acquire a deeper understanding of this conciliar passage when we read it in the light of Christ's own incarnation. The Decree *Ad gentes*, art. 10, teaches that the Church must implant itself among all peoples in the same way that Christ by his incarnation bound himself to the particular social and cultural circumstances of the people among whom he lived.

The history of the liturgy witnesses to the Church's incarnation in the culture and traditions of nations. The writings of scholars like A. Baumstark, E. Bishop, G. Dix, L. Duchesne, O. Casel, J. Jungmann, and M. Righetti, among several others, have drawn attention to the cultural underpinning of Christian worship.[1] Liturgists have become

---

[1] A. Baumstark, *Liturgie comparée: principes et méthodes pour l'étude historique des liturgies chrétiennes* (Chevetogne, 1953); E. Bishop, *Liturgia Historica* (Oxford, 1918), O. Casel, *Das christliche Kultmysterium* (Regensburg, 1960); G. Dix, *The Shape of the Liturgy* (London, 1986); L. Duchesne, *Les Origines du culte chrétien: Etudes sur la liturgie avant Charlemagne* (Paris, 1925); J. Jungmann, *The Early Liturgy to the Time of Gregory the Great* (Notre Dame, 1980); M. Righetti, *Manuale di storia liturgica* (Milan-Genoa, 1950–56).

increasingly conscious of the fact that Christian worship is so inextricably bound up with culture, that it is not possible to study its history nor celebrate it outside its cultural context. This is one of the consequences of the Church's incarnation, as it has been for Christ whose words and actions are understood in the context of the time in which he lived. This type of cultural consciousness has engendered a new approach to the study of Christian worship. There was a time when, under the influence of Amalar of Metz, who was active in the ninth century, liturgists explained rites and symbols in an allegorical way. Today we no longer make recourse to the passion narrative, as they did, in order to explain the meaning of such elements of the Mass as the *Gloria*, first reading, washing of hands, Eucharistic Prayer, breaking of bread, and commingling. These are now more adequately interpreted in the light of their historical origin.

Following art. 21 of the Constitution *Sacrosanctum Concilium*, we may say that there are three approaches to the study of liturgy, namely theological, historical, and pastoral. Though these three approaches have their specific areas of interest, they overlap and are mutually inclusive. The theology of the liturgy, for example, takes account of both historical developments and pastoral situations. History, on the other hand, unfolds the factors which underlie the Church's theological thinking and liturgical discipline. Lastly, pastoral liturgy builds solidly on theological and historical grounds. The study of any area of the liturgy should include history. We know that the postconciliar revision of liturgical books was strongly supported by historical data. The renewal of the liturgy was launched by Vatican II with an historical orientation. It is useful to remember, however, that history is grafted on people's culture. For this reason the study of liturgical history will be more integral and beneficial, if it is approached from the cultural epochs in which the Church lived.

Historical data need to be analyzed and interpreted.[2] The liturgical historian should thus be equipped with a critical mind vis-à-vis the development of rites. Every development has its historical justification, though not necessarily its value. Not every formulary, not every rite and symbol from the past, and not every feast that has been instituted has perennial significance for the Church. Thus the reform of

[2] A.-G. Martimort, "L'Histoire et le problème liturgique contemporains," *Mens concordet voci* (Tournai, 1983) 177–92.

the Roman Missal willed by art. 50 of the Constitution *Sacrosanctum Concilium* eliminated many of the medieval accretions which blurred the meaning and purpose of the Mass. Some formularies, though venerable in age, had to be modified in order to be more contemporary. The Instruction *Comme le prévoit* admits that "sometimes the meaning of a text can no longer be understood, either because it is contrary to modern Christian ideas (as in *terrena despicere* or *ut inimicos sanctae Ecclesiae humiliare digneris*) or because it has less relevance today (as in some phrases intended to combat Arianism) or because it no longer expresses the true original meaning as in some obsolete forms of lenten penance."[3] In the same way some feasts were suppressed, like the Finding of the Cross because of its legendary origin, or lowered in rank, like the feasts of the Immaculate Heart and Joseph the Worker because of their decreased political relevance.

Likewise the liturgical historian should be able to critique historical data in light of the principles of Vatican II. After the promulgation of the Constitution *Sacrosanctum Concilium* historians are called to examine their data in light of this document. Its basic principles include the following: the central position of the paschal mystery, the role of the word of God in the liturgy, active participation which involves the use of the vernacular, congregational singing and acclamations, and lay ministries, as well as the communal aspect of the sacraments and sacramentals. These are the conciliar principles with which historians are to judge whether the data they have at hand are still liturgically acceptable or not in the postconciliar Church. For example, the performance of a baroque Mass with choir and orchestra can reduce the assembly to a mute audience. This is obviously contrary to the principle of active participation.

In the course of centuries the liturgy has integrated local elements that still adorn it. Remarkable are the Greco-Roman influences on Christian worship during its formative stage. These elements need to be closely examined in order to discover their theological premises. They also need to be carefully reviewed in order to establish their relevance to today's world. Christian liturgy cannot consist merely of things from the past. In the process of examination and review it is useful to remember that sometimes the historical background of rites

[3] English text in *Documents on the Liturgy 1963–1979* (Collegeville, 1982) no. 24, 287.

and symbols more than the liturgical formularies accompanying them can be a more fruitful approach. For example, the rite of commingling at Mass is interpreted adequately by a recourse to its history rather than to its allegorical meaning.

The historical approach is also a valid way of evaluating and critiquing the implementation of Vatican II's liturgical reform. While its liturgical principles are unassailable, one can always raise questions on how they have been realized in the postconciliar books.[4] Not everything in the finished product is beyond reproach and ulterior improvement. In this context one might call into question some concrete instances of conciliar implementation by the Missal of Paul VI. Yet the historian may not ignore the fact that art. 50 of the Constitution on the Liturgy has willed a radical reform of the Missal of Pius V.

Lastly, the historical approach is useful for the correct interpretation of the conciliar agenda regarding the retrieval of the classical form of the Roman liturgy. This is an option that is articulated by the Constitution in arts. 21, 34, and 50 on the basis of historical studies done during this century on the Roman rite. By identifying its classical features the conciliar reformers were able to isolate the medieval accretions, particularly during the Franco-Germanic period. Critics have accused this option for being archeological and romantic. Objectively, however, the *romana sobrietas* and the practical sense of the postconciliar liturgy are realistic measures for fostering active participation and for encouraging local Churches to inculturate the new typical edition of liturgical books. Something similar happened from the eighth century onward when the Franco-Germanic Churches inculturated the classical form of the Roman liturgy.

THE JEWISH ROOTS

The beginnings of Christian worship are firmly grafted on the Jewish cult in the time of Jesus Christ.[5] That is why, the Jewish religion remains a constitutive element of our worship. Christian liturgy is un-

---

[4] A. Nocent, *Le renouveau liturgique. Une rélecture* (Paris, 1993).

[5] P. Grelot, *La liturgie dans le Nouveau Testament* (Paris, 1991); W. Oesterley, *The Jewish Background of the Christian Liturgy* (Oxford, 1925); R. Beckwith, "The Jewish Background to Christian Worship," *The Study of Liturgy*, C. Jones, ed. (London 1979) 39–51; E. Fisher, ed, *The Jewish Roots of Christian Liturgy* (New York, 1990) 39–51.

thinkable without the Jewish rites it inherited, without the psalms which the Church continues to pray, without the Jewish prayerful memorial of God's deeds expressed in an attitude of thanksgiving, praise, and supplications, and without the conviction that our worship represents the last phase of God's work in salvation history.

This period can be characterized, in the words of S. Marsili, as "continuity with the Jewish tradition, on the one hand, and Christian novelty, on the other."[6] This spirit of continuity and novelty explains the attitude of Jesus toward the cult of his people, an attitude of fidelity to Jewish traditions combined with the critical spirit of a reformer. We read in Matthew 5:17: "I did not come to abolish the law and the prophets but to bring them to perfection."

Jesus respected the sacrificial practices of his people. He did not reject temple sacrifices, but he taught his followers that such sacrifices should include reconciliation and communion with one's brothers and sisters (Matt 5:23-24). It is not out of place to imagine that as a faithful Jew he offered sacrifices and oblations, as on the feast of Passover. As long as the old dispensation lasted, he regarded the temple of Jerusalem as the "house of God," as the "house of prayer" (Matt 21:13; Mark 11:17). His violent reaction to those who defiled the holiness of the temple is proof of this (Mark 11:15). Yet it would seem that Jesus associated himself with the synagogue more than with the temple, perhaps because he did not belong to the priestly line of Aaron (Matt 4:23; Mark 1:38-39; Luke 4:16; John 5:59). We know that the prayer he composed for his disciples reflects the synagogal tradition of the *Shemoneh Ezreh* or *Amida*.

Like every faithful Jew, Jesus observed the sabbath. But in his arguments with the Pharisees he made it clear that the sabbath was instituted for people and that people were not made for the sabbath (Mark 2:27). Sabbath rest does not mean refraining from works of love toward those who are in need. Thus he healed the sick and performed miracles on the sabbath. And he declared: "The Son of man is Lord also of the sabbath" (Mark 2:28).

Lastly Jesus joined his people on their great festivals. He went up to Jerusalem to celebrate the Passover (Matt 26:17-19). He observed the day of Pentecost (John 5:1), the feast of the Tabernacles (John

[6] S. Marsili, "Continuità ebraica e novità cristiana," *Anamnesis* 2 (Casale Monferrato, 1978) 13–39.

7:10), and the Dedication of the Temple (John 10:22-23). Yet he announced that the time would come when people would no longer worship in Jerusalem (John 4:20-21), that the temple would be destroyed (Matt 21:1-3), and that true worshipers would worship the Father "in spirit and truth" (John 4:23-24). By this Jesus signified that to encounter God there would no longer be a need for the temple because God could be found in the heart of those upon whom the Holy Spirit had been bestowed. Perhaps his most astounding declaration on this matter was that his risen body would be the new temple (John 2:21), the "place" where all would encounter God in worship.

The reform of the Jewish cult did not consist only of critique and purification of some of its components. It involved something more profound. Jesus reinterpreted elements of his people's religion in the context of his own doctrine and mission. Thus the paschal meal was to be a meal in his memory, baptism was to be administered in the name of the Father, and of the Son, and of the Holy Spirit, and the Scriptures were to be read in the light of his person. Jesus did not eliminate them nor did he change their features, but he gave them a radically new meaning. In so doing he in fact instituted a new religion and a new form of worship, though he solidly established them on Jewish traditions. It is in this sense that we speak of continuity and novelty.

The disciples of Jesus followed the footsteps of their Master. We do not have any detailed description of the shape of the liturgy during the apostolic period, but the basic plan can be gleaned from several New Testament passages. Luke 24:13-35 reflects the Eucharist of the Apostolic Church which included the awareness that it was the risen Lord himself who explained the Scriptures and broke the bread. Baptism, which meant "washing of water by the word" (Eph 5:26) was administered "in the name of Jesus Christ" for the remission of sin and the gift of the Holy Spirit (Acts 2:38). The apostles laid hands on those who received a ministerial office in the community (Acts 6:6; 13:3; 1 Tim 5:22). The sick of the community were prayed over and anointed with oil by the presbyters "in the name of the Lord" (Jas 5:14-15). Christians were exhorted to sing psalms (Col 3:16; Jas 5:13). The first disciples continued to enter the synagogues on the sabbath (Acts 13:14) and to pray in the temple (Acts 3:1). Though they observed the sabbath, they gathered on Sunday for the preaching of the word and the breaking of bread (Acts 20:7). The apostle Paul, who was preaching in Asia Minor, hurried back to Jerusalem for the feast of Pentecost (Acts 20:16).

The actuations of the disciples, in imitation of Christ's own attitude, were marked by a sense of continuity with the Jewish tradition side by side the growing awareness of Christian novelty. Even after the temple of Jerusalem was razed to the ground in the year 70, the communities of Syria and Palestine continued to observe the Jewish cult together with Christian practices: sabbath and Sunday, synagogue and Eucharist, circumcision and baptism. Perhaps this was the context of the criticism by the author of *Didaché*, written in Syria around the year 90, against those who still observed the Jewish daily prayers and days of fasting.[7]

It is useful at this point to note that the temple, as long as it stood, was a point of reference to the first disciples. However, the synagogue more than the temple imprinted its mark on their worship which consisted largely of the preaching of the word. Indeed they considered the synagogue the nucleus of the Christian community. Even after they were excommunicated from synagogal fellowship, they spoke of their community, its leadership, and some of their rites in words that evoked the synagogue (Jas 2:2; 5:13-15).[8] But it was the domestic tradition in Jewish worship, which consisted mainly of the sabbath ritual meal, passover meal, and blessings, that had a lasting influence on Christian worship, particularly the preaching of the word (Acts 20:8) and the breaking of bread (Acts 2:46). Baptism also, as the occasion demanded, was administered at home (Acts 9:18; 10:22, 48). Thus what was distinctive of the Christian liturgy, namely preaching, baptism, and Eucharist, took place in a domestic environment.

The attitude of critical fidelity should accompany the study of Christian worship. Jesus did not abolish the traditions of his people, though he critiqued them in order to bring them to perfection. And the first disciples kept much of their religious traditions, though they saw in them the foreshadowing of Christ's mystery. The shape of Christian worship which we inherited from the past is part of our tradition, but its human components need always to be critiqued

---

[7] J. Audet, ed, *Didaché* (Paris, 1958) 234.
[8] S. Bacchiocchi, *From Sabbath to Sunday* (Rome, 1977) 157–9.

and, if necessary, purified. It can happen that liturgical norms and practices become another form of sabbath that ignores the basic law of love and service and forgets that it has been instituted to respond to human needs. It can also happen that in our liturgical celebrations we lose the sense of continuity with the Church's history and traditions or, on the other hand, become so complacent with their actual shape that we reject anything that looks new. The novelty of Christian worship is the eternal person and mystery of Christ, but these need to be reexpressed again and again in different languages, rites, and symbols in order to make the image of Christ in the liturgy more clearly visible in our time. The history of the liturgy attests to the fact that this was what the Church has done in the course of centuries.

CHRISTIAN WORSHIP IN THE GRECO-ROMAN WORLD

Coming out of the Jewish environment, the Church in the West had to face the challenges of evangelization presented by the culture and religions of Greeks and Romans.[9] How did the missionary Church cope with the new situation and what effect did such an encounter have on its worship? In many ways this question continues to present itself in various missionary circumstances. In recent history a foremost example was the tragic Chinese Rites controversy (1645–1939) revolving around the relationship between Christian liturgy and ancestral veneration which the Chinese consider the bedrock of their civilization.[10]

A certain tension could still be felt during the Greco-Roman period between fidelity to Jewish traditions and the Christian sense of independence. Such tension was present in the quartodeciman controversy. The Quartodecimans, who lived mostly in Asia Minor, kept the Easter feast on 14 Nisan, the full moon of springtime, regardless of whether or not it was Sunday. They based their theology on the typology of the paschal lamb which the Jews immolated on 14 Nisan. Easter for them meant Christ's sacrifice. Polycarp of Smyrna defended its apostolicity against Pope Anicetus who wanted them to observe Easter only on Sunday, the day of Christ's resurrection.

[9] A. Chupungco, "Greco-Roman culture and liturgical adaptation," Not 153 (1979) 202–18.
[10] F. Bontinck, La lutte autour de la liturgie chinoise aux XVIIe et XVIIIe siècles (Louvain, 1962); J. Dournes, L'Offrande des peuples (Paris, 1967).

Polycrates of Ephesus did the same in his debate with Pope Victor I, who in 196 threatened to excommunicate the Quartodecimans of Asia Minor. The controversy was resolved by the Council of Nicea in 325 which fixed Easter on Sunday in order that, as Constantine's letter on the Council affirmed, "there will be nothing in common between us and the hostile race of the Jews."[11]

Another trait of this missionary period was the Church's tenacious disdain of pagan religions. This attitude obviously originated in Jewish monotheism which regarded pagan religions as the creation of the devil. Justin Martyr, for example, accused the Mithraic rites of counterfeiting the Christian Eucharist with its initiatory meal of bread and water.[12] Tertullian, on the other hand, mocked the initiation baths of Isis and Mithras which, for their extravangance and expense, accomplished nothing, unlike Christian baptism which purified and effected salvation with a few words and at no expense.[13]

This negative attitude seems to be at work in those situations where the Church lives in a pagan environment. It is a measure of self-defense and an affirmation of its identity. Even today Christians in countries where they are a minority tend to avoid contacts with the rites of other religions, even if they are pertinent and can be suitably integrated into Christian worship. But soon after such a situation is overcome, as we observe in the fourth century when paganism began to weaken, the Church puts on a more open and discerning attitude toward pagan rites. This is the case with the mystery rites which exerted much influence on the development of Christian initiation, especially by the fourth century.[14] The Eleusinian rites, the Egyptian rites of Osiris and Isis, the Phrygian rites of Attis, and the Persian rites of Mithras all began to wane during the fourth century. This was the time when Christians began to borrow some of their linguistic and ritual elements.

---

[11] M. Richard, "La question pascale au IIe siècle," *L'Orient Syrien* 6 (1961) 177–212; W. Huber, *Passa und Ostern. Untersuchungenzur Osterfeier der alten Kirche* (Berlin, 1969); A. Chupungco, *Shaping the Easter Feast* (Washington, D.C., 1992) 43–59.

[12] Justin Martyr, *1 Apology*, c. 66, L. Pautigny, ed. (Paris, 1904) 140–2.

[13] Tertullian, *De Baptismo*, c. 2, R. Refoulé, ed., SCh 35 (1952) 65–6.

[14] Cf. E. Yarnold, "Baptism and the Pagan Mysteries in the Fourth Century," *HJ* XIII (1972) 247–67.

The mystery rites influenced the Christian thinking on the sacrament of baptism which in the time of Justin Martyr received the name φοτισμός or enlightenment. The mystery rites were in fact essentially a process of enlightenment. There existed a lexicon for initiation common to Christians and pagans. Both groups were familiar with words like λουτρόν or washing, μύομενος or initiate, μυστήριον or the rite, and μύστης or the person in charge of initiation. There were also resemblances in the components of initiation rites, like the scrutinies, the learning of sacred formulas, fasting, stripping, immersion, the putting on of white garment, and the meal of initiation. Other similarities are the *disciplina arcani* or the discipline of secrecy regarding the elements of initiation rites and the consequent practice of mystagogy after initiation in order to explain to the initiate what had taken place during the rite. There is no need to point out that while Christians and pagans shared in some instances the same vocabulary and rites, they meant radically different things.

This period is marked also by efforts to integrate into Christian worship those cultural elements that were not strict components of the pagan cult. Tertullian, for example, used the legal term *eieratio*, or cessation of contractual obligation, and such military terms as *sacramenti testatio* and *signaculum fidei* or promise of loyalty to the emperor, when he spoke about baptismal renunciation and profession of faith respectively. On the ritual side we have examples like the baptismal anointings, footwashing of neophytes, and the cup of milk mixed with honey. These rites, though employed also in mystery rites, were explained by Tertullian, Hippolytus of Rome, and Ambrose more from their cultural than their cultic context.[15] It is useful to note here that in most instances the cultural elements, whether religious or not, were vested with a new meaning through the method of biblical typology. We may consider this as the Church's way of inserting culture into the framework of salvation history. God continues to accomplish his saving plan in every age by making use of people's cultural heritage.

---

[15] These patristic examples are treated at greater length in section 3 of volume 2 under the heading: *Inculturation of the Liturgy*.

During this period we also observe the development of liturgical languages.[16] Outside Palestine and Syria κοινή, the popular type of Greek different from the literary or classical, was the language spoken by a good number of people both in the eastern and western parts of the Roman Empire. By the year 64, when the Church of Rome was established, κοινή was prevalent in the imperial city, not only among the eastern immigrants but also among the Romans themselves. Consequently the Church of Rome adopted it as its official and liturgical language. It will be recalled that during the first two centuries ten out of fourteen bishops of Rome were Greek-speaking.

The Latinization of the liturgy began in Northern Africa from the third century, thanks to the efforts of such writers as Tertullian, Cyprian, Arnobius, Lactantius, and Augustine. From them we inherited liturgical words like *plebs*, *sacramentum*, *ordo*, and *institutio*. It was also in Northern Africa around the year 250 that the first authorized Latin version of Scripture, often quoted by Cyprian, appeared for liturgical use. Pope Victor I (+203), an African by birth, made the first attempt to introduce Latin into the liturgy of the Roman Church. The result was a bilingual liturgy, Greek for the prayer formularies and Latin for the readings. This situation lasted until the fourth century during the papacy of Damasus I (+384), when Rome spoke Latin once again. However, sometime in the seventh century because of a new wave of migration from the East, the Roman liturgy became bilingual once more at least for the readings and some rites of catechumenate.

The shift from Greek κοινή to Latin and the transitional periods of bilingualism speak highly of the Roman Church's pastoral sensitivity. Though the shift to Latin in the fourth century came a hundred years later and the use of contemporary vernacular languages several hundred years after, one must admire the enterprising courage of the Roman Church whose veneration of its traditions is proverbial. Most probably it had not been easy for the Roman Church to abandon the language it had used in apostolic times and the age of martyrs. But its pastoral sense spurred it to decide in favor of a language the people understood. Nor was it without hesitation on the part of

[16] C. Vogel, *Medieval Liturgy: Introduction to the Sources* (Washington, D.C., 1986) 294–7; Th. Klauser, *A Short History of the Western Liturgy* (Oxford, 1979) 18–24, 37–47.

Vatican II to permit the use of the modern languages in the liturgy. This part of history teaches us that fidelity to tradition means adapting to the needs of people in every age and of every cultural tradition.

Another feature of this period was the domestic celebration of the breaking of bread, as Acts 2:46 and 20:7-12 narrate. Domestic liturgy was the tradition the disciples brought with them to the Greco-Roman world. The lector Emeritus admitted to the proconsul of Carthage during the persecution of 304 that "it is in my house that we hold the *dominicum*," that is, the Lord's meal.[17] Converts offered the use of their homes for the Eucharist. Among the Romans the traditional house was a four-sided structure built around an open courtyard with a well of water at the center. In large houses the *triclinium* or dining room could be easily rearranged for the Eucharist. Rome claims several such houses which can still be visited under the churches of John and Paul, Cecilia, Clement, and Pudentiana. When there were no persecutions, for these were sporadic, Christians bought houses and adapted them permanently for liturgical use. A famous example of such churches is the third-century house at Dura-Europos on the Euphrates. It had a function room which could contain a large eucharistic assembly and a smaller room for baptism.[18] The houses owned or acquired by Christians for liturgical use came to be known as *domus ecclesiae*, the house of the Church.

Whether it be for theological reasons or practical considerations, Christians did not celebrate in temples, whose *cella* would have been too narrow and dark and whose open colonnades would have been unsuitable for the meal. Nor did they celebrate in the dark underground rooms of the catacombs with the prospect of eating the Lord's supper amidst entombed bodies. They chose to continue the apostolic tradition of home Eucharists. Modern attempts to pattern the architectural design of new churches after temples of other religions seem to miss the point about the Lord's supper as a meal. The *domus ecclesiae* rather than the temple symbolizes the Christian concept of hospitality toward the strangers and the poor of the community with whom the Lord's meal is shared.

---

[17] *Acta Saturnini, Datii*, etc. PL 710–11.

[18] J. Boguniowski, *Domus Ecclesiae. Der Ort der Eucharistiefeier in der ersten Jahrhunderten* (Rome, 1986); N. Duval, "L'espace liturgiques dans les églises paléochrétiennes," *MD* 193 (1993) 7–29.

Thus the Eucharist, the distinctive celebration of Christians, was held at home because it is the meal of the household of God. This is a tradition that the liturgy has lost in the course of time. Its message, however, should continue to live on in our thinking about the eucharistic assembly as God's family, in our hospitality toward those who are strangers to the community, in our search for convivial fellowship with all regardless of their socio-economic status, and in our effort to provide people with a liturgical space where they can return to, as to their home, in order to refresh their tired spirits.

THE CONSTANTINIAN ERA

The general conditions that prevailed in the Church during the era of Constantine are well known. Free at last and a grateful recipient of imperial favors, the Church advanced with giant strides in every aspect of its life and mission. This period saw the flowering of patristic theology and the insertion of the Church into the cultural and socio-political stream of the Greco-Roman civilization. These factors exerted a profound influence on the shape of the liturgy. From an intimate household celebration the liturgy evolved into something both solemn and regal. Not only the Roman rite but also most of the Oriental rites at this time flourished within the framework of the imperial culture.[19]

The effects of the Constantinian benevolence toward the Church are immediately visible in the liturgy. After Constantine's conversion there came a dramatic shift from the simplicity of homes to the splendor of imperial basilicas.[20] These roofed structures were rectangular in shape and divided inside into three or five naves marked by rows of columns. At the far end was the apse where the emperor had his throne. Taken over by Christians, the domestic dining room gave way to the large public halls where there was ample room at the nave for the assembly and enough space in the sanctuary for the table, the ambo, the bishop's chair, and the seats for presbyters and ministers. The first Christian basilica was the Lateran palace, which Constantine gave as a gift to Pope Sylvester. The emperor ordered the construction of new basilicas on the Vatican hill where the apostle Peter was

---

[19] For further characterization, see J. Jungmann, "The Age of Constantine," *The Early Liturgy to the Time of Gregory the Great*, 12–198.

[20] R. Cabié, *The Eucharist*, vol. 2, *The Church at Prayer* (Collegeville, 1986) 7–123; E. Foley, *From Age to Age: How Christians Celebrated the Eucharist* (Chicago, 1991).

buried, at Ostian Way where the apostle Paul had been martyred, at the Campo Verano where the deacon Lawrence was buried, and in several other places outside the City such as Ostia, Albano, Capua, and Naples. On her part his mother Helena had the basilicas in Bethlehem, Nazareth, and Jerusalem constructed to commemorate aspects of Christ's life.

When Constantine decreed in 321 the observance of Sunday rest for the empire, the celebration of the Eucharist acquired a more solemn form.[21] The atmosphere and architectural ambience of basilicas demanded, at any rate, a more splendid form of celebration. The prayer formularies were rhetorically enriched in consonance with the ambient of the imperial hall. Oriental euchologies, like the *Euchologion of Serapion*, assimilated the literary traits of Hellenism: solemn and rhetorical, and a tendency to use abstract terms, like ineffable and infinite, for God. The Roman canon, which dates around this period, presupposes an ambient like the basilica. It has all the flourish of a grand Roman oration: solemn, hieratic, and literary, and the tendency to use juridical terms. As regards liturgical gestures, some of these were copied from the ones used in the imperial court, especially in Byzantium. Lastly, the space and environment of the basilica strongly influenced the development of liturgical music. While music in the house church had been rendered practically by anyone who could sing, it now required a trained choir. In the West, especially Rome, the choir was composed of clerics who were trained from youth to a very high technical standard of chant-singing.[22]

In 318 Constantine conferred on bishops civil jurisdiction over court litigations which involved Christians. Decisions handed by bishops were considered final. This implied that they, and to some extent the presbyters, had to be assigned a corresponding place in the civil hierarchy. Thus the clergy acquired the titles and insignia that state dignitaries enjoyed.[23] Examples of such insignia for bishops,

---

[21] W. Rordorf, *Der Sonntag. Geschichte des Ruhe- und Gottesdiensttages im ältesten Christentum* (Zürich, 1962).

[22] J. Quasten, *Music and Worship in Pagan and Christian Antiquity* (Washington, D.C., 1983).

[23] Th. Klauser, "Bischöfe auf dem Richterstuhl," *Jahrbuch für Antike und Christentum 5* (Münster, 1962) 129–74; Idem, *A Short History of the Western Liturgy*, 32–7.

particularly the bishop of Rome, are the imperial *cappa magna*, throne, *lorum* or the pallium, ceremonial maniple, *camelaucum* which developed into crown or miter, and gold ring. Bishops acquired the privilege to be greeted by a choir as they entered the basilica, to have their portraits hung in ecclesiastical offices, to be served at the throne with veiled hands, and to be honored with prostration and kissing of feet.[24]

The Constantinian period witnessed other liturgical developments. Worthy of note are the rites of Christian initiation which received their most developed ritual shape at this time. Both in the East and the West these rites were celebrated with great solemnity, especially during the Easter Vigil. Eusebius of Caesarea reports that Emperor Constantine, though still a catechumen, ordered huge torches to be lighted throughout the city on Easter night to honor the neophytes.[25] The description of the rites of initiation made by Cyril of Jerusalem and by Ambrose of Milan in their respective Sees shows such a solemnity and an organization as would not have been possible a century earlier.[26]

The integration of the Church in the socio-political structure of the Constantinian Empire had its effect also on the liturgical language. A remarkable case is the type of language used in the ordination prayers for bishops, presbyters, and deacons. Though these formularies appeared in the Veronese *libelli* around the year 558, they probably antedate the *libelli* themselves. The three formularies constantly use words borrowed from the socio-political system of the empire. These words are *ordo, gradus, dignitas*, and *honor* which are part of the ranking system among government officials. Parallel to this Roman system the clerical hierarchy was defined according to rank and the corresponding dignity of office and honor. Thus at this early period the ecclesiastical offices were regarded, in some way, as equivalents of the Roman institution. The Roman *senatus populusque* found its counterpart in the Church's *ordo populusque*, that is, the hierarchy and

---

[24] R. Berger, "Liturgische Gewänder und Insignien," *Gottesdienst der Kirche 3* (Regensburg, 1987) 309–46.

[25] *De Vita Constantini* IV, 22, *PL* XX 1169.

[26] Cyril of Jerusalem, *Catéchèses mystagogiques*, A. Piédagnel, ed., SCh 126 (1966); Ambrose of Milan, *De Sacramentis, De Mysteriis*, B. Botte, ed., SCh 25 (1961).

the faithful.[27] There is, of course, no question that even then the office of pastoral ministry or shepherding continued to be the basic role of persons in holy orders, but it was expressed in the socio-political language, insignia, and ceremonials of the Constantinian era.

Another trait of this period was the trend toward a relative uniformity among Eastern and Western Churches regarding the observance of some liturgical practices.[28] There were two chief reasons for this. The first was the exchange of liturgical resources among several Churches, especially in the East. Antioch, for example, played an important role in the development of the liturgy of Alexandria. Even after the separation of the Nestorians of the Syro-oriental rite from the Monophysites of the Syro-western rite, exchanges between the two groups continued in the area of liturgical rites and texts. Furthermore, several Syriac and Coptic euchologies were translations of the Greek formularies. And the Byzantine anaphora of St. Basil is actually an elaborated form of a shorter anaphora which was used in Alexandria.

The exchange of resources did not only enrich the liturgical tradition of the receiving Church; it also brought about a certain sense of universal communion among the Churches and respect for each other's traditions. Relative uniformity in the liturgy attests to the attitude of veneration with which the smaller local churches held the prayer formularies and other liturgical practices of such major sees as Jerusalem, Rome, Alexandria, and Byzantium.

For the Churches in the West the trend toward relative uniformity is explained by the tendency on the part of bishops to exercise control over liturgical texts, especially for the Eucharist. The underlying reason for this was the danger of heresy. We know that until then there had been greater freedom in composing formularies for use in the liturgy. The author of *Didaché*, Justin Martyr, and Hippolytus of Rome stated this as a fact. Hippolytus himself composed a eucharistic prayer, but he merely offered it as a model that the bishop did not have to recite from memory. All that Hippolytus required was sound

---

[27] D. Power, *Ministers of Christ and His Church* (London, 1969).

[28] B. Botte, "Le problème de l'adaptation en liturgie," *Revue du clergé africain* 18 (1963) 311–6; S. Marsili, "Unità e diversità nella Liturgia delle origini," *Anamnesis* 2, 41–5.

110

doctrine.[29] But by the time of Augustine of Hippo prayer formularies were being composed for circulation not only by those who had no expertise in the matter but also by heretics. He noted that unsuspecting people used them, when in fact they contained doctrinal errors.[30] The Council of Carthage decreed in 407 that the prayers to be used for worship should be those that had been approved by the council.

Fear of heresy was one of the chief factors for the ecclesiastical control of liturgical texts. Indeed, if these texts proclaim publicly what the Church believes, there is every reason to ensure their orthodoxy. The liturgy, after all, cannot be a theological forum where each presider is free to air his or her personal opinions. This seems to be a valid reason for the intervention by ecclesiastical authority on matters concerning the content of certain liturgical formularies.

A final point to consider in connection with the Constantinian era is the development of the liturgical calendar on the basis of the festivals observed in the empire.[31] Much earlier, around the year 120, the gnostic sect of Basilides already celebrated the Epiphany as the Christian counterpart of the Alexandrian festival in honor of Aion. This method of "Christianization" continued to be used in the succeeding centuries. Around the year 336 the Christians in Rome began to celebrate on December 25 the birth of Christ. In the Julian calendar the winter solstice fell on this day and was marked by the *Saturnalia* and since 274, also by the Mithraic *Natale solis invicti*. It is certain that the introduction of Christmas was part of the Roman Church's agenda of counteracting festivals of pagan origin. From the second half of the fourth century western Churches also kept the birth of John the Baptist on June 24, the day of the summer solstice. It is likely that the date was chosen to balance the two solstices. Another feast coming from this period which was directly influenced by a pagan festival is St. Peter's Chair in Rome. The *Roman Chronograph* of 354 assigns to February 22 the *Natale Petri de cathedra*. In February the

[29] Hippolytus, *Traditio Apostolica* 9, B. Botte, ed. (Münster, 1989) 28.

[30] Augustine, *De Baptismo contra Donatistas* 6, 47, CSEL 51, 323; A. Nocent, "Dall'improvvisazione alla fissazione delle formule e dei riti," *Anamnesis* 2, 131–5; A. Bouley, *From Freedom to Formula* (Washington, D.C., 1981).

[31] E. O. James, *Seasonal Feasts and Festivals* (New York, 1961); A. Adam, *The Liturgical Year* (New York, 1981); P. Jounel, *Le renouveau du culte des saints* (Rome, 1986).

Romans celebrated for eight days the festival of *Parentalia* in honor of their ancestors. Part of the celebration was a funeral meal called *charistia* or *cara cognatio* during which the ancestors were represented by an empty chair. This Christian counterpart was a way of honoring the apostle Peter, the ancestor in faith of the Church of Rome.

In conclusion, it can be said that the religious and socio-political culture of the era of Constantine has left an indelible mark on the Church and its liturgy. At this time the Christian liturgy became the liturgy of the Greco-Roman empire, celebrated in the splendor of the basilicas. This new form of liturgy was vested with the beauty and nobility of the imperial culture, with what was considered worthy of divine cult. Such types of celebration, with all the insignia, though modified, of the imperial past, can sometimes appear to people of today as something theatrical. But the basic question is whether we are able to separate the "imperial" shape from our liturgy without opening the door to banality, without disregarding the principle that divine worship deserves all that is beautiful and noble in human culture.

CONCLUSION

The early centuries in the history of the Christian liturgy can be considered formative under different aspects. Continuity with those Jewish traditions which Christ and the first disciples handed over to the Church will always be a characteristic trait of Christian liturgy. Underlying this assertion is a theological premise, namely that in the liturgy Christ, who associates the Church to himself, continues to exercise his priestly office whereby he fulfilled God's plan of salvation. In this sense the liturgy should be regarded as the last phase of God's interventions in salvation history. The liturgy cannot be understood outside the context of its Jewish origin.

The Greco-Roman period offers historical models to the Church as a missionary community. In imitation of this period the dialogue between the Church and the various cultures in the world must go on in a spirit of openness and, at the same time, critical evaluation. Furthermore, it should be remembered that our liturgy has inherited much of the cultural wealth of Greeks and Romans, and that much of it has passed the test of time. History teaches us to respect and even venerate sound traditions. At the same time this period tells us that it is part of our tradition as Church to inculturate the liturgy in our own times and, when called for, also to create new forms that are able to comunicate faithfully and effectively to the people of today the message of Christian worship.

The Constantinian era had a dramatic effect on the shape of the Christian liturgy both in the East and the West, as it had on the entire life and activities of the Church. The effect can be felt even today, despite centuries of changes in the shape of the liturgy. Again this era has become a solid pillar in our liturgical tradition. For most liturgical families it had a formative role and hence cannot be easily dismissed. This does not mean, however, that some of the cultural elements coming from that period, like the socio-political language, have not in fact outgrown their relevance. They may need to be reviewed in the spirit of Vatican II's liturgical renewal.

Bibliography

Adam, A. *Foundations of Liturgy: An Introduction to Its History and Practice.* Trans. M. J. O'Connell. Collegeville, Minn., 1992.

Bradshaw, P. *The Search for the Origins of Christian Worship.* London, 1992.

Jungmann, J. *The Early Liturgy to the Time of Gregory the Great.* Liturgical Studies 6. Notre Dame, Ind., 1959.

Righetti, M. *Manuale di storia liturgica.* Vol. 1, *Introduzione generale.* 3rd ed. Milan, 1964.

Srawley, J. *The Early History of the Liturgy.* 2nd rev. ed. Cambridge, 1949.

Wegman, H. *Christian Worship in East and West: A Study Guide to Liturgical History.* Trans. G. W. Lathrop. New York, 1985.

Manel Nin, O.S.B.

8

History of the Eastern Liturgies

I. INTRODUCTION

The faith life of a Christian community is expressed in a variety of sacraments and celebrations. The ensemble of gestures, words, and signs received and accepted by the Church makes up its liturgical celebration. The liturgy develops over the centuries with forms that are closely linked to the various cultures; thus the liturgy powerfully mirrors the cultural, theological, and even ethnic background of the various Christian communities.[1]

The liturgies of the Eastern Churches are often called "rites." The term is legitimate provided it refers to the entire lived experience — liturgical and theological — of a specific concrete Church, but it is inadequate if it simply refers to the possibility of celebrating the sacraments according to a liturgical usage recognized by the Latin Church as valid. The concept of rite (Byzantine, Syrian, Armenian, etc.) must be seen as a Church's theological-liturgical-cultural reality. It is *not* some theological-liturgical-cultural "suit of clothes" worn by the one Church in order to create an impression of variety and diversity. Accustomed as we are to the Latin Church with its apparent ritual unity, we may be surprised at the variety of liturgies in the Eastern Churches.

To understand something of these Churches' liturgical evolution, we need to take a quick look at their history. The origin of all Eastern Christian liturgies is closely linked to the development of the patriarchal sees: Rome in the West and in the East primarily Alexandria,

---

[1] R. G. Roberson, *The Eastern Christian Churches. A Brief Survey* (Rome, 1995).

Antioch, Constantinople, and Jerusalem, with Seleucia-Ctesiphon, Armenia, and Georgia in a secondary position. Moreover, the evolution of these liturgies was linked to the importance gradually assumed by the various patriarchal sees. The development began with those episcopal sees that stood out from the others by reason of their apostolic foundation. The early Churches tended to be clustered around the important episcopal sees, and as the circle gradually tightened, around those few sees that would later become what we call "patriarchates."

The great patriarchates with their distinctive organization — including juridic — slowly took shape over the centuries. The first mention of an episcopal see with wider jurisdiction comes to us from the sixth canon of the Council of Nicea (325), which recognized the much wider jurisdiction of the archbishops of Alexandria, Rome, and Antioch. Thus the major civil provinces of the empire also became the major episcopal sees. At the Council of Constantinople (381), the wider jurisdiction of the Sees of Rome, Alexandria, and Antioch was recognized; the episcopal sees of Asia Minor, Pontus, and Thrace still remained separate. Of special importance was the fact that the council placed the See of Constantinople, which was also the imperial see, after Rome.[2] From then on, Constantinople would extend its jurisdiction into the neighboring regions of Asia Minor, Thrace, and Pontus; this was solemnly ratified by the Council of Chalcedon (451). The council modified the territorial division of the East, accepted the full and wider jurisdiction of Constantinople over Asia Minor, Thrace, and Pontus, and enlarged the jurisdiction of Jerusalem, making it a patriarchate. Chalcedon marks the beginning of the stable arrangement later referred to as the "pentarchy" or five sees that were governed by patriarchs: Rome, Constantinople, Alexandria, Antioch, and Jerusalem.

In the origin and development of the various liturgies of the Eastern Churches, there has been an evolution that is not always easy to explain. From the celebration described in the *Didaché* or the anaphora found in the *Apostolic Tradition* to the celebration of the Divine Liturgy in the Byzantine Rite, there has been a progression —

[2] Canon 3 of the Council of Constantinople reads: "The bishop of Constantinople is to have the primacy of honor after the bishop of Rome, since this city is the new Rome."

or rather an evolution — which has left no trace in the documents or manuscripts, seeing that these have often come down to us in an incomplete state.[3]

As for the origin of the different Eastern liturgies, we can speak of two major phases.

1. The Earliest Period

Two great liturgical branches were already quite distinct at the beginning of the fourth century in the East: the Syro-Antiochene and the Alexandrine. A unity existed in both, centered around the Eucharistic Prayer.

a. Syro-Antiochene Branch. Liturgical evolution in the region of Antioch spread to every place where the Patriachal See of Antioch held authority. The result would be a liturgy that is a mixture of Semitic and Hellenistic elements. The Syro-Antiochene branch gave rise to three distinct liturgies:

1. The liturgy of Mesopotamia and Persia.
2. The liturgy of Antioch and Jerusalem.
3. The liturgy of Byzantium.

We find the most ancient Antiochene witnesses in such patristic texts as the *Didaché*, the *Apostolic Tradition*, several anaphoras, the catecheses of St. John Chrysostom, the Catechetical Homilies of Theodore of Mopsuestia, the *Peregrinatio Egeriae*, the catecheses of Cyril of Jerusalem, and the Homelies of Narsai of Edessa. The two main languages in this branch are Greek, which would attempt to dominate in Antioch, Jerusalem, and Constantinople, and Syriac (Eastern and Western dialects), which would remain the liturgical language in Persia, Mesopotamia, and at a certain point, in monastic circles near Antioch. Several anaphoras date from this first period of formation of the Antiochene liturgy: the Greek *Anaphora of St. James*, a text that must go back at least to the fourth century and which

---

[3] Baumstark, *Liturgie comparée*, 16–32. The author devotes the second chapter to the laws of liturgical evolution and proposes some rules for the evolution of the various liturgies: (1) a movement "from diversity to unity," in other words, from a diversity of texts, formulas, and rites there is a gradual tendency toward ritual unity; (2) an evolution "from sobriety to richness"; (3) a "discovery of the presence of new texts which gradually replaced those that were more ancient."

reflects the Jerusalem liturgy of that period;[4] the Syriac *Anaphora of St. James*, a Syriac version of the preceding with minor variations; the *Anaphora of Addai and Mari*, the *Anaphora of St. John Chrysostom* as well as others.

b. *Alexandrine Branch.* We have very little documentation for Alexandria compared to Antioch; the patristic texts are much more theological and much less liturgical.[5] The only clearly liturgical source from this period is the *Euchologion of Serapion of Thmuis*, a fourth-century Egyptian bishop. It contains the two parts of the Eucharist: the Liturgy of the Catechumens, and the Liturgy of the Faithful. It has two epicleses. The one before the institution asks that the "power of God" may descend upon the offerings; the one after asks that the "Logos of God" may descend upon the offerings.[6]

2. Period of Consolidation

After the fifth century, the various doctrinal and cultural currents led to a gradual diversification, or rather, mutual estrangement of the Churches and liturgical families. Antioch, although divided into two patriarchates (Chalcedonian and anti-Chalcedonian), would still remain a source of liturgical influence. During the Middle Ages the Ethiopian liturgy would be reformed based on Antiochene models. Jerusalem, too, would exercise its influence on the liturgies of Constantinople, Armenia, and Georgia. The various schisms and politico-ecclesial developments led to a liturgico-ecclesial situation in which there was an East Syrian group, an anti-Chalcedonian group, and a Chalcedonian group. From the fifth century on improvisation tended to disappear; texts and rites became fixed. After Chalcedon, the liturgy in Alexandria developed in two directions: Chalcedonian/Greek, which was to feel the strong influence of the Byzantine liturgy of Constantinople during the Middle Ages, and Coptic, which would go its own way, remaining faithful to its anaphoras of St. Mark, St. Basil the Great, and St. Gregory the

---

[4] Since the twelfth century it has been used only once a year (October 23) in Jerusalem, Cyprus, and Zakynthos.

[5] Alexandria gave the Church great theologians (Clement, Origen, Cyril, etc.), Antioch great preachers and mystagogues (Diodore, Theodore, John Chrysostom). See A. Olivar, *La predicación cristiana antigua* (Barcelona, 1991).

[6] Hänggi-Pahl, *Prex*, 128–33.

Theologian.[7] These last two are Antiochene in origin and tradition; however, owing to the anti-Chalcedonian sentiment linking Antioch with Alexandria, they come from Egypt. From Alexandria came the Ethiopian Rite, which would borrow elements from the Alexandrine and Antiochene liturgies and undergo Byzantine influence much later. The liturgy in Antioch, influenced by the Jerusalem liturgy through the Anaphora of St. James, developed into three great branches already mentioned: the liturgy of Antioch and Jerusalem, which would consolidate around the West Syrian liturgy; the liturgy of Mesopotamia and Persia, which would consolidate around the East Syrian liturgy; and the Byzantine liturgy.

The process of liturgical unification would also be slow in Byzantium; there are no texts prior to the ninth century in the codices that have come down to us. For a knowledge of the evolution of the liturgy, we must refer either to the descriptions of the Fathers in their catecheses and mystagogies, or to those of the liturgical commentators.

On the one hand, Chalcedon and the period following signaled the isolation or independent liturgical evolution of the non-Chalcedonian churches. On the other hand, the liturgy of Constantinople gradually came to dominate the Greek liturgies, that is, the liturgies of those Churches that accepted Chalcedon. In these episcopal sees, changes of liturgical texts or books were linked at times to socio-political changes — usually violent.

This period also marked the development not only of the Eucharist, but also the Office, mainly around the two centers of Jerusalem and Constantinople.[8] We find the first copies of lectionaries in Jerusalem around the middle of the fifth century. Around the beginning of the seventh century, the Liturgy of the Hours (ὡρολόγιον) developed, in accord with the various hours of prayer during the day. At the beginning of the eighth century, Constantinople had an Office for cathedrals and parishes. The cycle of weeks (ὀκτώηχος) was already developing around the seventh or eighth century, and there were τυπικά or books to regulate the liturgical usages in different

---

[7] This anaphora is addressed entirely to Christ; see Hänggi-Pahl, *Prex*, 358–73.

[8] Taft, *La liturgia delle ore*. I. H. Dalmais, "Origine et constitution de l'office," *MD* 21 (1950) 21–39, also summarizes the formation and development of the Office.

places. The most important τυπικά were originally associated with monastic rules[9] and come from the chief centers of monasticism.

Let us examine three of them: the τυπικόν of St. Sabas in Jerusalem, the τυπικόν of Studion in Constantinope, and the τυπικόν of the Great Church, also in Constantinople.

The τυπικόν of St. Sabas reflects the traditions of the Palestinian monasteries during their most flourishing period (fourth-sixth centuries). It presents a liturgy that is strongly monastic. In the night vigils, for example, Psalm 118 is given the place of honor. Thanks to the authority of the founder of the monastery from which it came, this τυπικόν spread to the Melkite Churches of Alexandria and Antioch, and in the twelfth and thirteenth centuries to the capital, Constantinople.

The τυπικόν of Studion — the monastery of that name founded in 463 in the capital — also reflects a strongly monastic structure. The Studion monastery was linked to the spiritual tradition of those monks known as ἀκοίμετοι ("sleepless ones") because they celebrated the liturgy twenty-four hours a day. This τυπικόν had an influence on Asia Minor, Mount Athos, Byzantine Italy, and even Russia.

The τυπικόν of the Great Church includes the offices celebrated in the church of the *Anastasis* in Jerusalem — until it was supplanted by the τυπικόν of St. Sabas — and in the church of Hagia Sophia in Constantinople. It contains the Divine Liturgy, Vespers, Matins, and various prayers used during Lent; it also contains the prayers of the priest and the people, who generally participated in responsorial form. This monastic influence on the cathedral office derives from the iconoclast struggles, in which the monks played a major role, and from the growing choice of monks as candidates for the episcopate.[10]

II. THE EASTERN CHURCHES AND LITURGIES

The various Christian Churches are often named according to their profession of faith. However, it would be more appropriate to label

---

[9] We may recall the clear liturgical prescriptions found in monastic rules such as those of St. Pachomius († 348), St. Basil († 379), and St. Benedict († 543), as well as the liturgical references in the writings of John Cassian (4th–5th century) and others.

[10] B. Luykx, "L'influence des moines sur l'office paroissial," *MD* 51 (1957) 55–81.

them according to their ethnic or geographic situation. In this regard it is worth recalling the divisions that arose in the Church following the Councils of Ephesus (431–43) and Chalcedon (451). We must also remember the gradual estrangement between East and West, an estrangement already signaled by the Photian Schism (863–879) and the schism of 1054.[11] We may say that the schism was caused over time by various factors. There was the East's lack of interest in the West, on the one hand, and the Crusades and the creation of the "uniate" Churches on the other.

1. The East Syrian Churches

Those Christian communities situated in Persia and Mesopotamia that are heirs to the exegetical and theological tradition of the See of Antioch are called the "East Syrian Churches." They have also been called "Nestorian" churches because their formulas of faith cite as masters such authors as Diodore of Tarsus and Theodore of Mopsuestia, both regarded by the imperial churches as Nestorius' teachers. The East Syrian Churches rejected the Council of Ephesus (431–433) and were the first to separate from the imperial Church. The founding of these churches probably dates to the beginning of the second century, but their greatest development took place under the Sassanid monarchy — from the beginning of the third century (a period of great development but also great persecution for these churches)[12] until the Arab invasions around 632. The metropolitan see of these churches was Antioch at first, and after the split, Seleucia-Ctesiphon. They were churches with a strong missionary thrust, their missionaries reaching as far as India and China.[13] These churches began to decline especially in the fourteenth century; in later centuries they suffered persecution from the Turks, Kurds, and Persians. Today the East Syrian Churches are found in Iraq, Iran, Syria, India, the former Soviet Republics, and the United States. The language of these churches was Syriac before the Muslim invasions,

[11] F. Dvornik, *Le scisme de Photius. Histoire et légende*, col. Unam Sanctam 19 (Paris, 1950).

[12] J. Labourt, *Le christianisme dans l'Empire Perse* (Paris, 1904).

[13] In 1625 a bilingual Syrian-Chinese stone tablet was found in Siganfu bearing the date 781. This stone tablet tells us that a fully organized church existed in China since 635.This church is said to have reached as far as Mongolia. See *PDOC*, art., *Église nestorienne*, 189–91.

when it was replaced by Arabic — although the eastern dialect of Syriac is still used in the liturgy. During the twelfth and thirteenth centuries, the East Syrian Churches numbered several million faithful in twenty-three metropolitan jurisdictions in Asia, China, and India. Today there are two centers, one in the mountains of Kurdistan and the other in India, the Syro-Malabar Church.[14] There is also the Chaldean Church, which is the East Syrian branch united with Rome. It is dependent upon the patriarch of Babylon of the Chaldeans, whose see is in Baghdad. Union with Rome took place under Yuhannan Sulaka in 1552, after several years of contacts.

The original cultural center of the East Syrian Churches — and thus of the East Syrian liturgy — was the city of Edessa, the axis of Semitic Christian culture which opened toward Persia and reached as far as India. Edessa was the seat of a most important theological school, one of whose greatest names would be St. Ephrem. The most important ecclesiastical center, especially after Edessa fell into Persian hands in 363, was Seleucia-Ctesifon, a city situated on the Tigris River.[15]

The East Syrian liturgy can be regarded as a liturgy with distant origins in the Syro-Antiochene branch, although gradual estrangement from that patriarchal see led this liturgical family to an evolution of its own.[16] Our knowledge of the various stages in the development of the East Syrian liturgy is based on two sources. For the early centuries there are the commentaries on the liturgy that we find in East Syria; for the later centuries we have the manuscripts (and later, the editions) that transmit the text of the Eucharist, the other sacraments and the Office.[17] Among the chief commentators on the East Syrian liturgy are Theodore of Mopsuestia († 428), author of an important body of catechetical homilies which also contains com-

---

[14] B. Vadakkekara, *Origins of India's St. Thomas Christians* (Delhi, 1995).

[15] P. Youssif, *La bibliographie classifiée de la liturgie syrienne orientale* (Rome, 1990).

[16] *PDOC* 329–34; C. Moussess, *Les livres liturgiques de l'Église chaldéene* (Beirut, 1955); F. Y. Alichoran, *Missel chaldéen* (Paris, 1982). I would also mention the edition of J.E.Y. de Qelllayta, which contains the texts of the three Eucharistic Anaphoras, various other blessings, and the consecration of an altar.

[17] The texts of the Office will be important in all Eastern liturgies, especially because of the links between all the Eastern Churches and monasticism. In the East, the only form of religious life — at least until recently — was monastic life.

mentary on the Eucharist;[18] Narsai of Edessa (fifth century), author of a series of metrical homilies rich in theological and liturgical content; Gabriel Qatraia (seventh century), author of a symbolic explanation of the Eucharist that provides good liturgical information; Pseudo-George of Arbela (ninth-tenth centuries), author of a highly symbolic commentary on the liturgy.

There are three important stages of liturgical evolution in the history of the East Syrian liturgy:

a) The reform of Catholicos Isho'yahb III (650–658) helped unify the various rites of the East Syrian Church. He codified the Office, using the major hours (Vespers, Vigils, and Lauds) almost exclusively and leaving the other hours to the monasteries. The latter were allowed to adapt Vigils by distributing the psalms in a way more suited to their customs.

b) The reform of Elia II (1176–1190) enriched the Office with a series of prayers after each psalm or group of psalms.

c) The reform of Yahballaha (1190–1223) put together the so-called *Gazza* ("treasury"), which is a collection of liturgical hymns.

2. The West Syrian Churches

Those churches that rejected the profession of faith of the Council of Chalcedon (451) out of faithfulness to the Christology of Cyril of Alexandria are called the West Syrian Churches. Belonging to this group is the Syrian Church of Antioch. It was organized by two important personages: Patriarch Severus of Antioch († 538) and Jacob Bar Addai († 578). In 543 Jacob declared a state of schism between this church, which used Syriac, and the church that would remain faithful to the Emperor Justinian (527–565), which used Greek and was called the Melkite Church. The Syrian Church, whether Orthodox or Catholic, is not very large, but there is a significant diaspora which is very important. At any rate, there are signs of a growing awareness of their own tradition and a renewed interest in liturgy and theology. Today there are about 2.5 million Syrian Orthodox in Iraq, Syria, Turkey, Lebanon, all parts of Europe, Latin America, and the United States.

---

[18] R. Tonneau and R. Devresse, *Les homélies catéchétiques de Théodore de Mopsueste*. Studies and Texts 145 (Vatican City, 1945).

As in the case of the East Syrian Churches, there is a West Syrian Church that was united with Rome in the seventeenth century. Today this Church has its own patriarchate and numbers about one hundred thousand faithful. To this tradition belongs the Syro-Malankara Church of India, whose liturgy is West Syrian.

The West Syrian liturgy is also called the Jacobite liturgy and is used by the West Syrian Churches, both Orthodox and Catholic, and to a large extent by the Maronite Church. It is a liturgy that brings together the theological-liturgical heritage of Severus of Antioch, patriarch of the city on the Orontes (512–518), who enriched the liturgy with many hymn-like compositions. We must also mention St. Ephrem († 373) as a source of many of the texts of this liturgy, along with Jacob of Sarug (451–521).

3. The Coptic and Ethiopian Churches

The Coptic Church is a non-Chalcedonian church, whose origins are quite obscure. It claims to have been founded by St. Mark and thus would be apostolic in origin. What is certain is that in 180[19] it had a well-organized episcopate with a bishop named Demetrius and a school of theology that would produce great theologians such as Clement and Origen. The Coptic Church, like the Syrian, also flourished in the centers of monasticism. The development of a Coptic literature took place at the end of the third century and especially during the fourth. At first this consisted of translations, but soon it also became an original body of literature, gradually developing alongside of and in contrast to the Byzantine Greek literature that prevailed in the capital, Alexandria. After Chalcedon, most of the Coptic Church accepted the non-Chalcedonian confession of faith. Already in 537 Alexandria had two patriarchs: one Chalcedonian and Melkite, faithful to the emperor, and one anti-Chalcedonian, which included all the Coptic communities and the chief monastic centers. The Coptic Church today is limited mostly to Egypt. Monastic life is flourishing in this church. It has suffered little outside influence, save for that of Syrian origin, owing to the fact that both Copts and Syrians are "monophysites." Today in Egypt there are two Coptic patriarchates: Orthodox and Catholic. The latter dates only from the end of the nineteenth century. The Coptic Orthodox number about

[19] Eusebius of Caesarea, *Historia Ecclesiastica*, VI.

8.5 million at present and the Coptic Catholics about two hundred thousand.

Our information about the liturgy in Alexandria is quite vague, especially for the first millennium.[20] As mentioned earlier, the Coptic Church, being non-Chalcedonian, was strongly opposed to Byzantium. The greatest development in the Coptic language took place in the fourth century, especially near monastic centers such as the White Monastery; associated with it are the names of Pachomius († 346), Shenute († 466), and Rufus of Shotep (late sixth century). The Coptic language develops the literary genre of "homily" (this term refers to homilies, biblical commentaries, and monastic catecheses) and includes translations of Greek texts.

Coptic became a liturgical language after the doctrinal controversies with Byzantium in the fifth century; even today it is a much-used liturgical language, although in many places Arabic has gained the upper hand. The Coptic liturgy is associated with the phenomenon of monasticism, and after the break following Chalcedon, especially the monastery of St. Macarius, which became the non-Chalcedonian patriarchal see, far from the capital, Alexandria.[21] The monastic culture that shaped the liturgy of the Coptic Church was of a popular nature, not overly learned, anti-Hellenic. It is a liturgy that is long, solemn, contemplative, and somewhat lacking in variety. The Coptic rite today is not much different from that celebrated in the monastic communities of Skete. There have been some influences, notably Syrian, such as those that took place during the patriarchate of Benjamin (626-655), who was Syrian by birth and promoted the literary development of Coptic. There were other reforms in the twelfth century under Patriarch Gabriel II ibn Turayk (1131–1145), who fixed the anaphoras in their present three forms. In the fifteenth century, Gabriel V (1409–1427) fixed the various celebrations in the form that is still used today.[22]

---

[20] *PDOC* 339–41; Hanna Malak, *Les livres liturgiques de l'Église copte*, in *Mélanges Eugène Tisserant III* (Vatican City, 1964) 1–35.

[21] H. H. Ayrout, *Regards sur le christianisme en Égypte hier et aujourd'hui*, in *Proche Orient Chrétien* 15 (1965) 3–42.

[22] Malak Hanna, "Le rôle de la divine liturgie eucharistique dans la vie de l'Église copte hier et aujourd'hui," *Proche Orient Chrétien* 23 (1973) 266–83.

The Ethiopian Church is another non-Chalcedonian church and is strongly dependent on the Coptic Church. It has always recognized the authority of the patriarch of Alexandria and was governed by a metropolitan chosen from among the Coptic monks. In 1959 an Ethiopian patriarch was elected, and today the authority of the patriarch of Alexandria is recognized as exclusively spiritual.

The beginnings of Christianity in Ethiopia are obscure. There were certainly Christians already in the fourth century, and it seems that Christianity arrived there via Coptic and Syrian missionaries. The liturgical documents from the first millenium have not come down to us since they were destroyed by King Amda Sion (1314–1344) and the various Islamic invasions.

The liturgical language is Ge'ez, and the liturgy is not a mere reproduction of the Coptic; there are in fact many influences, both Jewish and Syrian

4. The Armenian Church

Another non-Chalcedonian church is the Armenian Church, which solemnly condemned Chalcedon at the Synod of Dvin in 506. Armenia had been evangelized either by missionaries from Syriac speaking regions or by Greek speaking missionaries from Asia Minor, the most famous being St. Gregory the Illuminator. In 390, under Catholicos Sahag the Great, ties with the see of Caesarea in Cappadocia were definitively broken. The monk Mesrob (360–440)[23] invented the Armenian alphabet and translated the Bible and principal writings of the Fathers. Persecution, which has been the lot of the Armenian nation, has given rise to numerous diaspora. Today the Armenian Church is found throughout the world. It recognizes the patriarchal see or "Catholicosate" of Etchmiadzin in Armenia, together with two other Armenian Orthodox patriarchates: Jerusalem and Constantinople. There is also a branch of this Church in union with Rome, whose patriarch lives in Beirut.

In the realm of liturgy, we can say that the Armenian liturgy has been greatly influenced by the Churches of Jerusalem and Cappadocia; thus it is in the Syro-Antiochene tradition with Cappadocian influences.

---

[23] A monk and chorbishop, he received a good formation in Greek and devoted himself to the task of translating texts into Armenian.

5. Byzantine Churches

The various communities that remained faithful to the Christological teaching of Chalcedon gradually came under the liturgical influence of the see of Constantinople and became what would be called simply the Orthodox Churches: Constantinople, Antioch (Melkite), Alexandria (Melkite), and Jerusalem.

The name Byzantine churches refers to a group of churches dependent on the Patriarchates of Constantinople, Alexandria, Antioch, and Jerusalem — patriarchates that always remained faithful to Chalcedon. These churches are also called "Melkite" in contradistinction to the anti-Chalcedonian churches. Those Melkites dependent on the patriarchate of Antioch have always been very rooted in their own land, and despite exile and the diaspora (they gravitated to the regions of Lebanon, Syria, Iraq, and Turkey), they are among the most thriving of the Orthodox Churches. The Melkites of the patriarchate of Alexandria are Greek speaking and have never become part of the Coptic/Egyptian world. The Melkites of the patriarchate of Jerusalem, mostly Arabs, are found today in the Holy Land and are led by a hierarchy that is totally Greek. The primacy of the patriarch of Constantinople (also called the ecumenical patriarch) over the other Orthodox Churches is exclusively one of honor. He has direct jurisdiction over the Orthodox faithful in Turkey, Western Europe, America, Australia, and Mt. Athos. The Churches of Cyprus and Greece are autocephalous. As for the Orthodox Churches in the Slavic world, we may note that Bulgaria became a patriarchate in 927, Moscow in 1589. The Church of Romania became a patriarchate in 1924.

The term "Byzantine" includes a group of churches that today are spread throughout the world. They accept the first seven ecumenical councils and celebrate a common form of liturgy.

For a good knowledge of the history of the Byzantine liturgy, we must search the τυπικά, the collections of norms and descriptions regarding liturgical celebrations, which we have already mentioned. The three major τυπικά are that of the Great Church of Constantinople, that of St. Sabas, and that of the Studite monastery in Constantinople.[24] We must also know the history of Byzantium,

[24] R. Taft, *The Byzantine Rite*, 16–21.

especially that which is linked to two great centers. For the first center, Jerusalem, there are three important periods: the period before the Persian conquest (614), the time between the Persians and Moslems (614–638), and the period following the destruction wrought by Egyptian caliph Hakim (1009). For the second center, Constantinople, the important periods are these: the pre-iconoclast period; the time of the iconoclast crisis (eighth-ninth centuries); the period around the fall of Constantinople to the Crusaders in 1204, when many things were eliminated, created, or added to the liturgy, and a large number of hymns were introduced; the period around the fall of Constantinople to the Turks in 1453; and finally, the period of the Byzantine renaissance in Russia and Moldavia, when various editions of the τυπικόν of St. Sabas were made (1610, 1633, 1634, 1682). In Russia we have the reform of Patriarch Nikon, who tried to bring uniformity to the Slav-Byzantine liturgy through the use of Greek models. This reform would give rise to the schism of the Old Believers, who rejected it.[25]

6. The Maronite Church

The Maronite Church was born in, and always remained closely linked to the monastic circles adjacent to Antioch and Apamea, near the Orontes River in present-day Lebanon. The Maronite Church originated between the sixth and seventh centuries near the monastery of St. Maron. More than 530 monks underwent martyrdom in this monastery in the year 517. It is a church opposed to both the Melkites and the Syrian Jacobites; in the eighth-ninth century it became autonomous. The Maronite Church has always wished to be a bridge between East and West and has always been part of the Antiochene tradition. Its faithfulness to Rome has often led it to accept Latinization and has obscured its Eastern appearance to some extent. It is also a church strongly marked by monasticism; however, this is a monasticism with a distinctly missionary character.

---

[25] There are still over six million Old Believers *(starovieiskii)* today.

128

Bibliography

Assfalg, J., and P. Krüger, eds. *Petit dictionnaire de l'Orient chrétien (PDOC)*. Turnhout, 1991.

Baumstark, A. *Comparative Liturgy*. Rev. B. Botte. Trans. F. L. Cross. Westminster, Md., 1958.

Borgia, N. *Origine della liturgia bizantina*. Grottaferrata, 1933.

Bornert, R. *Les Commentaires byzantins de la divine liturgie du VIIe au XVe siècle*. Archives de l'Orient chrétien 9. Paris, 1966.

Botte, B., and others. *Eucharisties d'Orient et d'Occident*. 2 vols. LO 46–47. Paris, 1970.

Bouyer, L. *Architeturra e liturgia*. Bose, 1994.

Dalmais, I.-H. *Introduction to the Liturgy*. Trans. R. Capel. Baltimore, 1961.

_____. *Le liturgie orientali*. Rome, 1982.

_____. "Quelques grands thèmes théologiques des anaphores orientales." In B. Botte and others, *Eucharisties d'Orient et d'Occident*, 2:179–195. LO 46–47. Paris, 1970.

De Meester, P. *Studi di rito bizantino*. Bk. 1, pt. 4, Rituale-benedizionale bizantino. Rome, 1930.

Evdokimov, P. *La prière de Église d'Orient: Approches oecumeniques*. Paris, 1966.

Gelsi, D. "Liturgie orientali." *NDL* 983–1007.

Gonzalez Fuente, A. *Preghiere eucaristiche della tradizione cristiana*. Padua, 1983.

Hänggi, A., and I. Pahl. *Prex eucharistica: Textus e variis liturgiis antiquioribus selecti*. Spicilegium Friburgense 12. Fribourg, 1968.

Hanssens, J. M. *Institutiones liturgicae de ritibus orientalibus*. Rome, 1930.

Janeras, S. *Introductio in liturgias orientales* (pro manuscripto).

_____. *Bibliografia sulle liturgie orientali*. 1961–1967 (pro manuscripto).

Nin, M. "The Liturgical Heritage of the Eastern Churches." In *Catholic Eastern Churches: Heritage and Identity*. Rome, 1994.

Paprocki, H. *Le mystère de l'eucharistie*. Paris, 1993.

Raes, A. *Introductio in liturgiam orientalem*. Rome, 1962.

Salaville, S. *An Introduction to the Study of Eastern Liturgies*. London, 1938.

Taft, R. *Introduzione allo studio delle liturgie orientali: Bibliografia essenziale*. (manuscript). Rome, 1982.

____ . *The Liturgy of the Hours in East and West: The Origins of the Divine Office and Its Meaning for Today.* 2nd rev. ed. Collegeville, Minn., 1993.

____ . *The Byzantine Rite: A Short History.* American Essays in Liturgy. Collegeville, Minn., 1992.

Tisserand, E. *Petit paroisien des liturgies orientales.* Harissa (Lebanon), 1941.

Yousif, P., ed. *La bibliographie classifiée de la liturgie syrienne orientale.* Rome, 1990.

Anscar J. Chupungco, O.S.B.

9

History of the Roman Liturgy
Until the Fifteenth Century

THE EARLY SHAPE OF THE LITURGY IN ROME

The history of the Roman liturgy began with the spread of the Gospel in the Eternal City around the year 64. We possess significant data allowing us to reconstruct, to a point, the liturgical life of the Roman Church during the first three hundred years. Justin Martyr has recorded for us how the rites of Christian initiation and the Sunday Eucharist were celebrated in Rome before the year 165.[1] His description of the baptismal rite is meager but essential. It consisted of a pre-baptismal catechesis, prayer and fasting, washing in a pool (?) of water in the name of the Trinity (with a formulary that is evocative of an early creed), and Eucharist. His description of the Sunday Eucharist is more detailed. He mentions the following elements: readings from the writings of the Apostles and the prophets, homily, intercessions, presentation of bread and wine with water, a long prayer (representing the Eucharistic Prayer), Communion, and donations for the needy and the upkeep of community guests. He also mentions a presider (the bishop of Rome) and the ministries of lector and deacon. Justin further informs us that for these Sunday Eucharists people came from all over the city and the surrounding areas.

It is useful to note here that the third-century *Apostolic Tradition*, attributed to Hippolytus of Rome, offers greater details on liturgical practices ranging from initiation, Eucharist, and ordination to daily

---

[1] *1 Apology*, c. 61–62; 65, 67, L. Pautigny, ed. (Paris, 1904).

prayers. But we have no assurance that this book represents the liturgy in third-century Rome.

From archeology we know that the Christians of Rome met in the *domus ecclesiae*, the houses offered by converts for liturgical use. Celebrated are those found under the churches of John and Paul, Cecilia, Clement, and Pudentiana. The plan of these Greco-Roman houses made them suitable for the Eucharist, baptisms, and probably for catechetical instructions. In time of peace Christians even bought buildings and transformed them into *domus ecclesiae*. We are told that Emperor Alexander Severus (✝ 235) chose to sell to the Christians a public building, "for it would be better that a god, of whatever sort, be adored there rather than to use the building for the sale of drinks."[2]

As regards the eucharistic vessels, it seems that in the first century wicker baskets were used, since these were the normal bread containers used at home. One of the frescoes in the catacomb of Callixtus depicts seven baskets containing the eucharistic bread. Wine, on the other hand, was stored in pitchers or jars. These were often earthenware, though some were made of metal. By the early third century wicker baskets gave way to glass and metal patens. The *Liber Pontificalis* mentions in the notices on Pope Zephyrinus (✝ 217) and Pope Urban I (✝ 230) that the former required glass patens for the Eucharist and that the latter donated twenty-five silver patens.[3]

The language of the liturgy of Rome until the fourth century was generally the Greek κοίνή, though Pope Victor I (✝ 198) made efforts to introduce Latin. By the middle of the third century, a Latin version of the Scriptures was being used for the readings, while the prayer formularies were still in Greek. Little of this Hellenistic heritage survived. A brief quotation from the early Roman anaphora in Greek can be found in a writing of Marius Victorinus in 360.[4] It is interesting to note that while the liturgy did not make a complete transition to Latin until the papacy of Damasus I (✝ 384), the Roman Church had already adopted it around the year 250 as its official language.[5] From

---

[2] See R. Cabié, *History of the Mass* (Washington, D.C., 1992) 22.

[3] *Le Liber Pontificalis*, vol 1, L. Duchesne, ed. (Paris, 1955) 139, 143; see E. Foley, *From Age to Age: How Christians Celebrated the Eucharist* (Chicago, 1991).

[4] *Adversus Arium* II, 8, SCh 68, 416.

[5] C. Vogel, *Medieval Liturgy. An Introduction to the Sources* (Washington, D.C., 1986) 293–7.

then on until the reform of Vatican II, Latin would be stubbornly retained as the language of the Roman liturgy. Exceptions are the Roman liturgy in Slavonic authored in the ninth century by Cyril and Methodius, the request for vernacular liturgy made by Quirini and Justiniani in 1513, and the attempt by the Synod of Pistoia in 1786 to shift to Italian.

As regards the liturgical calendar, the Roman Church concentrated on Sunday as the day of the synaxis. On the day of the sun, as Justin Martyr had called it, the faithful gathered in one place for the Eucharist. It would seem that baptisms also took place on Sunday, as we can gather from the same writer who ties up baptism with the second part of the eucharistic celebration, that is, from the kiss of peace and the intercessions onward. The Quartodeciman controversy brought to evidence that the predecessors of Pope Victor I forbade for the Roman Church the celebration of Easter on 14 Nisan. The difference between them and Pope Victor was that they did not prohibit the Quartodecimans in Rome to keep their traditional date for Easter.[6] Pentecost as conclusion to Easter did not surface as a liturgical feast until the fourth century. However, the cult of martyrs which probably included the Eucharist and the Christianized form of *refrigerium* can be dated at least from the third century.[7]

The artistic representations in the *domus ecclesiae* and the catacombs have special value for the liturgical history of Rome for these murals reflect the biblical and theological themes of the liturgical celebrations. Examples from Scriptures are the sacrifice of Isaac, Moses drawing water from the rock, Jonah the prophet, the three young men in the furnace, Daniel among lions, Mary and the Child, the adoration of the magi, the baptism of Jesus, the Samaritan woman, the multiplication of loaves, the resurrection of Lazarus, the healing of the paralytic and the blind man, and the good shepherd. Other examples are the woman (Church) at prayer, baskets of bread loaves, fish, and boat. From these representations we are able to get an idea of how the Church of Rome based its liturgical rites of initiation and Eucharist on biblical themes and explained them accordingly. Their presence in the catacombs does not imply that these sacraments were

[6] A. Chavasse, *La liturgie de la ville de Rome*, 21–25.

[7] M. Augé, "I santi nella celebrazione del mistero di Cristo," *Anamnesis* 6, 247–59.

celebrated there. Rather, it underlines the relationship between Christian death and the sacraments.[8]

In many ways this early shape of the liturgy in Rome was not distinctive of the city. House churches, the basic plan for Christian initiation and the Eucharist, the liturgical calendar, liturgical furnishings and arts, and the use of Greek were common at this time to East and West. Several of these elements were developments of the original core of Christian worship. The Roman Church was rooted in the early Christian traditions and showed deep attachment to much of its Jewish heritage. Indeed the Roman liturgy, which evolved after the fourth century, was to a large extent a reworking of this original core. No wonder that as far as the twentieth century the Constitution on the Liturgy of Vatican II, art. 23, insists on retaining "sound tradition" while keeping the way open to "legitimate progress."

The era of freedom under Constantine caused frenetic development in every sector of the liturgy, but it did not produce the liturgy which we know today as the Roman liturgy. It was only toward the end of the fourth century that the liturgy in Rome acquired the cultural traits that strongly contributed to the formation of a Roman liturgy, a liturgy developed by Roman popes for the Roman people.

THE CLASSICAL ERA OF THE ROMAN LITURGY

The study of the Roman liturgy made by E. Bishop at the beginning of the twentieth century made scholars deeply aware of its original characteristics. These had been influenced by what he called "the genius" of the Roman people. Today we would speak of cultural values, linguistic and ritual patterns, and institutions or, in short, the components of the Roman culture around the fifth century.[9]

The adaptations made in the Roman liturgy beginning in the eighth century when the Franco-Germanic Churches adopted it obscured the original Roman genius. By the process of eliminating medieval accretions it became evident that the original core of the Roman liturgy was not dramatic but sober, not prolix in language and rites but simple, not symbolic in its gestures but practical and

---

[8] F. Van der Meer - C. Mohrmann, *Bildatlas der frühchristlichen Welt* (Gütersloh, 1959); A.-G. Martimort, "L'iconographie des catacombes et la catéchèse antique," *Rivista di Archeologia Cristiana* 25 (1949) 105–14.

[9] E. Bishop, "The Genius of the Roman Rite," *Liturgica Historica*, 2–9.

functional. Historians, like B. Neunheuser, would refer to this as the "pure" shape of the Roman liturgy.[10] The underpinning consideration here is that prior to the introduction of cultural elements from the Churches across the Alps, the Roman liturgy had possessed texts and rites that were proper to the people of Rome toward the fifth century.

The nomenclature "pure" Roman liturgy, however, is quite relative. We know that non-Roman elements had been introduced into the liturgy of Rome before the eighth century. Feasts, like the *Hypapante*, known today as the Presentation in the Temple, came to Rome from the East in the seventh century together with the Nativity of Mary.[11] The *Agnus Dei* for the fraction of bread became part of the Roman Mass during the papacy of Pope Sergius I (✝ 701) who was of Syrian origin. Although Rome was celebrated for its auto-sufficiency in several sectors, it was not totally estranged from developments that were taking place in other Churches, especially Jerusalem.

Another way to describe this period is to call it "classical." In ancient Rome the word *classicus*, from *classis*, referred to the superior cultural division of the Roman population. The *homo classicus* was a person who had been formed in the Greek and Roman philosophical thought and educated in classical grammar, rhetorics, and arts: in short, a person of culture. Today we speak of "classic" as the model or standard and authoritative expression of literature, music, painting, sculpture, and architecture according to the principles and methods of ancient Greeks and Romans. By definition "classic" is synonymous with such qualities as balance, restraint or sobriety, noble simplicity, orderliness, solemnity, and directness. These qualities define the classical Roman liturgy that began to evolve after the fourth century, thanks to the creativity of such Roman bishops as Damasus (✝ 384), Innocent I (✝ 417), Leo the Great (✝ 461), Gelasius (✝ 496), Vigilius (✝ 555), and Gregory the Great (✝ 604).

To have a deeper appreciation of the classical shape of the Roman liturgy it is necessary to examine closely its chief components. B. Neunheuser distinguishes two: the formal and the theological.[12] The formal components include the ritual elements, like the plan of the

[10] *Storia della liturgia attraverso le epoche culturali*, 55–70; see A. Triacca, "Tra idealizzazione e realtà: liturgia romana 'pura'?" *RL* 45 (1993) 413–42.

[11] P. Jounel, *Le renouveau du culte des saints* (Rome, 1986) 100–180.

[12] *Storia della liturgia attraverso le epoche culturali*, 64–6.

celebration, gestures, and symbols, as well as the corpus of liturgical texts, especially the euchological formularies. The theological components, on the other hand, embrace the doctrinal and spiritual message contained in the ritual elements and texts.

As a preliminary consideration, it is useful to note that upon these formal and theological components the Roman cultural values, patterns, and institutions of the fifth century have exerted a remarkable influence. Simplicity, sobriety, and practical sense are deeply etched in the rites, while the euchological formularies are marked by restraint, brevity, and directness. The detailed studies made by A. Chavasse of the classical shape of the Roman liturgy are most enlightening.[13]

As regards the formal components, we note that the classical Roman "genius" was very much at work in the papal Mass described by *Ordo Romanus I* which was compiled in the seventh century, though it represents an earlier material.[14] During the Eucharistic Prayer the pope stood at the altar alone (*surgit pontifex solus in canone*) and recited the prayer with no further ceremonies and without the assistance of hovering and ubiquitous masters of ceremonies. No candles were brought into the sanctuary at the words of consecration, no bells were rung, no incensation of the sacred species was made, and there were no genuflections and signs of the cross. At the doxology the archdeacon alone stood at the altar to raise the cup. During the entire canon all the "concelebrants" stayed in their places at the far end of the sanctuary.

Practical sense is present in the rituals of the papal Mass wherein the entrance, offertory, and Communion songs are regarded as songs of accompaniment. When the activities they accompanied were over, no less than the pope himself signaled to the choir master to stop singing: *respiciens ad priorem scolae annuit ei ut dicat Gloriam; et prior scolae inclinat se pontifici et inponit.* Altar cloths were not spread until the time of the offertory rite, and presumably they were removed after the celebration, as the Roman rite still does after the Eucharist on Holy Thursday. The washing of hands at the offertory, which acquired a symbolic meaning during the early Middle Ages, seems to have been dictated by table hygiene.

[13] A. Chavasse, *La liturgie de la ville de Rome du Ve au VIIIe siècle.*
[14] *Ordo Romanus I*, M. Andrieu, ed. (Louvain, 1965) nos. 29–50.

We gather from the description of *Ordo Romanus I* that there were two distinct cultural forces at work in the papal Mass. The entrance rite has the appearance of an imperial court ceremonial, but thereafter the native Roman quality of sobriety prevails. Thus the nucleus of the eucharistic liturgy, namely the word and the sacrament, remained practically untouched by the drama and pomp of the imperial court ceremonial.

As regards language we note that from the fourth to the late sixth century the Roman Church was in the process of developing the Latin liturgical language.[15] Those were centuries of an intense creativity that produced several classic prayers for eucharistic use, such as collects, prayers over the gifts, prayers after Communion, and prayers over the assembly. These texts have come down to us in medieval sacramentaries. A good number of these compositions are preserved in the *Roman Missal of Paul VI*. The chief authors of the early Roman texts were none other than the bishops of Rome: Damasus, Innocent I, Leo the Great, Gelasius, Vigilius, and Gregory the Great. The literary style of the formularies indicates that their authors received their education from the Roman schools of rhetorics, arts, and classical studies.

We are able to identify the rhetorical style that adorned these compositions.[16] One example is the *cursus* or the rhythmic arrangement of the final words of an oration with the scope of highlighting the cadences and thereby producing such sentiments as joy and wonder. Pope Leo the Great is celebrated for the use of the *cursus* in his orations and homilies. A classic example is the Christmas collect preserved in the Veronese Sacramentary: *Deus, qui humanae substantiae dignitatem et mirabiliter condidisti et mirabiliter reformasti.* . . . The final words *mirabiliter condidisti* and *mirabilius reformasti* are in the *cursus velox* which arouses the sentiment of admiration.[17] Another example is the binary succession of sentences, a kind of embolism which develops the theme of the oration. Pope Vigilius often used it for the prefaces. The following text is superb: *Nullis quippe forinsecus miseriis adfligemur, si vitia frenemus animorum; nec visibili dedecori subiacebit, qui*

---

[15] C. Mohrmann, *Liturgical Latin. Its Origin and Character* (Washington, D.C., 1957).

[16] M. Augé, "Principi di interpretazione dei testi liturgici," *Anamnesis* 1, 159–71.

[17] *Sacramentarium Veronense*, L. Mohlberg, ed. (Rome, 1978) no. 1239, 157.

foedis cupiditatibus obviaverit; nulla inquietudo praevalebit extrinsecus, si agamus corde sincero.[18] Another rhetorical style is antithesis which consists of contrasting concepts, as in a preface for the Ascension: *in caelos ascensio, humilitate discessio.*[19] A fourth example is *concinnitas* or the balance between parts of an oration through the thought or grammatical symmetry: *Plebs tua, Domine, sacramentis purificata caelestibus; quod sumit intelligat; quod gustu delibat, moribus apprehendat; quod iustis orationibus expetit, tua misericordia percipiat.*[20]

A cursory examination of the collects in the early sacramentaries reveals a language addressed to the intellect rather to the heart of the listeners. This is explained by their classical quality of sobriety. Probably only a few would link the following collect to the Christmas feast: *Deus, qui hanc sacratissimam noctem veri luminis fecisti inlustratione clarescere; da, quaesumus, ut cuius lucis mysteria in terra cognovimus, eius quoque gaudiis in caelo perfruamur.*[21] This text, composed for the winter solstice or the victory of light over the darkness of winter, understandably focuses on the element of light. But it requires special catechesis to show the association of the feast of Christmas to the winter solstice. One would have expected words about the child in the manger, the song of the angels, the shepherds. But the *romana sobrietas* preferred to speak of light.

The Roman Canon, which is quoted in part by Ambrose of Milan, is thoroughly imbued with the culture of classical Rome. Its language portrays the Roman taste for a certain gravity in speech as well as simultaneous redundance and brevity. Such phrases as *te igitur, hanc igitur,* and *unde et memores,* at the start of a sentence are elegant, hieratic, and solemn. The use of the title *Clementissime Pater* gives to the Roman Canon an imperial tone, and so does the phrase *supplices te rogamus ac petimus.* True to its sacrificial orientation, the Roman Canon uses pre-Christian sacrificial expressions like *accepta habeas.* It has incorporated also a pagan funeral inscription, namely *refrigerium lucis et pacis.* The legalistic Roman mentality resonates in the threefold declarations *haec dona, haec munera, haec sancta sacrificia inlibata* and *hostiam puram, hostiam sanctam, hostiam immaculatam.* Lastly, the

[18] Ibid., no. 501, 66.
[19] Ibid., no. 176, 22.
[20] Ibid., no. 1068, 135.
[21] *Le Sacramentaire grégorien*, J. Deshusses, ed. (Fribourg, 1971) 36, 99.

Roman Canon observes balance in its structure. Balance, which is akin to equanimity, was highly prized by the Romans. This is especially evident in the mementoes of the living and the dead and the double commemoration of saints before and after the narration of the Last Supper.[22]

The foregoing examples reveal how profoundly the Roman "genius" influenced the corpus of the early Latin texts. The result was an elevated Latin, a kind of *Kulturlatein* which was not probably accessible to people who spoke only the *Volkslatein*, who did not belong to the class of the *homines classici*. In short, the style of these compositions pertained to that segment of the Roman élite, the people of culture, the *homines classici*. This is an issue that will continue to vex historians and pastors alike as they search for a ritual language that is elevated and noble yet contemporary and accessible to the vast majority, if not to all.

As regards the theological components we note a certain sobriety and restraint toward the mystery of the Eucharist. In the *Ordo Romanus I* we do not come across external signs of adoration and reverence directed to the sacred species through such gestures as incensation, bowing, and genuflection. The one exception is at the entrance rite when with bowed head the pope or deacon pays respect to the sacrament which had been consecrated in a previous Mass.

Roman sobriety is even more striking in the language used by the early sacramentaries for the prayers after Communion. Whereas medieval prayers, often influenced by the eucharistic spirituality of the period, spoke of the sacramental bread and wine directly as the body and blood of Christ, the classical Roman prayers rarely mentioned them. These tended to veil the real presence with such words as *cibus et potus* (food and drink), *sacramentum, dona caelestia* (heavenly gifts), and *munera salutifera* (saving gifts).[23] It does not mean, of course, that the Roman Church did not believe in the real presence, but it was not part of the *romana sobrietas* to depict the eucharistic mystery with

---

[22] For bibliography and treatment of the Roman Canon, see A. Nocent, "La preghiera eucaristica del canone romano," *Anamnesis* 3/2, 229–45; see also E. Mazza: *The Eucharistic Prayers of the Roman Rite* (New York, 1986).

[23] Cf., for example, *Sacramentarium Veronense*, L. C. Mohlberg, ed. (Rome, 1978) nos. 4, 82, 86, 108. Cf., however no. 16 which speaks of *corporis sacri et praetiosi sanguinis libamine*.

vivid imagery. The Romans of the classical period would have been uncomfortable hearing the words "the body of Christ" and "the blood of Christ" as they received them at Communion time. The Latin formula for Communion in the *Apostolic Tradition* is, unlike the Sahidic version, indirect: *panis caelestis in Christo Iesu* for the bread, and *In Deo Patri omnipotenti, et Domino Iesu Christo, et Spiritu Sancto et sancta Ecclesia* for the cup.[24]

Another theological component that characterized the classical era of the Roman liturgy was the practice of stational Masses in the major basilicas and the titular churches at which the bishop of Rome presided. These Masses, celebrated on solemnities and particularly during Lent, were occasions to gather the clergy and faithful of Rome around their bishop. Stational Masses expressed the unity of the local church. And this unity was hightened by celebrations held in various basilicas and titular churches around the city. By the end of Lent the four corners of Rome would have been covered. Thus the unity of the local church was manifested in those places where the bishop and the people were gathered together for the Eucharist. Roman Lent with its spirit of penance and almsgiving gave these stational assemblies an ascetical and social dimension.[25]

To heighten further the sense of unity, the pope sent on Sundays the eucharistic *fermentum* to the presbyters in the titular churches of the city. Pope Innocent I explains in his letter to Decentius in 415 why the presbyters received the *fermentum: ut se a nostra communione maxime illa die, non iudicent separatos.*[26] For on Sundays, due to the pastoral ministry in their parishes, the presbyters could not join the pope in the stational church. Medieval writers have sometimes interpreted the subsequent commingling as a symbol expressing the union between Christ's body and blood, and hence of his resurrection.[27] But such an allegorical interpretation does not suit the symbolic "genius" of the Roman liturgy.

[24] *La Tradition Apostolique de Saint Hippolyte*, B. Botte, ed. (Münster 1989) no. 21, 56–57. Note that the Sahidic version has: *Hic est panis caelestis, corpus Christi Iesu* and *Hic est sanguis Domini nostri Iesu Christi.*

[25] A. Chavasse, *La liturgie de la ville de Rome*, 231–46.

[26] Ibid., 21–6; 60–7; J. Jungmann "Fermentum," *Colligere Fragmenta* (Beuron, 1952) 182–90.

[27] B. Capelle, "Fraction et commixtion," *MD* 35 (1953) 79–94.

The classical shape of the Roman liturgy attracted the attention of the eighth-century Franco-Germanic people who copied or imitated it and imported its books. In the twelfth century, when the Roman Church woke up to the realization that it had lost the classical shape of its liturgy because of Franco-Germanic influences in the city, efforts were made to recapture it. The postconciliar reform of Trent tried likewise, though with no appreciable success. It was with some kind of nostalgia that the eighteenth-century Synod of Pistoia attempted to restore it, except that the synod was condemned by Rome. Fresh efforts appeared at the beginning of the twentieth century in the liturgical movement that is now called "classical." Thanks to this movement the recovery of the classical shape of the Roman liturgy became part of Vatican II's agenda.

It is this classical shape that the Constitution on the Liturgy speaks about in art. 34: "The rites should be marked by a noble simplicity; they should be short, clear, and unencumbered by useless repetitions; they should be within the people's powers of comprehension and as a rule not require much explanation." The option for the classical form was taken to task, even during the council, for being somewhat archeological. A council father advised the conciliar commission on the liturgy to institute changes for reasons not of archeology but of pastoral care for which the council had been convened.[28] Yet in the thinking of those who framed the Constitution the pastoral care, which promotes active and intelligent participation, was addressed by the classical qualities of the Roman liturgy. Thus art. 50 directs that for the sake of "devout, active participation" the rites of the Mass are to be simplified, useless duplications eliminated, and useful and necessary elements restored to the vigor they had "in the tradition of the Fathers."

THE ROMAN LITURGY DURING THE FRANCO-GERMANIC PERIOD

Several factors tied the history of the Roman liturgy to the Franco-Germanic Empire and churches which flourished in northern Europe in the eighth century. If not for these factors the Roman liturgy would probably have remained a local liturgy for a local church and preserved its original classic quality.

[28] *Schema Constitutionis de Sacra Liturgia*, Modi II, 8 (Vatican City, 1963) 8.

After the conversion of King Clovis in 496, pilgrims, monks, clergy, and bishops from the north began to visit Rome. Impressed by the splendor of the Rome's liturgical celebrations, they brought home its usages. Thus the process of importing elements of the Roman liturgy, though sporadic and on purely private initiative, began. The phenomenon which we call today "inculturation of the Roman liturgy" has its origin at this time. The Roman classical shape came into contact with the new cultures of the northern people, and this encounter left profound marks, some of them indelible, on the Roman liturgy.

The process gathered force in the eighth century in the reign of Pepin III, called the Short (751–768) who tried to impose the Roman system on his empire. It is useful to note that during this period there existed in the Franco-Germanic Empire what C. Vogel has quite improperly described as "liturgical anarchy." Liturgical usages varied from diocese to diocese because the bishops had control of the shape of worship in their respective local churches.[29] The so-called Gallican liturgies, though sharing common non-Roman traits, were in fact never uniformly imposed in the empire. There was no central authority, like the post-tridentine Congregation of Rites or today's Congregation for Divine Worship, with power to regulate the development of the liturgy. The situation encouraged the importation of the Roman liturgical books, especially by the middle of the eighth century. These books were adapted, as it was to be expected, to the liturgical usages of the different churches. The result was the incursion of the Roman liturgy in the empire of Pepin the Short but in the variety of local adaptations. The Gelasian Sacramentaries of the eighth century, as they are called today, are the chief witnesses to this.

The role of Pepin the Short is commemorated by his son Charlemagne (774–814), who wrote in his *Admonitio Generalis* of 789 that his father had abolished the *gallicanus* in favor of the *cantus romanus* or the recitation of the Roman orations, in order to show unity with the Apostolic See. Charles the Bald, the last of the Carolingian emperors († 877), recalled that until the time of Pepin the churches in Gaul and Spain celebrated the liturgy differently from the Roman

[29] C. Vogel, "Les motifs de la romanisation du culte sous Pépin et Charlemagne," *Culto cristiano. Politica imperiale carolingia* (Todi, 1979) 17–20; J. Pinell: "La Liturgia gallicana," *Anamnesis* 2, 62–7.

Church.[30] Bishops were also involved in the process of romanization. Remedius of Rouen went to Rome in 760 and brought back with him the second cantor of the papal *schola cantorum* in order to teach the Roman *cantilena* to his clergy. Chrodegang of Metz, a great admirer of the Roman liturgy, visited Rome in 753 and introduced in his diocese the Roman chant and Order of Mass.[31]

Of great importance to the development of the Roman liturgy was the way the books were adapted to the Franco-Germanic situation. The *Gelasian Sacramentary*, Vat. Reg. lat. 316, carries two versions of the same formulary, one (no. 454) original Roman, the other (453) Gallicanized.[32] One notices the shift from the original *adoptionis spiritum* to the Gallicanized *sanctificationis spiritum*. This seems to indicate a new theological stress concerning the effect of baptism. On the other hand, the change from the original *puram servitutem* to *puram animam et purum pectus* seems to focus attention on the moral rather than the theological aspect of baptism in line with the people's moralistic approach to the sacraments. Finally the distance of these local churches from the center of Christendom seems to be the reason for the addition of the phrase *per universa mundi spatia* to the Gallicanized form.

Charlemagne, the protector of *iustitia Sancti Petri*, continued the reform of romanization and unification initiated by his father with a more decisive program. In 783 he requested Pope Hadrian I for a pure (*immixtum*) Roman sacramentary with the intention of replacing the mixed Gelasian sacramentaries that circulated in his empire. Copies were to be made from it as *ex authentico*. Two years later the pope sent him a Gregorian, hence papal, type of sacramentary. Perhaps the pope did not realize the emperor's intention. Being a papal book for stational Masses, it did not include several formularies, such as those of the Sundays after Epiphany and the octaves of Easter and Pentecost, not to mention things that were integral to the religious world of the Franco-Germanic people such as funeral

---

[30] *Capitularia Regum Francorum 1*, MGH (1835) 61; *Epist. ad Clerum Ravennatis, Mansi: Concilia* XVIIIB, 730.

[31] C. Vogel, *Medieval Liturgy. An Introduction to the Sources*, 119–20.

[32] *Sacramentarium Gelasianum*, ed. L. C. Mohlberg, RED, Fontes IV (Rome, 1981) 75.

Masses, votive Masses, and blessings.[33] On Benedict of Aniane († 821) fell the responsibility to fill in the lacunae with local elements at his disposal. These he collected as a supplement to the Roman sacramentary with the explanatory preface *Hucusque*. Unwittingly elements of the mixed Gelasian sacramentaries and the usages of the Franco-Germanic churches once again entered into the Roman book. Thus the program of romanization turned out to be a gallicanization of the Roman liturgy. The rest is part of the history of the liturgical books.

A similar phenomenon occurred in the case of the Roman ordines the first of which left Rome for the north sometime between 700 and 750. These ordines were eventually elaborated to form the pontificals in the broad sense of the word. A notable example is the Romano-Germanic Pontifical composed between 950 and 962 in the Benedictine Abbey of Mainz.[34]

This pontifical, which claims a particular interest for the history of the succeeding Roman pontificals, is a remarkable description of the liturgical state of the Franco-Germanic Churches. The Masses for energumens and various exorcisms reflect the spirit world in which they lived. The numerous sermons and the explanation of various liturgical items show the need of bishops and clergy for greater information. Likewise the blessings *ad diversa* reveal the people's religious attitude toward things and places they used. Practically everything that could be blessed was blessed: houses, sleeping quarters, kitchen, food, bath tubs, soap, field, animals, and so on. Startling are the blessings of the instruments of ordeal like the incandescent gridiron and boiling or else ice water.[35]

It was also at this time when the so-called liturgical "apologies" became a constant companion of priests when they celebrated the liturgy. These prayers were a form of self-deprecation and recognition of unworthiness on the part of the presiders. They were ubiquitous and were sometimes inserted even in the canon of the Mass. The most developed form is exhibited in the *Missa Illyrica* of 1030, published by Flacius Illyricus in 1557. Other examples are found in some

[33] J. Deshusses, "L'Evolution du sacramentaire," *Le Sacramentaire grégorien*, 61–74.

[34] C. Vogel, "Introduction générale," *Le Pontifical romano-germanique du dixième siècle* III (Vatican City, 1972) 28–55.

[35] Ibid. II, nos. 180–245, 333–80; nos. 246–52, 380–414.

of the ordines published by E. Martène.[36] The "apologies" form part
of the religious moralism that gripped several liturgical formularies
of the Franco-Germanic Churches.

But the Franco-Germanic people will for ever be admired for their
romanesque architecture, hymnody, and miniature arts. The church
edifices in Reims, Hildesheim, Essen, and Fleury, to mention a few
examples, combine the traditional Roman genius for sobriety and
functionality with the Franco-Germanic sense for harmony and dy-
namism. The hymn *Veni, Creator Spiritus* and the Easter sequence
Victimae paschali laudes are some of the stupendous compositions that
still resound in today's liturgical celebrations. The miniatures,
painted in vivid colors and with imagination or fantasy, decorate the
lectionaries and sacramentaries, a tradition that has survived in our
liturgical books.[37]

What took place at this period was the integration of the artistic,
dramatic, and spiritual genius of the Franco-Germanic people with
the imported classical Roman liturgy. By a turn of events in the tenth
century this gallicanized shape of the Roman liturgy entered the city
of Rome to gradually replace the classical form. The preparatory
liturgy commission of Vatican II proposed to eliminate much of
"these elements originating in the character of the Franco-Germanic
people and which the Roman Church later adopted."[38] We know,
however, that several of these foreign elements have survived the
liturgical reform of Vatican II because of their intrinsic value and pastoral usefulness. One must admit that in many ways they enriched
the classical Roman liturgy by infusing it with drama, poetry, and
symbolism.

As a final consideration, the Franco-Germanic period has relevance
particularly in those local churches whose culture differs from the
classical qualities of the reformed Roman liturgy. It serves as a his-

---

[36] *De Antiquis Ecclesiae Ritibus Libri* I (Hildesheim, 1967) cap. IV, Ordo
XXXIV–VII, 662–79; A. Nocent, "Les apologies dans la célébration eucharistique,"
Liturgie et rémission des péchés (Rome, 1975) 179–96.

[37] F. Müterich: "I libri carolini e la miniatura carolingia," 283–301; V. Elbern,
"Werke liturgischer Goldschmiedekunst in karolingischer Zeit," 305–36; C. Heitz,
"L'architettura dell'età carolingia in relazione alla liturgia sacra," 339–62, *Culto
cristiano. Politica imperiale carolingia*.

[38] *Schema Constitutionis de Sacra Liturgia*, Emendationes VI (Vatican City, 1963) 32.

torical model of inculturation, which in the thinking of the present legislation takes the revised Roman liturgy as its point of departure.[39]

THE ROMAN LITURGY FROM THE TENTH
TO THE FIFTEENTH CENTURY

Another development in the Roman liturgy began to take shape in the tenth century when it returned to the city in its Gallicanized form. Several factors, both political and religious, contributed to it. After the death of Louis the Pious in 840, the Franco-Germanic Empire went into crisis and collapsed in 887. The French part of the empire distanced itself from the German which Otto I (951–973) ruled with the religious fervor of the Carolingians. In 962 he went to Rome to be crowned emperor of the Holy Roman Empire and to inaugurate the *Renovatio Imperii*. There he discovered that the city was racked by political conflicts and suffered badly from the spiritual decadence of its head. The Roman clergy had accused Pope John XII (✝ 964) of simoniacal ordinations, of ordaining bishop a boy ten years of age, and of giving away to women of bad repute the Church's sacred vessels.[40] The following year Otto I went back to Rome accompanied by archbishops and bishops to institute reforms. What interests us here is the fact that his ecclesiastical cortege brought along the Gallicanized Roman liturgical books, with particular mention of the Romano-Germanic Pontifical. Furthermore as part of the Ottonian emperors' political strategy Germans occupied the see of Peter from 1046 to 1057: Clement II, Damasus II, Leo IX, Victor II, and Stephen IX. These popes celebrated the Roman liturgy in the Gallicanized form they had known in their homeland.

The Roman decadence was felt also in the indispensable area of manuscript writing. During the papacy of Gregory V (996–999) Rome did not have *scriptoria* to transcribe liturgical books. In exchange for

---

[39] *The Roman Liturgy and Inculturation.* IVth Instruction for the Right Application of the Conciliar Constitution on the Liturgy (nn. 37–40), (Rome, 1994) no. 36, 18.

[40] M. Andrieu, "La diffusion du Pontifical romano-germanique. Son adoption par l'Eglise romaine," *Les Ordines romani du haut moyen-âge*, vol 1 (Louvain, 1931) 512–15. Of Pope John XII *Liber Pontificalis* (II, 246–49) notes: *Iste denique infelicissimus, quod sibi peius est, totam vitam suam in adulterio et vanitate duxit.*

the privilege of immunity requested by the monks of Reichenau, he demanded to be regularly furnished copies of their liturgical books. Thus the Franco-Germanic liturgy became the liturgy of the Lateran Basilica.[41]

Outside developments in the liturgy also influenced to some degree that of Rome. The tenth-century monastic reform of Cluny led to a type of liturgical worship that grew longer and more solemn with the years. Though not everything Cluny practiced was originally its own, it succeeded in propagating as community activities devotions to the cross, the Eucharist, Mary, and the saints. It encouraged the multiplication of Masses, their "private" celebration in the lateral chapels of the church, and the recitation of psalms for benefactors. It was Abbot Odilo († 1049) who instituted the commemoration of the dead on November 2.[42]

Another outside development in the tenth century was the importance being given to dramatization in the liturgy. Examples of these are the Easter *visitatio sepulchri, officium peregrinorum,* and *hortolanus.* These forms of drama made use of the liturgical texts, like the sequences, and the *dramatis personae* were the liturgical ministers.[43]

Dramatization in the liturgy reveals the state of liturgical life of the high Middle Ages. It tells us that ordinary people no longer grasped the meaning of the liturgy and had to be helped with visual aids. The English *Regularis Concordia* explains that drama was intended for the ignorant and those new in the faith. Participation in songs and responses had began to wane. Burkhard of Worms († 1035) complained that people in church ignored the greeting and exhortation of the priest as they continued to chat among themselves. In 1078 Pope Gregory VII had to require people to bring an offering at least for solemn Masses. The twelfth-century *Ordo officiorum* of the Lateran Basilica decried the fact that the ancient practice of daily Communion during Lent, including Sundays, was not being observed by both

[41] C. Vogel, *Medieval Liturgy,* 230–39; M. Andrieu, "La diffusion du Pontifical romano-germanique," 515–17.

[42] K. Hallinger, "Progressi e problemi della ricerca sulla riforma pre-gregoriana," *Il Monachesimo nell'alto medioevo e la formazione della civiltà occidentale* (Spoleto, 1957) 257–91; J. Leclercq: "Culte et pauvreté à Cluny," *MD* 81 (1965) 33–50.

[43] K. Young, *The Drama of the Medieval Church* (Oxford, 1951); B. Berger, *Le drame liturgique de pâques* (Paris, 1976).

clergy and faithful. It thus prescribes Communion of the faithful at least three times a year.[44]

The accession of Gregory VII to the papal throne in 1072 had profound consequences for the liturgy of Rome. A defender of the liberty of the Church against investiture, he was also a reformer who combatted the two abuses which plagued the Roman clergy: simony and nicholaism. To counteract investiture he built the image and authority of the pope: feasts of holy popes were to be kept in every local church; bishops had to make an oath of allegiance to the pope before their ordination; the naming of the pope in the canon of the Mass was to be observed everywhere.[45] Part of his strategy in the reform of the clergy, besides the imposition of a quasi-monastic discipline, was to reestablish the traditional liturgical usages of the Church of Rome before the Germans took over its government. The return to the *regula sanctorum patrum*, the *ordo romanus*, and the *mos antiquus*, which he claimed to have studied, became the order of the day.[46] Some elements of the traditional usages concerned the order of psalmody, fasting on Saturday, omission of the *Alleluia* in Septuagesima, and the ancient *ordo* for the celebration of the Easter Vigil.

In the spirit of the Gregorian reform, the Roman liturgists of the twelfth century reworked the Romano-Germanic Pontifical using the method of elimination in an effort to restore the *romana sobrietas*. Things not pertaining to the scope of a pontifical, like didactic elements, or ran contrary to the Roman cultural sensitivity, like the Masses for energumens and the blessing of instruments of ordeal, were eliminated. The result was the Roman Pontifical of the twelfth century.[47] This book was propagated in other local Churches in Italy and north of the Alps by papal legates who went about implementing the decrees of Lateran Council I (1123) and by the popes themselves who before the reign of Innocent III (1198–1216) frequently

---

[44] B. Neunheuser, *Storia della liturgia*, 93–4.

[45] E. Cattaneo, "La riforma gregoriana," *Il Culto cristiano in occidente*, 231–42.

[46] *Regula Canonica*, G. Morin, ed., *Anecdota Maredsolana*, 2, series 1 (Paris, 1913) 459–60. Pius V invoked the *pristina sanctorum Patrum norma* for the Tridentine Missal of 1570; so did Paul VI for the Missal of 1970.

[47] M. Andrieu, *Le Pontifical romain au moyen-âge*, vol 1, 8–16; C. Vogel, *Medieval Liturgy*, 230–9.

148

went into exile in various parts of Italy and France. The rest is part of the history of the Roman liturgical books.

Although the work of the Roman liturgists of the twelfth century was not perfect in the sense that several Franco-Germanic elements survived, it is a proof that the Roman Church does not easily forget nor lay aside its classical genius and its traditions. Its openness to things new does not prejudice its attachment to the *regula sanctorum patrum*. The liturgical reform of Vatican II confirms this.

The reigns of Pope Innocent III and of Pope Honorius III (1216–1227) witnessed further development in the shape of the Roman liturgy. It is useful to set their reigns in the context of an age of intense spiritual and cultural activities represented by Dominic († 1221) and Francis of Assisi († 1226), the great scholastics led by Thomas Aquinas († 1280), the University of Paris, and the great cathedrals in Reims, Westminster, and Florence.

On his part Innocent III initiated a liturgical novelty. He instituted a type of liturgy that would respond to the particular situation of the Roman curia which at that time functioned as an itinerant administrative body. For their travels curia members needed portable liturgical books with a simplified format. For this purpose a missal now known as *Missale Curiae*, a pontifical, and a breviary were composed.[48] Clearly the intention of Innocent III was neither codification nor unification of liturgical usages. By a turn of circumstances, however, this type of liturgy was adopted by the Friars Minor who, besides being closely linked to the Roman curia, often found themselves also in an itinerant situation. Thus the liturgy of the Roman curia spread beyond the small group of ecclesiastics for whom Innocent III had originally intended it.[49] Its relationship with the famous 1295 Pontifical of Durand and the 1485 *Editio princeps* by A. Piccolomini and J. Burchard of Strasbourg is part of the history of the Roman liturgical books.

Intense spiritual and cultural activities continued well into the fourteenth and fifteenth centuries. These years were marked by the guilds, construction of numerous chapels and oratories, the appear-

[48] M. Andrieu, *Le Pontifical romain au moyen-âge*, vol II, 263–323; C. Vogel, *Medieval Liturgy*, 252.

[49] S. van Dijk, *The Origins of the Modern Roman Liturgy* (London, 1960).

ance of influential preachers and reformers like Savonarola († 1498),
the birth of the Renaissance, the works of the great masters like
Giotto († 1337), Dante Alighieri († 1321), and Filippo Bruneleschi
(† 1446). The invention of the printing press by Johann Gutenberg in
1445 contributed immensely to culture and religion, including the
liturgy. The *Editio princeps* of the Roman Pontifical was printed in
Rome in 1485. This period closes with the discovery of America in
1492. Yet these centuries shared much in human misery and
tragedies. The tenor of life, caused by political strifes all over Europe,
was violent. The Black Plague of 1380 and the Hundred Years War
(1337–1453) induced in the people a sense of pessimism. Lastly the
fall of Constantinople in 1453 rocked the confidence in the existence
of a Christian world. Because of this authors have called these centuries the "autumn of the Middle Ages."[50]

In the area of liturgy things were not better. Indeed there was
something insidious about this period. The external appearances
seemed healthy, but within was a dangerous malaise that announced
the total collapse of the Church's life of worship. It is important to
note, however, that much of the malaise with which this period was
afflicted was not a product of the time, but had its origin in the preceding centuries.

The following are some examples. Clericalism, which forced the
assembly to resort to private devotions during Mass, had made its
appearance already in the ninth century with the composition of the
plenary missals. The premise for these missals is that the presider did
everything by himself and privately, regardless of an assembly.[51] The
theology of the transubstantiation, which developed against the
heresy of Berengarius of Tours († 1088) confined the attention of
clergy and faithful to the moment of consecration. People sometimes
came to Mass with the sole desire to witness a miracle similar to the
one reported in Bolsena in 1236. Another example was the excessive
use of allegorism, which presented the Mass to the assembly as a
mere occasion to remember aspects of Christ's life. This period inherited it from the allegorism of Amalarius of Metz († 850) and Pope
Innocent III.

[50] J. Huizinga, *The Waning of the Middle Ages* (London, 1976).
[51] C. Vogel, *Medieval Liturgy*, 105–6, 156–9.

Likewise during this period the faithful's devotion to the Mass consisted in gaining its "fruits." Consequently Masses were multiplied in order to comply with the obligation arising from the stipends offered by the faithful and alas indulge at times in the abusive *Missa bi-*, *tri-*, or *quadrifaciata* or the several repetitions of the parts of the Mass before reciting once the canon of the Mass.[52] Finally this period witnessed the birth of the *devotio moderna* among the religious. It was a spirituality of a mystical type influenced by Master Eckhart († 1327), purely personal or unecclesial in the style of Thomas à Kempis († 1471), and strongly affective in expression. With the exception of Gertrude of Helfta († 1301), few knew how to nourish their spiritual and mystical life with the liturgy.

The fourteenth and fifteenth centuries were an interplay between light and shadow. Their external vitality hid the malaise of clericalism, exaggerated allegorism, misplaced devotion to the Mass, a form of spirituality that dispensed with the liturgy as its source, and most of all the loss of an ecclesial sense caused by individualism. This period tells us that when solid theological, ecclesiological, and liturgical foundations are absent in our liturgical activities, autumn has come and winter is not far away.

[52] S. Marsili, "Excursus I," *Anamnesis* III/2, 78–91.

Bibliography

Cattaneo, E. *Il culto cristiano in Occidente. Note storiche.* BELS 13. Rome, 1984.

Chavasse, A. *La liturgie de la ville de Rome du Ve au VIIIe siècle.* SA 112. Rome, 1993.

Dix, G. *The Shape of the Liturgy.* 2nd ed. Westminster, 1945. Reprint New York, 1982.

Duchesne, L. *Christian Worship: Its Origin and Evolution.* Trans. M. L. McClure. London, 1956.

Harper, J. *The Forms and Orders of Western Liturgy from the Tenth to the Eighteenth Century.* Oxford, 1991.

Jungmann, J. *The Early Liturgy to the Time of Gregory the Great.* Notre Dame, Ind., 1980.

Klauser, Th. *A Short History of the Western Liturgy.* Trans. J. Halliburton. 2nd ed. New York, 1979.

Mazza, E. *The Eucharistic Prayers of the Roman Rite*. New York, 1986.

Metzger, M. *Histoire de la liturgie. Les grandes étapes*. Paris, 1994.

Neunheuser, B. *Storia della liturgia attraverso le epoche culturali*. Rome, 1977.

Nocent, A. "La preghiera eucaristica del canone romano." *Anàmnesis* 3/2.

Schmidt, H. *Introductio in liturgiam occidentalem*. Rome, 1960.

Vogel, C. *Medieval Liturgy: An Introduction to the Sources*. Trans. and rev. W. Storey and N. Rasmussen. Washington, 1986.

Willis G. G. *A History of Early Roman Liturgy to the Death of Pope Gregory the Great*. London, 1994.

Keith F. Pecklers, S.J.

10

History of the Roman Liturgy from the Sixteenth until the Twentieth Centuries

There was significant liturgical activity at the beginning and end of this historical period, that is, from 1563 until 1614, and again from 1903 until 1962. Otherwise, the seventeenth, eighteenth, and nineteenth centuries witnessed little change in liturgical practice.

THE ROMAN LITURGY AT THE TIME OF THE REFORMATION

The sixteenth century was a time of tremendous reform. Martin Luther († 1546) criticized the Church's use of indulgences, the exaggerated cult of the saints, and a liturgical practice that had become pompous and removed from the people. In 1520, he wrote the second of his famous three treatises: "The Babylonian Captivity of the Church," which contains his interpretation of the sacraments. His thesis is already stated in the title. As the Jews were sent away from Jerusalem into captivity under the oppression of the Babylonian Empire, so in Europe, Christians were sent away from the Scriptures under the oppression of a papacy that had misused the sacraments, especially the Eucharist.[1] The treatise exposed three aspects of the Church's slavery: the denial of the chalice to the laity, the doctrine of transubstantiation, and the doctrine of the sacrificial character of the Mass. Moreover, Luther abolished private Mass and private

---

[1] "Introduction," "The Babylonian Captivity of the Church," in *Three Treatises* (Philadelphia, 1988) 116.

153

confession, called for a vernacular liturgy, and emphasized the priest-hood of the baptized.[2]

Though we normally consider the Reformation to be "Protestant" under the leadership of Luther, John Calvin († 1564), Ulrich Zwingli († 1531), and others, the Catholic Church experienced its own reformation through the Council of Trent and the founding of reforming orders like the Jesuits. We have already seen that the fourteenth and fifteenth centuries were a time of heightened clericalism and a lost ecclesial sense. The Mass had become a devotional practice. Eucharistic adoration was viewed as superior to eucharistic participation in its fullest sense, and liturgy's relationship to the daily life of Christians was lost. Religious individualism was on the rise and with it the proliferation of private Masses where the priest's reception of Communion was viewed as representative of those who did not communicate. By the beginning of the fourteenth century, the practice of Mass stipends offered to the priest for having a Mass said for one's particular intention was already well in place. The sixteenth-century Church was ripe for reform.

Symbolically, the Renaissance saw a growing interest in the theme of magic, of "natural" (i.e., good) magic and "demonic" magic.[3] Liturgical abuses increased. Those who attended Mass or those who paid a stipend to the presider were entitled to obtain the "fruits of the Mass." Although earlier medieval interpretations of those "fruits" were more benign, the Renaissance saw the list to include the following: "during the time one hears Mass one does not grow older . . . after hearing Mass one's food tastes better; one will not die a sudden death; the souls in Purgatory will not have to suffer while one is hearing Mass for them."[4] The Reformation emerged within such a milieu, reacting against what appeared to be poor doctrine and scandalous practice and against a cultural system which deprived Christians of personal freedom and direct access to God's mercy.[5]

---

[2] E. Cattaneo, *Il culto cristiano in Occidente* (Rome, 1978) 343–8.

[3] B. Cooke, *The Distancing of God: The Ambiguity of Symbol in History and Theology* (Minneapolis, 1990) 188–9.

[4] J. Jungmann, *The Mass of the Roman Rite: Its Origins and Development* (Dublin, 1986) I: 129, note 10.

[5] D. Power, *The Sacrifice We Offer* (Edinburgh, 1987) 40.

For the first time, religious orders founded in the sixteenth century were exempted from the obligation to pray the choral Office in order to be more apostolically available.[6] This meant architectural changes in the newly-constructed churches of those orders since choir stalls for the corporate praying of the Office were unnecessary. This also meant radical changes in the liturgical space. Church architecture in the late medieval period focused on the altar as shrine. The building was divided into clearly delineated areas. The nave for the laity and the choir where the Office was chanted was divided by a wooden partition, called a "roodscreen" (rood meaning cross) since a large cross often hung on or above the partition. As the nave and the choir were two separate architectural spaces, they were also treated separately according to church law: the choir (also called chancel) belonged to monks and clergy and the nave to the laity. In the distance beyond the choir was the altar.[7] Moreover, side chapels grew to facilitate the increase in private Masses, especially in churches of religious orders where there were many priests living in the same place.

Sixteenth-century church buildings, however, were seen as a single worship space. The removal of the chancel allowed for clear sightlines, and barriers between the assembly and the altar had vanished. The first monumental church of this new architectural style was the Jesuit Church of the Gesù in Rome, built between 1568 and 1575, soon to be imitated elsewhere. There was no roodscreen blocking the assembly's vision. The altar stood centrally in the apse for all to see. With the Jesuits' emphasis on preaching and catechesis, the spoken word rather than sung chant now became the priority, so the ambo was placed on the north wall in the center of the church. Concerns about acoustics and visibility were given greater attention because of the emphasis on the ministries of the Word, an emphasis that seemed "too Protestant" to some critics. This concern about acoustics is best demonstrated in a debate over what type of ceiling should be installed in the Gesù. The Jesuits wanted a ceiling of open wooden trusses because it would acoustically assist the preaching and catechesis. Cardinal Alessandro Farnese, benefactor of the church, preferred a stone vault ceiling. Cardinal Farnese won.

[6] J. Weiss, "Jesuits and the Liturgy of the Hours," unpublished Ph.D. dissertation, University of Notre Dame, 1992.

[7] J. White, *Roman Catholic Worship: Trent to Today* (New York, 1995) 6.

THE LITURGICAL REFORMS
OF THE COUNCIL OF TRENT

The Council of Trent lasted from 1545 until 1563. In light of Vatican II, the Tridentine council is often viewed as conservative and even reactionary. Indeed, its agenda included an affirmation of Catholic doctrine on such topics as the seven sacraments instituted by Christ as instruments of God's distribution of grace, and the propitiatory nature of eucharistic sacrifice as a response to Protestant reformers who held that the Mass was a "testament" of God's forgiveness. But the council also sought to correct some of the liturgical abuses witnessed and commented upon by those same reformers and even encouraged pastoral sensitivity regarding liturgical concerns such as the vernacular.[8] In attempting to challenge what was seen as a rampant subjectivity of the liturgy,[9] a rigid uniformity was enforced, so much so that the liturgy remained virtually unchanged until Vatican II. The call for liturgical uniformity overshadowed the pastoral dimension.

Liturgically, the Council of Trent dealt primarily with the Mass and the Liturgy of the Hours. In its disciplinary decree *De observandis et evitandis in celebratione missae,* passed in its twenty-second session on September 17, 1562, the council ordered that the most serious liturgical abuses be eliminated: Mass should be celebrated only in consecrated places, magical treatment of the consecrated host was to stop, disrespectful and inappropriate liturgical music was to cease, bishops were to keep an eye on their priests regarding stipends so that they did not profit inappropriately from a proliferation of Masses, superstition around the number of fixed Masses should cease. The reform of the missal was not mentioned. It was not until the twenty-fifth session when both the missal and breviary were discussed and then referred to the pope to be reformed.[10]

Pius IV delegated the task of reforming the missal and breviary to a commission whose proceedings no longer exist. In 1568 the

---

[8] H. Schmidt, *Liturgie et langue vulgaire. Le problème de la langue liturgique chez les premiers Réformateurs et au Concile de Trente* AGreg 53 (Rome, 1950).

[9] With the birth of the Reformation, many Catholic priests initiated their own reforms. In some parts of Austria, for example, the Eucharistic Prayer was eliminated altogether. Jungmann, I:134.

[10] Jungmann, 133–5.

Breviarium romanum ex decreto sacrosancti Concilii Tridentini restitutum, Pii V. Pont. Max iussu editum was promulgated followed two years later by the *Missale Romanum ex decreto ss. Concilii Tridentini restitutum, Pii V. Pont. Max iussu editum,* issued in July 14, 1570. Prior to the Council of Trent, Clement VII commissioned Francisco de Quiñonez, a Spanish cardinal, to produce a revision of the breviary. Quiñonez published his breviary in 1535 with the printed approval of Paul III. The breviary was intended for private recitation, and the psalter was divided into weekly segments without repetitions. The length of Scripture readings was increased and read in sequence. Saints' legends and votive offices were omitted along with elements more appropriate to choral recitation such as antiphons, responses, chapters, and intercessions. Many hymns were also omitted. The Quiñonez breviary soon became popular because it was simple, short, and easy to use, so much so that it was reprinted eleven times in the first year and over one hundred times in its thirty-two years of use.[11]

The breviary produced by the Tridentine commission was a return to the traditional Roman office albeit shortened and simplified. Choral elements were restored although hagiographical legends and the votive offices suppressed by Quiñonez were left omitted. The obligation to pray the offices of the Blessed Virgin and the Dead, along with the *Gradual* and Penitential psalms was removed. The sanctoral cycle was simplified.

The commission's goal regarding the reform of both the breviary and the missal was not the composition of new books but a return to tradition, to the ancient liturgy of the city of Rome. This included a cleansing of the liturgical calendar allowing for greater attention to feasts and seasons, and the removal of unnecessary or inappropriate texts added to the breviary and missal over the centuries. Prior to the council, saints' days were so abundant that they even took the place of Sundays. Only those saints' days celebrated in Rome prior to the eleventh century were accepted as legitimate for the new calendar. As a result, 157 days opened up on the liturgical calendar, excepting octaves. A number of votive Masses and sequences were likewise removed from the missal. Order was given to private prayers and

---

[11] R. Taft, *The Liturgy of the Hours in East and West: The Origins of the Divine Office and Its Meaning for Today* (Collegeville, 1986) 311.

gestures of the presider which had been multiplied due to excessive fervor and piety.[12]

The topic of liturgical music was also included in the agenda of the council. Prior to the council music was often used inappropriately in the liturgy, as background during the Eucharistic Prayer, for example, while the presider prayed the prayer privately. The council permitted only such music that had a particular function in the liturgy. Further, preference was given to communal or "conventual" Masses where the canons or the whole religious community celebrated together, over private Masses devoid of music and the other ministries. Perhaps most significant was the council's statement that the solemn celebration of Mass was to become the normative eucharistic liturgy rather than the unadorned "low Mass."[13]

These Tridentine reforms sought to bring about a liturgical uniformity both in theology and practice, and so rubrics were now printed for the first time at the beginning of both the breviary and missal, despite requests that permissions for regional differences in celebrations of the Roman rite be left to the local bishops involved. The 1502 *Ritus servandus in celebratione missae* of Johannes Burckard, papal master of ceremonies, was the source for the rubrics of the 1570 missal and substantially changed the face of Catholic worship far beyond the confines of Rome.[14]

The pastoral sense of the council participants and their genuine desire for reform within the Catholic Church should not be overlooked. By the time the decree on the Mass was formulated, bishops at the council had already recognized the importance of Communion by the whole assembly during Mass and this became one of the practical reforms desired out of the disciplinary decrees that were issued. Other decrees reveal discussion on the possibility of the use of the vernacular and on offering the chalice to the whole assembly during Mass.[15]

[12] R. Cabié, "The Celebration of the Eucharist in the West from the Council of Trent to Vatican Council II," in A.G. Martimort, *The Church at Prayer* vol II: *The Eucharist* (Collegeville, 1987) 175.

[13] Ibid.

[14] P. Jounel, "From the Council of Trent to Vatican Council II," *The Church at Prayer,* vol 1: *Principles of the Liturgy,* 67–8.

[15] J. Huels, "Trent and the Chalice: Forerunner of Vatican II?" *Worship* 56 (1982) 386–400. Decision on offering the chalice to the faithful was left to the Pope. In

While affirming that Latin was the language of mystery and the language of the Church, at least some of the bishops at the council were concerned that a large percentage of every liturgical assembly was unable to comprehend what was taking place. This concern was expressed in the twenty-second session (1562) when it was decreed that the liturgical readings and the mystery of the Eucharist should be explained to the people during Mass, at least on Sundays and feasts (no. 1554). Moreover, despite the "fruits" received because of so many private Masses celebrated throughout the world, the practice of Communion by the laity only once or twice a year was considered unsatisfactory.[16] Therefore, that same session expressed the desire that the faithful should communicate sacramentally at every Mass where they are present (no. 1552).

As for the doctrine of the Eucharist, there were no surprises. In 1551, during the thirteenth session, the doctrine of the real presence was reaffirmed (no. 1513) along with reservation of the sacrament in churches for veneration (no. 1520) and care of the sick (no. 1521). That same session affirmed the preeminence of the Eucharist over other sacraments (no. 1516) and the doctrine of transubstantiation (no. 1519). The twenty-second session affirmed the propitiatory nature of the eucharistic sacrifice (no. 1548) and that Christ offered himself in bread and wine to reveal his own priesthood in the order of Melchizedek (no. 1546). The Roman Canon was proclaimed free from error (no. 1550), and priests were reminded that water was to be mixed with wine in offering the chalice (no. 1553) as already prescribed in the Council of Florence.

Under the leadership of Gregory XIII, the liturgical calendar was revised in 1582. Two years later, the *Roman martyrology* was revised, relying on the ninth-century martyrology of Usuard and removing undocumented or historically inaccurate hagiographical accretions. A commission of ten worked on the new text, including the noted historian Cardinal Cesare Baronius, who published further revisions in

---

1564, permission was granted by Pius IV to Germany and several other European countries. Successors of Pius IV gradually revoked the permission, for Bavaria in 1570, and finally Bohemia in 1621. C. Constant, *La concession à l'Allemagne de la communion sous les deux espèces: Etude sur les débuts de la reforme catholique en Allemagne (1548–1621)* (Paris, 1923, 2 vols).

[16] Power, 128–9.

1586 and 1589. The martyrology was intended to be read in religious houses at the daily office of prime. No other liturgical book was revised as often as the martyrology since new canonizations and ongoing research required new editions of the text.[17]

In 1588, the Congregation of Sacred Rites was established by Sixtus V, along with fourteen other congregations. Responsibilities for the congregation included care for the celebration of the rites, the restoration and reform of ceremonies, the reform of liturgical books, regulating the offices of patron saints, the canonization of saints, the celebration of feasts, the reception of dignitaries to Rome, and the solution to liturgical difficulties raised by local circumstances.[18] Despite these different responsibilities, there is no question that the primary function of the congregation was to assist the goal of liturgical unification throughout the western world and to see to it that the newly instituted Roman rubrics were being faithfully observed.[19]

The Congregation of Sacred Rites also continued the reform of liturgical books begun at Trent. In 1596 the new *Roman Pontifical*, based on the thirteenth-century pontifical of French bishop William Durandus was published and made universally mandatory by Clement VIII. Four years later, in 1600, the first *Caeremoniale Episcoporum (CE)* was published, containing rubrics for liturgies involving a bishop. The *Roman Ritual (RR)* followed in 1614 as a type of pastoral manual: blessings of persons, places, or things, the administration of baptism, penance, marriage, extreme unction, processions, etc. The text was based largely on the 1523 text for priests by Dominican Alberto Castellani and on Cardinal Giulio Antonio Santori's 1601 ritual. Although Paul V encouraged bishops and priests to use the new ritual, it was not obligatory. As a result, with the exception of Italy, the *RR* was little known until the mid-nineteenth century, and even then, many dioceses had their own appendixes included up until Vatican II.[20]

---

[17] White, 12.
[18] F. McManus, *The Congregation of Sacred Rites* (Washington, D.C., 1954) 27.
[19] White, 12–4.
[20] White, 12.

THE ROMAN LITURGY DURING THE BAROQUE PERIOD

The religious culture of the seventeenth-century baroque was a culture of joyful celebration and feasting with pilgrimages and processions in richly adorned costumes, with a flamboyant church architecture and orchestral music, and with dramatic representations. The visual and the audio were of paramount importance in this sensual culture.[21]

Liturgically, it was a time of uniformity, or in the words of historian Theodor Klauser, a period of "rigid unification in the Liturgy and rubricism."[22] Reform of liturgical books continued with Clement VIII's new edition of the breviary in 1602 and a new missal in 1604, adding new saints' days and making corrections in the readings. Urban VIII issued a new breviary in 1632, revising the Latin hymns. New editions of the martyrology, missal, and pontifical were published in 1630, 1634, and 1644 respectively. The CE of 1600 was revised by Innocent X in 1650. Other than the revision of liturgical books, however, there was relatively little liturgical change.

The decline in liturgical activity during the baroque period gave way to a growth in eucharistic adoration. The RR of 1614 prescribed the tabernacle for the universal Church. Unlike the medieval hanging pyx in the form of a dove, baroque tabernacles tended to be rather substantial in size. With newly constructed churches free of barriers and the altar and tabernacle in clear sight, veneration of the reserved Eucharist took on a new appeal. The unified baroque interior did, indeed, gather people together in a way that the medieval worship space could not. The only difference was that it was the reserved sacrament rather than the liturgy itself that became the motive for the gathering. Liturgy became subordinate to the cult of the reserved Eucharist. The altar became a throne for the monstrance containing the sacrament and the interior of the church became a throne room. The altar itself played a subordinate role to the much more elaborate tabernacle and monstrance. The feast of Corpus Christi was the most important liturgical celebration of the Church

---

[21] B. Neunheuser, *Storia della liturgia attraverso le epoche culturali* (Rome, 1983) 122–3.

[22] T. Klauser, *A Short History of the Western Liturgy* (New York, 1981) 117–52.

year because in that feast the Church professed its belief in the real presence of Christ in the reserved sacrament.[23]

Jesuits, not only through their architecture but also through their ministries, promoted such eucharistic adoration. In fact, up until Vatican II, one of the few times of common prayer prescribed for Jesuits was eucharistic benediction on Sundays and feasts. The Congregation of Rites sought to challenge and suppress the baroque subordination of the Mass as a backdrop to the veneration of the reserved sacrament but this was not a battle easily won. Indeed, the tension continues today in some places where bishops insist that the reserved sacrament be centrally located in the liturgical space so that the assembly has view of the tabernacle during Mass.

Unlike the clear lines and noble simplicity of medieval architecture, baroque architecture was theatrical, known for its flamboyant movement, color, and detail, and its twisted columns as demonstrated in the baldachino of St. Peter's Basilica in Vatican City, designed by the baroque master, Gianlorenzo Bernini († 1680). Nothing was simple in baroque churches. Everything was designed to create effects and awaken the senses. Mission churches built during the seventeenth century were often copies of what the Jesuit and Franciscan missionaries had left in Portugal and Spain, so the baroque style soon made its way throughout the world.[24]

Musically, the age of the baroque was equally rich although the focus was more on theatrical performance than liturgical function. Occasionally, there were congregational hymns sung during low Masses. The *Cantual of Mainz* published in 1605 encouraged the incorporation of German hymns in the Mass, including hymns to be sung by the assembly in place of the *Gloria*, the *Sanctus*, etc. This tradition existed in Germany, especially in Bavaria even prior to the Reformation, eventually finding its way into the German high Mass. It escaped condemnation by church authorities because the presider continued to whisper the texts in Latin as the assembly and choir sang in German. New musical developments in harmony and counterpoint brought about newly composed Masses to be sung by one or more choirs, along with the use of other instrumentation besides the organ. Masses were composed for orchestras by such musical leaders

[23] Klauser, 138–9.
[24] White, 28–9.

as Mozart and Beethoven. The artistic accomplishments of Baroque music entertained liturgical assemblies, but congregants remained passive spectators and had little role in the liturgy itself.

One significant liturgical issue of the seventeenth century was that of the Chinese Rites Controversy[25] which demonstrated the tension between the Catholic culture of Europe and its encounter with the non-Christian cultures of Asia through the experience of Catholic missionaries. The controversy centered on two issues: the veneration of deceased parents and relatives, and the cult of Confucius. Early Jesuit missionaries like Matteo Ricci believed that the Chinese did not have to deny every aspect of their culture to accept Christianity, while later Dominican and Franciscan missionaries disagreed. The debate received a great deal of attention from the Congregation of Sacred Rites.

Back in Europe, the mid-seventeenth century witnessed the evolution of the neo-Gallican liturgies.[26] The term "neo-Gallican" has no reference to the earlier Gallican rites but refers to the country of origin. Beginning in 1667 with the *Ritual of Alet*, a number of dioceses in France published a series of service books with rubrics printed in French and with variations in content from diocese to diocese. A new ritual for the Archdiocese of Reims followed ten years later, along with a new breviary published in 1678 by the archbishop of Vienne, Henri de Villars. The breviary replaced antiphons and responsories with others taken from Scripture. A new breviary was published for the Archdiocese of Paris in 1680 followed by a new missal in 1684. A new monastic breviary for Cluny followed in 1686.[27]

The growth of the Jansenist movement with its rigoristic piety had its own influence on worship in France in the seventeenth and eighteenth centuries.[28] Founded by Cornelius Jansen (✝ 1638), bishop of Ypres, Jansenists argued that a serious preparation was required prior to the reception of Communion. This position was viewed by outsiders as challenging the practice of frequent Communion, while Jansenists believed they were encouraging a more informed liturgical participation. Although the movement had a number of supporters

---

[25] G. Minamiki, *The Chinese Rites Controversy from Its Beginning to Modern Times* (Chicago, 1985).

[26] F. Ellen Weaver, "The Neo-Gallican Liturgies Revisited," *SL* 16 (1986–1987) 62–5.

[27] White, 32.

[28] A. Adam, *Les Jansénistes au XVII siècle* (Paris, 1968).

among the bishops, it was condemned by several popes, Innocent X and Clement XI in particular. Jansenists battled with Jesuits over the sacrament of penance, accusing the Jesuits of being too lenient with the sacrament due to their adherence to probabilism. Jansenists argued for greater severity and stricter penances.

THE ROMAN LITURGY IN THE
AGE OF ENLIGHTENMENT

The enlightenment's emphasis on rationalism and logic was not a great help to the reform of the liturgy. This was a time of heightened individualism where the essential logic of the liturgy was sought in order to assist in personal moral formation. Despite Tridentine attempts to simplify the liturgical calendar and restore the celebration of Sunday to its proper place, the proliferation of feasts continued and many were assigned to Sundays. As for liturgical scholarship, ancient sacramentaries and the *Ordines Romani* were being discovered, studied, and published, thanks to the initiative of scholars like Cardinal Giuseppe Tomasi († 1713).[29] In 1741, attempting to re-launch the liturgical reform, Pope Benedict XV established a commission to recommend liturgical changes. Following their six-year project, the commission presented their report in 1747, but it was rejected by the Pope. Benedict XV then decided to take the matter into his own hands but died before being able to execute the liturgical reform he desired. Despite liturgical scholarship and attempts at reform, rigid liturgical rubricism continued, with the exception of the local liturgies of the French church.[30]

The biblical and patristic revival taking place in France and throughout Europe gave added incentive to return to the sources. Liturgical innovations continued to the extent that by the eighteenth century, 90 of the 139 dioceses in France had its own liturgy. French bishops viewed their approval of liturgical changes as similar to that of their predecessors who had exercised the same power in approving the study and revision of earlier liturgical texts.[31] Some German bishops followed the example of their French neighbors in reforming breviaries used in their dioceses according to the French model.

[29] I. Scicolone, *Il Cardinale Giuseppe Tomasi di Lampedusa e gli inizi della scienza liturgica* (Palermo, 1981).

[30] P. Jounel, "From the Council of Trent to Vatican II," 72.

[31] J. F. De Percin De Montgaillard, *Du droit et du pouvoir des évêques de régler les offices divins dans leurs diocèses* (Paris, 1686).

A very significant attempt at liturgical renewal came in 1786. Inspired by the Tuscan Grand Duke Leopold II and under the leadership of Scipio dé Ricci († 1810), bishop of Pistoia-Prato, the Jansenist-influenced Synod of Pistoia called for a return to the pristine liturgy of the early Church. The synod affirmed the independence of diocesan bishops to govern their own dioceses accordingly and that such governance took place according to the approval of the diocesan synod of the clergy. This was the position of the Gallican articles of 1682. Devotion to the Sacred Heart promoted by the Jesuits was opposed along with the cult of those saints and their reliquaries lacking historical foundation, and processions carrying reliquaries or images of the Madonna and the saints.

The synod encouraged the active liturgical participation of the faithful, introducing use of the vernacular, eliminating Masses taking place simultaneously in the same place, underlining the centrality of the Sunday and parochial Eucharist where the presider should proclaim the prayers in a loud, clear voice, and decreeing that Communion given to the faithful must be consecrated at that same Mass, rather than inappropriately relying on the convenience of the tabernacle. Baptismal preparation for parents and godparents was insisted upon, and it was considered preferable that baptisms took place at the Easter Vigil. Marriage preparation for couples was also decreed.

The synod was far ahead of its time. Indeed, the liturgical reforms bear a remarkable resemblance to liturgical concerns of Vatican II because both relied upon the same sources for their reforms: the liturgical tradition of the Church that ancient liturgical texts began to propagate. Unlike the Synod of Pistoia, however, Vatican II enjoyed a fifty-year preparation in the work of the liturgical movement. In 1794, eight years after the Synod of Pistoia, eighty-five propositions of the Synod were condemned by Pius VI in the bull *Auctorem fidei*. The first fifteen regarding the Church and its hierarchy were considered heretical while the rest were termed "false, scandalous," etc. Dé Ricci was subjected to public humiliation and was deposed as bishop in 1790. In fact, the people and clergy of the diocese were not in agreement with the decrees.[32]

---

[32] C. Bolton, *Church Reform in 18th Century Italy: The Synod of Pistoia 1786* (The Hague, 1969).

THE ROMAN LITURGY AND
THE PERIOD OF RESTORATION

Following the French Revolution, the Church in France was in a state of tremendous disarray. In 1833 Prosper Guéranger († 1875) refounded the Benedictine Abbey of Solesmes that had been suppressed during the revolution (1792). Guéranger's intent was that the new Solesmes respond to the needs of the contemporary Church while remaining faithful to the monastic rule and Church teaching.[33] It would also assist in bringing about ecclesial unity and uniformity in France in light of local liturgical innovations that he considered too Jansenist and Protestant since they were done without the permission of the Holy See. Unlike the rest of France, the Eucharist and hours at Solesmes were celebrated strictly according to the Roman rite. Guéranger advocated a return to Gregorian chant as the official liturgical music of the Church. In the 1870s, the monks of Solesmes embarked on a study of chant manuscripts by returning to medieval sources and purifying texts of accretions. The results of their research have proved to be a valuable contribution for the Church.

Despite Guéranger's conservatism, he is often considered to be the founder of the European liturgical movement. This is ironic since his approach was highly subjective, leading him to inaccurate liturgical conclusions. Some of the local French liturgies he opposed, for example, were later accepted by Vatican II and incorporated in the missal of Paul VI. Nonetheless, Guéranger's contribution was significant. He worked at restoring the liturgy as central to the monastic life. He educated many of the French clergy and laity through his nine-volume series, *L'année liturgique*, begun in Advent of 1841. In that same year, he initiated another major work, *Institutions liturgiques* which was more scholarly in tone. It must be noted, however, that unlike other liturgical pioneers, Guéranger failed to promote the fundamental liturgical principle of "full and active liturgical participation by whole assembly." Moreover, his work failed to rely on a patristic liturgical model and it lacked the social justice dimension, central elements of the liturgical movement in Europe and elsewhere.

[33] C. Johnson, *Prosper Guéranger (1805–1875): A Liturgical Theologian* (Rome, 1984) 147–89.

The influence of Solesmes was not limited to France but was carried into Germany as well, through the founding of the Benedictine abbey of Beuron and then its daughter house of Maria Laach. In many respects, Beuron closely resembled Solesmes. Founded in 1863 by Maurus and Placidus Wolter, these brothers initiated that same monastic and liturgical reform in Germany that Solesmes had offered to the church in France. The early years of the monastery at Beuron reveal concerns similar to those of Solesmes, a great respect for the classic Roman liturgy, for example. Beuron became famous for its Romanesque art and its art school founded by Desiderius Lenz, who was influenced by Giotto, El Greco, and others. Lenz worked at establishing artistic unity within one liturgical space, fostering the harmonic relationship between art and liturgy and encouraging others to do the same. Beuron also became involved in liturgical publishing. In 1884, Dom Anselm Schott published the first German-Latin missal, *Das Messbuch der Hl. Kirche*. In 1893 the *Vesperbuch* followed. Each volume contained numerous explanations taken from Guéranger's *L'année liturgique*.

The late nineteenth century witnessed a growth in liturgical scholarship. The review *Ephemerides liturgicae* was founded in 1887 and three great collectors of liturgical texts, the Surtees Society, the Henry Bradshaw Society, and the Alcuin Club Collections were founded in 1884, 1891, and 1899, respectively.

THE CLASSICAL LITURGICAL MOVEMENT

The early years of the twentieth century saw the coming of age of the liturgical movement in Europe and gradually in other parts of the world. Although Guéranger is sometimes called the founder of the European liturgical movement, most historians agree that the real founder was the Belgian Benedictine, Dom Lambert Beauduin, monk of Mont César (founded in 1899), and the date for the movement's inception was 1909 at the *Congrès national des ouvres catholiques* at Malines, Belgium, when Beauduin delivered his historic address, *La vraie prière de l'église.* In that conference, he called for full and active participation of all Christians in the Church's life and ministry, particularly the liturgy. He took as his mandate one of the statements from the *motu proprio* of Pius X, *Tra le sollecitudini*, promulgated on 22 November 1903, which described the liturgy as "the Church's most important and indispensable source," and called for greater liturgical participation. Although the *motu proprio* dealt primarily with the issue of Gregorian chant as the "supreme model for sacred music," its call for greater liturgical participation by the whole Church was far more influential. Beauduin claimed the papal document as the "magna carta" of the liturgical movement.

Two years after the promulgation of the *motu proprio*, the same pope promulgated *Sacra Tridentina synodus*, reiterating the Tridentine call to sacramental communion by the faithful. The document led to the return of many Catholics to the practice of weekly and even daily Communion and fostered an awareness of the reception of Communion as integral to liturgical participation. With the promulgation of *Quam singulari* in 1910, Pius X lowered the age for first Communion to the "age of reason," i.e., when the child had reached age seven. In 1911, the apostolic constitution *Divino afflatu* called for a reordering of the psalter in the breviary, and it was reformed again in 1914.

In 1910 Beauduin founded *La vie liturgique* and was joined by other monks of Mont César in initiating the annual *semaines liturgiques* (liturgical weeks) in 1912. In 1914, he published his only book, *La piété de l'église,* which was a public declaration of the liturgical movement, offering it solid theological and ecclesiological grounding. Several years earlier, another Belgian Benedictine monastery, Maredsous (1872), had already earned a reputation in liturgical publishing with the 1882 edition of the first French-Latin missal, *Missel des fidèles* by Dom Gérard van Caloen, rector of the abbey school.[34]

In the Rhineland, Maria Laach became a center of German liturgical scholarship and reform. In 1913, before becoming abbot, Ildefons Herwegen († 1946) met a group of young laymen who expressed the desire for greater liturgical participation. One year later, the new abbot invited that same group back to the monastery for holy week of 1914, where they celebrated together the dialogue Mass for the first time.[35]

---

[34] B. Botte, *Le Mouvement liturgique: Témoignage et souvenirs* (Paris, 1973) 18–23.

[35] A. Häußling, "Die betende Kirche. Maria Laach und die deutsche Liturgische Bewegung," in *Erneurung der Kirche aus dem Geist der Liturgie* (Maria Laach, 1992) 15–26.

Herwegen, together with two of his monks, Cunibert Mohlberg and Odo Casel († 1948), and in collaboration with Romano Guardini († 1968), Franz Dölger, and Anton Baumstark pioneered the German liturgical movement. In 1918 they organized a three-fold series of publications: *Ecclesia Orans, Liturgiegeschichtliche Quellen,* and *Liturgiegeschichtliche Forschungen.* Three years later, they initiated the periodical *Jarbuch für Liturgiewissenschaft.* A theoretician, Casel wrote hundreds of articles and books in the next thirty years, the most famous of which was *Das cristliche Kultmysterium.* In that text he spoke of the sacraments as mysteries, believing that Christian sacraments were rooted in the Greek mystery cults. Although this theory is no longer held today, his interpretation gave way to a positive and rich view of the Church as the mystical body of Christ that expresses itself relationally and symbolically through sacramental participation. Casel's theory was hotly debated. Guardini published his classic work *Vom Geist der Liturgie* in 1923. Under Herwegen's direction, the first *missa recitata* was celebrated in the crypt of the abbey church on August 6, 1921, presided over by the prior, Albert Hammenstede. This Mass included the praying of the ordinary parts of the Mass in common and the participation of the assembly in the offertory procession.

Liturgical renewal of the early twentieth century was not limited to Belgium, France, and Germany but was spreading elsewhere. The first Netherlands Congress on Liturgy took place at Breda in 1911, leading to the founding of the Liturgical Society of the Dioceses of Haarlem (1912) and Utrecht (1914), and the Dutch Liturgical Federation in 1915. In Austria the liturgical movement grew under the leadership of Augustinian Canon Pius Parsch († 1954). Based at his monastery of Klosterneuburg, Parsch integrated the liturgical scholarship of Germany with the pastoral concerns of Austria in a common goal of biblical and liturgical renewal. That renewal was fostered through two important publications: *Das Jahr des Heiles* (begun in 1923), a commentary on the missal and the breviary for the entire liturgical year, and *Bibel und Liturgie* (founded in 1926), which promoted the relationship between Bible and liturgy and encouraged a wider knowledge of Scripture among Catholics.

In Italy, the monks of Finalpia, Savona, fostered the liturgical apostolate through their important review *Rivista liturgica* in which many of the Italian liturgical pioneers communicated their ideas on the renewal of the liturgy. Founded in 1914, the journal continues to be published today. Two leading figures in the Italian liturgical movement were Emmanuel Caronti, O.S.B. and Ildefonso Schuster, O.S.B. In 1919, Schuster wrote his *Liber Sacramentorum* which consisted of historical and liturgical notes on the Roman missal, addressed primarily to the clergy. Caronti grounded ecclesial piety in a solid liturgical spirituality in his text *La pietà liturgica*. His greatest contribution, however, was the widely acclaimed *Messale festivo per i fedeli*. This missal helped a large number of Italian Catholics to encounter the richness of the Church's worship by assisting their understanding of the liturgical texts and thereby enhancing an appreciation of the liturgy itself.[36]

The liturgical movement began to take shape in other European countries as well[37] with different emphases according to the cultural and ecclesial climate within each country. In particular, there were significant developments in Spain, Portugal, Switzerland, England,[38] Czechoslovakia, Hungary, and Poland.[39] Such cultural diversity was best seen through liturgical architecture. The French Church of Notre Dame du Raincy designed by Auguste Perret, a secular architect well-known as a master of reinforced concrete construction, was dedicated in 1923 and marked the beginning of the movement in modern liturgical architecture. Perret's influence soon spread beyond France. In Switzerland, examples include Karl Moser's Church of St. Anthony, Basel, and Fritz Metzger's Church of St. Charles, Luzerne, and in Germany, Rudolf Schwartz's chapel at Burg Rothenfels designed in collaboration with Romano Guardini, and his Church of Corpus Christi, Aachen. Germany took the lead in initiating the dialogue between theologians and architects through the influence of Maria Laach and individuals such as Guardini.[40]

---

[36] F. Brovelli, *Ritorno alla liturgia: Saggi di studio sul movimento liturgico* (Rome, 1989) 231–2.

[37] For a recent survey of the liturgical movement within Europe, see R. K. Fenwick and B. Spinks, *Worship in Transition: Highlights of the Liturgical Movement* (Edinburgh, 1995).

[38] D. Gray, *Earth and Altar* (Norwich: Alcuin Club Collections 68, 1986).

[39] J. Sroka, *L'apport de l'abbé Michel Kordel au mouvement liturgique polonais* (Roma: SL.D. dissertation, Pontifical Liturgical Institute of Sant' Anselmo, 1973.)

[40] P. Hammond, *Liturgy and Architecture* (New York, 1961) 50–66.

The liturgical movement was not limited to Europe, but found its way across the Atlantic to the Americas, as well. In 1926 the liturgical movement in the United States was launched at Collegeville, Minnesota, under the leadership of Virgil Michel, O.S.B. († 1938), in collaboration with William Busch, Martin Hellriegel, Gerald Ellard, S.J., and others.[41] In 1933 the Brazilian liturgical movement was initiated in Rio de Janeiro by Martinho Michler, O.S.B., in collaboration with Beda Kecheisen, O.S.B., Polycarpo Amstalden, O.S.B., Hildebrando Martins, O.S.B., and others.[42] The movements in Brazil and the United States were both marked by a strong pastoral emphasis, highlighting the relationship between liturgy and social action. In both countries annual liturgical weeks were a source of support and encouragement for liturgical pioneers and promoters, and in both countries a pastorally-oriented periodical was immediately founded as an important tool in promoting liturgical renewal. *Orate Fratres* (later *Worship*) was founded in 1926 to foster a deeper understanding of and wider participation in the liturgy through articles, editorials, announcements of lectures and conferences, "letters to the editor," etc. In 1934, the weekly *Folheto litúrgico* was founded at Sao Paolo initially including only the liturgical texts for Sunday to promote the dialogue Mass, but gradually also including occasional instructions on the Mass to promote a better liturgical understanding.[43]

The liturgical renewal was given support in the 1928 apostolic constitution on sacred music *Divini cultus*, which argued that the faithful should not attend the liturgy passively as "silent spectators" but as active participants, singing with the presider and choir. Although such documents assisted the work of the liturgical pioneers, their task remained difficult and controversies often became normative. Germany offers an interesting example. In 1934 the pastoral journal *Liturgisches Leben* was founded in Berlin by university chaplain Johannes Pinsk († 1957) to forge the relationship between liturgy and daily life. Increasingly, the journal encouraged Christian social re-

[41] K. F. Pecklers, *The Liturgical Movement in the United States of America: 1926–1955* (Collegeville, 1995).

[42] J. Ariovaldo da Silva, *O Movimento Litúrgico no Brasil: Estudo Histórico* (Petrópolis, 1983).

[43] Ibid., 58–9.

sponsibility, especially in light of the rise of Nazism.[44] Some within the German church began to publicly criticize the liturgical movement for such activism, as in M. Kassiepe's book *Irrwege und Umwege im Frömmigkeitsleben der Gegenwart*. Responding to the controversy, a Liturgical Working Party was initiated including such members as Romano Guardini and Josef Jungmann. The controversy continued and was brought to the German hierarchy in 1942. The result was the establishment of a national liturgical commission which, in addition to members of the Liturgical Working Party, also included monks from Beuron and Maria Laach. The group served as a liaison between members of the liturgical movement, the German bishops, and the rest of the German church. In 1943 Cardinal Betram, archbishop of Breslau, requested permission from the Holy See for the reform of the ritual, the breviary, and other liturgical books. Cardinal Maglione, the Vatican secretary of state responded by approving the *Gemeinschaftsmesse* (community Mass) and stated that the Holy See "sympathetically tolerates" the *Deutsches Hochamt* (sung Mass) which included the singing of vernacular hymns contrary to the rubrics.[45]

Interest in liturgical research and education grew in the 1940s. In the United States, the first national liturgical week took place in 1940 at Holy Name Cathedral, Chicago, with 1,260 participants. The *Centre de pastorale liturgique* was founded in Paris in 1943 under the leadership of A.-M. Roguet, O.P., and Pie Duploye, O.P., and soon became a center of liturgical activity. Two years later, the centre initiated its well-known publication *La Maison-Dieu* which continues to the present. Meanwhile in Austria, Josef Jungmann, S.J. († 1975), was writing his classic work, *Missarum Sollemnia*. The two-volume text took six years to complete, from 1939 to 1945, and was published in 1948. Balthasar Fischer was the first to hold a chair of liturgy in the

[44] A number in the German liturgical movement strongly opposed Nazism. Although Hans A. Reinhold is considered more a pioneer of the liturgical movement in the United States, he attributed his own liturgical formation to Maria Laach and ultimately had to flee Germany because of his outspoken criticism of Nazism. Finding his way to the United States, Reinhold was largely responsible for instilling a strong social consciousness in the American movement during the 1940s.

[45] V. Funk, "The Liturgical Movement: 1830–1969" in P. Fink, *The New Dictionary of Sacramental Worship* (Collegeville, 1990) 702–3.

University of Trier's theological faculty in the academic year 1946–1947. Johannes Wagner founded the Liturgical Institute in that same year, serving as its first director, while at Maria Laach, the Herwegen Institute for the Promotion of Liturgical Studies was inaugurated with the publication of the well-known *Archiv für Liturgiewissenschaft*. Michael Mathis, C.S.C., began the first American academic program in liturgy in the summer of 1947 at the University of Notre Dame in Indiana. In 1951 the Liturgical Institute at Trier initiated its *Liturgisches Jahrbuch*.[46]

One finds few names of women in the history of the liturgical movement. It would seem that all the liturgical pioneers were men and almost all were Benedictine. This was not the case. True enough, women were excluded from the academic world until relatively recently, so those specialists who set the agenda for the liturgical reform were primarily men. But it must also be noted that women were often involved in different facets of the liturgical movement. In Belgium, for example, the Abbey of Wépion was founded in the 1920s to introduce the "modern woman" to the richness of the liturgical life. The abbey became a liturgical center not only for Belgian women, but for German and French women, as well. In Germany, most of the early work on the index for *Jahrbuch für Liturgiewissenschaft* was done by Agape Kiesgen († 1933), a Benedictine nun from Herstelle. In fact, Kiesgen collaborated with Odo Casel on a number of projects. Another nun of Herstelle, Aemiliana Löhr († 1972), who wrote over three hundred articles, poems, and books, is known for having composed some of the best meditations for Sundays and feasts throughout the 1930s. At Maria Laach, Abbot Herwegen encouraged one of his monks, Athanasius Wintersig († 1942) to write *Liturgie und Frauenseele*. The book explicitly discussed the important role of women in the liturgical movement. One finds regular contributions by women in the liturgical periodicals *Bibel und Liturgie, Liturgische Zeitschrift*, and *Liturgisches Leben*.[47] In the United States, examples include Justine Ward and

[46] H-C. Schmidt-Lauber, "Begriff, Geschichte und Stand der Forschung," in Schmidt-Lauber und K-H. Bieritz, *Handbuch der Liturgik: Liturgiewissenschaft in Theologie und Praxis der Kirche* (Leipzig, 1995) 23–6.

[47] T. Berger, "The Classical Liturgical Movement in Germany and Austria: Moved by Women?" *Worship* 66 (1992) 234–6.

Georgia Stevens, R.S.C.J., who founded the Pius X School of Liturgical Music in 1916, as well as Adé Bethune, Dorothy Day, Catherine DeHueck, Sara Benedicta O'Neil, Mary Perkins Ryan, and Nina Polcyn Moore, all of whom contributed significantly to that liturgical movement.[48]

Liturgical research and pioneering were supported by several significant papal documents in that same period. As World War II was raging, Pius XII issued his encyclical *Mystici Corporis Christi* in 1943, which emphasized the corporate nature of the Church as the body of Christ. This fundamentally Pauline doctrine promoted by nineteenth-century German theologians of the Tübingen school and used by liturgical pioneers as the theological basis for liturgical renewal was highly controversial prior to the encyclical because some believed it threatened the hierarchical structure of the Church. In that same year, the encyclical *Divino afflante Spiritu* was issued allowing for the use of modern exegetical methods for the study of Scripture. Four years later, in 1947, Pius XII issued *Mediator Dei,* the first encyclical exclusively devoted to the liturgy. Although the document cautioned against liturgical abuses and upheld the Latin liturgy, it officially recognized the liturgical movement and inaugurated a series of liturgical changes that would lead to the Vatican II.

In 1947 Belgium received permission for the celebration of evening Mass on Sundays and holydays. The Diocese of Bayonne, France, received approval for the recitation of the complete *introit* psalm, and a Latin-French edition of the *RR* was also approved. One year later, the Belgian Diocese of Liège received permission for the same ritual. The Japanese bishops were given permission to allow evening Masses also in 1948, and daily evening Masses were approved for some parts of Poland. The translation of the *MR* of 1570 (except for the Roman Canon) into Mandarin Chinese was approved by the Holy See in 1949, and India was given permission for evening Masses and a shorter eucharistic fast. In 1950 a shorter form of the breviary was approved for use in Holland, while the Austrian, French, and German bishops requested permission for the restoration of the Easter Vigil to Holy Saturday evening. A restored Easter Vigil was approved as an experiment on February 9, 1951, with the document *Ordo Sabbati*

[48] N. Mitchell, "The Amen Corner," *Worship* 68 (1994) 64–72.

Sancti. In 1953 and 1957 the apostolic constitutions *Christus Dominus* and *Sacram communionem* respectively, gave permission for evening Mass and a shortened eucharistic fast to the universal Church.[49]

In 1955 Pius XII's encyclical on liturgical music *Musicae sacrae disciplina* approved the use of vernacular hymns during Mass, but far more significant was the full restoration of the Holy Week rites, promulgated for Palm Sunday 1956. This was seen as a landmark accomplishment for liturgical pioneers. Odo Casel did not live long enough to see his foundational work on the paschal mystery come to fruition. He died in 1948, just after intoning the *Exsultet* during the Easter Vigil at the Benedictine convent of Herstelle. The revised rites of Holy Week left much work to be done. Prior to 1955, liturgies of the paschal triduum were normally celebrated in the morning with only a small number of the faithful present. Now that those liturgies had been transferred to the evening, Catholics needed to be catechized as to why participation in those rites was so important.

In 1951 the first international liturgical congress took place at Maria Laach, followed by Odilienberg in 1952, and Lugano in 1954. In 1956 the first international pastoral liturgical congress was held at Assisi. This was a historic meeting. Presided over by the prefect of the Congregation of Sacred Rites, Cardinal Gaetano Cicognani, the congress gathered together over fourteen hundred participants from five continents, including eighty bishops and six cardinals. Among the presentations, the talk by Josef Jungmann, "The Pastoral Idea in the History of the Liturgy," and that of Cardinal Augustin Bea, "The Pastoral Value of the Word of God," were considered the most significant.[50] Only several years later, Vatican II's *Sacrosanctum Concilium* would echo many of the same concerns articulated at the Assisi Congress. Two primary concerns surfaced during the congress: the issue of a vernacular liturgy and the reform of the breviary. Both topics brought about lively discussion and even heated debate during the congress.[51] At the end of the gathering, participants travelled to Rome for an address by Pius XII, where he stated that the movement

[49] Funk, 706–8.

[50] *The Assisi Papers: Proceedings of the First International Congress on Pastoral Liturgy, Assisi-Rome, September 18–22 1956* (Collegeville, 1957) 18–31.

[51] A. Bugnini, *The Reform of the Liturgy: 1948–1975* (Collegeville, 1990) 12.

was a sign of God's providence and of the presence of the Holy Spirit in the Church, bringing people closer to the mystery of faith and the grace that comes through liturgical participation.[52]

Pius XII died on October 9, 1958 and John XXIII was elected pope. On January 25, 1959 the new pope announced Vatican II. On June 6, 1960, a preparatory commission on the liturgy was established with Cicognani as president. One month later, Annibale Bugnini, C.M. († 1982) was appointed secretary.

The commission began its work immediately, creating subcommissions on the following topics: (1) the mystery of the liturgy in relation to the Church, (2) the Mass, (3) eucharistic concelebration, (4) the Divine Office, (5) sacraments and sacramentals, (6) calendar reform, (7) use of Latin, (8) liturgical formation, (9) liturgical participation by the laity, (10) cultural and linguistic adaptation, (11) simplification of liturgical vesture, (12) liturgical music, and (13) liturgical art.[53] When the time came to appoint members for the various subcommissions, many members of the liturgical movement were chosen. Names such as Godfrey Diekmann, O.S.B. (St. John's Abbey, Collegeville, Minnesota, U.S.A.), Balthasar Fischer (Trier, Germany), Joseph Gelineau, S.J. (Paris, France), Anton Hänggi (Fribourg, Switzerland), Josef Jungmann, S.J. (Innsbruck, Austria), Frederick McManus (Washington, D.C., U.S.A.), Cipriano Vagaggini, O.S.B. (Bologna, Italy), Johannes Wagner (Trier, Germany) appeared on the roster of the preparatory commission.

The preparatory commission designed the *schemata* for the reform of the liturgy which was presented to Vatican II.[54] Between October 22 and November 13, 1962, council participants spent fifteen general meetings discussing liturgical reform. A series of amendments delayed the process, thus it was not until the end of the second session, on December 4, 1963, that Paul VI promulgated *Sacrosanctum*

---

[52] *Christ the Center of the Church's Liturgy, Address by His Holiness, Pope Pius XII, to the Delegates of the First International Congress on Pastoral Liturgy assembled in Vatican City, September 22, 1956.* Trans by the Vatican Press Office (Clyde, Mo: Benedictine Convent of Perpetual Adoration, 1957).

[53] Bugnini, 15–16.

[54] C. Braga, "La preparazione della Costituzione *Sacrosanctum Concilium*," in A. G. Martimort, *Mens concordet voci* (Paris, 1983) 381–403.

Concilium,[55] approved by a vote of 2,147 to 4. Following an introduction, the first chapter of the constitution outlines the general principles for the reform, followed by concrete directives on the Eucharist in the second chapter. Chapter 3 deals with the other sacraments and sacramentals, followed by the Liturgy of the Hours (ch. 4), the liturgical year (ch. 5), liturgical music (ch. 6), and liturgical art (ch. 7). The doctrine of the Church as the mystical body of Christ that theologically girded the liturgical movement prior to the council gave way to a new vision of the Church as the people of God.

On January 29, 1964, a new commission was established by Paul VI to assist in the implementation of the new liturgical reforms throughout the world. Called the *Consilium ad exsequendam Constitutionem de sacra Liturgia* and chaired by the archbishop of Bologna, Cardinal Giacomo Lercaro, the international *Consilium* comprised fifty cardinals and bishops and over two hundred liturgiologists. Annibale Bugnini, C.M., served as secretary. That commission was given the task of revising liturgical books according to the new directives of the council, of teaching the whole Church about the renewed liturgy and the call to full and active participation. Change came quickly, not only regarding the vernacular, but in many other areas, as well. The work of the *Consilium* lasted for five years when in 1969, it was replaced by the Congregation for Divine Worship.

In the forty-five years prior to Vatican II, many men and women throughout the Church labored tirelessly for a renewal that would call clergy and laity alike into full and active liturgical participation. Liturgical pioneers like Beauduin, Casel, and Michel died before they could witness the results of their initiative. Other pioneers who promoted such things as a vernacular liturgy were happy to see their dream become a reality. All those efforts were crowned with the promulgation of *Sacrosanctum Concilium*. The difficult task of implementation was yet to come. Thirty-five years later, we are still learning the significance of those liturgical reforms and the social responsibility implied in our liturgical "Amen."

[55] W. Baraúna, *The Liturgy of Vatican II*, 2 vols (Chicago, 1966); H. Schmidt, *La Costituzione sulla Sacra Liturgia: testo, genesi, commento, documentazione* (Rome, 1966).

Bibliography

Cattaneo, E. *Il culto cristiano in Occidente*, 371–378. Rome, 1978.

Klauser, Th. *A Short History of the Western Liturgy*. Trans. J. Halliburton. 2nd ed. New York, 1979.

Martimort, A.-G., ed. *The Church at Prayer*. Collegeville, Minn., 1987.

Neuner, J., and J. Dupuis. *The Christian Faith in the Doctrinal Documents of the Catholic Church*, 413–428. Staten Island, N.Y., 1981.

Neunheuser, B. *Storia della liturgia attraverso le epoche culturali*. Rome, 1983.

Power, D. *The Sacrifice We Offer: The Tridentine Dogma and Its Reinterpretation*. Edinburgh, 1987.

Taft, R. *The Liturgy of the Hours in East and West*. Collegeville, Minn., 1987.

White, J. *Roman Catholic Worship: Trent to Today*. New York, 1995.

Jordi Pinell i Pons, O.S.B.

11

History of the Liturgies in the Non-Roman West

I. THE FORMATION OF THE LATIN RITES

1. Diversification through a Process of Ecclesial Maturity
The process of diversification of the rites of the Christian liturgy took place through the positive affirmation of particular values in specific churches within the unanimous tradition in what is essential. Christianity had spread through communities closely related to their place of origin or residence and to their historical and cultural components. Discrepancies did not produce differences among local churches in terms of planning communitarian prayer, celebrating the Lord's memorial, administering the sacraments, and organizing a calendar of seasons and feasts. Instead, this was brought about by a progressive theological and pastoral understanding of the mysterious reality that Christ had entrusted to the Church in the sacraments.

The ongoing, in-depth understanding of their meaning inspired a more refined elaboration of those signs which helped Christians to establish contacts with God, according to the dictates of their own faith. Thus, the churches continued to be rooted in their particular history as they used the cultural means which characterized them. In that general evolutionary process, there were frequent contacts and exchanges between metropolitan sees, but in any case, the formation of local liturgies occurred spontaneously and autonomously.

2. Culmination of the Homiletic Period
In the Western Mediterranean region the phenomenon of liturgical creativity appeared in the middle of the fifth century at the height of

the "homiletic period," that is to say, when, for all practical purposes, public allocution addressed directly to the assembly was already replacing the form of instruction of a treatise to be read and learned in private. In all of this, one implicitly finds a new appreciation for the "praying ecclesial assembly" as the medium for transmitting revealed truth, the place and privileged moment for the Holy Spirit's salvific action. From then on, the formularies intended for ecclesial prayer and the eucharistic celebration became privileged documents of Christian thinking. People were already beginning to experience that participation in the liturgy constituted a first-rate pedagogical tool indispensable for completing the pre-baptismal catechesis.

3. Product of Particular Circumstances

The ceremonial organization of the celebrations of the Office, the Mass, and the sacraments (every *ordo's* schema) and the list of fixed or variable texts (readings, canticles, and euchology) were mostly the work of clergymen who were familiar with the practices and customs of various churches. Thus, the quality and success of those fundamental elements depended on their authors' skill and talent. For the most part, the uniqueness of local liturgies was the result of the choices made by their authors at a determined time in their evolution.

4. All the Churches Did Not Have the Same Luck

All the Western churches did not succeed in attaining full development. There is nothing left of what might have been the liturgies of Latin Africa or Aquileia. Little has been preserved of what was beginning to be organized as the liturgy of Benevento. Some liturgical rites for the so-called "Celtic rite" for Ireland were compiled, but their content does not show that a lot of creativity took place there. We will see shortly that circumstances were not equally favorable or adverse to the three liturgies that we will consider: the Ambrosian, the Gallican, and the Hispanic.

5. The Mass and the Office Are Not Distinguished in the Same Way

The Office is that part of the liturgy in which local churches show the greatest freedom and independence. In the service of common prayer, they invent forms that inspire while nourishing personal spirituality, as they combine scriptural phrases and images with church-composed poetic and euchological texts inducing reflection. Thus, we find hymns, antiphons, responses, and prayers from different genres which are subsequently presented in wisely organized structures. The greatest care in the plan of the celebration applies to the rites of the sacraments.

Local liturgies are more similar in terms of the celebration of the Eucharist. This is undoubtedly because of the close ties uniting all the churches with the universal tradition. However, even in this case, it should be indicated that while the Ambrosian Mass is close to the Roman Mass in its structure, by nature of their variable texts the Gallican and Hispanic Masses differ from them. Their configuration is so similar that variable parts of the Hispanic rite could easily be used in the Gallican rite, and vice versa, Gallican prayers could be used in the Hispanic rite.

6. Current Interest

Local Latin liturgies provide a focus for our present study especially from a doctrinal point of view. The contemplation of Christ's mystery according to the liturgical year inspired their authors to write spiritual reflections comparable to those of the treatises and homilies of the patristic period. The events or situations conditioning their genesis, evolution, and decadence are also valuable because they serve now as models to help in pastoral orientation.

The three rites we will examine have not been equally preserved. The Ambrosian rite in its entirety — Mass, Office, and ritual — continues to be used in the area where it was created. On the other hand, the daily celebration of the Hispanic rite — Mass and Office — was limited to the Mozarabic Chapel of the Cathedral of Toledo. Occasionally, that Mass is celebrated in other parts of Spain.

The Office, the Mass, and the ritual of the Ambrosian church have been renewed according to the guidelines of Vatican II. The Hispanic-Mozarabic ritual has also been revised.

Today, it would be impossible to celebrate Mass according to the Gallican rite. Only the readings and the euchology have been preserved. The manuscripts of the antiphonary were not kept. As a result, we lack the songs which were part of the celebration. The sources pertaining to the Gallican rite have been totally lost.

II. THE AMBROSIAN LITURGY

1. Name and Origin

The well-known figure of St. Ambrose gave his name to the local liturgy of Milan. Some of the pieces intended for sacred songs which the saintly doctor and bishop composed at the same time as he promulgated his hymns may have brought about the institution of the music school whose influence subsequently spread to Rome, Benevento, Tarragona, and Seville. Most likely, the criteria used to select the Scripture of the Milan rite, at least for Lent and Easter, came from a fourth-century tradition contemporary of Ambrose.

But Milan's autonomous liturgy also reflected the Roman creativity of the fifth century, when Milan's euchological school adopted the principle of a variation for the preface and the prayers of the Mass such as the experiment St. Leo had introduced in Rome.

2. The Eucharistic Prayer of De Sacramentis

By interpreting the Eucharistic Prayer quoted by St. Ambrose in *De Sacramentis* (IV, 5–6) as an incipient version of the "Roman canon," one can assume that a common liturgy co-existed at that time in Rome and Milan. Nevertheless, the canon which was definitively re-worked in Rome in the middle of the fifth century, could never have resulted from a mere stylistic evolution of the text that Ambrose had known. There are differences between the two texts due to distinct euchological traditions. The Roman canon differs from *De Sacramentis* in very specific points that make it closer to other traditions like the Alexandrian school among others. The Eucharistic Prayer adopted in the Ambrosian rite was not the one from the *De Sacramentis*, but rather from the Roman canon according to the Gregorian version with some variations introduced in Milan.

3. Precedents of an Ambrosian Sacramentary

Historical circumstances did not favor a quick and opportune formation of these particular liturgical books. A schism had taken place for doctrinal reasons and the most representative part of the Milan church had to emigrate to Geneva (571), from where it would not return until 649. Meanwhile, both the Gelasian and Gregorian forms of the Roman sacramentary had been written and promulgated, and both models were to have a strong impact on the eventual options of the Ambrosian compilers.

Yet, at the petition stage, the euchological output for the Ambrosian Mass had been very prolific. Occasionally, there were imitations or variations on Roman texts, but quite frequently new and original ideas emerged. Compared with the formal and juridical language of Roman euchology, the texts of the Ambrosian rite stand out because of a literary style and a lexicon closer to poetry. The structure of the Mass differed from that of the Roman rite in some unimportant though significant details.

The Ambrosian compilers knew the Gelasian model. That prevented them from proceeding with criteria as restrictive and austere as those which characterized the codification of the Gregorian version. They took greater and better advantage of their pre-existing patrimony in editing the Ambrosian sacramentary.

4. *Autonomous and Wise Make-up of the Office*
While it is true that the Ambrosian church had always been subject to what was happening in the Roman rite in the establishment and subsequent evolution of the Mass, it also showed greater freedom in organizing ecclesial praise.

It kept very ancient principles in its selection of psalms and canticles as fundamental elements. It worked out the schemes so that the blend of genres (psalmody, reading, poetry, euchology) would intensify the fervor of the praying community. Also contributing to this fervor was the variety of the forms of singing, from simple psalmodic antiphons to others with a more complex melody, attaining the great responsory, an authentic concert piece as a meditation song. The form of the *responsorium prolixum* presupposed a centonization of the text, and the Ambrosian school became masterful in that technique. Its models were taken as examples by the music schools of Rome and Spain.

Some external influences were imposed upon the Ambrosian Office by its contacts with Benedictine monasteries during the tenth and eleventh centuries. Those were mostly the simultaneous accumulation of various systems of psalmody. The severe Romanizing reform imposed by the Council of Trent affected one of its most significant parts. The unified celebration of the vigil and the morning praise, making the Ambrosian Office resemble venerable examples of some

Eastern rites and also the Hispanic rite, was divided into two separate celebrations without taking into account that the perfect balance of the previous structure was destroyed.

In spite of all, until now, the Ambrosian breviary represented one of the most interesting realizations of the Divine Office, created and preserved with a strong identity of the Church which had designed it. The revision done at the suggestion of Vatican II has been most respectful of the values of its own tradition. Thus, in *Diurna Laus*, we still find the work of a church which, from its most remote origins, was able to harmonize music, word, and gesture with great ability and skill in order to present the mystery of communitarian prayer.

III. THE GALLICAN LITURGY

1. Name and Place of Origin

The term "Gallican" liturgy was established in the seventeenth century by J. Thomasius and I. Mabillon, editors of several of its main sources. It did, in fact, refer to a local liturgy that had emerged in the Mediterranean region of the Gauls and was based on traditions from the Latin ambit, common to those that gave rise to the Hispanic rite.

Later on, other authors incorrectly applied the adjective "Gallican" to elements developed in agencies of Central Europe. These were songs, prayers, rubrics, and ceremonies which gradually filtered into the liturgical books of the Roman rite, from the time the latter was officially adopted in Charlemagne's court and imposed in his whole empire. These elements derived from Nordic piety and from a spirituality proceeding from the British Isles rather than from the Latin culture of the patristic period.

Here, we will refer to what must be considered strictly Gallican and only to what involves the subject matter of two liturgical books: the lectionary and the sacramentary.

2. Construction of the Gallican Peculiarity

The philological analysis of the texts intended for the eucharistic celebration leads us to believe that the greatest and best period of its creativity took place between the end of the fifth century and the middle of the sixth. The Wolfenbüttel palimpsestic lectionary, the oldest of the Latin liturgical texts, also corresponds to the same period.

In order to understand one of the oddest peculiarities of the Gallican rite, we have to recall what was occurring in Rome, whose pattern was increasingly forced upon other Latin churches from then on.

The preface had always been set in all the liturgies. Thanksgiving was considered as an integral and unchangeable part of the Eucharistic Prayer, and it developed in accordance with the style and theme of the corresponding anaphora. From the middle of the fifth century, Rome experimented with and established the custom of a variable preface according to the specific themes of the feast, followed by the set canon which we all know. At the same time, there also appeared changeable short prayers to be recited at several predetermined parts of the celebration: (a) when the assembly gathers before God, (b) at the conclusion of the litanies of universal intercession, (c) at the offering of bread and wine, (d) after Communion, (e) before the assembly is dismissed. Copies of the *libelli missarum* circulated throughout the West. In them, we can observe the interconnected while distinct groups of five prayers and a preface which make up the formulas for a Mass.

Without knowing that reality achieved in the Roman rite, the evolutionary process leading to the Gallican-Hispanic system would have been inconceivable. The variability of the preface, on one hand, and the plurality of texts forming a unified whole on the other, suggested the fragmentation of the Eucharistic Prayer into always varying parts.

3. *Alternance of* Praefatio *and* Collectio

Another important step in characterizing the Gallican rite occurred with the frequent and multiple use of euchological texts addressed to the assembly. These texts already had precedents in the urban liturgy of Rome — calling for fasts and vigils, for example — but the Gallican and Hispanic liturgies applied them in more varied and important ways. One of the most specific texts of both rites — the Gallican *praefatio*, the Hispanic *oratio admonitionis* — introduced a pastoral liturgical style establishing an ongoing communication between the celebrant and the assembly.

In their terminology, the Gallican sources specify if the text is a prayer rising up to God, the *collectio*, and if it is an exhortation addressed to the faithful, the *praefatio*. Although the output of the early Gallican euchological school was not prolific, it was extremely valuable. It does show an original and profound theology of the Eucharist as sacrifice and fulfillment of the Lord's institutional mandate.

4. Irregular and Difficult Codification

However, in the absence of a metropolitan see to offer a solid basis, without the indispensable support and seeing that it was systematically replaced by the Roman rite, the Gallican liturgy quickly lapsed into unavoidable decadence.

The codification of its liturgical books achieved between the middle of the seventh and eighth centuries was rushed, uneven, and overly conditioned by the models of the Roman sacramentary. In the venerable Karlsruhe fragment, edited by F. G. Mone, which corresponds more to the petition stage than to the codification of the books, it is difficult to distinguish what is genuine from later imitations.

Eager to produce a book resembling the Roman canon, the compiler of the so-called *Missale Gothicum* used inferior adaptations to fill up unavoidable lacunae. The Milan and Munich manuscripts took from the Hispanic liturgy what they did not find in their own. Following the example of the Bergamo Sacramentary and other similar books of the Ambrosian rite, the Bobbio Missal combined the lectionary and the sacramentary. But Bobbio's Missal is Gallican only until the preface. From the *Sanctus* on, it proceeds with the Roman canon.

Something similar occurs with the so-called *Missale Gallicanum Vetus*, which rarely includes texts corresponding to the *Post Sanctus* and to the *Post Secreta*. Romanization is even greater in the *Missale Francorum* since it adopts a strictly Roman structure by which it arranges texts of Roman origin. Yet, both missals, the *Missale Gallicanum Vetus* and the *Missale Francorum* contain authentically Gallican texts for Holy Week and ministerial ordinations.

The codification of the lectionary is not totally homogeneous either. There are fewer similarities between the already mentioned Wolfenbüttel, Luxueil manuscript, the monumental Luxeil lectionary copied two centuries later, and other small extant fragments from the same area.

IV. THE HISPANIC LITURGY

The Hispanic liturgy, better known as "Mozarabic" and also called "Visigothic" by some, largely developed during the sixth and seventh centuries, with the successive contributions of three metropolitan sees located in three different areas of the Iberian Peninsula: Tarragona, in the east, Seville in the south, and Toledo in the center.

1. Formation Time

The barbarian invasions and doctrinal disputes against the invaders' Arianism had delayed its development in relation to the other local Latin liturgies. But, thanks to the relative religious peace obtained with the Visigoths' official conversion to Catholicism in the Third Council of Toledo (589), there flourished in the kingdom an authentic Latin humanism, fostered by the court which contributed indirectly to the expansion of the Catholic liturgy.

While it is true that the phenomenon of liturgical creativity occurred later in Spain than in other Mediterranean churches, it is also true that it lasted much longer there. By observing what was happening in other places, the Hispanic fathers had been able to verify the effectiveness of the liturgy as a means to inculcate authentic doctrine in the consciences of the faithful. This is why euchology, hymnody, and the biblical centonizations of sacred chant became favorite literary genres. In fact, together the euchological texts and hymns make up the most important literary legacy of that geographical area during the sixth and seventh centuries.

2. Contribution of the Local Councils

In Spain the churches' solicitude to carry out liturgical celebrations wisely and in the best possible way also manifested itself in the attention that the councils devoted to the subject. The councils of the Tarragona province issued decrees concerning the liturgy in the first half of the sixth century and from 589 on, so did the councils of Toledo until the middle of the seventh century.

As a result, the literary and doctrinal work of the fathers of the Hispanic churches and the councils' legislation converged in the formation of the rites. However, the documentary value of the conciliar decrees does not only have a strictly disciplinary character.

In writing the canon establishing the recitation of the Creed within the eucharistic celebration, placing it precisely in the part of the Mass corresponding to the Communion rite, St. Leander of Seville justified his decision with theological and pastoral reasons. His brother, St. Isidore, would follow his example. In his early years, the latter had written a treatise *De Ecclesiasticis Officiis,* which can be considered as the first "liturgy manual" in history. In it, he showed that he was well informed about the liturgical customs of other Western churches. Years later, having attained full maturity in erudition and pastoral experience, Isidore presided over the Fourth Council of Toledo (633) and drafted its documents. Each of the seventeen canons devoted to liturgical matters carefully illustrated the prescriptions equally imposed by the council to all the churches of the kingdom with historical documentation and doctrinal arguments.

One of the clearest objectives seen in the liturgical canons of the Fourth Toledo Council was to eliminate some peculiarities of the Braga see, which had been introduced during the Swabian rule. Wanting to dissociate themselves from the Catholic churches of the Visigothic camp, the Catholic churches of the northeast of the Peninsula under the Swabian rule had appealed to Rome during the papacy of Vigilius (538) under the guise of a simple consultation in order to clear up some doubts. Following the guidelines they received, they were baptizing by a triple instead of a single immersion as it was done elsewhere; they were using a set Eucharistic Prayer, namely the Roman canon; they rejected hymns and other poetic texts; they sang the *alleluia* before, not after the gospel; they gave the blessing at the end of Mass, not before Communion, etc. In 585, the Braga province and its churches had come under the Visigothic rule. Yet, after seventy-eight years, the Fourth Toledo Council still detected romanizing remnants and it took great care to eliminate them.

The Tenth Toledo Council (656) established an annual feast on December 18 in honor of the Virgin Mary. This time, St. Ildefonse, author of a treatise on Mary's virginity, played an important role in the council and he wrote the corresponding canon. Later, when he was archbishop of Toledo, he composed the texts for the Office and the Mass of that feast.

3. Exchanges among Various Sees and with Other Liturgies
Despite that attitude of strong defense of what was typically their own and authentic, the Hispanic churches never lost contact with the

distant Eastern liturgies — Alexandrian, Antiochan, or Syro-Chaldean — and with the nearest liturgies of southern Gaul, Milan, and Rome. The Hispanic liturgy was affirming itself while it always remained connected with universal tradition.

Provinces exchanged their respective works. The uniformity often called forth by the council in terms of the liturgy was limited to the ecclesiastical province. Lists of biblical pericopes, chants, and euchological texts of the Office and the Mass were made known, and all of this became shared patrimony. But every metropolitan church arranged this in its own style. In the sources that have come down to us in manuscripts from the same tradition, there are relatively important differences in composition.

After a long period of constant creativity during which texts circulated from one church to another as petitions, the compilation of the liturgical books took place at the end of the seventh century. Their revision and definitive codification was attributed to St. Julian of Toledo, who died in 690.

4. Under Arab Rule

The Arab invasion (711) suddenly interrupted what could have been a normal evolutionary process of the Hispanic rite. Some clerics were able to emigrate and take liturgical books with them. A book of prayer for the Office from Tarragona is still kept in Verona. Other codices enriched the libraries of monastic schools where the Carolingian cultural movement flourished. In this way, texts of Hispanic origin were used to prepare the Roman Germanic pontifical.

A bastion of resistance against the Islamic occupation was established in Asturias. As soon as this basis for the future Reconquest was consolidated, in 790, Alfonso the Chaste decreed the restoration of the Palatine liturgy in Oviedo, just as it had been celebrated in Toledo.

When they were fleeing from the Moors, the Hispanic émigrés had taken refuge in Septimania. Armed and led by the Franks' military chiefs, they had liberated both sides of the Eastern Pyrenees in 782. From there, they conquered successively all the counties of the *Hispanic Marchia*, and these counties formed Catalonia. Benedictine monasteries settled in the liberated regions where they introduced the Roman rite. Elements of the Hispanic rite subsisted in the liturgical codices of the Roman rite which were copied there, specifically the parts corresponding to the calendar and the ritual.

On the other hand, the ancient rite continued to be celebrated in the part of Spain occupied by the Arabs and in the new kingdoms of Leon, Castile, and Navarre. Many of the codices and liturgical fragments of the ancient Hispanic rite copied during the tenth and eleventh centuries in Leon, San Millán de la Cogolla, San Juan de la Peña, Santo Domingo de la Calzada, and Santo Domingo de Silos are still preserved.

The manuscripts show that there was a renewal of music that had taken place in the tenth century. Leon and San Millán were the main centers. That renewing movement implied a certain degree of creativity. The ancient songs were not merely transcribed; they were enriched by new verses.

There was an attempt to extend creativity to the field of euchology, but in view of the low cultural level of the time, high quality texts could not be expected. The Masses grouped in the third part of the *Liber Ordinum* and some of the devotional prayers *ad miserationes* for the *Liber Horarum* (monastic Office) are probably the result of that endeavor.

5. Accusations of Adoptionism

During the eighth century, an unfortunate doctrinal polemics between people from liberated and occupied Spain, had grave consequences for the old Hispanic rite.

Elipando, the archbishop of Toledo, assuming the chief responsibility in matters of Catholic orthodoxy in the area of Spain occupied by the Moors, believed he had the obligation to correct Mignecio who was in charge of one of the southern episcopal sees. In Elipando's intention to explain that the Word had assumed human nature in his own person, he was using the verb "adopted" and the phrase *adoptivus homo* to indicate Christ's human nature.

These expressions reminded Beato de Liébana of an ancient heresy called "adoptionism." Beato was a writer from the Cantabrian region of free Spain, and he was already well known in the Frankish kingdom for his commentary on the Book of Revelation.

The polemics worsened to the point that it gave rise to four councils: Ratisbon (792), Frankfurt (794), Rome (798), and Aachen

(798–800). Condemned on various occasions, Felix de Urgell was hurt the most by all of this, for no other reason than his stubbornness in supporting Elipando.

To justify the use of the word *adoptio* and the expression *adoptivus homo,* three letters (in 792, 798, and 799) were sent to the bishops of the Frankish kingdom and personally to Alcuin. Although one of the letters was signed by a group of Spanish bishops and another by Felix de Urgell, Elipando had written the three letters. They almost always cited the same texts, fragments from the Hispanic liturgy attributed to Spanish authors whose orthodoxy could not be doubted. In fact, Alcuin did not find any error in those excerpts. However, he did not realize either that some quotations were not pertinent. Two of the texts cited by Elipando did not apply the concept of "adoption" to Christ, but to Christians, "children of God by adoption" in virtue of sanctifying grace.

"Adoptionism" never existed in the Mozarabic church. But its liturgy, seemingly so different from the Roman liturgy, could not easily avoid the suspicion surrounding it even though such an accusation represented the greatest historical absurdity that could be perpetrated.

6. Toward Suppression

Nevertheless, the fact is that Pope John X (914–918) sent a legate named Zanellus to Spain to examine the liturgical books in use there. All he was able to observe was that the words of consecration were not exactly the same as those of the Roman Missal. They were actually St. Paul's words in 1 Corinthians 11:24-26. Another visit by Cardinal Hugo Candido on behalf of Pope Alexander II (1068) was also ineffective.

However, for Gregory VII (1073–1085) the existence of a different liturgy in Spain was not a matter of doctrine, but of discipline. Based on what was happening in the East, he thought he could infer that the diversity of rites entailed the division of powers. The fact that Spain had its own liturgy limited the range of his reform program. His legates imposed the substitution of the old rite by the Roman rite in the monasteries of San Salvador de Leyre in the Navarre kingdom (1067) and of San Juan de la Peña in Aragon (1071). The pope prevailed on King Alfonso VI to call a council in Burgos (1080). In it, the

suppression of the so-called "Gothic" rite was decreed for the kingdoms of Leon and Castile.

7. *Relative Survival of the Rite*

In their desire to remain faithful to their ancestors' religious tradition
to celebrating Christian worship and participating in it, Hispanics
who were in the part of Spain occupied by the Moors had to pay a
special tribute to local authorities. They were designated under the
name of "Mozarabs." In recognition of their merits, when Toledo was
liberated (1085), King Alfonso VI conceded to the Mozarabs the privilege of continuing to celebrate the ancient Hispanic rite in the six
parishes existing in Toledo in spite of the suppression decreed by the
Council of Burgos.

The archbishop of Toledo, Bernardo de Sahagún (1085–1124), tried
to revoke that privilege. But, the Mozarabic communities which had
been joined at the beginning of the thirteenth century by many emigrants from southern Spain and from North Africa, tenaciously defended their sacred rights.

The scribes of Sts. Justa and Rufina and of St. Eulalia parishes continued to renew the liturgical books of the ancient rite during the
twelfth and thirteenth centuries until the beginning of the fourteenth
century.

8. *Two Traditions*

The manuscripts copied in Sts. Justa and Rufina parish differ from the
codices copied in St. Eulalia parish and from those proceeding from
the north of the Peninsula (Tarragona, Leon, San Millán, and Silos).

The A tradition, represented by most of the manuscripts, reveals a
better and more elaborate compilation of the liturgical books intended for the Divine Office and the eucharistic celebration. But the B
tradition, represented by the manuscripts of Sts. Justa and Rufina,
presents undeniable signs of archaisms and cannot be in any way
considered as a distorted version of the other tradition.

In view of its size, the A tradition could only be the result of St.
Julian of Toledo's work of codification. In the B tradition, several
signs lead us to identify the liturgy as it was celebrated in the metropolitan church of Bética (Andalusia) which Southern emigrants
brought with them to Toledo and which they zealously followed in
the Toledan parish dedicated to the two Sevillian martyrs.

9. Cardinal Cisneros' Restoration

When Cardinal Francisco Ximénes de Cisneros became archbishop in 1495, he became immediately aware of the religious and cultural value of the Mozarabic liturgy. He also observed that it was in danger of disappearing. In order to insure that it would continue, he established the Mozarabic Chapel. He assigned it an altar-chapel in the cathedral for the Office and the Mass according to the Mozarabic rite to be celebrated there daily, and he put Canon Alfonso Ortiz in charge of the printed edition of the missal and the breviary.

The *Missale mixtum, secundum regulam beati Isidori, dictum mozarabes* appeared in 1500 and the *Breviarium secundum regulam beati Isidori* in 1502. The Missal was re-edited in Rome in 1755 with a presentation and explanatory notes by Alexander Lesley, a Jesuit. Lesley's re-edition was reproduced in Migne's Latin Patrology, volume LXXXV.

Later on, in 1804, the archbishop of Toledo, Cardinal Francisco Antonio de Lorenzana, also published a new corrected edition of the Missal under the title *Missale Gothicum secundum regulam beati Isidori Hispalensis episcopi*. Cardinal Lorenzana himself had already re-edited the breviary in Madrid in 1775 under the title of *Breviarium Gothicum secundum regulam beati Isidori*. Migne's Latin Patrology reproduced this revised version of the breviary in volume LXXXVI.

10. Revision of the Missal

On July 12, 1982, Cardinal Marcelo González Martín appointed a committee whose mission was to revise the Hispanic rite Missal according to what Vatican II had suggested. The new edition of the *Missale Hispano-Mozarabicum* in four volumes was approved by the Roman Congregation of Divine Worship on July 17, 1988.

On one hand, the revision consisted in eliminating extraneous elements and the distortions which had been introduced in the Ordinary of the Mass of the 1500 edition, and on the other hand, in integrating all the contributions of ancient sources from both traditions. All the manuscripts were used for that revision.

The new edition and the accompanying guidelines facilitated the occasional or relatively regular celebration.

Bibliography

I. THE FORMATION OF THE LATIN RITES

King, A. A. *Rites of Western Christendom.* Vol. 4, *Liturgies of the Past.* Milwaukee, 1959.

Klauser, Th. *A Short History of the Western Liturgy.* Trans. J. Halliburton. 2nd ed. New York, 1979.

Pinell i Pons, J. "Liturgie locali antiche (origine e sviluppo)." *NDL* 776–783.

_____. *Preci eucaristiche occidentale: Testi delle liturgie ambrosiana, gallicana e ispanica. Sintesi di uno studio letterario-dottrinale.* Rome, 1984.

II. THE AMBROSIAN LITURGY

Biffi, G. "Il nuovo messale della Chiesa ambrosiana: Spirito e principi della sua riforma." *Ambrosius: Bollettino liturgico ambrosiano* 2 (1976) 81–99.

_____. "La riforma del Messale Ambrosiano: Metodo e risultati." *Not* 13 (1977) 12–28.

_____. "La 'ambrosianità' della nostra 'Liturgia delle Ore.'" *RL* 70 (1983) 234–236.

Borella, P. *Il rito ambrosiano.* Brescia, 1964.

Cattaneo, E. *Il breviario ambrosiano: Note storiche ed illustrative.* Milan, 1943.

Dell'Oro, F. "Il nuovo Messale della Chiesa ambrosiana." *RL* 64 (1977) 524–623.

_____. "Annotazioni in margine alla 'Diurna laus.'" *RL* 70 (1983) 236–256.

_____. "La ristampa aggiornata del Messale ambrosiano del Vaticano II." *RL* 75 (1988) 637–712.

Triacca, A. *I prefazi ambrosiani del ciclo 'De tempore,' secondo il Sacramentarium Bergomense: Avviamento ad uno studio critico-teologico.* Rome, 1970.

_____. "La liturgia ambrosiana." *Anàmnesis* 2:88–110.

III. THE GALLICAN LITURGY

Griffe, E. "Aux origines de la liturgie gallicane." *ButLitEc* 52 (1951) 17–43.

Pinell i Pons, J. "Anàmnesis y epìclesis en el antiguo rito gallicano. *Didaskalia* 4 (1974) 3–130.

_____. "Gallicana, liturgia." *DPAC* 2, cols. 1425–1431.

Porter, W. S. *The Gallican Rite.* Studies in Eucharistic Faith and Practice 4. London, 1958.

Thibaut, J. B. *L'ancienne liturgie gallicane, son origine et sa formation en Provence aux Ve et VIe siècles.* Paris, 1929.

IV. THE HISPANIC LITURGY

Aldazábal, J. "La misa en el rito hispano-mozárabe renovado." *Ph* 175 (1990) 57–77.

Pinell i Pons, J. "Las fórmulas conclusivas y de enlace complementarias del sistema de textos variables en la Misa del antiguo rito hispánico." *Paschale Mysterium: Studi in memoria dell'abate Prof. Salvatore Marsili (1910–1983)*, 139–168. SA 91. Rome, 1986.

———. "La estructura de la misa en rito hispánico, herencia de la tradición universal y de su propia historia." *Not* 267 (October 1988) 471–727.

———."Credo y comunión en la estructura de la misa hispánica, según disposición del III Concilio de Toledo." *Concilio III de Toledo. XIV Centenario 589–1989*, 333–342. Toledo, 1991.

———. "El oficio catedral hispánico." *Ph* 175 (1990) 9–37.

———. "El Misal Hispano-Mozárabe: Nueva edición revisada." *Ph* 191 (1992) 367–380.

Rivera Recio, F. "La controversia adopcionista del siglo VIII y la ortodoxia de la liturgia mozárabe." *EphLit* 47 (1933) 506–536.

———. "Gegorio VII y la liturgia mozárabe." *RET* 2 (1942) 3–33.

Sancho, J. "El leccionario de la Misa en la liturgia hispánica renovada." *Ph* 175 (1990) 39–56.

Part III

Liturgical Sources
A. Documents and Books

Basil Studer, O.S.B.

12

Liturgical Documents of the First Four Centuries

Liturgical historians are not of one mind when it comes to defining what is a liturgical book. Still they do agree in their emphasis on two elements: a liturgical book is one that is composed for liturgical use and is in fact used in a local church's liturgical celebration.[1] However, no such books are found in the first four centuries, when the only book used was the Bible, parts of which were read in the Sunday assembly[2] or on other occasions. On the other hand, enough evidence exists that we can get a fairly clear idea of the major rites that became fixed relatively early, at least in their essential elements. Christian writers from that period have transmitted liturgical formulas, some of which are still used, such as the Apostles' Creed or other baptismal creeds,[3] as well as the Roman canon and other Eucharistic Prayers.[4] At any rate, a good number of texts contain information about how the ministers or faithful prayed and to which models they turned for their liturgical prayer.

For a better understanding of these basic assertions, we must take into account the distinction usually made by liturgists between the period of creativity, when cultural expressions were freely improvised, and the period when rites and prayer formulas were gradually fixed. In the first period the president of the assembly prayed

---

[1] I. Scicolone, "Libri liturgici," *NDL* (1984) 701–13.

[2] See the very early testimony of Justin, *Apol.* 1, 67, 3.

[3] J.N.D. Kelly, *Early Christian Creeds* (London, 1972).

[4] A. Chupungco, *Canone Romano*: *DPAC* i, 572–6.

spontaneously in the name of all, as Justin attests,[5] even though he drew inspiration from scriptural formulas or others that were already traditional. These were adapted, if necessary, to the various circumstances of language and culture. But on the level of ritual, traditions already seem more established, although we notice a certain proliferation of secondary rites.[6] During the second period ritual details underwent further development; the major prayers took on an increasingly more definite shape. Two factors determined this evolution. Concern for orthodoxy, and to some extent esthetics, led more influential bishops such as Basil, Chrysostom, and Augustine, to propose prayer models to their brother bishops.[7] On the other hand, the episcopal liturgy in the great centers often became a model for presbyteral celebrations in the secondary churches.

Since the role of Scripture and Jewish tradition in the gradual transition from spontaneous to fixed forms of liturgical celebration is discussed elsewhere, we shall not go into it here. But it will be remembered that it is really the patristic evidence which makes clear that the liturgies of all Churches go back more or less to Judaeo-Christian origins.[8] We should also note that this transition did not happen everywhere at the same time, and so we must be flexible in assigning a date, viz., third-fourth century. At any rate, in this article we shall consider documentary evidence from the first four centuries. But it is not necessary to present all the evidence for the liturgical life of that period in chronological order. It is better to group it according to literary genre, keeping to chronology only within individual groups. Thus it is easier to grasp each document's particular importance.

1. CHURCH ORDERS

Concern for the organization of the community's daily life appears quite soon in the history of the early Church. A need was felt to regulate the common life of its members, the manner of receiving guests

[5] Justin, *Apol.* 1, 67, 5.

[6] See especially the rite for baptism, whose essentials are already fixed in the *Didaché* 7, 1, but which undergoes further development in the second century, as attested by Tertullian in his *De baptismo* and in the *Traditio Apostolica*.

[7] See the studies of the so-called Liturgy of St. Basil in *CPG* 2905. For Augustine, see M. Klöckener, *Das eucharistische Hochgebet bei Augustinus:* FS C. P. Mayer (Würzburg, 1989), 461–95.

[8] See C. Giraudo, *Eucaristia per la Chiesa* (Rome, 1989).

and strangers, and aid for the poor and sick. In particular there was an effort to order common prayer so as to avoid all confusion. These concerns found juridical or, as we would say, canonical, expression in the so-called *church orders*.

A trail of evidence for these can be found in all patrologies, even though unlike other ancient Christian writings, they do not strictly belong to the history of early Christian literature.[9] In fact, most of these "canonical" writings are anonymous and owe their origin to compilers. Put together mostly during the third and fourth centuries in Syria and Egypt, these collections are closely related to each other. The later ones are essentially reworkings of earlier ones. Their authors, in fact, did not intend to preserve the traditions they received but to adapt them to new circumstances in their communities. We should note in this regard that concern to regulate the community's daily life soon becomes a concern to guarantee its hierarchical order. Thus we can speak of a living literature. Finally, these collections are distinguished by their pseudepigraphal character. They were issued under apostolic authority. At first this claim was meant only to stress their conformity to apostolic teaching. But with time greater emphasis was placed on their apostolic origin, and they were attributed to Clement of Rome, Hippolytus, individual apostles, and even Jesus himself.

Although these documents are collections and pseudepigraphal in nature, they deserve to be considered as the first. More than other writings, they bear witness to the historical evolution of rites and liturgical prayers, at least for those times and places where they originated. Their compilers, by issuing them under apostolic authority, filled the lacuna existing between the authority of Sacred Scripture, which was accepted during the second century, and the authority of synods, which would not be recognized until the fourth century.[10] At any rate, these documents' pseudepigraphal nature certainly contributed to their acceptance by local churches which were more or less important. It is not easy to interpret this "canonical" evidence. The original versions have not always been completely preserved. Often we must turn to much later translations from Syriac,

[9] B. Altaner and A. Stuiber, *Patrologie*, § 64. "Kirchenordnungen und liturgische Texte."

[10] G. Schöllgen, *Kirchenordnungen*, 21

Latin, or other languages.[11] We must also exercise care when judging the acceptance of documents that were already a collection. The new compiler has not only placed them in a different setting but has also frequently modified individual chapters. Finally, we must not forget that in condemning certain abuses and insisting on certain rules, the compiler has presented personal ideals but not described the actual situation in the community.

a. Didaché

The Teaching of the Twelve Apostles, usually called the *Didaché*, has been described as a manual of catechetics, liturgy, and discipline (Rordorf). It was probably composed around the end of the first century near Antioch in Syria. It includes three parts and an epilogue. The first part consists of a moral instruction of Jewish origin, which has been Christianized: the teaching on the Way of Life and the Way of Death (1–6). The second part deals with baptism, Christian fasting, daily prayer, and prayers of thanksgiving (7–10). Especially noteworthy is the fact that baptism is administered with a trinitarian formula. As for the prayers before and after meals, we are not sure if these are Eucharistic Prayers. In any case, their structure, which is borrowed from Jewish tradition, can help us to understand better the later Eucharistic anaphoras. The third part contains disciplinary prescriptions concerning hospitality, the ministers of the community, and the Sunday celebration (11–5). The work ends with an eschatological admonition (16).

Its liturgical orientation is evident in the chapters on baptism, the prayers of thanksgiving, and the Lord's Day. But the other chapters are not without liturgical interest. In fact, the moral instruction is presented with a view to baptism (see 7, 1) and so is pre-baptismal in nature. The same is true for fasting and prayer. The teacher speaks about the position of prophets and their relation to bishops and deacons, after alluding to their liturgical ministry (10, 7).[12] Finally, the epilogue urges the community to gather frequently in order to be ready for the parousia of the Lord, whose hour no one knows (16, 1f).

[11] The most famous example is the *Traditio Apostolica*.

[12] See also 15, 1 where the subject changes from Sunday to the appointment of bishops and deacons. It is significant that in the *Apostolic Constitutions* (VII 26, 6) the prophets are replaced by presbyters.

No doubt this first Church Order, although it reflects only the situation in one minor local church, sheds a great deal of light on the beginnings of the Christian liturgy. It helps us recognize its Jewish background. As prototype of a whole series of "canonical" documents, it also helps us understand how from the very beginning Christian communities felt the need for liturgical and disciplinary rules and prescriptions.

b. Traditio Apostolica

According to Quasten, the *Apostolic Tradition* must be considered a document of inestimable value for our knowledge of church institutions and Christian life during the first centuries.[13] Today, however, this assessment is challenged or at least nuanced in two respects. On the one hand, the document's Roman origin, defended by its editor B. Botte and also held by V. Loi and M. Simonetti, is more or less strongly questioned by G. Kretschmar, M. Metzger, and W. Geerlings. On the other hand, B. Botte's reconstruction of the text, which J. Quasten and J.M. Hannsens considered valid, has been seriously criticized by P. Nautin and W. Geerlings. M. Metzger considers it fanciful (*un document fantôme*).[14]

The document's structure is not very clear. Based on the titles, which according to Botte are ancient, it is divided as follows: Prologue, in which the author defends the tradition of his community against certain innovations; Church Order (1–21), including rituals and prayers for the ordination of bishops (2–4), presbyters (7), and deacons (8), as well as the catechumenate and Christian initiation (15–21); Prescriptions for community banquets (22–30); Various prescriptions (31–42); Epilogue, in which the author insists again on the value of tradition.

Given the contents of this document, there is no way to deny its unique importance for the history of liturgy. But what is needed is an interpretation of its texts that takes into account the fact that Botte's edition is a reconstruction based primarily on the fourth-century Latin version. The Eastern additions, possibly lost in the Latin version, must also be considered. Those who would say that Hippolytus of Rome compiled the *Apostolic Tradition* should not forget that the

[13] J. Quasten, *Patrologia* I (Rome, 1967) 35.
[14] M. Metzger, art.cit.: *EO* 5 (1988) 242. See 248ff; 254f.

writings attributed to him are divided into two blocks: the so-called Eastern writings and the writings mentioned in the list on the chair of the "statue of Hippolytus." Only writings from the second block may be used for an *auctor per auctorem* explanation. Furthermore, the importance of the *Apostolic Tradition*, which certainly existed in some form, is also a result of its acceptance by later compilers and translators.[15]

c. Didascalia Apostolorum

The *Didascalia Apostolorum*, written around the year 230 by a bishop in Syria, was only partially transmitted in Greek — in the *Apostolic Constitutions* (I–VI). On the other hand, it was completely preserved in other languages, especially in a Syriac version, which must antedate the middle of the fourth century. Also important is a partial Latin version, which may go back to the end of the fourth century. Dealing with a large number of disciplinary questions, it insists strongly on freedom from the Law (24f). As for its liturgical elements, the chapters on the bishop's duties, including those toward penitents (4–14), are especially interesting. Other subjects of interest include the organization of the liturgical assembly (12), deacons and deaconesses (16), and the discipline of fasting (21).

d. Canones Ecclesiastici Apostolorum (CPG 1739)

The *Canones Ecclesiastici Apostolorum*, also called the *Apostolic Church Order*, are a brief work that, like the *Didaché*, includes the teaching on the Two Ways (4–15), a part on church ministries (16–22), and a part on the role of the laity, men and women (23–30). It goes back to the third or fourth century and reflects conditions in Syria or Egypt.

e. Constitutiones per Hippolytum — Canones Hippolyti

The *Constitutions of Hippolytus*, also known as the *Epitome*, have been incorporated into Book VIII of the *Apostolic Constitutions*, the *Canons of Hippolytus* and the *Testamentum Domini*. They may reflect the situation in the Roman Church, but they leave many unanswered questions. Nowadays the *Canons of Hippolytus* are regarded as prior to the *Apostolic Constitutions*.

---

[15] See the information in *CPG* 1737.

f. Constitutiones Apostolorum (CPG 1730)

The rather extensive work known as the *Apostolic Constitutions* is the first of the pseudo-apostolic canonical collections. Written around the end of the fourth century in northern Syria, it is presented by its compiler (compilers?) as the final document of the so-called Council of the Apostles (Acts 15), edited by Clement of Rome. It includes pre-Nicene canonical and liturgical texts, specifically the *Didascalia* (I–VI), the *Didache* (VII, 1–32), the *Traditio Apostolica* (VIII), and the *Canoni Apostolici* (VIII, 47). As documentary evidence for the liturgy of the first four centuries, it is of considerable importance. It contains a nearly complete eucharistic ritual (VII–VIII) and many prayers not found in the received sources. These are mostly from the author himself. Those texts borrowed from earlier collections have obviously undergone later development. The compiler's modifications and additions become more substantial in the third book, and in the last two books they predominate. Of a stylistic nature, they add to the number of biblical quotations, show greater respect for the community's new situation, highlight the apostolic origin of the documents, and adapt them to the compiler's own theology. However, this last point is still debated by specialists. At any rate, the author's theology should not be called Arian, even though it does not really reflect orthodox belief at the time of its composition. The Quinisext Synod (692) had already rejected certain of the collection's passages as heretical interpolations. On the other hand, its apostolic origin was never questioned in antiquity. Thus it is not surprising that the collection was translated, at least in part, into various languages.[16]

There are also other canonical collections, such as the *Collectio Veronensis* (CPG 1731), the *Sinodos Alexandrina* (CPG 1732), and the *Octoeuchos Clementinus* (1733). But these collections are later than the year 400, although they may contain earlier documents. The same is true of the *Testamentum Domini* (CPG 1743).

2. MYSTAGOGICAL CATECHESES

As attested by several NT writings, especially the Acts of the Apostles, baptism and admission to the Christian community were from the very beginning preceded by instruction on faith in Jesus Christ as Lord and Savior, and the Christian life. In the course of the

[16] See *CPG* 1730.

second century, evidence for this intellectual preparation becomes more frequent and more specific. We know this primarily from the *Didaché*, the *Epistle of Barnabas*, Justin's *Apology* (ch. 61), and Irenaeus's *Demonstration of the Apostolic Preaching*.

As we already see in the Letter of Paul to the Romans (ch. 6) and the Gospel of John, the very earliest pre-baptismal instruction included an explanation of Christian initiation — in other words, baptism and the Eucharist. Justin, in the liturgical chapters of his *Apologia* (chs. 61–7), and Tertullian, in his *De baptismo*, give clear information about the method used in the sacramental catecheses. According to them, Christian rites are best explained in virtue of their names (baptism: regeneration, illumination), their natural symbolism (water cleanses and gives life), their biblical prefigurations (the manna of the Israelites foretells the Eucharist), and analogies with other data of faith (the Eucharist is compared to the incarnation of the Word). In his *De oratione*, Origen clearly states that this way of emphasizing the *ratio sacramenti* and the biblical figures — to use Tertullian's expression (*De bapt.* 9) — is similar to biblical exegesis which explains texts according to their literal sense and their deeper sense.[17] Augustine, with his doctrine of *sacramentum-similitudo*, would put the finishing touches on this type of patristic reflection.[18]

The most beautiful evidence for the interpretation of the major Christian rites is found in the so-called mystagogical catecheses of the fourth and fifth centuries. This name, attested in the manuscript tradition, is used to describe catecheses that were given mostly during Easter week to the newly baptized. The expressions *mystagogy* ("initiation to the mysteries") and thus *mystagogical catecheses* ("discourses on the mysteries") became popular when Christian authors definitively accepted the mystery language long used in Judaeo-Christian exegesis.

Among the mystagogical catecheses, first place belongs to those attributed to Cyril of Jerusalem (d. 387). They may, however, be from his successor John; in any case, they were given rather late.[19] In five catecheses, the preacher and bishop of the Holy City develops the following topics: (1) the renunciation and baptismal profession, (2)

[17] B. Studer, *L'esegesi doppia in Origene: ASE* 10 (1993) 427–37.
[18] Ibid., 427f, with Augustine, *Epist.* 98, 9.
[19] See the discussion of their authenticity in Sch 126, 18–40.

the mystery of baptism, (3) the chrism, (4) the body and blood of Christ, and (5) the eucharistic celebration. In developing these topics, which correspond to the structure of initiation in Jerusalem, he remains close to the ritual and biblical method. Especially interesting is the way he refers to the primordial waters, the Exodus, the Passover, the Jordan, and the wedding feast at Cana.[20]

Another famous example is the baptismal catecheses of John Chrysostom (d. 407). These discourses were given by the greatest preacher of the Greek Church around the year 390 in Antioch, center of the Eastern world. Some of these have become available only more recently, thanks chiefly to the research of A. Wenger. Among the catecheses reprinted in Migne and published by him, two are post-baptismal. However, they are not mystagogical in the strict sense. Instead they present the authentic Christian life of a baptized person according to the Letters of Paul, who was Chrysostom's spiritual master.

At almost the same time, Theodore, who later became bishop of Mopsuestia (d. 428), also gave catechetical homilies in Antioch. Among these homilies, which have come down to us only in Syriac, ten are commentaries on the baptismal creed, one is an interpretation of the Lord's Prayer, and five are initiations into the mysteries: baptism (2), anointing (1), and the Eucharist (2). Since (unlike those of Chrysostom) they stress the symbolic meaning of the rites, they constitute the major evidence for initiation as celebrated in late fourth-century Antioch. Moreover, the information we have from Theodore is supplemented by the catecheses of Proclus, bishop of Constantinople (d. 446). To grasp the full significance of these beautiful catecheses, we must remember two things. On the one hand, Theodore, who is considered the most outstanding representative of "historical" exegesis, gives a surprisingly "allegorical" interpretation of the details of the liturgy. For example, he compares the procession with the offerings to Christ's journey to his passion. He sees the deacons as representatives of the angels who are present at the liturgical assembly. On the other hand, presupposing a quasi-apocalyptic view of the world, he distinguishes two καταστάσεις: the world of corruption and the world of life. He sees the liturgical celebration as anticipating the life of heaven: baptism is a figure of eternal rebirth, the

[20] J. Daniélou, *Catechesi*, 161ff.

Eucharist is a figure of the angelic liturgy, and the whole of Christian life is a figure of our final union with Christ and God.

Finally, we have the most famous example from the Latin Church, the baptismal catecheses of Ambrose of Milan (d. 397). These are preserved in two works whose authenticity is no longer questioned today: the *De sacramentis* and the *De mysteriis*. These sermons by the great bishop of Milan deserve special attention for two reasons. First, they allow us to reconstruct the entire ritual of the church of Milan, which was mother of a liturgical family. Second, they also furnish information about the Roman Liturgy, as their reference to the Roman canon demonstrates. This information, we should note, can easily be supplemented by the Easter sermons of bishops who lived near Milan: Zeno of Verona (d. ca. 372), Chromatius of Aquileia (d. 407), Gaudentius of Brescia (d. 410), Peter of Ravenna (d. 450), and Nicetas of Remesiana (d. after 414). On the other hand, Ambrose's catecheses are distinguished by their theology, which is not only profound, but later had a great influence on Western sacramental theology. We may recall the following points: Christ, true God and creator, is presented as the *auctor sacramentorum*; baptism and the Eucharist appear, in the context of his exegesis of the Canticle of Canticles, as a personal encounter with Christ; the "heavenly" words spoken by the priest are efficacious; thus the Eucharist is also a *remissio peccatorum*.

3. PATRISTIC PREACHING
It is neither possible nor necessary here to compare the history of Christian liturgy with that of patristic preaching. It suffices to point out a few facts that show how a good knowledge of the latter can be useful for study of the former.

Like other phenomena in the life of the Church, the preaching of the Fathers grew up in a Jewish matrix. But the path that leads from synagogue teaching to acceptance of the rhetoric of Greece and Rome was quite long. From its beginnings, which are reflected, for example, in the two letters attributed to Clement of Rome, to sermons that reflect the school of Libanius and Donatus, a complex process of linguistic and homiletic inculturation was at work. First, we notice some hesitation in the use of the words πίστις, εὐσέβεια, and ἐλπίς, which Christian writers owe to the Septuagint, and the other use they received from the classics. The fact that the word δόξα is translated into Latin by the four terms *maiestas, claritas, gloria,* and *honor*, and the fact that *sacramentum* does not correspond in any simple way to μυστήριον are perhaps even more interesting.[21] It is also instructive to compare rhetorical forms inherited from the Bible, such as the parallelism of the psalms, and those borrowed from ancient rhetoric, such as antithesis. What literary research finds in the sermons of the Fathers holds true for much of the liturgy. The major difference between the two areas lies in the fact that the homiletic evidence is much more abundant than the liturgical; that is why the history of liturgy owes so much to the history of homiletics.[22]

Perhaps it is trivial to point out that for an understanding of a text it is not enough to know its author; we must also have some idea about the people to whom the text is addressed. Indeed, the word is word in the full sense only if it reaches its destination and is heard and understood. This basic hermeneutic principle is especially true in the case of preaching. Proclaiming and explaining the Word of God, the preacher stands before his audience of faithful, who are sympathetic or at least curious. He hears their reaction and is applauded or even criticized. This fact has been the subject of much study, either in general works on patristic preaching or in monographs on individual writers: the Cappadocians (Bernardi), Ambrose (Graumann), Augustine (Van der Meer, Pellegrino), and many others. We need not consider the details in these descriptions of the Fathers of the Church and their audience. Instead we should stress that for a knowledge of the elements of the liturgical assembly, it is much more useful to study the public to whom these homilies were addressed than to conduct research on other documents or on the liturgical texts themselves. Indeed, the information found in the studies of individual authors is taken from the sermons themselves — and not only from the preachers' own remarks, their manner of addressing their audience and perhaps adapting themselves to its expectations, but also from its reactions as these may have been written down by the secretaries who were taking notes during the sermon. Part of a sermon

---

[21] B. Studer, *Spätantike lateinische Übertragungen griechischer christlicher Texte und Themen:* V. Warnach (ed.), *Hermeneutik als Weg heutiger Wissenschaft* = Salzburger Studien zur Philosophie, *Bd.* 9 (1971) 87–115.

[22] C. Mohrmann, *Études sur le latin des chrétiens,* 4 vols. (Rome, 1958–1977); W. Dúrig, *Pietas liturgica* (Regensburg, 1958).

was its description of the assembly: the large crowd, their joy or per-haps sorrow, not to mention that preachers sometimes had to com-plain at the small number of those present.

We may also recall that the practical thrust and timeliness (the *hodie*) of the liturgical celebrations is apparent from the sermons given during them. But we have already dealt with this in our dis-cussion of the Fathers and the liturgy. Still it is useful to add one more word on the transmission of the sermons of the Fathers. As al-ready mentioned, preachers spoke extemporaneously. The text was established by secretaries or perhaps some devout members of the faithful. The notes were preserved in the episcopal archives. Before being circulated, they may have been revised by the preacher him-self. The authors or others saw to their publication — usually in col-lections — or else inserted the texts into their writings. Such was particularly true in the case of Ambrose. This method of transmitting sermons could also have its drawbacks. We are not always sure about a text's authenticity and integrity. Before using the sermons of the Fathers, we must clarify the circumstances of their transmission, using Patrologies, modern editions or lists such as the *Clavis Patrum Latinorum et Graecorum*, or Frede's list of ecclesiastical authors.[23]

4. THEOLOGICAL TREATISES AND BIBLICAL COMMENTARIES

Until the middle of the second century, non-canonical Christian literature had an exclusivly practical thrust. It consisted of letters, homilies, and exhortations of various kinds. But after the year 150, writings of a more theoretical nature appeared. These may be di-vided into treatises and biblical commentaries. The first group in-cludes apologies, which are replies to particular questions that may have been raised by adversaries, and controversial or polemical works, which are attempts at summarizing a series of problems. The second group is divided into *quaestiones et responsiones* and commen-taries, which may be either written or oral (homilies).

Among these writings, treatises dealing with liturgical questions are naturally of greater interest here. We find them at the beginning

[23] See the *Claves* published by Brepols; H. J. Frede, *Kirchenschriftsteller, Verzeichnis und Sigel* (Freiburg, 1995); P. Verbraken, *Études critique sur les sermons authentiques de Saint Augustin* (Steenbrugge, 1976).

of the third century. First of all, we should mention Tertullian's *De baptismo*. In defending the *religio aquae* (religious use of water) against certain opponents of baptism, he describes the baptismal ritual of Carthage, explains the chief scriptural texts, speaks of the conditions for the administration of baptism, and defines the principle of liturgical sacramentality.[24] This theology of baptism was supplemented by Cyprian's letters upholding the non-validity of baptism administered by heretics. The concern of these two great authors, however, was not limited to first penance. They also spoke of second penance, that is, readmission to the sacraments of those who after baptism were excommunicated for grave sins. Tertullian dealt with this question in his treatise *De paenitentia*, and Cyprian in some of his letters, especially the *De lapsis*. Cyprian's letter 63 is also important for the Eucharist. Refuting certain bishops who were opposed to the use of wine, the bishop of Carthage (d. 258) emphasizes several basic principles of the theology of the Eucharist: its institution by Christ, its connection with the Last Supper and thus its sacrificial character, and the role of the celebrant as representative of Christ. While these writings are highly polemic (as was later the case with Augustine's anti-Donatist works, especially his *De baptismo*), others are more irenic. Among the latter we should note the treatises in which Tertullian, Origen, Cyprian, and others spoke of prayer, especially the Our Father.[25] Two things should be emphasized here. On the one hand, we must always remember that the explanation of the Lord's Prayer was linked more or less closely to baptism. On the other hand, it is worth noting that Origen's *De oratione*, which deals with private prayer, also contains precious information about the community's official worship. Certain prayer gestures are explained, as well as the direction to face while praying, and the sacredness of the place.[26] While Western writers show great concern about the major liturgical rites of baptism and the Eucharist, Eastern writers devote less time to

[24] P. A. Gramaglia (ed.), Tertullian, *Sul battesimo* (Rome, 1979); E. Evans, *Tertullian's Homily on Baptism* (London, 1964) XXIII–XXVIII.

[25] A. Hamman, *La prière. Les trois premiers siècles* (Tournai, 1963); E. von Severus, *Gebet: RAC* 8 (1972) 1134–1258; V. Grossi, *Tertulliano-Cipriano-Agostino. Il Padre nostro* (Rome, 1980); A. Pollastri, *Padre nostro: DPAC* II, 2565ff (bibliography).

[26] Origen, *Orat.* 31f. See W. Gessel, *Die Theologie des Gebetes nach "De oratione" von Origenes* (Munich, 1975).

these questions *(OE)*. However, Eusebius of Caesarea left a treatise on the Easter Solemnity *(CPG* 3479), Gregory of Nyssa included some chapters on the sacraments in his Great Catechesis, and Gregory Nazianzen and John Chrysostom spoke about the priesthood.[27]

Besides these works which may be called liturgical treatises, there are many others which were not written to clarify liturgical questions, yet examined aspects of the early liturgy at close range. First, we must mention the Apologies. In order to refute the accusations of atheism and immorality that pagans were uttering against Christianity in the second century, Justin described Christian initiation and the Sunday liturgy, giving a very profound explanation.[28] Later, in his *Apologeticum*, Tertullian sang the praises of the Christian assembly.[29] His *Ad uxorem* contains additional information and is also an impressive expression of the meaning of Christian marriage.[30] Equally interesting is Origen's *Contra Celsum*. In the eighth book of this extensive apology, the Alexandrian teacher discusses the nature of true spiritual worship.[31] Such worship demands knowledge of the one true God. With his strong tendency toward spiritual interpretation, Origen defends a purely spiritual meaning for the temple, altar, and statues. But when it comes to sacred times, he does not seem to place as much emphasis on spiritual interpretation. Although advocating the ancient ideal according to which the perfect Christian celebrates Sunday, Good Friday, Easter, and Pentecost every day, he admits that the simple faithful, who cannot reach this lofty ideal, need symbols and annual feasts to remind them at least occasionally of the Logos of God.[32] Thus Origen not only established the basis for

---

[27] Gregory of Nyssa, *Catech. Mag.*, 33–7; Gregory Nazianzen, *Or.* 1–3; John Chrysostom, *De sacerdotio (CPG* 4316).

[28] Justin, *Apol.* 1, 61–67. See the commentary by C. Munier, *L'Apologie de saint Justin Philosophe et Martyr* = Paradosis 38 (Fribourg, 1994) 127–41, with an updated bibliography.

[29] Tertullian, *Apologeticum*, 39.

[30] Tertullian, *Ad uxorem* II, 8. See B. Studer, *Zur Hochzeitsfeier der Christen in den westlichen Kirchen der ersten Jahrhunderete* = SA 93 (Rome, 1986) 51–85.

[31] See M. Fédou, *Christianisme et religions païennes dans le Contre Celse d'Origène* (Paris, 1988) especially 299–375.

[32] Origen, *C. Cels.* 8, 23. See also Origen, *Com. Io.* 13, 18, 109–13; *Hom. Num.* 23, 4: PG 12, 749C–751A.

a theology of feasts[33] but also provided fundamental elements for the theology of the sacraments.[34] We must also mention a famous text of Augustine, even though it is later than the year 400. In his *De Civitate Dei* — the greatest apology of Christian antiquity — he draws inspiration from Porphyrius's *Ad Marcellam* and shows that the Christian sacrifice consists in the *caritas* made possible by the passion of the one and only Mediator, made real in the Church's daily Eucharist.[35] Both Eastern and Western writers, when discussing questions of faith or morals, often touched on aspects of the celebration and meaning of the liturgy. We have discussed these writings elsewhere in our explanation of the saying *lex orandi-lex credendi*. Finally, it should be remembered that while interpreting Sacred Scripture, Christian exegetes also raised questions of a liturgical nature. They did this because they were explaining biblical texts to a liturgical assembly, or because they had to comment on Old or New Testament passages concerning liturgical realities, such as John 3 and 6 or 1 Corinthians 11, or because certain puzzling words would inspire them to give allegorical or typological interpretations of a liturgical nature. In this area, we recommend consulting the indexes in the editions of the Fathers, or lists of biblical quotations such as those in the *Biblia Patristica*.

5. HISTORIOGRAPHY AND HAGIOGRAPHY

During the first three centuries there was not much development in Christian historical writing. But with the end of the great persecutions (311–12) there came a great flowering of this literary genre, so suited to the needs of the Christian religion. The celebrated pioneer was Eusebius of Caesarea (d. ca. 340).[36] Basing himself on a large number of historical documents, he attempted to show in his *Historia Ecclesiastica* how the Christian religion had definitively triumphed under Constantine the Great. In his pursuit of this apologetic and edifying aim, Eusebius provided a great wealth of documentary

[33] See W. Schütz, *Der christliche Gottesdienst bei Origenes* (Stuttgart, 1984) 40–5.

[34] H. U. von Balthasar, *Le mysterion d'Origène: RSR* 26 (1936) 513–67; 27 (1937) 38–64.

[35] See B. Studer, *Das Opfer Christi nach Augustins De Civitate Dei X, 5–6: SA* 79 (Rome, 1980) 93–107 (bibliography).

[36] G. Bosio et al., *Introduzione ai Padri della Chiesa, Secoli III e IV* (Turin, 1993) 173–202.

evidence, without which we would know very little about the first three centuries. Part of this unique information is the amount of data on the Christian liturgy: baptism, the Eucharist, the cult of the martyrs, as well as the existence and structure of buildings for worship (the basilicas). This evidence is supplemented by the *Vita Constantini* and the *History of the Martyrs* of Palestine. We should note that in his historical writings Eusebius not only informs us about many liturgical facts but also proves to be an extremely valuable witness to liturgical terminology. He testifies especially to the growing acceptance of mystery language.

Eusebius's *Historia Ecclesiastica* was imitated by a series of Greek and Latin authors, almost all of them after 400.[37] However, their works are less important for knowledge of the history of the liturgy, given that their documentary evidence, perhaps original, no longer constitutes a practically exclusive historical source.

The historical works of Eusebius can be supplemented by hagiographic writings dating back to the first four centuries. With regard to the martyrs, specialists distinguish between "passion narratives," which are faithful accounts of the martyr's death; "judicial acts," which are more or less lengthy reports of the processes at which the martyrs were condemned; and "epic and romantic legends," where history gives way to fantasy and fiction. In addition, specialists insist on the differences between earlier and later writings, between writings of Latin origin and those of Greek origin.[38] We cannot enter into this vast area here. Anyone who would use these writings, which were meant primarily for edification of the faithful, must be aware of the complex nature of early hagiography. From the viewpoint of liturgical history, these documents are of some interest for three reasons. They reflect the liturgical practice of the time inasmuch as they end with doxologies[39] or contain quasi-liturgical prayers, as in the *Martyrdom of Polycarp*.[40] They also attest to the cult of the martyrs and

---

[37] See the information in P. Siniscalo, *art. cit.* We should especially note the *Historiae Ecclesiasticae* of Gelasius of Caesarea and Rufinus of Concordia, written shortly before and shortly after 400.

[38] V. Saxer, *Atti, Passione, Leggende: DPAC* II, 2140–9.

[39] See for example the *Martyrium Polycarpi* 23, 3; *Acta Iustini* 6; *Acta Martyrum Scillitanorum*, 17; *Passio Perpetuae et Felicitatis*, 21, 11; etc.

[40] *Martyrium Polycarpi*, 14, 1–3.

their relics.[41] Later they would include the *Gesta martyrum* in order to explain to pilgrims the origin of the martyrs' shrines.[42] Finally, certain Passions, such as the *Passio Perpetuae*, were written to be read at liturgical assemblies.[43] In some churches, for example those of Africa, reading of the Acts and Passions of the Martyrs was part of the Liturgy of the Word. In Rome such readings were allowed only at the martyrs' tombs or in presbyteral churches — not in the papal liturgy.

During the fourth century lives of holy monks and bishops were added to the martyrologies. Among the most famous were the *Life of Anthony*, written by Athanasius and twice translated into Latin,[44] and the first *Life of Pachomius*, which along with his *Praecepta*, letters, and catecheses, also translated into Latin, formed the basis of Pachomian monasticism.[45] While the *Life of Anthony* merely attests to the beginning of the cult of saints who were not martyrs of blood but martyrs of conscience, the documentary evidence on Pachomius tells us about the liturgy of the Egyptian monks. Gregory of Nyssa's eulogies dedicated to Gregory the Wonderworker, Athanasius, his brother Basil, Ephrem, and Meletius of Antioch cannot really be called lives of these holy bishops. But they do have a hagiographic quality, especially the first, which circulated under the title *Vita Gregorii Thaumaturgi* (CPG 3184).[46] At any rate, they contain many liturgical elements, including richly detailed evidence on the meaning of Christian feasts, information on the Eucharist, Christian funerals, and banquets in honor of the martyrs. Gregory of Nyssa also eulogized his sister Macrina. In this work he has also left us valuable informa-

---

[41] See especially *Martyrium Polycarpi*, which according to T. Baumeister, *Heiligenverehrung: RAC* 112–5, already contains all the elements of the cult of the martyrs.

[42] T. Baumeister, *Heiligenverehrung: RAC* 127.

[43] *Passio Felicitatis*, 1, 5–6. For the question of the liturgical reading of hagiographic writings, see B. de Gaiffier, *La lectures des actes des martyres dans la prière liturgique en occident: ABoll* 72 (1954) 134–66.

[44] G.J.M. Bartelink (ed.), *Vita di Antonio* = C. Mohrmann (ed.), *Vite dei Santi* = Scrittori Greci e Latini (Rome, 1974).

[45] A. Veilleux, *La liturgie dans le cénobitisme pachômien au quatrième siècle* = SA 57 (Rome, 1968).

[46] B. Studer, *Das christliche Fest, ein Tag der gläubigen Hoffnung: SA* 95 (Rome, 1988) 517–29, especially 523–8, with the respective quotations.

tion about monastic prayer, the *lucernarium*, prayers for the dying, and funeral ceremonies.[47]

Among the works of historiography and hagiography we can also include the *Itineraria* that appear during the fourth century. The Greek and Latin term *historia* had two meanings in antiquity: investigation and narration. Both meanings have to do with both past and present. Basing themselves on written evidence, historians presented the past (*res gestae*); basing themselves on visits to the places or on eyewitnesses, they explained in detail what they had seen and experienced.[48] In this sense, descriptions of journeys are historical writings. Since they concern the cult and shrines of the saints, they also share essential elements of hagiography. Two *Itineraria* come from the fourth century: the *Itinerarium Burdigalense* to Jerusalem (333) and the *Itinerarium Egeriae* (381–384). The second is certainly more important, also from a liturgical point of view.[49] It contains a wealth of information on the holy places of Egypt and Palestine, especially those in the vicinity of Jerusalem.[50] There are also detailed descriptions of the liturgy in the Holy City (Dedication, Epiphany, Holy Week, Paschal Time).[51]

6. ECCLESIASTICAL CORRESPONDENCE AND CHRISTIAN POETRY

Since the beginning of Christianity, a huge number of letters have been exchanged between Christian communities and their leaders. Beginning in the third century, the bishops of Alexandria would send Easter Letters every year to the communities in Egypt, announcing the date of Easter.[52] Toward the end of the fourth century, the bishops

[47] E. Giannarelli (ed.,) *La Vita di s. Macrina* (Milan, 1988) Index, s.v. *preghiera*.

[48] See B. Studer, *La cognitio historialis di Porfirio nel De ciuitate Dei di Agostino: Studia Ephemeridis Augustinianum* 50 (Rome, 1995) 529–53, especially 537–48.

[49] A. Hamman, *Egeria: DPAC* I, 1108, with bibliography. In addition there is P. Maraval, *Égérie, Journal de Voyage: SCh* 296 (Paris, 1982); E. Bermejo Cabrera, *La proclamacion de la escritura en la liturgia de Jerusalem. Estudio terminologico del "Itinerarium Egeriae"* = Studium biblicum franciscanum. Coll.maior 37 (Jerusalem, 1993); N. Natulucci (ed.), *Egeria, Pellegrinaggio in Terra Santa* = Biblioteca Patristica (Florence, 1993).

[50] See P. Maraval, *Égérie*, 56–117: a reconstruction of Egeria's journey, worked out using the later versions of Valerius and Paul the Deacon.

[51] See P. Maraval, *Égérie*, 367ff: Analytic Index, 2. Liturgie.

[52] P. Évieux, in *SCh* 372, 73–118, especially 111f.

of Rome began to address themselves officially not only to the Western Churches, but also to those of the East in so-called decretal letters.[53] These writings deserve special attention inasmuch as they emanated from important communities, mother churches or missionary centers, or from bishops who enjoyed great authority and in one way or another expresssed the consensus of all the Churches. Certainly they contain the clearest expression of the Fathers' thought and its pastoral orientation to current realities. We can distinguish between letters in the strict sense, whether official or personal, and treatises composed in epistolary form.[54]

We cannot go into detail on the correspondence from the patristic era. A few examples must suffice to show that letters from the communities or the great bishops constitute a major source for the history of liturgy. At the end of the first century, the community in Rome wrote to the community in Corinth appealing for harmony. This so-called *Prima Clementis* shows how the faithful in Rome prayed; the Jewish origins of the Christian liturgy are also clearly apparent.[55] The letters of Cyprian, "primate" of Carthage (d. 258), are also of great importance. These first letters from a bishop deal with many liturgical questions (penance, Eucharist, baptism, the cult of the martyrs).[56] The Easter Letters in which the bishops of Alexandria, beginning with Demetrius (188–230), announced the date of Easter, not only emphasize the paschal mystery but also deepen the notion of the Christian feast.[57] Noteworthy among Basil of Caesarea's extensive correspondence is a letter on frequent Communion.[58] Knowing that Ambrose took great care to organize the daily life and liturgy of the churches in northern Italy, it is not suprising to find in his many letters much information of a liturgical nature: the question of Easter (ex.coll. 13), references to liturgical chant (75A, 34), fasting (ex.coll.

---

[53] B. Studer, in *Patrologia* III, 546–57 (*DPAC* II, 2664ff).

[54] M. Pellegrino, in NBA 21, XXV–XXXVIII.

[55] A. Jaubert, in SCh 167, 139ff.

[56] V. Saxer, *Vie liturgique et quotidienne à Carthage vers le milieu du IIIe siècle* (Vatican, City, 1969).

[57] P. Évieux, in SCh 372, 73–118, especially 111f.

[58] Basil, ep. 93 (a. 372). The bishop of Caesarea also takes positions on baptism, matrimony, and ordination. But he does this especially with regard to the canonical requirements for the administration of these sacraments. See Y. Courtonne, *S. Basile et son temps* (Paris, 1973), 456–90; 521–25.

13, 11), or the liturgical functions of the priest.[59] There are also many letters and epistolary treatises in which Augustine[60] develops his ideas on the criteria to be used in judging liturgical rites (ep. 54), the sacramental meaning of the paschal feast (ep. 55), the relationship between faith and baptism (ep. 98), prayer (ep. 139), the euchological terminology of 1 Timothy 2:1 (ep. 149, 2, 11–7), and, of course, the much-debated question of baptism (ep. 166).[61] Among the papal letters, those of Leo I deserve special attention. They concern the date of ordinations and repetition of the Eucharistic sacrifice (ep. 6), the baptismal liturgy (ep. 16; 168, 1), the date of Easter (ep. 121), and the administration of sacramental penance (ep. 108; 167f).[62]

To shorten our discussion considerably, we may say that the letters of the Fathers of the Church are to a great extent a "personal" source for their liturgical thought. Of course that is even more true for the Christian poetry that developed during the fourth century.[63] We already have evidence for the first three centuries that chants and hymns borrowed from the Bible or composed by Christian authors were sung at liturgical assemblies.[64] However, we know much more about the practice of the imperial Church. It is said that Arius had his faithful sing verses as a way of spreading his theological ideas.[65] Augustine refers to something similar in the case of the Donatist, Parmenianus.[66]

---

[59] R. Gryson, *Le prêtre selon saint Ambroise* (Louvain, 1968) especially 235–93, but also elsewhere, with references to various letters, e.g., 76, 4.8.23.25.

[60] Augustine himself introduces some of his letters into his "books." See G. Bardy (ed.), *Augustin, Les révisions:* BA 12, 39f.

[61] W. Roetzer, *Des Hl. Augustinus Schriften als liturgie-geschichtliche Quelle* (Münster, 1931).

[62] T. Jalland, *The Life and Times of St. Leo the Great* (London, 1941) 399–410.

[63] A. Dihle, *Die griechische und lateinische Literatur der Kaiserzeit* (Munich, 1989) 581–90: "Liturgische Dichtung"; J. Fontaine, *Naissance de la poésie dans l'Occident chrétien* (Paris, 1981).

[64] J. Quasten, *Patrologia* I (Casale, 1975) 143–56: "Gli inizi della poesia cristiana," with references to the hymn "Phos hilaron" (2nd cen.) and the papyrus Oxyrhynchus XV, n. 1786 (3rd cen.). See also A. Hamman, *Phos Hilaron: DPAC* II, 2777.

[65] *CPG* 2028, and J. Quasten, *Patrologia* II (Casale, 1973) 15f.

[66] Augustine, *Epist.* 55, 18, 34. On this subject, see W.H.C. Frend, *Parmeniano: DPAC* II, 2686f.

More important from a liturgical point of view were the hymns of Hilary and Ambrose, which have been described as "a kind of 'back-lit picture' of the Arian controversy."[67] The three hymns by the bishop of Poitiers that were discovered in 1885 have no history. Ambrose's fourteen (?) authentic hymns "created a 'fixed form' of Latin liturgy," which lasted a millennium and a half.[68] Reflecting the various currents of the Latin poetic tradition as it was renewed and perpetuated during the fourth century, the poetry of Prudentius is obviously the high point of early Christian Latin poetry. The ballads of the *Peristephanon*, dedicated to the Spanish, Roman, and other martyrs, are a singular witness to the veneration of the saints. Although later than the year 400, at least as to their definitive publication, they do testify to the "liturgical sense" of the fourth-century Latin Church. The extent to which the latter was open to the values of ancient poetry is confirmed by the epigraphs of Damasus, also composed in honor of the martyrs and placed near their tombs.[69] Poetry occupied an even more important place in the Eastern Church.[70] However, we do not know the names of the fourth-century authors. Ephrem, the most famous hymnographer of the Syrian Church, is an exception.[71] While it is true that his poems are more like sermons composed in verse, they became a model for Byzantine liturgical poetry. If we could be sure of the authenticity of a poem on virginity and a hymn addressed to Christ, we could also count Gregory Nazianzen among the fourth-century liturgical poets.[72]

Early Christian literature contains a great wealth of documentary evidence on the history of Christian worship. Even though we do not find books in the strict sense during the first four centuries, the writings of Christian authors of the period allow us to get an idea of that time in history when the liturgy of the Eastern and Western Churches was formed in its essentials. But to properly evaluate these unique sources and take advantage of their riches, we must be conscious of their great literary variety and study them in their ecclesial and cul-

---

[67] J. Fontaine, *Inni/innologia: DPAC* II, 1881ff. (bibliography).
[68] J. Fontaine, art.cit., 1782.
[69] C. Pietri, *Damaso: DPAC* I, 883ff.
[70] A. Dihle, *Literatur,* 584: on the Eastern origins of liturgical chant.
[71] Ibid., 585.
[72] Ibid., 583.

tural setting. Only on these two conditions can we fully understand how the liturgy of the apostolic communities became the liturgy of the Churches.

Bibliography

CHURCH ORDERS

Bradshaw, P. F. *Kirchenordnungen*. Vol. 1, *Altkirchliche*. *TRE* 18 (1989) 662–670.

CPG 1730-1743 (editions and critical studies).

Faivre, A. "La documentation canonico-liturgique de l'Église ancienne." *RSR* 54 (1980) 204–215; *RSR* 54 (1980) 273–297; *RSR* 55 (1981) 31–42.

_____. *Ordonner la fraternité: Pouvoir d'innover et retour à l'ordre dans l'Église ancienne* = Histoire. Paris, 1992.

Giraudo, C. *La struttura letteraria della preghiera eucaristica*. Analecta Biblica 92. Rome, 1981.

Hanssens, J. *La liturgie d'Hippolyte: Documents et études*. Rome, 1970.

Schöllgen, G. *Zur Entstehung und Entwicklung der frühchristlichen Kirchenordnungen*. FCh 1:13–21. Freiburg, 1991.

DIDACHE

CPG 1735.

De Halleux, A. "Les ministères dans la Didachè." *Irén* 53 (1980) 5–29.

Niederwimmer, K. *Didache*. Kommentar zu den Apostolischen Vätern 1. Göttingen, 1989.

Rordorf, W., and A. Tuilier, eds. *La doctrine des douze Apôtres (Didachè)*. SCh 248. Paris, 1978. (See *DPAC* 1:947f.).

Schöllgen, G. "Didache: Zwölf-Apostel-Lehre." FCh 1:23–139. Freiburg, 1991.

TRADITIO APOSTOLICA

Botte, B., ed. *La Tradition Apostolique de saint Hippolyte: Essai de reconstitution*. LQF 39 (see SCh 11bis, 1968). Münster, 1963.

Geerlings, W. *Traditio Apostolica*. FCh 1:141–313. Freiburg, 1991 (bibliography).

Magne, J. *Tradition Apostolique sur les "charismes" et "Diataxeis des saints apôtres."* Origines chrétiennes 1:193–225. Paris, 1975.

Metzger, M. *Nouvelles perspectives pour la prétendue Tradition Apostolique. EO* 5 (1988) 241–259 (see SCh 320 and 336; *ALW* 33 (1991) 290–294.

Nuove richerche su Ippolito. Studia Ephemeridis "Augustinianum" 30. Rome, 1989.

DIDASCALIA APOSTOLORUM

CPG 1738.

DPAC 1:948ff.

Rahner, K. *La penitenza nella Chiesa*, 483–522. Rome, 1968.

TRE 18 (1989) 665ff.

CANONES ECCLESIASTICI APOSTOLORUM

CPG 1739.

DPAC 1:577ff.

Faivre, A. *Naissance d'une hiérarchie, 143–153*. Paris, 1977.

LThK 1 (1993) 871ff.

CONSTITUTIONES PER HIPPOLYTUM

CPG 1741, 1742.

DPAC 1:827.

TRE 18 (1989) 667ff.

CONSTITUTIONES APOSTOLORUM

CPG 1730.

Metzger, M. *Les Constitutions Apostoliques*. 3 vols. SCh 320 (1985); 329 (1986); 336 (1987).

Schöllgen, G. Bibliography in *LThK* 1 (1993) 872ff.

MYSTAGOGICAL CATECHESES

A. General Bibliography

Cesana, F. *L'eucaristia nei Padri: La catechesi eucaristica del II al VII secolo*. Milan, 1982.

Daniélou, J. *La catechesi nei primi secoli*. Turin, 1969.

Dragon, G. *Naissance d'une capitale: Constantinople et ses institutions de 330 à 451*. Paris, 1974.

Hamman, A. *L'initiation chrétienne*. Paris, 1980.

Mazza, E. *Mystagogy: A Theology of Liturgy in the Patristic Age*. Trans. M. J. O'Connell. New York, 1989.

Olivar, A. *La predicación cristiana antigua*. Barcelona, 1991.

Paverd, F. van de. *Zur Geschichte der Messliturgie in Antiocheia und Konstantinopel gegen Ende des vierten Jahrhunderts*. OCA 187. Rome, 1970.

Rentinck, P. *La cura pastorale in Antiochia nel IV secolo*. AGreg 178. Rome, 1970.

Riley, H. M. *Christian Initiation: A Comparative Study of the Interpretation of the Baptismal Liturgy in the Mystagogical Writings of Cyril of Jerusalem, John Chrysostom, Theodore of Mopsuestia and Ambrose of Milan.* Washington, 1974.

Ruffini, E., and E. Lodi. *"Mysterion" e "sacramentum": La sacramentalità negli scritti dei Padri e nei testi liturgici primitivi.* Nuovi saggi teologici 24. Bologna, 1987.

Schütz, W. *Geschichte der christlichen Predigt.* Berlin, 1972.

Studer, B. *Soteriologie der Kirchenväter.* HDG 3/2a:144–156, 181–190. Freiburg, 1978.

_____. "Mistagogia/Mistero." *DPAC* 2 (1984) 2264–2266 (bibliography).

Zinconce, S. *Studi sulla visione dell'uomo in ambito antiocheno (Diodoro, Crisostomo, Teodoro, Teodoreto).* L'Aquila, 1988.

B. Bibliography for Cyril of Jerusalem († 387)

Bosio, G., ed. *Introduzione ai Padri della Chiesa. Secoli III e IV,* 247–260 (bibliography). Turin, 1993.

CPG 2:3585ff.

Fernandez, D. *Diversos modos de presencia de Cristo en los catequesis de san Cirilo de Jerusalen. EstTrin* 9 (1975) 245–272.

Piédagnel, A., and P. Paris, eds. *Catéchéses mystagogiques.* SCh 126 (1966) and 126bis (1990). Paris, 1966.

Röwekamp, G., ed. *Cyrill von Jerusalem: Mystagogische Katechesen.* FCh 7. Freiburg, 1992.

Yarnold, E. "Cyrillus von Jerusalem." *TRE* 8 (1981) 261–266.

C. Bibliography for John Chrysostom († 407)

Bosio, G., ed. *Introduzione ai Padri della Chiesa. Secoli III e IV,* 390–435 (bibliography). Turin, 1993.

Corsato, C. "Dottrina battesimale nella catechesi di San Giovanni Crisostomo." *StudPad* 23 (1976) 270–296.

CPG 2:4305–4995, esp. 4460–4472: Catecheses ad illuminandos.

Finn, Th. M. *The Liturgy of Baptism in the Baptismal Instructions of John Chrysostom.* Washington, 1967.

Fittkau, G. *Der Begriff des Mysteriums bei Johannes Chrysostomus: Eine Auseinandersetzung mit dem Begriff des "Kultmysteriums" in der Lehre Odo Casels.* Bonn, 1953.

Kaczynski, R. *Das Wort Gottes in Liturgie und Alltag der Gemeinden des Johannes Chrysostomus.* Freiburger theologische Studien 94. Freiburg, 1974.

Sartore, D. "Il mistero del battesimo nelle catechesi di S. Giovanni Crisostomo." *Lateranum* 50 (1984) 359–395.

SCh 50 bis (Paris, 1970); 366 (Paris, 1990—bibliography and introduction). English translation with commentary: ACW 31 (1963) under the direction of P. W. Harkins.

Wenger, A. "Jean Chrysostome." *DSp* 8 (1974) 331–355.

D. Bibliography for Theodore of Mopsuestia

Bosio, G. *Introduzione ai Padri della Chiesa. Secoli IV e V,* 389–409. Turin, 1995.

CPG 2:3827–3864, esp. 3852: "Homiliae catechetichae."

Bruns, P., trans. *Theodor von Mopsuestia, Katechetische Homilien.* FCh 17:1/2. Freiburg, 1995.

Tonneau, R., and R. Devreesse. *Les homélies catéchétiques de Théodore de Mopsueste.* Photocopy of Ms. Migana Syr. 561, translation, introduction, index = ST. Vatican City, 1949.

E. Bibliography for Ambrose († 397)

Banterle, G., trans. *Spiegazione del Credo, I sacramenti, I misteri, La penitenza.* SAEMO 17. Milan, 1982.

Calcaterra, C. *La catechesi pasquale di Ambrogio di Milano.* Milan, 1973.

Dassmann, E. "Ambrosius von Mailand." *TRE* 2 (1978) 362–386.

Jacob, C. *"Arkandisziplin," Allegorese, Mystagogie: Ein neuer Zugang zur Theologie des Ambrosius von Mailand.* Frankfurt, 1990.

Mara, M. G. "Ambrogio." *DPAC* 1 (1983) 147–152.

Schmitz, J., ed. *De sacramentis = Über die Sakramente; De mysteriis = Über die Mysterien / Ambrosius, De sacramentis-De mysteriis.* FCh 3. Freiburg, 1990 (bibliography).

PATRISTIC PREACHING

Baus, K., and E. Ewig. *The Imperial Church from Constantine to the Early Middle Ages.* New York, 1980.

Beatrice, P. F., ed. *Cento anni di bibliografia ambrosiana (1874–1974).* Milan, 1981.

Bernardi, J. *La prédication des pères cappadociens: Le prédicateur et son auditoire.* Paris, 1968.

Daniélou, J. *La catéchèse aux premiers siècles.* Paris, 1968.

Graumann, T. *Christus Interpres: Die Einheit von Auslegung und Verkündigung in der Lukaserklärung des Ambrosius von Mailand.* Berlin, 1994.

Monachino, V. *La cura pastorale a Milano, Cartagine e Roma nel secolo quarto.* Rome, 1947; 2nd ed., 1973.

Olivar, A. *La predicaciòn cristiana antigua.* Barcelona, 1991.

Sachot, M. "Homilie." *RAC* 16 (1991/2) 148–175 (172/5: bibliography).

Salzmann, J. C. *Lehren und Ermahnen: Zur Geschichte des christlichen Wortgottesdienstes in den ersten drei Jahrhunderten.* WUNT 59. Tübingen, 1994.

Schütz, W. *Geschichte der christlichen Predigt*. Berlin, 1972.

Sottocornola, F. *L'anno liturgico nei sermoni di Pietro Crisologo*. Ravenna, 1973.

Van der Meer, F. *Augustine the Bishop*. Trans. B. Battershaw and G. R. Lamb. New York, 1962.

THEOLOGICAL TREATISES AND BIBLICAL COMMENTARIES

Di Berardino, A., and B. Studer, eds. *History of Theology*. Vol. 1, *The Patristic Period*. Trans. M. J. O'Connell. Collegeville, Minn., 1997.

Studer, B. *Die frühchristliche Literatur bis zur konstantinischen Zeit*. NHL.

———. *Die theologische Literatur vom 4. bis zum 7. Jahrhundert*. NHL.

HISTORIOGRAPHY

Dihle, A. *Greek and Latin Literature of the Roman Empire from Augustus to Justinian*. New York, 1994.

Siniscalco, P. "Storiografia." *DPAC* 2:3319–3326 (bibliography).

Studer, B. In A. Di Berardino and B. Studer, eds. *History of Theology*. Vol. 1, *The Patristic Period*, 270f. Trans. M. J. O'Connell. Collegeville, Minn., 1997.

HAGIOGRAPHY

Bastiaensen, A.A.R., et al., eds. *Atti e passioni dei martiri*, vii–xlix. Scrittori greci e latini. Rome, 1987.

Baumeister, T. *Heiligenverehrung* I: *RAC* 14:96–150. *Heiligenverehrung* II: *RAC* 14:150–183.

Saxer, V. "Agiografia." *DPAC* 1:80–83.

———. "Atti, Passione, Leggende." *DPAC* 2:2140–2149.

ECCLESIASTICAL CORRESPONDENCE AND CHRISTIAN POETRY

Dihle, A. *Greek and Latin Literature of the Roman Empire from Augustus to Justinian*. New York, 1994.

Fontaine, J. *Naissance de la poésie dans l'Occident chrétien*. Paris, 1981.

———. "Inni/innologia." *DPAC* 2:1781ff. (bibliography).

Pellegrino, M. "Introduzione alle lettere di Agostino." NBA 21. Rome, 1969. vii–cvii.

Studer, B. "Lettere dei papi." *DPAC* 2:2664ff. (bibliography).

———. In A. Di Berardino, and B. Studer, eds. *History of Theology*. Vol. 1, *The Patristic Period*, 292ff. Trans. M. J. O'Connell. Collegeville, Minn., 1997.

Elena Velkova Velkovska

13

Byzantine Liturgical Books

Current editions of the Byzantine liturgical books reflect the complex evolution and radical transformations experienced by the Constantinople tradition over a thousand years, from the fifth to the sixteenth century. The Byzantine rite, like the Roman, represents a synthesis of extremely diverse cultic and cultural traditions. Therefore we shall describe the books of each core tradition together with the books that have resulted from their repeated encounter.

I. BOOKS FROM THE ANCIENT CONSTANTINOPLE CATHEDRAL TRADITION

1. Psalter
The psalter contained the 150 psalms of the Septuagint and fifteen biblical canticles arranged in units called "antiphons." For this reason it was also sometimes called the antiphonary (ἀντιφωνάριον). Each antiphon was composed of a variable number of psalms with respective refrains and constituted the psalmodic *pensum* of the Liturgy of the Hours. Its organization has sometimes been attributed to the patriarch Anthimos (535–36). After the psalms came the fifteen biblical canticles proper to Constantinople and some appendices with chants and prayers. The earliest copy preserved is the famous Chludov Psalter (11th cen.), known for its valuable miniatures.

2. Gospel
The book used for liturgical proclamation of the gospel has always been an object of special veneration in Byzantine churches because it is a sign of Christ's presence. It is kept on the altar to indicate the

indissoluble link between the table of the Word and the table of the Bread and Cup.

As in the West, the earliest group of gospel codices is represented by the continuous text of the four evangelists (τετραευαγγέλιον) in the order Matthew, Mark, Luke, and John. This is followed or preceded by several tables indicating which pericopes are to be read. Beginning in the eighth century, lectionaries (εὐαγγέλιον, ἐκλογάδιον τοῦ εὐαγγέλίου) developed alongside the *tetraevangelion*. The pericopes were arranged in the order of their reading during the liturgical year: John, Matthew, Luke and Mark.

The earliest gospel lectionaries give pericopes only for Saturdays and Sundays during the year, for weekdays between Easter and Pentecost, and for the chief memorials of the Proper of the Saints. Only much later do lectionaries appear with pericopes for weekdays after Pentecost, with the exception of Lent, which was always aliturgical. This development depends on how often the Eucharist was celebrated. Even today it is not celebrated daily in all places but is restricted mainly to Saturdays, Sundays, and feastdays.

The readings are divided into four periods: the Gospel of John is read from Easter until Pentecost; the Gospel of Matthew from the Monday after Pentecost until the Sunday after September 14 (Exaltation of the Holy Cross); the Gospel of Luke from the Sunday after the Exaltation until Lent; the Gospel of Mark is read during Lent, with a few exceptions. Later it was also read on weekdays (Monday-Friday) beginning with the thirteenth Sunday after Pentecost.

Each of the three cycles (Saturday, Sunday, and Weekday), divided into four periods, follows the principle of semi-continuous reading. Holy Week and the Proper of the Saints, of course, have special readings.

3. Praxapostolos

This is a lectionary for the Eucharist containing pericopes from Acts (Πράξεις), the Letters of Paul (ἀπόστολος) — hence the Greek name πραξαπόστολος — and at a later period the Catholic Epistles, but not the Apocalypse. As in the gospel, the pericopes are arranged according to the Proper of the Season and the Proper of the Saints. The Proper of the Season begins with the Easter Eucharist and ends with the Easter Vigil of the following year; the Proper of the Saints, on the other hand, begins on September 1, which was the ancient Byzantine New Year.

The books are divided as follows: from Easter to Pentecost the Acts of the Apostles are read; on the thirty-second through the thirty-sixth Saturdays and Sundays after Pentecost, the readings are from the Pauline *corpus*; during Lent the Letter to the Hebrews is read; on the pre-Lenten Saturdays and Sundays and during Holy Week, the readings are special.

As we have already seen with regard to the gospel, the weekday cycle is later. In the concrete case of the *Praxapostolos*, it was arranged by distributing according to the principle of semi-continuous reading what remained of the Pauline *corpus* and the Letter to the Hebrews, including also the Catholic Epistles. This has given rise to various editorial possibilities in the manuscripts. These are embodied in as many groups, linked to the eucharistic rhythms of each local church during the time after Pentecost: a Saturday-Sunday lectionary, a Saturday-Sunday-Weekday lectionary, or simply a Weekday lectionary.

One characteristic of the *Praxapostolos* is its many rubrical directions. It should be noted that in our Bibles today the order of the books (Acts, Romans, Corinthians, etc.) follows that of the Byzantine *Praxapostolos*.

4. *Prophetologion*
The disappearance of the Old Testament reading from the Eucharist during the seventh century gave rise to the development of the Book of Prophecies (προφητολόγιον), whose earliest witness is *Sinai gr. 7* (9th cen.). This lectionary contains the Old Testament pericopes — often with musical notation — for Vespers and the vigils of major feasts, Vespers for weekdays (Monday–Friday), and Tersext for Lent. It also includes the psalms with their antiphons and the responsories between the readings (προκειμένα and Alleluia) for the Eucharist, together with many rubrics.

5. *Euchologion*
The Greek term (εὐχολόγιον) literally means "collection of prayers." This liturgical book contains the presidential prayers for the Eucharist, for the sacraments, and for blessings or consecrations of persons and things reserved to the bishop and/or priest. It corre-

sponds to the ancient *Sacramentarium* of the Roman Church. The earliest known copy is the codex *Barberini gr. 336* (8th cen.) from southern Italy, which is kept in the Vatican Library.

From an esthetic and formal point of view, the Byzantine *Euchologion* has come to us in the two forms of codex and scroll. Although, as we have mentioned, the codex is attested since the eighth century, we should note that the liturgical use of scrolls can lay claim to a certain antiquity. We need only think of the famous hymns or κοντάκια by Romanos the Melodist, a deacon in Constantinople before 518.

Some years ago L. W. Daly suggested that the liturgical use of scrolls be seen as an imitation by the Church of the practice of the imperial chancery. This was based on the parallels he established between the *kontakia* and *chrysobulls*. Briefly, the εὐχαί presented to God by the Church in the liturgy were supposedly written in a format identical to that used in civil *petitiones*. The *kontakia* then are a kind of elite *Euchologion* with a few special liturgical formulas, at first reserved to a prominent celebrant such as a bishop or patriarch.

Manuscript tradition for the *Euchologion* exists in one of two recensions: paleo-Byzantine and neo-Byzantine. The latter arose after the iconoclast controversy, and its earliest manuscript is from 1027 (Paris, Coislin 213). Each recension is in turn divided into Italian (Calabria-Campania, Calabria-Sicily, Salento) and Eastern (Sinai, Palestine, Greece). Each of these bears signs of distinct influences from the rite of Jerusalem.

6. Synaxarion

This collection of hagiographic material is arranged according to the sequence of feasts and memorials (σύναξις) from September 1 to August 31. It was "edited" in the ninth century under the sponsorship of Emperor Constantine VII Porphyrogenitus (913–959) in the context of the post-iconoclast liturgical reform. One famous *Synaxarion* has been improperly called the *Menologion* of Basil II (see below). In the twelfth century, verses by Christopher of Mytilene were added.

7. Rubrics

There is no separate *codex rubricarum* in the Byzantine cathedral tradition, but the directives for individual celebrations may be found, as we have seen, in the body or appendix of the lectionaries (gospel, *Praxapostolos, Prophetologion*), or incorporated into the *Synaxarion*. The most important collections of rubrics known today are included in the manuscripts *Patmos 226* and *Jerusalem Hagios Stauros 40:* codices P and H of the *Synaxarion*. Juan Mateos, who edited codex H, entitled his work the *Typicon de la Grande Église*, but this is not strictly correct, since τυπικόν is a term that belongs to the monastic rubrical tradition.

The rubrics contained in the *Synaxarion* are exceptionally important for a knowledge of the development of the stational liturgy of Constantinople, which revolved around the basilicas and imperial buildings. Times, routes, and participants are given. Also interesting are the rubrics for the proclamation of the Word at the Eucharist and those for the cathedral Liturgy of the Hours.

In addition to the *corpus* of rubrics apportioned among various books as needed, directories (διάταξις) were established in the eleventh century in a metropolitan context. These were for the patri-archal liturgy, whose increasingly complex development required detailed regulations.

II. BOOKS FROM THE PALESTINIAN MONASTIC TRADITION

1. Psalter

Unlike the cathedral tradition of Constantinople, the Palestinian monastic psalter, also called the Psalter of the *Anastasis*, is divided into twenty sections or "sessions" (καθίσματα), which in turn are sub-divided into three or more subsections (στάσεις) of three psalms each. The result is that each session is the same length. The number of verses is generally given at the end of each section or subsection. The 150 psalms are followed by 11 of the 15 canticles of the cathedral psalter, arranged in a Canon of nine odes. The earliest known witness to this type of psalter is *St. Petersburg gr. 216* from the year 862.

2. Horologion

This is the Book of Hours (ὡρολόγιον) of the monastery of Mar Saba in Jerusalem. It contains the ordinary invariable parts (psalms and hymns) for Vespers, ἀπόδειπνον, μεσονύκτικον, Matins, Prime, Terce, Sext, and None (the order may vary). Depending on the individual manuscripts, the ordinary is followed by various appendices containing hymns. The *Horologion* reflects a strictly monastic Liturgy of the Hours and does not envision the presence of a priest celebrant. The earliest example, which dates back to the ninth century, is codex *Sinai gr. 863*.

III. THE STUDITE AND SABAITE SYNTHESES

In the year 799, at the height of the iconoclast controversy, the monk Theodore and some of his companions moved from Sakkoudion, Bithynia (Asia Minor), to the Constantinople monastery of Stoudios, whose name he would later take. To assure adequate support for his iconodule position, Theodore appealed to Patriarch Theodore of Jerusalem, who sent some monks from Mar Saba to Stoudios. Thus they brought to Constantinople the prayer *horaria* of Palestine, which upon contact with the cathedral rite gave birth to the so-called Studite tradition. This process led to new "editions" of liturgical books already noted and to the creation of others.

1. Books Resulting from the Monastic-Cathedral Synthesis

For the celebration of the Eucharist, the Studite monks kept the cathedral *Euchologion*, gospel, and *Praxapostolos*. They did the same for the Liturgy of the Hours but distributed the prayers at Vespers and Orthros according to the Palestine *Horologion*. From Mar Saba the Studites adopted the psalter divided into sessions, but they interpolated refrains from the cathedral antiphonary between the psalm verses.

2. Hymnals

One of the monks who arrived in Constantinople with Theodore from Mar Saba was Theophanes Graptos (778–845), a hymnographer of exceptional talent. With him the consolidated hymn tradition of Palestine, already distinguished by the names of Andrew of Crete (d. 720), John of Damascus (d. 780), and Cosmas of Maiouma (d. 787), moved to the banks of the Bosphorus. There in Stoudios it was able to grow, thanks to Theodore himself and his brother Joseph, who later became metropolitan of Thessalonica.

a) Oktoechos-Paraketike. This hymn cycle is fifty-six days long and is divided into eight sections of a week each. It is called the Eight Tones (ὀκτώηχος) because each weekly section of hymns is sung according to one of the eight tones of Byzantine liturgical music. The cycle of the *Oktoechos* begins on the first Sunday after Pentecost and is interrupted on Friday of Carnival Week. However, it remains in effect on all the Sundays of Great Lent and Eastertime, except for Palm Sunday and Easter Sunday.

The Sunday hymn cycle of the Eight Tones is often attributed to John of Damascus but is certainly older, even though it also contains material from him. Parallel to the original Sunday *Oktoechos* there also developed a weekday series of hymns, called the *Parakletike* ("consolation"), which completed the cycle of fifty-six days.

b) Triodion-Pentekostarion. This contains the hymns for pre-Lent, Lent, Holy Week, and Eastertime. Originally conceived as one volume called simply the *Triodion*, it was later divided into two parts: the name *Triodion* was reserved to the section ending with Holy Saturday, and the name *Pentekostarion* was given to the section covering the fifty days of Easter. The name *Triodion* (τριώδιον) comes from the fact that during Lent the Canon for ὄρθρος (Vigils-Lauds) calls for the singing of just three biblical canticles with their respective odes.

c) Menaia. This collection of hymn texts contains the propers for the cycle of fixed feasts (μηναῖον, "monthly") arranged in twelve volumes according to the Byzantine calendar, which runs from September 1 until August 31. The *Menaia* may contain only selected texts for major feasts, or they may be complete and contain texts for every day. The earliest copies date back to the ninth century. Among them are the manuscripts *Messina gr. 175* and *Sophia, Dujec Center gr. 350.*

d) Musical Collections. Many hymn texts of the *Triodion*, *Pentekostarion* and *Menaia* have been gathered into special collections according to their textual-musical genre. Thus we have the collection of *stichera* for Vespers and Lauds (στιχηράριον), *kontakia* (κοντακάριον), and musical models for the Canons of *Orthros* (εἰρμολόγιον).

3. Menologion

This hagiographic collection, arranged by months (μηνολόγιον), contains the lives of the saints and patristic homilies read mostly at *Orthros* (Vigils-Lauds) or at other celebrations of the Hours, for example during Holy Week, as directed by the *Typicon*. The *Menologion* was compiled during the ninth century at the height of the Studite era, but the edition produced by Simeon Metaphrastes ("the Translator") during the second half of the tenth century is important enough that the book's manuscript tradition is usually divided into pre- and post- Metaphrastes. But Metaphrastes's work was adapted in turn, giving rise to the so-called Imperial *Menologion* from the time of Emperor Michael IV Paphlagones (1034–1041).

4. Typikon

Conflicts between the Proper of the Season and the Proper of the Saints, made more complicated by the increasing number of books used in the Liturgy of the Hours, would be regulated from now on by a new book of rubrics, the τυπικόν.

a) Studite Typikon. After Theodore's death, liturgical life in the monastery of Stoudios was entrusted to the brief prescriptions contained in the Rule (ὑποτύπωσις) composed by his disciples. The first real Studite *Typikon* we know of comes from the eleventh century and was drawn up by the hegumen Alexis, who was patriarch from 1025 to 1043. This *Typikon* is now available only in a contemporary Slavic translation, an eloquent sign of its spread throughout the Byzantine world. The first Studite *Typicon* in Italy dates from the second half of the twelfth century, although Theodore's Rule had already reached there by the first half of the tenth century.

b) Sabaite Typikon. This *Typikon* is the result of a renewed influence of the Mar Saba Laura on the Studite *Typikon*, in particular following the interlude of the Latin Empire in Constantinople. This influence is especially noticeable in the reintroduction of the Vigil between Saturday and Sunday. It is given such prominence that it occupies the first chapter of the *Typikon*. In the fourteenth century the Athonite recension of this book became the norm for the Byzantine rite during the Hesychast period. From the Holy Mountain it spread throughout the entire Byzantine world, paradoxically regulating even celebrations in secular churches. The only exception was southern Italy which remained faithful to the Studite *Typikon*, which is still followed today in the monastery of Grottaferrata near Rome — the only place in the world.

IV. PERIOD OF STABILIZATION AND UNIFICATION

With the fall of Constantinople in 1453 and the invention of printing, the various Greek liturgical books assumed definitive shape in the fifteenth century — naturally in their Byzantine-Sabaite form. Over the course of a few decades, the Venetian printing houses of the

Calliergi and Sabio published the entire series of liturgical books: *Horologion* (1509 and 1523), *Parakletike* and *Triodion* (1522 and 1525), Psalter (1524), *Oktoechos* (1525), *Euchologion* (1525?), *Menaia* (1526-36), Gospel (1539), *Apostolos* (1542), and *Typikon* (1545).

Stablization and the progressive spread of the Venetian editions has marked the history of the Byzantine tradition until our own day. Among the chief consequences, the first was the canonization, as it were, of a single local tradition to the detriment of many others still alive and well. The Venetian printers generally established the manuscript tradition of the Greek Mediterranean (it was closer at hand), with no attempt at comparison or correction based on other witnesses.

Thus the invention of printing hindered the organic development of the liturgical heritage, at the same time laying down the premises that would lead to the Byzantine rite becoming a monolithic and fixed block. Except for minor rubrical details, there was no possibility of legitimate liturgical pluralism, which until then had enjoyed free reign. The individual churches had practically no role in this process except to affix their formal *imprimatur*, while everything was left to the initiative and will of the printers.

The advent of printing served to accentuate a process already noted in the Orthodox world: the anthologizing of liturgical books. These tended to become complete. Although this process never produced books of the kind found in the West after Trent, nevertheless extracts from different liturgical books were often collected into a single volume, usually for the Liturgy of the Hours.

V. REFORMS AND REVISIONS

The historical, religious, and political phenomenon known today as uniatism, which since the late sixteenth century has resulted in the division of some churches into two obediences or jurisdictions, Roman and Orthodox, also favored in time the publication of separate liturgical editions. In fact, in the seventeenth century a special Roman congregation was created, headed by a cardinal, whose purpose was to correct (as was said at the time) the Greek liturgical books. This congregation remained active until the end of the nineteenth century. Breaking with the earlier tradition of confessional neutrality, the commission made certain dogmatic adjustments, obviously from a Tridentine viewpoint. It suppressed some texts or struck from others the names of dead authors not in communion with the Church of Rome.

Moved by needs disproportionate to the size of the project — such as the need to provide liturgical books for Albanian immigrants to Italy — the congregation during its long life actually promoted the critical study of Byzantine hymns and liturgical rules. Except for the editorial changes just mentioned, the books it had printed are generally considered good from a philological point of view.

On the Greek Orthodox side, during the most acute phase of a theological dispute, the monk Bartholomew of Imbros published a *Typikon of the Great Church* in 1838. This is nothing more than a drastic shortening of the Sabaite monastic *Typikon*, which was considered, not without reason, as unsuitable for parish celebrations. The edition met with great success, judging from the number of reprintings (1851, 1868, and 1884). Finally, in the context of a larger project to reform the liturgical books sponsored by the Ecumenical Patriarch Joachim III (1878–1894), the definitive edition of 1888 was published, thanks to the editorial work of Constantine, protocantor of the Great Church.

Unfortunately this Orthodox revision, like that of the Roman congregation, was not immune from editorial changes made under the banner of confessional intransigence.

VI. PROSPECTS

From what we have said thus far, it is clear that the history of the liturgical books during the last four centuries moves in a distinctly rubrical — if not rubricist — direction, at least in some churches. Only one principle of adapatation is considered: that the celebrant or cantor may *shorten* some parts of the celebration, but always within the framework of the customs of their particular church.

But the idea of reform of the Byzantine liturgical books is not new, even though it was spoken of with less insistence in the past — perhaps because people were conscious of a certain hypersensitivity on the part of the Orthodox in the area of liturgical renewal. It must not be forgotten that the reform in Russia by Nikon and, more recently, the adoption of the Gregorian calendar were carried out at the cost of internal schisms that are still with us. In fact, based on the documents of the preparatory commissions for the Pan-Orthodox Synod, the question of reform of the liturgical books — even what was earlier suggested on reorganization of the readings — has now been limited to discussion concerning the periods of fasting.

In any case, when we speak of reform of the liturgical books among the Orthodox, we must not imagine any kind of major change in the celebration. It would be no more than a matter of revising the texts of the individual books from a philological point of view in order to eliminate inconsistencies and inaccuracies.

However, there are new particular liturgies, such as the liturgy of New Skete Monastery in the United States and the French liturgy which follows the Gallican rite.

Bibliography

Allatius, L. *De libris et rebus ecclesiasticis graecorum dissertationes et observationes variae.* Paris, 1646.

_____. *De libris ecclesiasticis Graecorum dissertationes duae . . . ad editionem Cramoisianam Paris. MDCXCIV, additis notis, supplemento & indice atque elencho alpahabetico Melodorum Graecorum recusae, cura Jo. Alberti Fabricii.* Hamburg, 1717.

Beck, H. G. *Kirche und theologische Literatur im byzantinischen Reich.* Handbuch der Alterumwissenschaft 12:245–262. Munich, 1959.

Cappuyns, R. "L'histoire des livres liturgiques grecs." *Studi bizantini e neoellenici* 4 (1940) 470–473.

Federici, T. "Libri liturgici orientali." *Anàmnesis* 2:217–223.

Pantelakis, E. "Les livres ecclésiastiques de l'Orthodoxie." *Irén* 13 (1936) 521–557.

Taft, R. *Selected Bibliography on the Byzantine Liturgy of the Hours.* OCP 48 (1982) 358–404.

I. Books from the Constantinople Cathedral Tradition

PSALTER

Schneider, H. "Die biblischen Oden in christlichen Altertum." *Biblica* 30 (1949) 28–65.

_____. "Die biblischen Oden seit dem sechsten Jahrhundert." *Biblica* 30 (1949) 239–279.

_____. "Die biblischen Oden in Jerusalem und Constantinopel." *Biblica* 30 (1949) 433–452.

Strunk, O. "The Byzantine Office at Hagia Sophia." *Dumbarton Oaks Papers* 9–10 (1955–1956) 175–202, esp. 200–201.

Taft, R. *Selected Bibliography on the Byzantine Liturgy of the Hours. OCP* 48 (1982) 358–404.

_____. "Mount Athos: A Late Chapter in the History of the Byzantine Rite." *Dumbarton Oaks Papers* 42 (1988) 179–194, esp. 181.

GOSPEL

Aland, K. *Kurzgefasste Liste der griechischen Handschriften des Neuen Testaments.* Berlin, 1963.

Braithwaite, W. C. "The Lection-System of the Codex Macedonianus." *JThS* 5 (1904) 265–274.

Guillaume, D. *Saint Évangile conforme a celui qui est lu dans les Églises.* Rome, 1979.

Gy, P.-M. "La question du système des lectures de la liturgie byzantine." *Miscellanea liturgica in onore di Sua Eminenza il Cardinale Giacomo Lercaro,* 2:251–261. Rome, 1967.

Velkovska, E. "Lo studio dei lezionari bizantini." *EO* 13 (1996).

PRAXAPOSTOLOS

De Vries, I. *The Epistles and the Tones of the Byzantine Liturgical Year.* Eastern Churches Quarterly 3 (1954).

Junack, K. "Zu den griechischen Lektionaren und ihrer Überlieferung der Katholischen Briefe." *Die alten Übersetzungen des Neuen Testaments, die Kirchenväterzitate und Lektionare,* 498–589. Arbeiten zur neutestamentlichen Textforschung 5. Berlin–New York, 1972.

PROPHETOLOGION

Texts

Engberg, S. G. *Prophetologium. Pars altera: Lectiones anni immobilis.* Copenhagen, 1980–1981.

Zuntz, G., and G. Engberg, eds. *Prophetologium.* 2 vols. Monumenta Musicae Byzantinae, Lectionaria 1. Copenhagen, 1939–1981.

Studies

Engberg, S. G. "The Greek Old Testament Lectionary as a Liturgical Book." *Cahiers de l'Institut de Moyen Âge grec et latin* 54 (1986) 39–48.

Høeg, C., and G. Zuntz. "Remarks on the Prophetologion." AA. VV. *Quantulacumque: Studies Presented to K. Lake,* 189–198. London, 1937.

Taft, R. *A Selected Bibliography on the Byzantine Liturgy of the Hours,* no. 171.

Zuntz, G. "Das byzantinische Septuaginta-Lektionar." *Classica et mediaevalia* 17 (1956) 183–198.

EUCHOLOGION

Texts

Dmitrievskij, A. *Opisanie liturgiceskih rukopisej hranjasihsja v bibliotekax pravoslavnago Vostoka*. Vol. 2, *Euchologia*. Kiev, 1901. Reprint Hildesheim, 1965.

Goar, J. *Euchologion, sive Rituale Graecorum complectens ritus et ordines Divinae Liturgiae*. Editio 2a. Venice, 1730. Reprint Graz, 1960.

Parenti, S., and E. Velkovska. *L'eucologio Barberini gr. 336*. BELS 80. Rome, 1995.

Studies

Daly, L. W. "Rotuli. Liturgical Rolls and Formal Documents." *Greek, Roman and Byzantine Studies* 14 (1973) 332–338.

Grand Euchologe et Arkhiératikon. Trans. D. Guillaume. Parma, 1992.

Parenti, S. "Euchologion." *Lexikon für Theologie und Kirche* 3, col. 976. Freiburg, 1995.

Taft, R. *The Byzantine Rite: A Short History*, 52–56. Collegeville, Minn., 1992.

SYNAXARION

Texts

Delehaye, H. *Synaxarium ecclesiae Constantinopolitanae e codice Sirmondiano, nunc Berolinensi, adiectis synaxariis selectis*. Propylaeum ad Acta Sanctorum, Novembris. Brussels, 1902.

Studies

Luzzi, A. *Studi sul sinassario di Costantinopoli*. Studi e testi bizantino-neoellenici 8. Rome, 1995.

Noret, J. "Ménologes, Synaxaires, Ménées: Essai de clarification d'une terminologie." *AB* 86 (1968) 21–24.

Pieralli, L. "Synaxarium Ecclesiae Constantinopolitanae: La famiglia C." *OCP* 60 (1994) 399–470.

RUBRICS

Dmitrievskij, A. *Opisanie liturgiceskih rukopisej hranjasihsja v bibliotekax pravoslavnago Vostoka*. Vol. 1, *Tupikav*. Kiev, 1895. Reprint Hildesheim, 1965. 1–152.

Mateos, J. *Le Typikon de la Grande Église. Ms. Sainte-Croix Nᵒ· 40*. 2 vols. OCA 165–166. Rome, 1962-1963.

Taft, R. "The Pontifical Liturgy of the Great Church According to a Twelfth-Century Diataxis in Codex British Museum Add. 34060. *OCP* 45 (1979) 279–307; 46 (1980) 89–124. Reprinted in *Liturgy in Byzantium and Beyond*. Collected Studies Series 493. Brookfield, Vt., 1995.

II. Books from the Palestinian Monastic Tradition

PSALTER

Taft, R. *Selected Bibliography on the Byzantine Liturgy of the Hours. OCP* 48 (1982) 358–404, nos. 86, 87.

_____. "Mount Athos: A Late Chapter in the History of the 'Byzantine Rite.'" *Dumbarton Oaks Papers* 42 (1988) 181–182.

HOROLOGION

Texts

Black, M. *A Christian Palestinian Syriac Horologion (Berlin MS. Or. Oct. 1019)*. Texts and Studies, n.s. 1. Cambridge, 1967.

Mateos, J. "Un horologion inédit de Saint-Sabas. Le Codex sinaïtique grec 863 (IXᵉ siècle)." In *Mélanges E. Tisserant*. Vol. 3, *Orient chrétien*, 47–76. ST 233. Vatican City, 1964.

Studies

Egender, N. Introduction to *La prière des heures: Hôrologion*. La prière des églises de rite byzantin 1. Chevetogne, 1975.

Taft, R. *Selected Bibliography on the Byzantine Liturgy of the Hours. OCP* 48 (1982) 358–404, nos. 62, 63, 66-67, 70, 73, 75-76, 88, 90, 94, 101, 108, 110.

III. The Studite and Sabaite Syntheses

OKTOECHOS-PARAKLETIKE

Text

The Hymns of the Octoechus. Parts I-II. Monumenta Musicae Byzantinae, Transcripta 3 and 5. Copenhagen, 1940, 1949.

Studies

Hannick, Ch. "Le texte de l'Oktoechos." *Dimanche. Office selon les huits tons: Oktoechos*, 37–60. La prière des églises de rite byzantin 3. Chevetogne, 1972.

TRIODION-PENTEKOSTARION

Text

Follieri, E., and O. Strunk. *Triodium Athoum.* Monumenta Musicae
Byzantinae, Transcripta 9. Copenhagen, 1975.

MUSICAL COLLECTIONS

Follieri, E. *Initia hymnorum ecclesiae Graecae.* 5 vols. in 6. ST 211–215. Vatican
City, 1960–1966.

Szövérffy, J. *A Guide to Byzantine Hymnography: A Classified Bibliography of
Texts and Studies.* 2 vols. Medieval Classics: Texts and Studies 11–12.
Brookline, Mass., and Leyden, 1978–1979.

MENOLOGION

Ehrhard, A. *Überlieferung und Bestand der hagiographischen und homiletischen
Literatur der griechischen Kirche von den Anfängen bis zum Ende des 16.
Jahrhunderts.* 3 vols. TU 50–52. 3/1: Leipzig, 1937–1943; 3/2: Berlin, 1952.

Halkin, F. *Bibliotheca hagiographica graeca.* 3 vols. Subsidia hagiographica 8a.
Brussels, 1957³.

STUDITE TYPIKON

Taft, R. *Selected Bibliography on the Byzantine Liturgy of the Hours.* OCP 48
(1982) 358–404, nos. 29, 35, 37-38, 42-44, 47.

SABAITE TYPIKON

Text

Dmitrievskij, A. *Opisanie liturgiceskih rukopisej hranjasihsja v bibliotekax
pravoslavnago Vostoka.* Vol. 3. Kiev, 1901. Reprint Hildesheim, 1965.

Studies

Taft, R. "Mount Athos: A Late Chapter in the History of the 'Byzantine Rite.'"
Dumbarton Oaks Papers 42 (1988) 187–194.

PERIOD OF STABILIZATION AND UNIFICATION

Follieri, E. "Il libro greco per i greci. Le imprese editoriali romane e
veneziane della prima metà del Cinquecento." *Venezia centro di medi-
azione tra Oriente e Occidente (secoli XV–XVI): Aspetti e problemi,* 2:482–508.
Florence, 1977.

Korolevskij, C. "La codification de l'office byzantin: Les essais dans le passé."
OCP 19 (1953) 25–58.

Raes, A. "Les livres liturgiques grecs publiés a Venise." *Mélanges Eugène Tisserant.* Vol. 3, *Orient chrétien, deuxième partie,* 209–222. ST 233. Vatican City, 1964.

Tomadake, N. B. "L'edizione dei libri ecclesiastici greci (soprattutto liturgici) in Italia, a cura di religiosi greci ortodossi durante i secoli XV e XVI." *La Chiesa Greca in Italia dall'VIII al XVI secolo. Atti del Convegno Storico Interecclesiale,* 685–721. Bari, 1969.

REFORMS AND REVISIONS

Korolevskij, C. "Liturgical Publications of the Sacred Eastern Congregation." *Eastern Churches Quarterly* 6 (1945–1946) 87–96, 388–399.

_____ . "L'édition romaine des Ménées grecques: 1881–1901." *Bollettino della Badia Greca di Grottaferrata,* n.s. 3 (1949) 30–40, 153–162, 225–247; 4 (1950) 15–16.

Ploumidis, G. "Il libro liturgico (-biblico) greco e slavo. Scelte ecclesiastiche e tecnica editoriale." *Rivista di Bizantinistica* 2 (1992) 65–79.

Radovic, A. "Réformes liturgiques dans l'Église de Grèce." *Liturgie de l'Église particulière et liturgie de l'Église universelle,* 261–273, esp. 265–266. BELS 7. Rome, 1976.

Raes, A. "Les notices historiques de l'horologe grec." *AB* 68 (1950) 475–480.

Raquez, O. "La Congrégation pour la correction des livres de l'Église orientale (1719–1862)." *Sacra Congregatio de Propaganda Fide Memoria Rerum,* 2:514–534. Rome, 1972.

PROSPECTS

Federici, T. "Revisione dei libri liturgici nell'Oriente oggi." *Not* 15 (1979) 640–654.

Sargologos, G. "L'altération des textes liturgiques grecs." *Gestes et paroles dans les diverses familles liturgiques,* 235–278. BELS 14. Rome, 1978.

Manel Nin, O.S.B.

14

Other Liturgical Books in the East

In this section we shall list in schematic fashion the books used in the non-Byzantine Eastern liturgies. It must be said that the various editions of the liturgical books are especially associated with the Eastern Churches that are in communion with the Church of Rome, whereas in the Orthodox Churches the liturgical books in many cases are still in the manuscript stage.

I. EAST-SYRIAN LITURGICAL BOOKS[1]

The principal East-Syrian liturgical books may be grouped as follows:

Hudra (cycle). Contains the texts for all the offices of all feasts.

Gazza (treasure). Contains liturgical compositions for the offices of Vigils (*lelya*).

Kashkull (contains everything). Contains the texts of the *Hudra* as well as those for weekdays.

Warda (rose). A collection of poetic texts used as antiphons.

Ktaba daqdam wadbatar (book of before and after). Contains the texts for Sundays beginning with Easter.

Three Lectionaries: Old Testament, Epistles, and Gospel Book.

Naqpayatha drase (supplement to the mysteries). Contains chants for the celebration of the liturgy.

---

[1] See *PDOC* 329–34; C. Moussess, *Les Livres Liturgiques de l'Église Chaldéene* (Beirut, 1955); F. Y. Alichoran, *Missel Chaldéen* (Paris, 1982). I would also mention the edition of J.E.Y. de Quellayta, which contains the texts of the three eucharistic anaphoras and various other texts for blesssings and the consecration of an altar.

II. WEST-SYRIAN LITURGICAL BOOKS[2]

Ktobo d'anaphuras (book of anaphoras). Contains the prayers and anaphoras recited by the priest.

Diaconal. Book with the deacon's parts and the people's responses.

'Atiqto (Old). Contains the Old Testament readings.

Shliho (Apostle). Contains readings from the Letters of Paul, divided into three cycles: Sundays, movable feasts, immovable feasts, and weekdays.

Gospel Book. Divided into three cycles like the "Apostle."

Fanqitho. Contains the collection of liturgical texts for feasts during the year; it is subdivided into seven volumes.

Shimo (simple). Book for the weekly offices.

Psalter.

Book of Sedri (orders). The *Sedro* is a text recited by the priest, containing an introduction and homiletic type of admonition that refers to the feast being celebrated or the day of the week.

Book of Homilies.

III. COPTIC AND ETHIOPIAN LITURGICAL BOOKS[3]

1. Coptic Liturgical Books

There are twenty-one liturgical books in the Coptic liturgy, a sign that the different books and traditions are still very poorly codified.

Euchologion. Contains formulas for the Eucharist with the three anaphoras in use (St. Basil, St. Gregory, and St. Cyril), for Matins and for the Office of Vespers.

Diaconal. Variable parts of the deacon and the people.

Katameros. A lectionary in three parts: one for Sundays, feasts, and weekdays, one for Lent, and one for Easter and Pentecost.

Synaxarion. A kind of martyrology read at Mass after the reading from the Acts of the Apostles in order to show the continuity of salvation history.

Al-Tasafir. Arabic translation of the readings for Mass, with a series of commentaries on these.

Al-Mawa'iz. An anthology of homiletic texts from the patristic tradition.

[2] See *PDOC* 334–9.

[3] See *PDOC* 339–41; Hanna Malak, "Les Libres Liturgiques de l'Église Copte," *Mélanges Eugène Tisserant III* (Vatican, 1964) 1–35.

Al-Tamagid. Hymns and doxologies for saints' feasts.

Al-Mayamir. A series of homilies describing the feast being celebrated.

Al-Sirah. Biographies of the saints read after the *Al-Mayamir*.

Chants for Feasts. Chants sung during Communion.

Processional. Used for processions on the two feasts of the Holy Cross and on Palm Sunday.

Horologion. Ordinary parts for the seven hours of the Office.

Annual Psalms. Contains odes and Theotokia for the days of the week and the doxologies for saints' feasts.

Psalms for Khoiak. Contains proper offices for the month of Khoiak (before Christmas), dedicated to Our Lady.

Difnar. Contains a *menologion* with brief notes about the saints being celebrated and hymns for the saints' feasts.

Book of Chants. Contains hymns for Vespers and Matins of certain annual feasts.

Office of Laqqan. A book of blessings: for water on the feast of Epiphany, for Holy Thursday, and for the feast of SS. Peter and Paul.

Liturgy of Holy Week. Contains the prayers for Holy Week, from the Saturday of Lazarus to Easter Sunday.

Book of the Holy Pascha. Contains the lectionary for Holy Week.

2. *Ethiopian Liturgical Books*[4]

Missal. Contains about twenty anaphoras.

Manuals. There are several: for penance, matrimony, and the anointing of the sick.

Deggua. An antiphonal with psalms, antiphons, and other texts for the Office.

Soma Deggua. The antiphonal for Lent.

Antiphonal. Used for feasts.

Office. The common.

Synodos. A list of saints' feasts.

IV. ARMENIAN LITURGICAL BOOKS[5]

Tonacʿoycʿ. The Armenian version of the Greek τυπιχόν, that is, the book containing the rules for feasts and liturgical celebrations.

---

[4] See *PDOC* 341–3.
[5] See *PDOC* 343–4.

Horhdatetr (book of the mysteries). The missal containing the Liturgy of St. Athanasius, which is used by the Armenian Church.

Casoc^c. The lectionary containing the biblical pericopes for celebrations.

Zamagirk^c. The Book of Hours corresponding to the Greek ὁρολόγιον.

Sarakan. The antiphonary containing the variable parts of the Office and the *Tagaran*, which is a hymnal containing the variable parts of the Eucharist.

Mastoc^c. The ritual of the Armenian Liturgy.

Pontifical. Contains the parts pertaining to the bishop.

Synaxarion (a kind of martyrology).

Bibliography

Assfalg, J., and P. Krüger, eds. *Petit Dictionnaire de l'Orient Chrétien (PDOC)*. Turnhout, 1991.

Baumstark, A. *Comparative Liturgy*. Rev. B. Botte. Trans. F. L. Cross. Westminster, Md., 1958.

Dalmais, I.-H. *Introduction to the Liturgy*. Trans. R. Capel. Baltimore, 1961.

_____. *Les liturgies d'Orient*. 2nd ed. Rites et symboles 10. Paris, 1980.

Gelsi, D. "Orientali, liturgie." *NDL* 983–1007.

Hänggi, A., and I. Pahl. *Prex eucharistica: Textus e variis liturgiis antiquioribus selecti*. Spicilegium Friburgense 12. Fribourg, 1968.

Hanssens, J. M. *Institutiones liturgicae de ritibus orientalibus*. Rome, 1930.

Janeras, S. *Introductio in liturgias orientales* (pro manuscripto).

_____. *Bibliografia sulle liturgie orientali (1961–1967)*. Pro manuscripto.

Nin, M. "The Liturgical Heritage of the Eastern Churches." In *Catholic Eastern Churches: Heritage and Identity*. Rome, 1994.

Raes, A. *Introductio in liturgiam orientalem*. Rome, 1962.

Salaville, S. *An Introduction to the Study of Eastern Liturgies*. London, 1938.

Sauget, J. M. *Bibliographie des liturgies orientales (1900–1960)*. Rome, 1962.

Taft, R. *The Liturgy of the Hours in East and West: The Origins of the Divine Office and Its Meaning for Today*. 2nd rev. ed. Collegeville, Minn., 1993.

Yousif, P., ed. *A Classified Bibliography on the East Syrian Liturgy*. Rome, 1990.

Cassian Folsom, O.S.B.

15

The Liturgical Books of the Roman Rite

Every craft has its tools, and one of the essential tools for the study of the liturgy is a good grasp of liturgical books. This allows for a profound understanding of the sources of the liturgy, a *sine qua non* for tracing the development of the tradition. It is under this heading that liturgical books will be presented here: as essential tools of the trade, each having its own name, its own history, its own specific typology[1] or use. For the sake of clarity, the vast material under discussion will be divided into four major sections: books used for Mass, for the Liturgy of the Hours, for the good ordering of the liturgy, and for other sacraments and rites.

BOOKS USED FOR MASS

At first, the various books used for Mass existed separately: the sacramentary, possibly including the canon (for the priest or bishop), the lectionary (for the lectors), the antiphonary (for the cantors), and the calendar (for reference use). Only gradually were these many books gathered together into a single book, the Missal.

I. THE SACRAMENTARY

A. The so-called Verona Sacramentary
Our first sacramentary is really not a sacramentary at all, but a collection of *libelli* or booklets, each of which had originally been used

---

[1] By "typology" we mean the literary genre of a given document, the characteristics of this particular *type* of document in its historical context and actual use. Cf. L. Genicot, *Introduction*, TS 1 (Brepols, 1972) 8.

quite independently of the other. Thus it is a precursor of the sacramentary, properly so-called.

1. *Edition*: L. C. Mohlberg - L. Eizenhöfer - P. Sifrin, *Sacramentarium Veronense*, RED Series Maior, Fontes I (Rome, ³1978).

2. *Date of manuscript*: 600–625; Date of composition: 561–574.

3. *Description*: This book is structured according to the months of the year. Since the manuscript is defective, the text begins part way through the month of April; it ends with the month of December. The temporal and sanctoral cycles, along with certain sacramental rites are intermixed in a rather disorganized manner.

4. *Typology*: The Veronense is not arranged in such a way as to be used directly in the liturgical action itself. Rather, it is a collection of *libelli* from various different periods. A *libellus* is a small booklet containing a number of euchological texts: the formulary for a single Mass, for example, or a collection of formularies for different Masses, or a group of texts for some other kind of ritual action. In the Veronense, the presence of many different formularies for the same feast day indicates that the celebrant had a wide selection to chose from. This is a kind of liturgical resource book.

There are two kinds of *libelli*: (1) In the pre-sacramentary period, a *libellus* was single page, or a booklet of several pages containing the orations composed for a given feast or a given church. These *libelli* are the link between "structured improvisation" and the fixed texts of later sacramentaries. The Veronense is a collection of this type of *libellus*. (2) In the sacramentary period, there were still *libelli* in circulation, but these tended to be extracts of the sacramentaries themselves, for the use of priests who were traveling missionaries or pilgrims,[2] or for the celebration of various votive Masses.[3]

5. *History*: The Veronense is a private collection of authentic Roman *libelli*, which before their compilation in this book, were collected and kept in the Lateran archives. Originally, this collection was for papal use; later it was modified for the use of priests in the titular churches

---

[2] Examples of this type are the Stowe Missal (mid-seventh century, Celtic liturgy) and the Mone Missal (ca. 650, Gallican liturgy) cf. Vogel, *ML* 38.

[3] Examples of this type are the glagolitic (i.e., using the cyrillic alphabet) Missal of Kiev (9th century, based on a Roman prototype of the 6th–7th century) and the Votive Sacramentary of Alcuin (8th–9th century) cf. Vogel, *ML* 38.

of Rome. In modern times, the manuscript was discovered in the chapter library of Verona by Scipione Maffei in 1713. Already in 1735, with the edition of Bianchini, it was attributed to St. Leo the Great. While St. Leo surely is the author of some of its formularies, the attribution of the entire work to him has been shown to be erroneous. The most recent edition is that of Cunibert Mohlberg and collaborators (1956); the third edition (1978) was reprinted in 1994.

There has been a great deal of speculation as to the origins of this book. Some scholars have taken as their point of departure an analysis of particular formulas, striving to date the text on the basis of the literary style of a given pope, the theological content of the orations, and contemporary civil and ecclesiastical history. For example, it has been demonstrated that certain formularies can be attributed to St. Leo the Great (440–461) based on his literary and theological style,[4] to Pope Gelasius (492–496) based on his struggle against the pagan celebrations of the *lupercalia*,[5] and to Pope Vigilius (537–555) based upon the historical crisis of the siege of Rome by the Ostrogoths under King Witiges from July 537 to March 538.[6] Other scholars have based their research upon the book considered as a whole, as it has come down to us. According to this method, A. Chavasse has convincingly argued that the compilation as we now have it is actually an untidy combination of two different collections, one following the temporal and sanctoral cycle, the other supplying formularies for the liturgy of the hours, sacraments, and other rites (that is, the beginnings of a pontifical or ritual). On the basis of internal evidence, Chavasse proposes that this compilation was made during the papacy of Pope John III (561–574).[7]

The fact that later sacramentaries contain orations that are found also in the Veronense does not necessarily mean that there is a direct link between the one and the other. Taking into account the nature of this book, that is, a collection of *libelli*, it is more accurate to speak of

[4] J. Pinell i Pons, "Teologia e liturgia negli scritti di S. Leone Magno," *EO* 8 (1991) 137–81.

[5] B. Capelle, "Retouches gélasiennes dans le sacramentaire léonien" in *RB* 61 (1951) 3–14. Cf. also Gélase Ier, *Lettres contre les lupercales: Dix-huit messes du sacramentaire léonien*, G. Pomarès, ed., SCh 65 (Paris, 1959).

[6] A. Chavasse, "Messes du Pape Vigile (537–555) dans le sacramentaire léonien," *EphLit* 64 (1950) 161–213; 66 (1952) 145–219.

[7] Chavasse, "Le sacramentaire dit léonien," 183–5.

an indirect connection, since the other sacramentaries were able to draw upon the same kinds of *libelli* which were in circulation at the time. Thus, it cannot be said that the Veronense is a direct source for the Gelasian or the Gregorian sacramentaries.

B. The Gelasian Sacramentary

While the title of this sacramentary is *Liber sacramentorum Romanae Ecclesiae ordinis anni circuli,* since the edition of Muratori in 1748, it has been commonly called the "Gelasian Sacramentary" because it was thought that Pope Gelasius I (492–496) was its author. There is but one manuscript, the *Reginensis 316* of the Vatican Library. The conclusion is missing from the *Reginensis 316*, however, and is supplied instead by *Codex latinus 7193* of the Bibliothèque Nationale of Paris.

1. *Edition*: L. C. Mohlberg, *Liber sacramentorum Romanae Ecclesiae ordinis anni circuli,* RED Series Maior, Fontes IV (Rome, ³1981).

2. *Date of manuscript*: ca. 750, copied in the monastery of Chelles, near Paris. Date of composition: 628–715. *Terminus a quo*: after the pontificate of Pope St. Gregory the Great († 604), since the canon of the Mass contains additions made by St. Gregory; after the recovery of the relics of the Holy Cross by Emperor Heraclitus in 628, since the sanctoral includes the feast of the *Exaltatio Sanctae Crucis*. *Terminus ad quem*: before the pontificate of Pope Gregory II (715–731), since the Gelasian does not contain formulas for the Thursdays during Lent, introduced by the same pontiff.

3. *Description*: There are two distinguishing characteristics of this book: (1) It is clearly divided into three parts: the liturgical year; the sanctoral cycle, including a set of commons and the Masses of Advent; and the Sundays of the year, including the canon, Masses for various occasions, and other *varia liturgica*. (2) Frequently there is an "extra" oration after the Collect and before the Secret. Various theories have been proposed to explain this. Most recently, Chavasse argues that it serves as the concluding oration of the universal prayers.[8]

4. *Typology*: This is a sacramentary properly so-called, compiled for use during the liturgical action, containing the necessary texts for the

---

[8] A. Chavasse, "A Rome, au tournant du Ve siècle, additions et remaniements dans l'ordinaire de la messe," *EO* 5 (1988) 25–42.

248

bishop/priest for Mass, other sacraments, the liturgy of the hours, and various other occasions.

5. *History*: An analysis of the content of this sacramentary shows that it is a mixed book in two senses: (1) It is a Roman book to which many Gallican elements have been added. This is not a "pure Roman" sacramentary, therefore: the original Roman source has not come down to us. (2) The Roman base itself is mixed; that is, is a combination of papal and presbyteral elements. It is important to note that there were two liturgical traditions developing at the same time in Rome: one papal (Gregorian), the other presbyteral (Gelasian).

Chavasse proposes that the Gelasian Sacramentary was compiled for a single church out of the twenty-five titular churches which existed in Rome at the time: St. Peter in Chains.[9]

The Gelasian Sacramentary was used in Rome during the seventh century and the first part of the eighth. Before the papacy of Gregory II (715–731), it was brought to Gaul, where various Gallican elements were added.[10] Because of the widespread influence of this sacramentary in Gaul in the eighth century it is reasonable to conjecture that it must have arrived there by the end of the seventh. It would seem that this sacramentary was instrumental in the romanization of the Gallican liturgy even before the reforms of Pepin the Short (751–768). It is therefore an important witness to the "Roman-Frankish" rite which was gradually developing north of the Alps.

C. The Gelasian Sacramentaries of the Eighth Century
The Gelasian Sacramentary was not the only sacramentary being used by the church in Gaul in the mid-eighth century however. For another Roman sacramentary, a Gregorian of the Paduense variety (cf. below), had arrived on the scene as well. Rather than choose between one or the other, a decision was made to combine the two and make a new book, including certain Gallican and monastic additions. The archetype of this book has not come down to us. This family of sacramentaries is called the "Gelasian Sacramentaries of the Eighth Century" and can be divided into two groups: (1) The first group contains only one book: the Gellone Sacramentary. (2) The second

---

[9] Chavasse, *Le sacramentaire gélasien*, 332–9.
[10] Vogel, *ML* 66–7.

group contains all the rest: the most important being the St. Gall, Triplex, Rheinau, Phillipps, Angoulême, and Monza Sacramentaries. The difference is this: the second group derives from a systematic revision of the first group, in the course of which the majority of the doublets which had occured from combining the two sources (old-Gelasian and Gregorian-Paduense) were eliminated.

Group one

1. *Edition*: Ad. Dumas - J. Deshusses, *Liber sacramentorum Gellonensis*, CCL 159–159A (Turnhout, 1980).

2. *Date of manuscript*: ca. 790–800. Date of composition: ca. 760–770.

3. *Description*: The Gellone Sacramentary is clearly divided into two parts: the first part is the sacramentary proper, in which the temporal and sanctoral cycles are intermingled as in the Gregorian tradition, not separated as in the Gelasian tradition. The second part is a ritual-pontifical containing various episcopal blessings, orations according to monastic usage, an order of baptism, and an abbreviated martyrology.

4. *Typology*: Because of the presence of the large collection of episcopal blessings, the text as we have it was probably intended for a bishop. On the basis of both internal and external evidence, Deshusses proposes that the manuscript was copied for Bishop Hildoard (790–816) of the cathedral of Notre-Dame of Cambrai. The manuscript is handsomely illuminated.

5. *History*: It is proposed that the book was originally compiled in a monastic milieu, at the initiative of King Pepin the Short, as part of his plan for the liturgical unification of his kingdom. The monastic connection is clear from a number of specifically monastic feasts and rituals. Evidence points to the monastery of Flavigny in Burgundy, founded in 742.

Group two, Editions:

St. Gall:	L. C. Mohlberg, *Das fränkische Sacramentarium Gelasianum in alemanischer Überlieferung*, LQF *Quellen* I–II (Münster, 1918).
Triplex:	O. Heiming, *Das Sacramentarium Triplex*, LQF 49 (Münster, 1968).

Rheinau:	A. Hänggi - A. Schönherr, *Sacramentarium Rhenaugiense* (Fribourg, 1970).
Phillipps:	O. Heiming, *Liber sacramentorum Augustodunensis*, CCL 159B (Turnhout, 1984).
Angoulême:	P. Saint-Roch, *Liber sacramentorum Engolismensis*, CCL 159C (Turnhout, 1987).
Monza:	A. Dold - K. Gamber, *Das Sakramentar von Monza* (Beuron, 1957).

D. The Gregorian Sacramentary

While there is not sufficient evidence to claim that Pope St. Gregory the Great himself compiled this sacramentary, it can be demonstrated that he composed orations, and that he possibly compiled an earlier, less-structured version of this text.[11]

1. *Edition*: J. Deshusses, *Le sacramentaire Grégorien*, 3 vols., SF 16,24,28 (Fribourg, ²1979).

2. *Date of manuscript*: Deshusses uses *Cameracensis 164* as his base text, which is a copy of the original Hadrianum, executed ca. 811–812 in Cambrai during the episcopacy of Bishop Hildoard. Date of composition: It seems that the primitive redaction of the Gregorian took place during the pontificate of Pope Honorius I (625–638).

3. *Description*: Instead of being divided into three distinct books, as was the Gelasian sacramentary, the Gregorian combines the temporal and sanctoral cycles. Usually there are three orations only for each Mass: the *oratio*, *super oblata*, and *ad completa* or *ad complendum*. Sometimes there is also a *super populum*. Prefaces are greatly reduced in number. The stational churches are clearly indicated. When there is a procession, there is a special collect for the initial gathering at the stational church before the procession begins.

4. *Typology*: Initially, this sacramentary was for the personal use of the pope, or his representatives, organized with a view toward the liturgical celebrations in the stational churches of Rome. Hence the

---

[11] Deshusses, *Le sacramentaire Grégorien*, I, 52; H. Ashworth, "The Liturgical Prayers of St. Gregory the Great," *Traditio* (1959) 107–61; H. Ashworth, "Further Parallels to the Hadrianum from St. Gregory the Great's Commentary on the First Book of Kings," *Traditio* (1960) 364–73.

sacramentary was not intended for, nor suitable for, all the needs of a normal parish.

5. *History*: The somewhat complex history of this book can be divided into two periods: before and after the middle of the eighth century.

Before the middle of the eighth century.: The situation can be described most simply by using the example of a tree: There is a common trunk, which later divides into several branches. The common trunk has its roots in St. Gregory the Great († 604). In the sanctoral, there are a number of feasts which, according to the *Liber Pontificalis*, were introduced after St. Gregory but before 638, which points to the pontificate of Pope Honorius I (625–638), as mentioned above. The feast of the Presentation (*Hypapanti*) could not have been introduced before the pontificate of Pope Theodore (642–649).

The first branch to break off (ca. 670–680) is the so-called Type II branch. According to Chavasse, this revision was made for St. Peter's in the Vatican, which would explain why it had such authority and such a wide diffusion in the late seventh and early eighth century. It is this version of the Gregorian Sacramentary which found its way to Gaul, and was used in conjunction with the old Gelasian to form the Frankish or Gallicanized Gelasian of the eighth century. The Type-II Gregorian adapted the papal sacramentary for presbyteral use, and therefore, borrowed elements from the Gelasian and other sources in order to make up what was lacking for the parish setting. The best example of this Type II branch of the Gregorian family is a sacramentary in the archives of Padova, hence the name *Paduense*.

The main trunk kept growing however. During the pontificate of Pope Leo II (682–683), Masses for St. George and St. Peter in Chains were added. These Masses are not present in the *Paduense*. In the pontificate of Pope Sergius (687–701) three Marian feasts (Annunciation, Assumption, Nativity) were given greater solemnity by means of adding a procession. Originally these formularies were inserted as *libretti*, and when the codex was recopied (ca. 690) they were integrated into the text. The old copy, now out of date, was put aside. This older version of the Gregorian also made its way over the Alps. The best example of this Type I branch of the Gregorian family is the sacramentary of Trent.

The common trunk continued its natural growth. Pope Gregory II (715–731) added formularies for the Thursdays of Lent. This was the state of the Gregorian Sacramentary without further major developments up until the pontificate of Pope Hadrian I (772–795).

After the middle of the eighth century.: Charles, King of the Franks (king 768–800; emperor 800-814), following in the footsteps of his father, Pepin the Short, saw a unified liturgy as a means of establishing a unified kingdom. The Gallicanized Gelasian, however, was a clumsy book, and created more disorder than unity. So ca. 783, Charlemagne sent a request via Paul the Deacon (a monk of Monte Cassino on his way from the court back to Italy) to ask Pope Hadrian for a pure Roman sacramentary. The pope searched in the Lateran archives for the most authentic copy of the Gregorian Sacramentary available, and sent it to Charlemagne in 785–786 via Abbot John of Ravenna. The book arrived safely at Aix-la-Chapelle (Aachen) where is was known as the *Hadrianum* (third branch of the Gregorian family). This exemplar served as a model for many copies; the original itself, however, has not come down to us.

The Carolingian liturgists were puzzled with the new sacramentary, however, for two reasons: (1) The Latin of the Roman exemplar was somewhat corrupt, and needed to be corrected. (2) Being a papal sacramentary, the book did not contain many of the things necessary for ordinary parish use, and hence needed a supplement. The man who organized this work (ca. 810–815) was the monastic reformer, St. Benedict of Aniane († 821). The supplement is clearly distinguished from the sacramentary itself by an explanatory preface beginning with the word *Hucusque* (up to this point). The supplement can be divided into two parts: (1) a *florilegium* of texts assembled to fill in the lacunae of the *Hadrianum*, and (2) a long series of prefaces, a collection of episcopal blessings, and the rites for minor orders. The sources of the supplement are as follows: the Gallicanized Gelasian of the eighth century, the pre-*Hadrianum* Gregorian Sacramentary (Type I), the so-called Missal of Alcuin (a collection of votive Masses), other Gallican sources, the Visigothic liturgy (the family of Benedict of Aniane was of the Visigothic aristocracy), and Benedict's own liturgical compositions.

The *Hadrianum* and its supplement did not immediately replace the already existing liturgical books in use north of the Alps: i.e., the Frankish or Gallicanized Gelasians, the old Gelasian, and the Gregorian Sacramentary of the Type II branch. In fact, what gradually came about was a new fusion of these various traditions.

E. The Mixed Gregorians of the Tenth and Eleventh Centuries

The so-called "mixed Gregorians" or "Gelasianized Gregorians" are a new synthesis of the *Hadrianum*/Supplement and the Frankish *Gelasian* of the eighth century (which, it will be recalled, is a combination of the old-Gelasian, the Paduense type Gregorian, plus Gallican and monastic usages). This type will be described in greater detail below, in the section on the missal. For the moment let it suffice to say that with the Ottonian reforms in the second half of the tenth century, these mixed Gregorian sacramentaries return to Rome, and there become the new standard.

II. THE LECTIONARY

1. *Introduction*: Just as there was a special book for the priest or bishop, so also there were special books for the lectors. The terminology used for these books is somewhat complex, hence a somewhat lengthy introduction is necessary.

The structure of the Liturgy of the Word is clearly attested to as early as the second century (First Apology of Justin, chap. 67). But there is a long way from that simple reference to the earliest extant Roman lectionaries of the seventh century.

There are two basic ways of reading the Scriptures during the Eucharistic celebration: a simple *lectio continua*, or passages chosen specifically for the liturgical season or feast. In the earliest period the bishop or priest had a considerable role in the choice of the readings, but with the gradual development of the liturgical year and the stational liturgies of Rome, there was a parallel development of a system of fixed readings. The early existence of such systems, even before the compilation of the sacramentaries, can be deduced from homilies of the Fathers and other historical evidence, such as inventories of sacred furnishings and liturgical books.[12]

There are three different methods for indicating the liturgical readings: marginal notes, capitularies, and lectionaries properly so-called. In the first system, notes are made in the margin of a codex of the Bible. In the second, the Scripture selections are listed according to the initial and final word of the passage. The third method is the lectionary properly so-called in which the entire biblical passage is writ-

[12] Cf. Chavasse, "Evangéliare" 177–9.

ten out, these passages being arranged according to the established order of the cursus of readings. These three methods did not follow each other consecutively, but in fact, existed side by side for many centuries, until the lectionary finally came to dominate. The oldest Roman texts providing an organized system of liturgical readings are capitularies from the seventh and eighth centuries.

2. *Typology*: The first system of marginal notes presupposes that the Bible itself is a liturgical book, that is, used directly in the liturgical celebration itself. In the second system of capitularies, the list of pericopes could be appended to the liturgical book itself (the *Apostolum* or the *Evangelia*), or could exist separately as a kind of companion booklet (*comes*). The liturgical book itself received all the honor it was due; the Book of the Gospels in particular was not only reverenced in the liturgical celebration, but frequently was also beautifully illuminated and richly bound. The book of non-gospel readings rarely received the same lavish attention as the Book of the Gospels. In the third system, that of the lectionary properly so-called, the fact that the readings were written out in full and in order, had obvious advantages of practicality and ease of use. A disadvantage, however, was that with the normal growth and development of both the temporal and sanctoral cycles, a lectionary could become outdated more readily than a Book of the Gospels.

3. *History*: Because of the vast number of manuscripts involved, the enormous task for liturgical scholars has been to classify them and draw from them some kind of coherent synthesis. Most noteworthy in this area have been the labors of Frere, Klauser, and Chavasse.

To begin with, three basic distinctions can be made: there are manuscripts which contain only the pre-gospel readings (whether from the Old Testament or from the New Testament Epistles), manuscripts which contain only the gospel readings, and manuscripts which contain both (these books have an extremely variable nomenclature). What may be surprising to modern sensibilities is that the epistolary tradition and the evangeliary tradition developed separately from one another. When later on the two lists were combined, they did not always correspond.

At the risk of oversimplifying a very complex history, the following synthesis is presented according to three stages of development.

Stage 1

1. Corresponding sacramentary: *Gelasianum Vetus*
2. *Epistolary*: The oldest representative of this stage is the Comes of Würzburg (composition: ca. 600–650, manuscript ca. 700).[13] The manuscript is in two parts; the first part is an epistolary, and that is what concerns us here. The second part is an evangeliary, but from a later period and not directly related to the epistolary with which it is bound. The Comes of Würzburg is of great importance because it is the oldest extant witness of the Roman lectionary system, having such ancient characteristics as the absence of Masses for the Thursdays during Lent, and the designation *Dominica vacat* for the second Sunday of Lent.
3. *Evangelary*: None extant, although traces can be found in Type *Pi* of Stage 2 (cf. below).

Stage 2

1. Corresponding sacramentary: *Gregorianum*
2. *Epistolary*: The most important representative of this stage is the Comes of Alcuin (composition: ca. 626; manuscript: beginning of the ninth century).[14] This text has come down to us in two forms: (1) the epistolary itself, based on the Comes of Würzburg, a clearly Roman document, and (2) a later supplement, added in the third stage (cf. below) when the epistolary arrived in the kingdom of Charlemagne along with other liturgical books; the supplement is based on the Comes of Murbach (cf. Stage 3).
3. *Evangelary*: According to the research of Klauser,[15] there are three types of evangeliary in this stage: type *Pi* (composition: ca. 645; manuscripts: ca. 700), to which the evangeliary of the Würzburg manuscript corresponds;[16] type *Lamda* (composition: ca. 740; manuscripts: ca. 800); and type *Sigma* (composition: ca. 755; manuscripts ca. 800).

---

[13] Edition: G. Morin, "Le plus ancien comes ou lectionnaire de l'Eglise romaine," *RB* 27 (1910) 41–74. For a description, cf. Vogel, *ML* 339–40.

[14] Edition: A. Wilmart, "Le lectionnaire d'Alcuin," *EphLit* 51 (1937) 136–97. For a description, cf. Vogel, *ML* 340–2.

[15] Edition: T. Klauser, *Das römische Capitulare Evangeliorum, I: Typen* (Münster, ²1972). For a description, cf. Vogel, *ML* 342–4.

[16] Edition: G. Morin, "L'évangéliaire de Wurtzbourg," *RB* 28 (1911) 296–330.

1.   Corresponding sacramentary: Frankish Gelasian of the eighth century

2.   *Combined Epistolary and Evangelary*: When the Roman liturgy made its way over the Alps in the eighth century, the *capitularia* made the journey as well, but as two separate books: the epistolary and the evangeliary. There they were combined. Careful study on the part of Chavasse and others has demonstrated the existence of two principal families of this third stage; A, which is the Roman foundation (ca. 700) and B, which is the Franco-Roman synthesis (ca. 700–740).[17] There are a number of representatives of this stage of combined capitularies or lectionaries: (a) Klauser's type *Delta* (composition: ca. 750; manuscripts: end of the eighth century); (b) the Comes of Murbach (epistolary based on the Comes of Alcuin, evangeliary based on the Gospel texts of Stage 2);[18] (c) the Lectionary of Corbie (also called the Comes of Leningrad);[19] and (d) the Liber Comitis of Paris, also called the Verona Lectionary, or the Lectionary of Monza.[20]

Once having achieved this third stage of development, the lectionary remained remarkably stable over the succeeding centuries. In fact (via the liturgical consolidation of the Roman curia in the thirteenth century), the lectionary of the *Missale Romanum* 1570 can be traced directly back to this Franco-Roman synthesis.

The massive reform of the lectionary in the *Missale Romanum* 1970[21] had its seeds in a study week of the Fourth International Congress on the Liturgy, held at Mont César in Belgium in 1954.[22]

[17] A. Chavasse, "Les plus anciens types du lectionnaire et de l'antiphonaire romains de la messe," *RB* 62 (1952) 7–28.

[18] Edition: Wilmart, A. "Le *comes* de Murbach," *RB* 30 (1913) 25–69. For a description, cf. Vogel, *ML* 347.

[19] Edition: H. Frere, *The Roman Epistle-Lectionary* (Oxford, 1935) 1–24. For a description, cf. Vogel, *ML* 340.

[20] Edition: R. Amiet, "Un Comes carolingien inédit de la Haute-Italie," *EphLit* 73 (1959) 335–67. For a description, cf. Vogel, *ML* 344.

[21] Bugnini, chap. 26.

[22] K. Hughes, *The Monk's Tale: A Biography of Godfrey Diekmann, O.S.B.* (Collegeville, 1991) 158–9.

III. THE ANTIPHONAL

1. *Introduction*: Music has always been a part of solemn liturgy. In addition to euchological texts to be prayed, and scriptural texts to be read, there are also scriptural/poetic texts to be sung. To the sacramentary and lectionary, therefore, we must now add the antiphonal.

Because the repertoire of music for Mass grew out of an oral tradition, however, there is precious little evidence for written texts before the eighth century. The historian must rely on sketchy information from conciliar legislation, ecclesiastical history, the *Liber Pontificalis*, the *Ordines Romani*, and other medieval documents. John the Archcantor of St. Peter's (fl. ca. 680), whose accuracy historians sometimes question, wrote that the collection of chants for Mass and Office was begun by Pope Damasus (366–384) with the help of St. Jerome, and was expanded and developed by St. Leo the Great (440–461), St. Gelasius (492–496), St. Gregory the Great (590–604), and others, including various abbots of the monastery of St. Peter's.[23] While St. Gregory the Great did not compose the chant that bears his name, it seems clear that he gathered together and organized the existing corpus of liturgical music as part of the general ordering of the liturgy which took place during his pontificate.

2. *Typology*: Amalarius of Metz (780–850), in observing the discrepancies between Roman and Frankish terminology, provides us with some important information. He notes that "the volume which we call an "antiphonary" the Romans call by three names":[24] the *cantatorium* (containing the gradual psalm), the *responsoriale* (containing the responsory for the offertory), and the *antiphonarium* (containing the antiphons for the introit and communion). What the Romans had in separate books, Amalarius knew as a single volume. The terminology for the various types of chant books is somewhat fluid.

While we are concerned primarily with codices, earlier forms of writing chant texts and music are the *rotulus* (written on a continuous roll of paper or parchment) and the *libellus* (a booklet of indetermi-

---

[23] M. Righetti I,263–70.

[24] Amalarius, *Liber de ordine antiphonarii*, Prologus 17 in I. M. Hanssens, *Amalarii Episcopi Opera Liturgica Omnia*, t.1 (Vatican City, 1948) 363. Cf. also Vogel, *ML* 357.

nate size, as we have seen earlier).[25] The actual codices containing liturgical chants Michel Huglo classifies as either single or composite.

Single: (1) *Liber antiphonarius* (eighth century and following): this book could contain chants for both Mass and Office, following the complete cursus of the liturgical year. From the twelfth century onward, these books grew to an enormous size, and were placed on large stands in the center of choir, so that text and music could be read from a distance by a number of cantors. These books are often very beautifully illuminated. (2) *Cantatorium*: a book for the soloist, containing the chants between the readings (gradual, alleluia). Since the chant was usually memorized, this book did not have a purely practical function, but also conferred a certain honor upon the intervenient chants; often the cantatorium was richly illuminated, sometimes with a cover of carved ivory (hence the name *tabula*). (3) *Liber gradualis*: the book containing the proper chants of the Mass, and after the tenth century, also the ordinaries. (4) *Processionale*: (end of eleventh century and following): a collection of chants, in a small portable book for the use of the cantor, for occasional processions (February 2, Ash Wednesday, Good Friday, Major Litany of April 25, rogation days) and the Sunday procession (between Terce and Mass).

Composite books are a combination of several single books, either juxtaposed to one another, or actually integrated or fused together: (1) *Graduale*, without notation, bound just in front of the sacramentary. (2) Tables of Gradual texts, either preceding the sacramentary or integrated into it as marginal notes. (3) Sacramentary-Gradual: a combination of euchology and chants. (4) Lectionary-Gradual: a combination of readings and chants. (5) *Libelli* of tropes and sequences: these poetic compositions developed ca. mid-ninth century. (6) Tropary and Prosary: a whole book containing tropes and proses. (7) Tropary-Prosary-Processional. (8) Gradual fused with other books of the Mass, or in other words, a notated Missal. (9) Breviary-Notated Missal: containing everything needed for both Mass and Office. (10) Collections made for special occasions or special places (sanctuaries or places of pilgrimage, for example).

Even from these very sketchy lists, one can see how rich and varied the liturgical books of chant can be.

---

[25] Huglo, *Les livres* 63–75.

3. *History*: The most ancient texts of the antiphonal date from the eighth and ninth centuries, edited by Hesbert in parallel columns.[26] A clue in one of the manuscripts — a rubric for the seventh Sunday after Pentecost which says: *Ista ebdomata non est in antefonarios romanos* — leads to the conclusion that at the time of its compilation, there were older manuscripts of the same kind which were considered more authentically Roman, which did not contain the Mass *Omnes gentes* (the first words of the Introit). Hesbert then classified all manuscripts *without* the Mass *Omnes Gentes* as Family A (Roman), and all the manuscripts *with Omnes Gentes* as Family B (Franco-Roman). The Franco-Roman Antiphonal thus corresponds directly to the lectionary of Stage Three and the Frankish-Gelasian Sacramentary. The careful research of Chavasse has shown that behind the eighth-century recension traces can be found of an antiphonal that corresponds to Stage Two, while other traces allow us to go back as far as Stage One as well. This shows that the antiphonal and the lectionary developed together, and that the final synthesis of Stage Three was a result of the integrating efforts of the Carolingian liturgical reform.

The first antiphonals were not notated, since the melodies were memorized. During the ninth century, however, a system of musical notation developed. At first, these were simply musical signs (neumes) written above the liturgical text. Later, these neumes were written within a system of lines, so as to indicate more clearly changes of pitch. Also in the ninth century we see the diversification of the chant repertoire into two basic groups: East (German and Slavic) and West (romance languages), corresponding to the division of the empire in 843. The two groups have a common patrimony, but differ somewhat in both texts and music. With the passing of time, each diocese or monastery (wherever there was a church of major size or importance) developed its own personalized antiphonal: some parts of which were very uniform, other parts showing a great deal of diversity. Standardization came with the centralized religious orders such as the Cistercians, Dominicans, and Franciscans.[27]

---

[26] Edition: R. J. Hesbert, *AMS* (Brussels, 1935).
[27] Huglo, *Les livres* 84–94.

Musicologists divide the history of chant into four periods:[28] (1) The classical period is marked by the fusion of two different chant traditions in the eighth and ninth centuries; the new synthesis is what we call "Gregorian" chant. (2) The post-classical period from the ninth to the twelfth centuries is characterized by the development of a system of notation and the development of new musical forms, including polyphony. (3) The period of decadence is a rather long one: from the end of the Middle Ages to the nineteenth century. The development of measured music and modern major and minor tonalities led to the decline of the freer chant rhythms and the tonality of the eight modes. By the time of the Council of Trent, the level of liturgical music had reached a low point. Although attempts were made to reform the chant repertoire, the publication of the Medici Edition of the Roman Gradual in 1614–1615 codified a state of decadence which was to last for three centuries. (4) The period of restoration is closely associated with the monastery of Solesmes, founded in 1833, and the research of the monks on ancient chant manuscripts. After his Motu Proprio *Tra le sollecitudini* in 1903, Pope St. Pius X charged the monks of Solesmes to make an official edition of the chant books: the *Kyriale* came out in 1905, the *Gradual* in 1908. The research of Solesmes has continued throughout the twentieth century, and has not ceased with the publication of the post-Vatican II *Graduale Romanum* in 1974.

IV. THE CALENDAR

Ancient liturgical books, whether sacramentary, lectionary, or antiphonal, did not have a calendar inserted at the beginning of the text: This was a development of the Middle Ages. Although we find this development first in French lands from the ninth century onwards, it does not become a Roman custom until the twelfth century. The study of the calendar can be sub-divided according to its major types: as a separate document, and as inserted into various other liturgical books. This does not imply a strict chronological development from the first type to the second, however, since both types existed side by side for some time.

Separate document: In the ancient Church, there were two kinds of documents for keeping track of feast days: the calendar, an actual list

---

[28] Turco, *Il canto gregoriano* I, 23–39.

of feasts observed by a given church or diocese; and the martyrology, which is a more general compilation. In early documents, however, the distinction between the two is not always clear. The oldest evidence for the Roman calendar is two lists, a *depositio episcoporum* and a *depositio martyrum* included in the Philocalian Chronicle of 354. In addition, Frere has shown that the ancient origins of the Roman calendar are to be found in various lists of *tituli*, lists of stational churches and churches where a collect was said as part of the stational procession, and the arrangement of the seven *diaconiae* of ancient Rome. The *Liber Pontificalis* provides other data: for example, how the calendar is related to the growth of suburban cemeteries and shrines. Of course, the liturgical books themselves are an important source for the development of the temporal and sanctoral cycles. A description of ancient calendars, both Roman and non-Roman, can be found in Righetti and Jounel. This information is very important for an understanding of the cult of the saints and the life of the local church.

Inserted into various other liturgical books: Jounel's study is important for the twelfth century, Van Dijk's research is key for the thirteenth century. From the liturgy of the papal court, a direct path is paved for the Roman calendar of the post-Tridentine liturgical reforms.[29] The process of forming the post-Vatican II calendar is described in some detail by Bugnini.

V. THE MISSAL

1. *Introduction*: How the sacramentary, lectionary, and antiphonal came to be united in one volume is the topic of this section, along with the complex history of this new liturgical book: the missal.

2. *Typology*: As is so often the case, the terminology here is somewhat fluid. The word "missal" during the medieval period can mean a sacramentary, or a collection of Masses bound together in a *libellus*. Our modern understanding of the missal as a book for the priest which contains texts for the euchology, readings, and chants of the Mass for the entire span of the liturgical year, plus music for the parts

[29] Cf. also the proposals for calendar reform under Pope Pius XII: Sacra Rituum Congregatio, *Memoria sulla Riforma Liturgica*, Sectio Historica 71 (Vatican City, 1948) as well as the third supplement to the *Memoria* (Sectio Historica 79).

sung by the priest is a later concept, usually expressed by the terms *missale plenarium* or *missale completum*.

How did these various books come to be fused together? There are several stages in this gradual process, which however, are not to be understood as progressing consecutively from one to the other. Instead, the different forms existed side by side for long centuries. (1) From the ninth century following, we find sacramentaries with marginal notes indicating the *incipit* of the chants taken from the antiphonal. (2) *Libelli missarum* are important antecedents of the *Missale plenarium*. These collections for certain feasts, votive Masses, or other special occasions could contain the euchology, the readings, and the texts of the chants. Such *libelli* appear already very early on; the famous palimpsest from Monte Cassino is such an example, dating from the eighth century.[30] (3) Another system was to juxtapose the different books (sacramentary-lectionary or sacramentary-antiphonal or various other combinations), binding them together in a single volume. (4) The system that finally prevailed was a fully integrated Mass book, with the orations, readings, and chants all inserted in their proper place according to the order of the Mass. Vogel points out that toward the end of the ninth century, missals start to become more numerous than sacramentaries; by the first half of the twelfth century, sacramentaries are a minority; by the thirteenth century, sacramentaries are an exception; by the fourteenth century, they are merely an archaic remnant.

Why did these books come to be fused together? Among the most common theories are these: (1) the development of the private Mass,[31] (2) the obligation on the part of the priest to recite all the parts of the Mass, even if these parts were sung by the schola or read by the lectors,[32] (3) pastoral usefulness and the development of the

---

[30] A. Dold, *Vom Sakramentar, Comes und Capitulare zum Missale* (Beuron, 1943). Note that this is not a "missal" in the modern sense of the word, but rather a *libellus*.

[31] O. Nussbaum, *Kloster, Priestermönch und Privatmesse* (Bonn, 1961) and A. Häussling, *Mönchskonvent und Eucharistiefeier*, LQF 58 (Münster, 1973). But according to historical evidence, private and votive Masses were celebrated centuries before the advent of the *Missale plenarium*. It is more likely, therefore, that the private Mass simply followed the evolution of the Missal rather than determined it. Cf. Jungmann, *The Mass of the Roman Rite*, I,216 and Van Dijk-Walker, *The Origins* 61.

[32] Palazzo 124; Nocent, *LL* 169; Vogel, *ML* 105.

care of souls in small parishes away from large diocesan or monastic centers,[33] (4) the influence of priestly piety and the concern to omit nothing.[34]

3. *History*: The history and development of the Roman Missal can be divided into four stages: (1) the Gregorian-Gelasian synthesis (ninth–twelfth centuries), (2) the various traditions of the thirteenth-century, (3) the post-Tridentine Missal, (4) the post-Vatican II Missal.

<u>Stage 1</u>: The sacramentary, lectionary, and antiphonal which eventually come together to form the missal all have their origins in the Franco-Roman synthesis described earlier: the Frankish Gelasian sacramentary of the eighth century, the Franco-Roman Lectionary, and the Franco-Roman Antiphonal. But with the advent of the Gregorian Sacramentary north of the Alps and its subsequent Supplement, there was a new synthesis of the Gregorian/Supplement and the Frankish Gelasian: what Bourque calls the "gelasianized Gregorian sacramentary" of the tenth and eleventh centuries. It is important to note the differences between the Frankish Gelasian of the eighth century, and the Gelasianized Gregorian of the tenth century. The Frankish Gelasian included the following elements: (1) the old-Gelasian, (2) the Gregorian of the second type (e.g., *Paduense*), that is, an adaptation of the papal sacramentary for use in presbyteral churches, (3) Frankish elements, and (4) monastic elements. The Gelasianized Gregorian, on the other hand, has the Gregorian and its Supplement as a base, with certain blocks of material taken from the Frankish Gelasian. It is important also to keep in mind the two major Roman traditions that are behind these multiple combinations of sources: the urban tradition (basically Gelasian) and the papal tradition (Gregorian). (Note, however, that the Type II Gregorian represents an adaptation of the papal tradition for use in the urban parishes). While these two traditions existed amicably side by side in Rome, north of the Alps the situation was more complex: The existence of two different traditions, both claiming to be Roman, caused no end of difficulty. This will become apparent when examining the somewhat chaotic situation of the thirteenth century.

---

[33] Van Dijk - Walker, *The Origins* 65.
[34] P. Borella, "Verso il messale plenario," *EphLit* 67 (1953) 338–40.

According to Bourque, these mixed Gregorians may be classified according to three categories: (1) those in a direct line to the later *Missale Romanum*, forming a kind of bridge from the Hadrianum/Supplement to the thirteenth century Missal of the Roman Curia (and thence to the first printed *Missale Romanum* of 1474 and the 1570 Missal of Pius V), (2) the exuberant types, which while retaining the Hadrianum/Supplement, considerably augment it with formularies which do not appear in the later *Missale Romanum*, and (3) the eccentric types, which have no direct connection with the later *Missale Romanum*. Those in a direct line have these characteristics: they contain the additions to the sanctoral from the Supplement of Benedict of Aniane, they contain various votive and Requiem Masses, they have a reduced number of prefaces, and in general, they remain faithful to the formularies of the *Hadrianum* and Supplement.[35] While we are interested in tracing the direct line, one must not lose sight of the fact that these direct, exuberant, and eccentric types existed side by side.

Stage 2: According to the detailed analysis of Van Dijk, by the year 1275, the city of Rome knew four liturgical customs: the papal court, St. Peter's in the Vatican, the reform of Cardinal Orsini (later Pope Nicholas III), and the Lateran Basilica. (1) The papal court resided at the Lateran Palace, usually celebrating the liturgy in the pope's private chapel, the *Sancta Sanctorum*. The tradition of the papal court itself went through four distinct phases during the thirteenth century: (a) Innocent III reorganized the Divine Office during the last years of his pontificate (1213–1216), but the Mass itself was not touched. (b) Honorius III (1216–1227) revised the office again; this "breviary of Honorius" was adopted by the Friars Minor in 1230, and is known as the Regula Breviary. The Mass liturgy was not revised by Honorius either, although he did issue a missal. This "missal of Honorius" was adopted also by the Franciscans in 1230, and is known as the Regula

---

[35] One of the manuscripts in the direct line which frequently receives attention is Codex 65 of the Lateran Archives, the so-called "Lateran Missal," edited in 1752 by Azevedo. Bourque follows the commonly held theory that this missal is from the 11th century, and Vogel follows his lead. However, Kennedy (corroborated by Van Dijk) has shown that this is actually from the 13th century. The manuscript is an important witness to the pre-curial Missal, but its late date requires that the conclusions of Bourque and Vogel in its regard be modified.

Missal. (c) The missal of Honorius was revised at court in the 1240s since compared with the breviary, the missal was by this time much out of date. (d) The Regula books were also revised, by the fourth minister general of the Franciscans, Haymo of Faversham in 1243–44, and a second edition was published in the years 1250–1260. The result of these historical developments is a certain amount of confusion: each church or monastery following the tradition of the papal court had its own particular combination of new books and old. (2) St. Peter's in the Vatican represents an ancient and venerable tradition, distinct from that of the papal court. In general, books from St. Peter's represent the Old-Roman rite, the urban rite that St. Peter's had used for centuries, although towards the end of the century, Haymonian rubrics were also used. The other churches of the *Urbs* followed the Old-Roman tradition up to the 1250s and in some cases, even longer. But then there was a sudden change, and the old books disappeared. Why? (3) In the mid 1250s, the liturgy of the papal court was making serious inroads into the urban tradition. According to the research of Van Dijk,[36] John Cardinal Orsini, later Nicholas III, resisted the change, and in an effort to save the urban rite, devised a compromise: a new urban liturgy which combined the urban and papal rites, that is, the two traditions of the Vatican basilica and the Lateran palace. Nicholas III died in 1280, and with the fourteenth century transfer of the papacy to Avignon, his local reform came to naught. (4) The Lateran Basilica, served by Canons Regular, had its own liturgical tradition, distinct from that of the papal court. The origins of this tradition lie in the urban basilica liturgy of the previous century.

These four liturgical traditions, all of them Roman, mutually influence one another in the thirteenth century. But it is the papal tradition which comes to dominate, while the urban tradition practically disappears. The revised missal of the Franciscans was approved by Clement V (1305–1314) and adopted by the papal chapel. This missal forms the basis for the first printed missal of 1474, with the title: *Missale secundum consuetudinem Romanae Curiae*.

Stage 3: The reason why a reform of the missal was so necessary at the time of the Council of Trent was because the enormous variety

---

[36] Van Dijk, "The Urban and Papal Rites," 420.

from one diocese to another, or even within the same diocese, caused a great deal of confusion, was a source of scandal, and contributed to abuses. The Council of Trent, in Session XXV (1652) discussed the reform of the liturgy. A commission was formed, under the guidance of Archbishop Leonardo Marini, but since the members of the commission could not agree upon the criteria to adopt for the reform, and because it was necessary to bring the council to a close, the whole project was turned over to Pope Pius IV (1559–1565). With the death of Pius IV, the project passed to Pope St. Pius V (1566–1572), who added new members to the commission, and in July 1570, promulgated the new missal. The research of Frutaz has shown that a certain Guglielmo Cardinal Sirleto was instrumental in the reform of the missal: In the Vatican Library there is an incunabulum of 1497, the *Missale secundum morem Sancte Romane Ecclesie*, which contains the corrections of Cardinal Sirleto written in his own hand. This 1497 missal is substantially the same as the *editio princeps* of 1474. The major change in the 1570 missal was the modification of the calendar.[37] After Pius V, the missal received other minor modifications under Clement VIII (1604), Urban VIII (1634), and Benedict XV (1920): rubrical adjustments, the addition of formularies for newly canonized saints, and the addition of four prefaces. The 1948 *Memoria sulla Riforma Liturgica* of the Sacred Congregation of Rites concentrated principally on a reform of the calendar and the breviary, dedicating only three pages to the missal. In these pages, reference is made to the effect that calendar changes would have on the missal; there is also a brief discussion of the various themes of the liturgical movement concerning pastoral practice and the celebration of Mass.[38]

Stage 4: The desire of the Council Fathers of Vatican II for a *recognitio* of the *Ordo Missae*, other ritual actions, the lectionary, the prayer of the faithful, etc. (*SC* 47–58); the subsequent work of the *Consilium ad exsequendam Constitutionem de sacra Liturgia*; the translation of the missal into numberless vernacular languages; and other developments of the last thirty years — all these areas require ongoing and serious study.

---

[37] Cf. E. Focke and H. Heinrichs, "Das Kalendarium des Missale Pianum vom Jahre 1570 und seine Tendenzen," *TQ* 120 (1939) 383–400.

[38] Sacra Rituum Congregatio, *Memoria sulla Riforma Liturgica*, Sectio Historica 71 (Vatican City, 1948) 304–6.

Just as the books used for Mass were originally separate and distinct (the sacramentary, the lectionary, and the antiphonal) and only with the passing of time became fused into a single book (the missal), so also with the books used for the Liturgy of the Hours: the various books for the euchology, the readings, and the chant were only gradually fused into a single book: the breviary.

I. BOOKS FOR THE CHANT

A. Psalter

1. *Introduction*: We begin with the psalter, since it is the oldest liturgical book of the Divine Office, and forms its fundamental nucleus. In the Latin-speaking rites, three different translations of the psalter were to be found: two for liturgical use, the other for the purpose of study. All three are related in some way to the person and work of St. Jerome (ca. 342–420). (a) St. Jerome himself relates that he made an initial revision of the *Vetus latina* (Itala) psalter: whether this is the *Psalterium Romanum*[39] or not is contested.[40] The Roman psalter was diffused widely in Italy and also in Spain. (b) Jerome's second revision of the psalter was made ca. 389–392: This was a correction of the Latin version based on the Hexaplaric Greek text of the LXX. In Gaul, the Itala version was used until the end of the sixth century, when St. Gregory of Tours (ca. 540–594) introduced this second revision of St. Jerome into his cathedral; its wide diffusion in Gaul gave it the name *Psalterium Gallicanum*. It was the Gallican psalter that Alcuin introduced into the Vulgate, and hence this version came to dominate, even in Italy, from the ninth century onward. In Rome, Pope Sixtus IV (1471–1484) limited the use of the Roman psalter to the city of Rome and environs. After the reforms of Pius V, the Roman psalter was restricted even further to the Basilica of St. Peter.[41] (c) Around 392, Jerome made a fresh translation *iuxta hebraicam veritatem*.[42] This

[39] For a critical edition, cf. R. Weber, *Le Psautier Romain et les autres anciens psautiers latins*, CBL X (Vatican City, 1953).

[40] Cf. C. Estin, *Les Psautiers de Jérôme* (Rome, 1984) 25–8.

[41] S. Bäumer, *Geschichte des Breviers* (Freiburg-im-Brisgau, 1895). The French translation is being used here: *Histoire du Bréviaire* (Rome, 1905), rpt. 1967. Cf. I, 355–7.

[42] For a critical edition, cf. H. de Sainte-Marie, *Sancti Hieronymi Psalterium iuxta Hebraeos*, CBL XI (Vatican City, 1954).

was never used in the liturgy, however, since the earlier versions were already in common use.

2. *Typology*: It is important to distinguish between a *biblical psalter* and a *liturgical psalter*. A biblical psalter contains the 150 psalms, pure and simple, these being divided into five books. A liturgical psalter, on the other hand, is characterized by various additions made to the biblical psalter, such as the Old Testament canticles for Lauds, the New Testament canticles (*Benedictus, Magnificat, Nunc Dimittis*), other ancient hymns (*Gloria, Te Deum*), etc. In addition, a liturgical psalter, by means of the decoration of the initial letter of a given psalm, frequently indicated the distribution of the psalms according to the different days of the week. Salmon calls this type of psalter a *psalterium per ferias*, and reserves the term *liturgical psalter* to those in which the psalms are actually removed from their biblical order, and distributed among the various hours of the day.[43]

3. *History*: The development of the liturgical psalter is very gradual. By the twelfth century, antiphons and verses are often added in the margin or the free space between the psalms. Bit by bit, other elements are added in their respective places: invitatories, responsories, *capitula*, and the *incipit* of hymns. Other additions to the psalter are psalm titles, giving an interpretive key to the psalm along Christological and spiritual lines, and psalm collects, serving the same function.[44]

From the Carolingian period onward, we find psalters joined to various other liturgical books, forming psalter-collectars, psalter-hymnals, psalter-antiphonals, and other combinations. Thus the psalter acts as one of the fundamental nuclei of the future breviary, attracting other books of the office to its central core. From the twelfth century onward, another system of organizing the psalter becomes common: the psalms arranged not according to the days of the week, but according to the liturgical hour: that is, for vigils (*nocturnalis liber*), for lauds (*liber matutinalis*), for the day hours (*diurnale*), and for vespers (*vesperale*). It is not uncommon, however, to have

---

[43] P. Salmon, *Les manuscrits liturgiques latins de la Bibliothèque Vaticane*, ST 251 (Vatican City, 1968), I,xiv–xv.

[44] For psalm collects, cf. L. Brou, *The Psalter Collects*, HBS 83 (London, 1949). There is an African series (5th c.), a Roman series (6th c.), and a Spanish series (7th c.). For psalm titles, cf. P. Salmon, *Les "Tituli Psalmorum" des manuscrits latins*, CBL XII (Vatican City, 1959). Cf. also Martimort, "La prière des heures," 220–2.

different systems existing side by side. In the thirteenth century, the Breviary of the Roman Curia attains prominence, and eventually the fusion of the psalter into a complete breviary becomes the norm.

B. Antiphonal

1. *Introduction*: The name *antiphonarium* is used equivocally for the Mass antiphonal, the Office antiphonal, or a combination of both; hence special care is needed to distinguish clearly the content of the book in question. The edition of the ancient Mass antiphonals was done by Hesbert in 1935; almost thirty years later, he published an edition of the ancient Office antiphonals as well.

2. *Typology*: The antiphonal for the Liturgy of the Hours, following the order of the liturgical year, contains the texts and/or music for invitatories (for matins), antiphons (for the psalms), responsories (after the readings), and versicles (after the hymns). The incipits of the psalms and hymns may also be included, as well as certain rubrical directions. The way in which the antiphons and responsories are organized depends on which of the two major systems is being followed: monastic or cathedral. Hesbert accordingly divides his study according to these two different repertoires. The antiphonal is intended for the choirmaster or cantors: the choir itself would have known most of the repertoire by heart. The oldest antiphonals (ninth century) were not notated; it is not until the tenth-eleventh centuries onward that we find antiphonals with musical notation above the text.[45]

3. *History*: For the sake of clarity, it is useful to distinguish between the textual and musical elements of the antiphonal.

   Music: There is a certain amount of debate about the origins of Gregorian chant, as distinguished from old-Roman chant. Van Dijk has argued convincingly that the difference between the two parallels is the difference between the presbyteral/titular usage and the papal usage in Rome. Old-Roman chant is urban, Gregorian chant is papal.[46]

---

[45] The oldest manuscript (without notation) is the Antiphonal of Compiègne (between 860 and 880), Roman cursus. The oldest notated manuscript is the Antiphonal of Hartker (end of 10th-beginning of 11th c.), monastic cursus. Cf. Hesbert, *CAO* I,xvii–xix and II,vi–ix.

[46] S.J.P. Van Dijk, "The Urban and Papal Rites in Seventh and Eighth-Century Rome," *SE* 12 (1961) 414–5.

The Franco-Roman synthesis achieved in the ninth century, therefore, is not simply a synthesis of Gallican and Roman elements, but a synthesis of urban and papal elements as well. Huglo has shown that after the death of Charlemagne and the subsequent division of the empire, the chant developed along two different tracks, determined by geographical boundaries: the eastern part of the empire and the western part. While at first the chant was transmitted from one generation to the next by oral tradition, a system of notation gradually developed, which changed the physical arrangement of the antiphonal. The first notated manuscripts simply write in the musical notation above the text. Later, a staff is added, of one, two, and then four lines. This means that the text must be smaller to allow space for the lines of music. In the thirteenth century square notation develops, and this new method of musical notation spreads rapidly. By the fourteenth century the antiphonal has become fused with other office books to form the breviary, although the older form of the antiphonal as a separate book perdures for centuries afterwards.

Text: The antiphonal for the Office does not derive from a single archetype, but rather from a common repertoire that was added to as time went on. In the Romano-Germanic synthesis, however, the antiphonal for the Office never gained the same official status and authority as the liturgical books for Mass. As a result, there was much variety. While the order of the antiphons remained fairly stable from one place to another, the order of the responsories varied a good deal. In addition, the verses of the responsories did not always correspond to the content of the responsory itself. Shortly after the death of Charlemagne († 814), these inconsistencies prompted various initiatives of reform. Helisachar, the archchancelor of Louis the Pious (814–840), along with Nedibrius, bishop of Narbonne, undertook a reworking of the verses. Their reform took root in the western part of the empire, especially in southern France, while the eastern tradition maintained the old verses. In some places, both systems were combined together. These things troubled Amalarius (ca. 780–850) as well, who observed the discrepancies between the antiphonal of Metz and the Roman antiphonal of Corbie. Taking elements from both, he proposed a new antiphonal entirely; this reform attempt did not survive its author, but disappeared in the mid-ninth century. In Lyon, the deacon Florus and Archbishop Agobard (fierce opponents of Amalarius) worked to reform the antiphonal as well, substituting all non-biblical responsories with others taken from Sacred Scripture. The tradition of Lyon retained this characteristic thereafter. The development of those religious orders with a strong central government had implications for liturgical books in general and the antiphonal in particular. An exemplar kept in the main house of the order served as the model for all subsequent copies, and thus a certain standardization resulted. In the thirteenth century, the choice of the Franciscan order to follow the usage of the Roman curia had far-reaching implications for the Roman rite. But this pertains to the history of the breviary.

C. Hymnal

1. *Introduction*: The hymn functions as an interpretive key to the liturgical hour or the feast being celebrated: such compositions are often of great poetic beauty and theological richness. While there is an abundant bibliography on the hymn *per se*,[47] there is rather little on the hymnal and its development.[48]

2. *Typology*: For our purposes, the definition of the term "hymn" is being restricted to those poetic, metrical, compositions used in the Liturgy of the Hours. (Such compositions used elsewhere, such as in processions or devotions, can also be called hymns). The hymnal, a collection of these hymns for the Divine Office, appears in two forms: either joined to another book, or contained in a separate and distinct volume. The oldest hymnals which have come down to us are composite books: frequently psalter-hymnals, or hymnals joined to books of orations or readings. In the case of non-liturgical psalters, the hymns usually come at the end of the manuscript, while in the case of liturgical psalters, the hymns are interspersed throughout the various hours. The hymnal as a separate book gradually disappears from the scene after the fusion of the different books of the office into the one book of the breviary.

---

[47] Cf. the bibliographies provided in the following studies: P. Salmon, "La prière des heures," *EP 1961*, 824–5; A. G. Martimort, "La prière des heures," *EP 1983*, IV,231; and especially J. Szövérffy, *Latin Hymns, TS* 55, Turnhout 1989, 11–28.

[48] For the manuscript tradition, cf. J. Mearns, *Early Latin Hymnaries: an index of hymns in hymnaries before 1100* (Cambridge, 1913); P. Salmon, *Les manuscrits* I,49-58; K. Gamber, *CLLA*, SFS 1, 2 vol. (Fribourg, ²1968) II,602–5.

3. *History*: The origins of Latin Christian hymnody are to be found in the third-sixth centuries. Of all the hymn writers from this period who can be identified (St. Hilary of Poitiers, St. Ambrose, Prudentius, Sedulius, Venantius Fortunatus, St. Gregory the Great)[49] it is St. Ambrose who has the greatest authority:[50] St. Benedict, when speaking of hymns, calls them *ambrosiani* (Rule of St. Benedict 9:4 and 12:4). From this early period, however, no collection of hymns has come down to us. It is not until the sixth century that we have evidence of a distinct repertoire of hymns; traces can be found in the monastic rules of St. Benedict, St. Caesarius of Arles, and his successor St. Aurelian.[51] The oldest hymnal we have is from the Celtic rite, seventh century, followed by a psalter-hymnal of the Gallican rite, dating from the latter part of the eighth century.[52] According to Gneuss, up until the ninth century, there were two basic types of hymnal used in Western Europe: The first one derived from the Ambrosian tradition, and is reflected in the monastic rules just mentioned; the second coming from the Franco-Germanic or Gallican tradition. Both of these types were replaced at the time of Louis the Pious by a new hymnal, which has been attributed to St. Benedict of Aniane, but was probably worked on first by Alcuin, at the monastery of St. Martin in Tours.[53] The use of hymns in the liturgy of the hours, accepted early on in monastic circles, did not find universal acceptance elsewhere. Certain dioceses, such as Braga and Lyon, saw in such poetic compositions a departure from the purity of the Sacred Scriptures. In Rome,

[49] For a general overview, cf. Righetti II, 589–598; for a full-length study, cf. J. Fontaine, *Naissance de la poésie dans l'Occident Chrétien: esquisse d'une histoire de la poésie latine chrétienne du IIIe au VIe siècle* (Paris, 1981).

[50] J. Fontaine, ed., *Ambroise de Milan, Hymnes: texte établi, traduit et annoté* (Paris, 1992).

[51] St. Benedict (Rule, chaps. 9-18) states that each hour has its own hymn, but does not identify any of them; cf. *Benedicti Regula*, ed. R. Hanslik, CSEL 75 (Vienna, 1977) 53–74. The Rules of St. Caesarius (chap. 66) and St. Aurelian (*ordo quo psallere debeatis*) indicate a specific repertoire: cf. Caesarius of Arles, S. *Caesarii Arelatensis Episcopi Regula Sanctarum Virginum*, ed. Germanus Morin (Bonn, 1933) 22–3; St. Aurelian of Arles, *Regula ad monachos*, PL 68:393.

[52] For the Celtic hymnal, cf. Cod. C 5 inf. of the Biblioteca Ambrosiana, Milano, ed. F. E. Warren, *Antiphonary of Bangor*, HBS 4 (London, 1893); (Gamber, *CLLA* I,146, #150). For the Gallican hymnal, cf. Codex Vat. Regin. lat. 11, ed. Tommasi, Opera II (Roma, 1747) 351–434 (Gamber, *CLLA* II,583, #1617).

[53] Cf. Gy, "Le Trésor," 25.

hymns did not become part of the Office until the gregorian reforms of the eleventh century. While there is a great deal of variety in the hymn repertoires of the Middle Ages, both concerning text and melody, the development of the breviary in the thirteenth century brought about a certain standardization. The corpus of hymns did not remain static, however, but throughout the late Middle Ages, the neo-classical movement of the Renaissance, and the modern period, had both spurts of growth (with the canonization of new saints and introduction of new feasts) as well as times of pruning (with various reform movements).[54]

II. BOOKS FOR THE ORATIONS

A. *Introduction*: There is not just one nucleus of the Divine Office, the psalter — but also another, the collectar. That is, both the psalter and the collectar (and the lectionary as well, as will be shown below) gradually attracted other elements of the Office around themselves. These varied origins must be considered when studying the formation of the breviary.

As usual, the terminology is variable. Depending on the manuscript's place of origin, this book can be called *collectarium, collectarius liber, collectaneum, orationarius, orationale,* and *portiforium*.[55]

B. *Typology*: The collectar is the book the celebrant uses in the Divine Office, usually containing both *capitula* (short Scripture readings for Office) and concluding orations. Its function is parallel to that of the sacramentary: to give the celebrant the texts he needs for the carrying out of his part in the sacred action. Throughout history, there is a great deal of diversity in the contents of this book and in the way it is combined with other liturgical books. Gy points out that this variety indicates a response to different needs: for example, to supply the celebrant with the readings and prayers he needed for choir and sometimes also for pastoral work, to establish a definite ordo for the

---

[54] For collections of ancient hymns, cf. especially G. M. Dreves - Cl. Blume - H. M. Bannister, *Analecta Hymnica Medii Aevi*, 55 vols. (Leipzig, 1886–1922). For the hymnal in the 1971 *Liturgia Horarum*, cf. A. Lentini, *Hymni instaurandi Breviarii Romani* (Vatican City, 1968); Idem, *Te decet hymnus: l'Innario della "Liturgia Horarum"* (Vatican City, 1984).

[55] A 7th–8th c. predecessor is the *rotulus orationum*, in use in northern Italy. Cf. the Rotulus of Ravenna, Gamber, *CLLA* I, 317–8, #660.

Office, to provide the necessary elements for the recitation of Office outside of choir, etc.[56]

C. *History*: There is a clear development from sacramentaries, to simple collectars, to what Salmon calls enriched collectars. *Sacramentaries*: All the ancient sacramentaries contain orations for the Liturgy of the Hours, whether connected with specific feast days, or included in a series of *orationes vespertinales seu matutinales*, or found in lists of *aliae orationes*.[57] *Simple collectars*: The oldest collectars simply culled these orations from the sacramentaries and gathered them together in separate *libelli*.[58] In the ninth century, with the multiplication of proper collects for the specific liturgical hour or the feast being celebrated, the repertoire of orations increased. At the same time, the gathering together of *capitula* took place, and from the tenth century onward, *capitula* are rarely found separate from the collectar. There are two kinds of collectar-capitulary: the first, in which the two elements are included as two independent blocks of material, the second, in which orations and *capitula* are integrated together according to the order of the liturgical year. *Enriched collectars*: To this original base of material, other elements are soon joined: sacraments and rites which pertain to the *Rituale/Pontificale*, devotional prayers such as appear in the *libelli precum*,[59] blessings (of ashes, candles, palms) which today are found in the missal. In the eleventh century the calendar is often joined to the collectar, as well as antiphons, verses, responsories, and hymns (or at least their *incipit*).[60] In addition, a kind of *ordo officii* was often added: a description of the office of Sundays and weekdays, sometimes with readings and responsories included. In

[56] Cf. Gy, *Collectaire*, 448.

[57] Cf. Salmon, *L'Office Divin*, 23–4 for a detailed summary.

[58] The oldest example of such a collectar is the 8th c. fragment found in ms. Sangallensis 349, edited by O. Heiming, "Das Kollektarfragment des Sangallensis 349, s.5-36, saec. VIII," *Mélanges liturgiques offerts au R. P. Dom Bernard Botte O.S.B.* (Louvain, 1972) 175–203.

[59] Cf. A. Wilmart, ed., *Precum Libelli Quattuor Aevi Karolini* (Rome, 1940); Gamber, *CLLA*, II,612–3, #1698; K. Gamber, *CLLA: Supplementum* (Fribourg, 1988) 166, #1698.

[60] For published collectars of this type from the English tradition, cf. E. S. Dewick, ed., *The Leofric Collectar*, HBS 45 (London, 1914); E. S. Dewick - W. H. Frere, eds., *The Leofric Collectar compared with the Collectar of St. Wulfstan*, HBS 56 (London, 1921); A Correa, ed., *The Durham Collectar*, HBS 107 (London, 1992).

fact, a study of the manuscripts shows every possible combination: psalter-hymnal-collectar, collectar-hymnal, collectar-ordo, collectar-ritual, collectar-pontifical, even one example of an collectar-evangeliary (these gospel readings being used at the end of Matins on Sundays and feast days). Certain combinations of these liturgical books constitute a kind of primitive breviary.

III. BOOKS FOR THE READINGS

The division proposed here between scriptural, patristic, and hagiographical readings is not quite as neat and clean in the actual liturgical books. Because of this difficulty of terminology, the content of these books must be examined on a case by case basis.

A. Scriptural Readings

1. *Introduction*: It is important to distinguish between long readings for Vigils, and short readings, or *capitula*, for all the other hours. We have already seen that early on, the *capitula* were joined to the collects in a single book, for the use of the hebdomadarian.[61] In this section, we will treat primarily the books containing the readings for the night Office.

2. *Typology*: These books were intended for the lectern in choir, containing the long scriptural readings for the night Office. The scriptural text was divided into various sections, depending on a number of factors. During the summer season, when the nights were shorter, the readings were shorter also; but for the rest of the year the longer readings were retained. On Sundays and feast days there were three nocturns, with a corresponding increase in the number of readings. Of course, differences between the monastic and cathedral office must be taken into account.

3. *History*: There are two basic stages: the use of the Bible itself as a liturgical book, and the formation of a lectionary properly so-called.

Originally, it was the Bible itself that was used during the night Office. The Rule of St. Benedict refers simply to the codex of the Bible placed on the lectern (RB 9). The passages to be read were often indicated by marginal notes in the codex itself. There are a few rare ex-

---

[61] There are a few examples of books containing *capitula* independent of the collectar: cf. Martimort, *Les lectures*, 75, n.20. For manuscripts of collectar-*capitula* in addition to those cited by Gy, cf. Martimort, *Les lectures*, 76.

amples, however, of the books of the Bible arranged, not according to the order of the Vulgate, but according to the liturgical order of the night Office.[62] Unlike the history of the Mass lectionary, for the Office there is no evidence of any lists of pericopes, forming an intermediate stage between the Bible itself and the lectionary. Instead, there are *ordines*, indicating which books of the Bible were to be read, and when, throughout the course of the liturgical year. The earliest evidence of this kind is *Ordo Romanus* XIV, which represents the usage of the Basilica of St. Peter's in the second half of the seventh century (and perhaps going back even farther), followed by *Ordo Romanus* XIII-A, representing the usage of the Lateran in the eighth century.[63] Since these two traditions are different from one another, some scholars propose the theory that OR XIII is a later adaptation of OR XIV. However, it is important to keep in mind the existence of the double liturgical tradition in Rome, urban and papal, which would explain the differences, without implying any necessary literary dependence between these two *ordines*. It is the system of the Lateran, later adapted and abridged, which remained in the Roman Breviary until 1970.

In the course of time, there was a gradual shortening of the scriptural readings for various reasons. For example, with the development of the Office and the accretion of various new elements, there was a corresponding need to cut back on other areas where possible. In addition, at certain moments in the history of spirituality devotional readings were preferred to the Scriptures. In any case, in the eleventh century a certain shortening of the readings took place, without necessarily being connected with the development of the portable breviary in the twelfth century. It is in this context that the Office lectionary developed. While certain ancient Mass lectionaries included indications for the Office readings as well,[64] in this period, the Office lectionary is an independent book, although, as mentioned earlier, its contents were not necessarily exclusively scriptural readings.

[62] Milan, Biblioteca Abrosiana E 51 inf. (11th–12th c): cf. Martimort, *Les lectures*, 73.

[63] For OR XIV, cf. Andrieu, *Les "Ordines Romani" du haut moyen âge*, vol. 3 (Louvain, 1974) introduction 25–35, text 39–41. The text, according to ms V, begins thus: "Legitur autem omnis scriptura sancti canonis ab initio anni usque ad finem in ecclesia sancti Petri hoc ordine." For OR XIII-A, cf. Andrieu, vol. 2, introduction 469–78, text 481–8.

[64] Salmon, *L'Office divin au Moyen Age*, LO 43 (Paris, 1967) 27.

B. Patristic readings

1. *Introduction*: Although important monographs have been written on the use of patristic readings for the Office, and excellent catalogues of manuscripts have been published,[65] an overall history of this liturgical book has yet to be written. Frequently enough, the homilaries themselves do not give sufficient information about how they were used. Martimort points out the importance of consulting customaries and ordinals, as well as manuscripts of the breviary, in order to obtain a more accurate understanding of the place of these books in the liturgical celebration.[66] Another topic of interest is the role played by homilaries in the transmission of patristic texts. In short, there is a considerable amount of work to be done in this field.

2. *Typology*: As usual, there are important distinctions to be made. Not every collection of homilies or sermons is the liturgical book we call a homilary. A homilary is organized according to a particular cursus of readings, following the cycle of the liturgical year. Its content is predominantly patristic readings, although as mentioned above, there are very few "pure" homilaries: scriptural and/or hagiographical readings may also be included. Sometimes the homilary is intended for non-liturgical use: for the preparation of preachers, for *lectio divina*, for exegesis, or for table reading. In the liturgy, the homilary can be used for Mass (for the sake of unlearned clergy who would read a homily of the Fathers instead of preaching themselves) or for the night office of the Liturgy of the Hours (and in terms of the number of readings, we must distinguish between the monastic and cathedral office). For the night office, there are two ways of reading the Fathers: (1) the *lectio continua* of a patristic text, as a commentary on a given book of the Bible: this did not require a separate liturgical book, as the reading was taken directly from the writings of the Fathers, or (2) a patristic homily for a particular feast day or for the gospel text to be used at Mass: this second system did require a separate book, organized according to the liturgical calendar: that is, the

---

[65] Gamber, *CLLA*, II, 594–602; Salmon, *Les manuscrits*, IV, 3–74 (patristic readings mixed together with scriptural and hagiographical readings); Grégoire, *Homéliaires Liturgiques*.

[66] Martimort, "La lecture," 313–4.

homilary. Of course, a given homilary could be used in many different circumstances: Mass, Office, the monastic refectory. There is much
flexibility.

3. *History*: The sermons or homilies (the terms are interchangeable) of
certain Fathers were gathered together early on. The preaching of St.
Augustine is a notable example of this; his homilies were widely diffused and imitated. There are many collections of sermons from
North Africa: these made their way into Europe through two important centers: Naples and Arles.[67] The first evidence we have of the
liturgical use of patristic readings is the Rule of St. Benedict (first half
of sixth century), where he prescribes this reading for Vigils.[68] Since
this practice does not come from the earlier monastic tradition, from
what source does St. Benedict draw upon? Since he borrows other
liturgical customs from the tradition of the Roman Church, perhaps
this one comes from the same source? In fact, the *Ordines Romani* XIV
and XIII-A mentioned above, shed light on this question also. OR
XIV:10 (St. Peter's, second half of seventh century), at the end of the
list of scriptural books to be read at Vigils, adds laconically: *Tractatus
vero sancti Hieronimi, Ambrosi, ceterorum Patrum, prout ordo poscit, leguntur.*[69] Chavasse proposes that an entire family of later homilaries
all derive from a sixth-century homilary of St. Peter's.[70] Bouhot sug-

---

[67] Cf. Barré, "Homéliaires," col. 600–1. St. Caesarius of Arles made a collection
of the sermons of St. Augustine for the use of his clergy.

[68] RB 9:8.

[69] Manuscripts from the northern tradition (St. Gall, Paris) add the hagiographical readings: *similiter tractatus, prout ordo poscit, passiones martyrum et vitae patrum
catholicorum leguntur* (Andrieu III, 41). The later OR XIII-A expands the list. For
example in the context of the Vigils of Christmas, OR XIII-A:13 says: *Deinde leguntur sermones vel omelias catholicorum patrum ad ipsum diem pertinentes, id est
Agustini, Gregorii, Hieronimi, Ambrosi vel ceterorum* (Andrieu II, 486).

[70] A. Chavasse, "Le calendrier dominical romain au VIᵉ siècle," *RSR* 41 (1953)
96–122; Idem, "Un homéliaire romain du VIᵉ et du VIIᵉ siècle: Le Sermonnaire des
Saints-Philippe-et-Jacques et le Sermonnaire de Saint-Pierre," *EphLit* 69 (1955)
17–24; Idem, "Le Sermonnaire d'Agimond," Kyriakon, *Festschrift Johannes
Quasten*, t.2 (Münster, 1970) t.2, 800-10; Idem, "Le Sermonnaire Vatican du VIIᵉ
siècle," *SE* 23 (1978–79) 225–80; Idem, "Un homiliaire liturgique romain du VIᵉ
siècle," *RB* 90 (1980) 194–233.

gests that before this homilary, there weren't any, as such, in the Latin Church.[71]

Although in this early period there are no two homilaries exactly alike, it is possible to group them into categories according to their historical period: Barré classifies them as (1) patristic, (2) Carolingian, and (3) medieval.[72] (1) The patristic homilaries can be further classified into three types: those which depend upon the homilary of St. Peter's, those derived from the homilary of Paul the Deacon, and others which fit neither category. Among those depending on St. Peter's are the homilary of the Basilica of St. Peter, written by Leo *qui Schifo vocatur* (tenth century), the homilary of Agimond for the Basilica of Ss. Philip and James (ca. 730), the homilary of Eginon of Verona (ca. 796–799) and the famous homilary of Alan of Farfa (ca. 760–770).[73] Representing a completely different tradition is the homilary of Paul the Deacon, commissioned by Charlemagne. In this case, Charlemagne did not call for a Roman exemplar, but left the compiler a free hand. In this homilary, in addition to a different selection of readings, there are two innovations in respect to the Roman homilary: (1) There is but one patristic text per day, instead of several to chose from (with some exceptions for the greater feasts); and (2) for all the Sundays of the year and many feast days as well, a homily on the gospel of the day is provided, including a couple of verses from the Gospel itself just before the patristic text. While this homilary was never imposed universally, it was adopted by a large number of dioceses and monasteries; it was this homilary, in an abridged version, that found its way into the breviary. While the homilary types of St. Peter's and of Paul the Deacon are the most widespread, they are not the only ones: there are ancient homilaries from other traditions as well.[74] (2) The Carolingian homilaries are noteworthy because they were intended for personal reading, not for liturgical use or preaching. (3) The medieval homilaries, which flourished especially in the eleventh-twelfth centuries, are usually patristic homilaries completed by borrowings from the Carolingian tradition and from more recent

[71] J. P. Bouhot, "L'Homéliaire de Saint-Pierre du Vatican au milieu du VIIe siècle et sa postérité," *Recherches augustiniennes* 20 (1985) 87–115.

[72] Barré, "Homéliaires," col. 601–5.

[73] Martimort, *Les lectures* 83–6.

[74] Martimort, *Les lectures*, 86–7.

elements. Again, there is a great deal of variety from one geographical area to another. In central and southern Italy, the tradition of St. Peter's predominates. In areas where Charlemagne's influence was greatest, the homiliary of Paul the Deacon predominates. There are other traditions in France, Anglo-Saxon lands, and other parts of Italy.[75] The new religious orders have an important role to play in the standardization of the homiliary repertoire within their order.

C. Hagiographical readings

1. *Introduction*: Because hagiographical texts were the last type of reading to be admitted into the night Office in the Roman tradition, they are rarely found as a separate liturgical book. Instead the hagiographical readings are usually inserted into homiliaries, either as a supplement of some kind, or integrated into the course of the liturgical year.

2. *Typology*: The book known as the *passionary* or *legendary*, containing the acts of the martyrs and the lives of the saints, is not, in the first place, a liturgical book. As Philippart has demonstrated, this book was also used in the monastic refectory; *ad collationem*, that is, in the assembly of the brethren before Compline; in the work place, where one monk would read while the others were engaged in manual labor; and for private reading.[76] In non-Roman traditions, hagiographical readings were used both for Mass and Office. Roman usage never permitted non-Scriptural readings at Mass, and was very slow to admit hagiographical readings into the Office. Because the passionary was used in such varied contexts, in order to assert that a given manuscript is a liturgical book used in choir, the book itself must contain indications that it was, in fact, so used. Among such indications are: (1) the division of the text into lessons (three, six, nine, or twelve, depending on the particular context); (2) the presence of other elements of the liturgical celebration in the same book (e.g., scriptural or patristic readings); (3) the title of the book, sometimes specifying that it was used for the Office.[77]

---

[75] Barré, "Homéliaires," cols. 603–605; Martimort, *Les lectures*, 89–94.

[76] Philippart, *Les légendiers*, 112–7.

[77] Martimort, *Les lectures*, 100–1.

3. History: The liturgical use of hagiographical readings: As already mentioned, the custom of reading the *passiones* of the martyrs and lives of the saints for Office is not Roman in origin. There is abundant information, however, about this type of text as used in North Africa, Spain, Gaul, and Milan. We restrict ourselves here to the Roman tradition.

The earliest Roman reference to hagiographical readings in the liturgy is an explicit rejection of them. The decretal of pseudo-Gelasius (sixth century) says that according to ancient custom, and because of the anonymity of the texts in circulation and their dubious accuracy, such books are not read in the holy Roman Church (cf. DS 353). In the year 598, St. Gregory the Great, responding to a request of Eulogius of Alexandria for a copy of the *gesta* of the martyrs, replies that in the Roman archives he could only find one small volume.[78] The *Ordines Romani* confirm that even in the seventh century, hagiographical readings were not the Roman custom, whereas the Gallican recensions of the Roman texts include the *passiones martyrum et vitae patrum catholicorum*.[79] But finally, the ancient strictness gave way, and Rome adopted this practice as well. OR XII (ca. 800) shows that the reading of the *passio* or *gesta* of a saint was now customary on the feast day of that saint, in the church where the relics were venerated, and that Pope Hadrian I (772-795) extended this practice to the Basilica of St. Peter's.[80] From the eighth century onward, this literary genre developed rapidly, responding to the parallel development of the cult of the saints and the veneration of their relics. By the twelfth century, the Lateran Ordo of Prior Bernard indicates a hagio-

[78] Gregorii I Papae Registrum Epistolarum, MGH, *Epistolarum Tomus II* (Berlin, 1899) 29.

[79] OR XIV:10 in the Roman original and the various recensions north of the Alps (Andrieu III, 41). There is a more extensive description of the celebration of saints' feastdays in OR XVI:10-12 and OR XVII:76-78 (both *ordines* "Gallicanized," from the end of the 8th c.). Cf. Andrieu III, 148 and 185–6.

[80] OR XII:24–5 (Andrieu, vol.2, 465–6). Pope Hadrian in a letter to Charlemagne, touches indirectly on this question. After rejecting Lives of the Saints which did not have a known and approved author, and therefore, lacked any authority, the pope adds: *Magis enim passiones sanctorum martyrum sacri canones censuentes ut liceat etiam eas legi, cum anniversarii dies eorum celebrantur.* Epistolae Hadriani I Papae, MGH, *Epistolarum Tomus V* (Berlin, 1899) 49. Cf. De Gaiffier, "La lecture," 142.

graphical reading for all the numerous feasts of saints which by this time weighed down the calendar.[81]

The book of hagiographical readings:[82] In the beginning, these texts were written down in *libelli,* containing the acts of one or several martyrs, for use in the churches where these saints were honored. These *libelli* were gradually gathered together in larger collections, whose terminology is somewhat flexible: *acta martyrum, passiones martyrum, passionarium, vitae sanctorum.* When these texts are finally taken into the liturgy, compiled for the Office, and organized according to the liturgical year, then we have the liturgical book called the legendary. These rarely existed by themselves however, usually joined either to the biblical readings, the patristic readings, or both. Thus the full lectionary for the Office is formed.

D. Lectionary

Beginning in the tenth century and continuing to the twelfth century, the lectionary for Office gradually develops: that is, the amalgamation of the scriptural, patristic, and hagiographical readings to make a more or less organized whole. It must be stressed, however, that there is a great deal of variety in the contents of these lectionaries, depending on the usages of the local monastic or diocesan church. That is to say, unlike the lectionaries for Mass, no single lectionary for Office (before the advent of the breviary) ever became the generally accepted standard for the Roman rite.

The breviary begins to be formed in this same period of time. Salmon suggests that in addition to the psalter and the collectar functioning as a kind of core or nucleus for the formation of the breviary, the lectionary served the same purpose, attracting to itself various other elements of the Divine Office according to local circumstances.[83] The success of the breviary, in fact, explains why the complete lectionary, as a liturgical book in its own right, never became widespread.[84]

---

[81] L. Fischer, ed., *Bernhardi . . . Ordo officiorum ecclesiae Lateranensis* (Munich, 1916). Cf. nn. 249–54; 260–2; 264–72; 282–99, as cited in Martimort, *Les lectures,* 99–100.

[82] In this section, I am following Salmon, *Les manuscrits,* ix–x.

[83] Salmon, *L'Office divin au Moyen Age,* 60–1. Cf. also Martimort, *Les lectures,* 103–5.

[84] Salmon, *Les manuscrits* IV, viii.

IV. THE BOOK FOR THE CHAPTER OFFICE

1. *Introduction* (*the origins of the chapter office*): The chapter office is a synaxis which takes place in communities of monks or secular canons usually after Prime, but sometimes also after Terce. This always includes a liturgical office, which is sometimes followed by a chapter of faults and a distribution of the daily work assignments. This liturgical office is comprised of readings: the martyrology, the rule (which on Sundays or feasts days could be substituted by the gospel of the day and a homily), and the necrology. This *officium capituli* is a late-comer on the liturgical scene. It is not present in the Rule of St. Benedict. The earliest extant source is OR XVIII, an eighth-century document from a monastery in Gaul, which indicates that Prime was said in the dormitory, after which a section of the Rule of St. Benedict was read, with the superior giving an explanation of the text.[85] Other evidence is present in the Rule of Chrodegang (742–766) and canon 69 of the Council of Aix-la-Chapelle (817):[86] these texts pertain to collegiate churches of the secular clergy. The structure of the chapter office at this time includes (1) the martyrology, and (2) the rule and an explanation of the rule (or the gospel and a homily on the gospel). A third element, the reading of the necrology, was added later.[87] The earliest evidence for an actual book for this chapter office comes from the ninth century. Palazzo points out the constant dynamic in liturgical studies: namely, that liturgical action leads to the creation of the conditions necessary for that action: in this case, a separate space for the synaxis (the chapter room) and a separate liturgical book.[88]

2.*Typology* (the book of the chapter office): This ninth-century book is the so-called Martyrology of Usuard, written around 858 by a monk of Saint-Germain-des-Prés in Paris.[89] It includes a prologue, a marty-

---

[85] OR XVIII:3–4 (Andrieu, vol. 3, 205).

[86] Lemaître, "Liber Capituli," 629–30; Palazzo 174–5.

[87] For a description of the chapter office, cf. Martène, Book I:5, *De capitulo in De Antiquis Ecclesiae Ritibus Libri*, 4 vol. (Antwerp, 1736–1738); (rpt. Hildesheim, 1969) IV, col. 52–65. Lemaître gives a summary of the structure and content of Martène's text in "Liber capituli," 634.

[88] Palazzo, 175.

[89] J. Dubois, ed., *Le martyrologe d'Usuard: Texte et commentaire*, Subsidia hagiographica 40 (Brussels, 1965).

rology, hymns in honor of St. Germain, a list of the abbots of the monastery written in the margin, the Rule of St. Benedict, and the necrology. The title "martyrology," therefore, is misleading: the book is a *liber capituli*, which had a very wide diffusion, and became the archetype and model for subsequent versions. The four elements of martyrology, lectionary, rule, and necrology form the content of this type of book, although the order varies and all four elements are not always present. The term *liber capituli* itself is very rare; the oldest reference is in a thirteenth-century catalogue of books of the monastery of Cluny. Otherwise, the title tends to refer to only one of the book's component parts, such as the martyrology, or the rule. Since titles are misleading and terminology is variable, it is the content of the book which must be our guide. Perhaps one reason for the scarce attention paid to this liturgical book is that up until the thirteenth century, it was a question of local usage only. In 1266 this custom was adopted at a general chapter of the Friars Minor, after which it was then introduced into the Roman liturgical books.[90]

3. *History (of the book's component parts)*:

Martyrology: The martyrology as such existed long before it became part of the chapter office. This type of document may be defined as a collection which announces day by day, usually on the anniversary of death, the saints who are honored on that day. The origins of this usage are connected with the reading of the diptychs in the liturgy. The fact that the martyrology was sometimes bound together with the sacramentary and sometimes with the rule, indicates the various uses of this text. The oldest martyrology in the west is the so-called *martyrologium hieronymianum*, compiled in Italy in the second half of the fifth century. This contains only the day of the feast and the name of the place or cemetery where the saint was venerated. Such scanty information did not satisfy, and with the organization and extension of the chapter office, a martyrology with more detailed information was desired. This is the origin of the historical martyrologies, St. Bede the Venerable (673–735) being the first to compose such a text, followed by others who set out to complete the work Bede had begun. Usuard of Saint-Germain-des-Prés took the earlier

---

[90] Lemaître, "Liber Capituli," 626.

martyrologies and made a new synthesis;[91] it was his work that was adopted by Baronius as the base text for the official edition of the Roman Martyrology in 1584.[92]

Necrology: The necrology, as the martyrology, follows the Roman calendar, independent of the liturgical year. It is a list of the names of the faithful departed, to be used in the daily commemoration of the deceased members of a particular religious community or group of communities. From the Carolingian period onward, new forms of commemoration of the dead developed, giving rise to new liturgical practices both at Mass and Office. The development of new books testifies to the codification of these practices in a specific liturgical context: the chapter office.[93] Although the terminology is variable, the necrology is to be distinguished from the obituary, which is a more administrative kind of document, containing information about the endowment provided for Masses, and the revenues obtained from this endowment. In medieval books for the chapter office, the necrology usually comes after the martyrology or the rule. To this day monasteries retain this custom, although where the chapter office has been discontinued, the reading of the necrology takes place in another context, such as the refectory.

V. THE BREVIARY

1. *Introduction*: Just as in the case of the Mass the different books for orations, readings, and chants gradually came together to form the one book of the missal, so also in the case of the Office: the many and various books came together to form the one book of the breviary. This did not happen in a systematic fashion as something planned out and organized. Rather, as mentioned earlier, a single book (be that the psalter, the collectar, or the lectionary) served as a kind of nucleus, and other books tended to gravitate around this core of ma-

---

[91] For a list of the modern editions of ancient martyrologies cf. Dubois, *Martyrologes d'Usuard*, 35–45 (rpt. of "Introduction à la révision du martyrologe Romain," *Not* 21 [1985] 91–101; citation in question on 100–1).

[92] For a description of editions of the martyrology after 1584 — the corrections made by Pope Benedict XIV, the *editio typica* of 1913, the *editio prima post typicam* of 1922, up to the present day — cf. Dubois, *Martyrologes d'Usuard*, 24–6 ("Introduction," 90–2).

[93] Cf. Palazzo, 174.

terial. The breviary in its complete and integrated form does not appear until the thirteenth century.

2. *Typology*: The word "breviary" in ancient texts must be treated rather carefully. In itself, it simply means a shorter compendium of texts: this term usually referred to Office texts, but sometimes could refer to Mass texts as well. Common expressions are *epitomata sive breviaria, breviarium parvum itinerarium* (for taking on a journey), *breviaria portatilia* (portable, as opposed to the large book intended for choir), or *breviaria de camera* (for private recitation). Other terms such as *libelli officiales* or *manuales* were also used. As the name implies, the breviary was a unified and/or shortened version of the Office, but there were two kinds: breviaries of imposing size for choir and breviaries of modest dimensions for private recitation. Choir breviaries maintained the long readings for vigils, and were only shorter than their predecessors in that they eliminated *ad libitum* choices, reducing everything to a standard repertoire. Portable breviaries, on the other hand, greatly abbreviated the readings, included only the *incipit* of antiphons, responsories, and other texts, and omitted musical notation, all in an effort to reduce the size of the book. Early attempts to gather various books of the Office together into one volume simply juxtaposed one book or fascicle after the other, but this was a clumsy arrangement which was soon abandoned. The fused or integrated breviary was much easier to use, with each part of the Office in its proper place according to the unfolding of that particular liturgical hour and the order of the liturgical year.

3. *History: Thirteenth century*: The breviary tradition of the Roman curia was given new impetus by the liturgical reforms of Pope Innocent III (1198–1216). He promulgated an ordinal for the daily services of the papal court, including both Mass and Office, which was compiled somewhere between 1213–1216.[94] The instructions from this ordinal gradually found their way into the breviary itself, resulting in a rubricated breviary of the papal court. The rapid growth of the Franciscan order, the desire for uniform liturgical practice, and the advice of Cardinal Hugolin (the future Gregory IX), led St. Francis to adopt the liturgy of the papal court as the uniform liturgical

---

[94] Edition of this text: S.J.P. Van Dijk - J. H. Walker, *The Ordinal of the Papal Court from Innocent III to Boniface VIII and Related Documents*, SF 22 (Fribourg, 1975).

observance of the Franciscans, one exception being the use of the Gallican psalter instead of the Roman psalter. Meanwhile, during the pontificate of Honorius III (1216–1227), the court breviary was corrected and simplified, with a more universal use in mind. The friars, after the promulgation of their Rule in 1223, were able to obtain portable breviaries for their use, but they were given old copies, which did not contain the most recent corrections. In 1230 the Franciscans made their own edition, the so-called "Regula Breviary," but the outdated copies remained in circulation. Thus in the 1230s, at least three versions of the breviary were in use: the pre-Innocent book, the revision of Honorius III, and the Franciscan adaptation. In 1243–1244, the Minister General Haymo of Faversham addressed this confusing situation by issuing a corrected ordinal of the breviary. Because of the widespread and rapid diffusion of the Franciscan order, this breviary of the papal court was carried to every corner of Europe. Pope Nicholas III (1277–1286) imposed this breviary on the other churches of the city of Rome, which until then had followed the more ancient usage.

Sixteenth century: Although used widely, the breviary of the Roman curia was neither obligatory nor universal. In the fourteenth to sixteenth centuries, many local breviaries remained in use, and frequently enough, side by side with the Roman breviary. New compositions for the feasts of local saints, along with local usages for the temporal cycle were inserted into the breviary of the Roman curia according to the best judgment of the given compiler. In the fourteenth century, the Avignon captivity and the Great Schism had their negative influence on the Office, including much uncertainty and disorder concerning rubrical directives and actual practice. John of Arze, a theological consultor for the Council of Trent addressed the cardinal legates in August 1551 concerning the problems of the Divine Office.[95] His observations can be summarized in three points: (1) Because of the enormous growth of the sanctoral cycle, the Sunday office and ferial office were being neglected, which meant that the entire psalter was hardly ever recited. (2) The accumulation of several offices on the same day — the Little Office of the Blessed Virgin Mary, the Office of the dead, the gradual psalms, the penitential

---

[95] For these observations, cf. Baümer-Biron, *Histoire du Breviaire*, II, 95.

psalms, in addition to the regular Office — was far too burdensome. (3) The substitution of legendary and apocryphal material for the reading of Scripture, along with the use of other dubious texts (antiphons, hymns, and responsories), compromised the integrity of the Office. In response to this situation, there had already been numerous attempts at reform. The humanists, who found the style of the Office detestable, sought to return to the classical purity of the Latin language. It must be said that while some of the humanist attempts were praiseworthy, others were not. For example, in the desire to use strictly classical expressions, they sometimes tried to render the content of the Christian faith in the language of Greco-Roman paganism.

In any case, a revised hymnal was issued in 1525 (not obligatory) with the support of Pope Clement VII. The humanist reformers, and in particular, Bishop Zaccaria Ferreri of Campobasso, had in mind to correct the entire breviary, but Ferreri died in 1524, and his manuscript was lost in the Sack of Rome in 1527. Pope Clement VII did not give up, but entrusted the reform of the breviary to the Spaniard Francisco Quiñonez, titular cardinal of Santa Croce in Gerusalemme. His charge was to revise the canonical hours, restoring them to their ancient form if possible, to suppress prolix and problematic texts while remaining faithful to the usages established by the Fathers, so that clerics would no longer have an excuse for neglecting the duty of the prayer of the hours. Quiñonez began work in 1529, and finished it in 1534, just before the death of Clement VII. It was published in 1535 and approved for the private recitation of secular priests by Pope Paul III. In its content, it was a return to a broader reading of the Scriptures and the use of ecclesiastical texts which were historically accurate. In its simplified structure, however, it was a radical departure from the tradition, and as such, despite its popularity, received massive criticism from the Fathers of the Council of Trent. The then-reigning pope, Paul IV, when he had been bishop of Chieti, had also worked on a reform of the Breviary for the use of the new Congregation of the Theatines. His criteria were much more traditional however, and he suppressed the Breviary of Santa Croce in 1558, to be replaced by his own reform. But he himself died a year later, before bringing the project to completion.

In the third session of the Council of Trent (1563), the reform of the breviary was discussed, and a commission was formed for this work.

But desirous of bringing the council to a close, the Council Fathers entrusted the task to the Holy See. Since Pope Pius IV died in 1564, it was left to his successor, St. Pius V, to complete the work. New criteria for the reform of the breviary were established, in sharp contrast to the criteria of Quiñonez: (1) Nothing essential should be taken away from the old Roman Breviary. (2) The task was not to create a new breviary, but to restore the old one to its pristine state. (3) Those elements which were later additions were to be suppressed. This new breviary was published by Pius V in July 1568.[96]

Twentieth century: The Roman Breviary of 1568 had reduced the number of saints' feast days to 138. In the centuries that followed, with the continued development of the sanctoral cycle, the number increased once again, thus impairing the desired equilibrium between the temporal and the sanctoral cycle. By the time of Benedict XIV (1740–1758), the number of saints' feast days had risen to 228. In the nineteenth century, the reform of the breviary had been on the agenda of the First Vatican Council, but the council was suspended before such things could be discussed. Pope St. Pius X (1903–1914) established a commission to revise the breviary, according to two criteria: the restoration of the ferial office to its rightful place, and the celebration of the feasts of saints according to their proper rank. The result was a lightening of the daily office with a new distribution of the psalter, along with the institution of a mixed office: using the office of the day for the psalmody, and from the *capitulum* on, using the sanctoral office. This new breviary was promulgated in November 1911. During the pontificate of Pius XII, shortly after the publication of Mediator Dei (1947), the Sacred Congregation of Rites was charged with preparing a proposal for liturgical reform. In its published report, it returned to the thorny question of the relationship between the temporal and sanctoral cycle, and devoted well over a hundred pages to the question of the Roman Breviary[97] A supplement to this report some years later describes the results of a world-wide consultation of four hundred metropolitan sees about an *aggiornamento* of

[96] The *Breviarium Monasticum* was revised along the lines of the *Breviarium Romanum*, and was promulgated by Pope Paul V in 1612.

[97] Sacra Rituum Congregatio, *Memoria sulla riforma liturgica*, Sectio Historica n.71 (Vatican City, 1948). Cf. the section on the Roman Breviary, 169–304.

the traditional structure of the Divine Office.[98] Thus when in 1963, *Sacrosanctum Concilium* 83–101 spoke about a renewal of the Divine Office, the way had been well prepared.[99] The new *Liturgia Horarum*, while in some areas revolutionary, is very realistic and manageable. All the liturgical hours for a given day can be prayed without undue burden. At a distance of twenty-five years, it is possible to evaluate both the positive and negative elements inherent in the liturgical book itself, and the actual use of the book in daily practice.

BOOKS USED FOR THE GOOD ORDERING OF THE LITURGY

To have all the necessary books containing the prayers, the readings, and the music both for Mass and for Office is still not enough, for the question remains: How are these liturgical actions to be carried out? The rites and ceremonies must unfold in a certain order, according to certain norms, some of which are universal, others of which are local. Therefore, alongside the liturgical books already discussed, there is yet another category, namely books which describe, with a certain amount of detail, all the liturgical celebrations of the Church: Mass, Office, sacraments, and other rites. The purpose of these books is the good ordering of all the ritual actions of a given community. There are three major types of book in this genre: *ordines*, ordinals, and ceremonials.

I. ORDINES

1. *Introduction*: The *ordines* are usually small booklets or *libelli*, whose purpose is limited to describing a single liturgical action. The *Ordines Romani* published by Andrieu are the best known example of this type of book. The first *ordines* appear at the end of the seventh, beginning of the eighth century.

2. *Typology*: An ordo is a text which gathers together all the information necessary for the carrying out of a given liturgical action, including the *incipit* of the various texts, along with rubrical directions,

---

[98] Sacra Rituum Congregatio, *Memoria sulla riforma liturgica*, Sectio Historica n.97, Supplemento IV: Consultazione dell'episcopato intorno alla riforma del Breviario Romano (1956-1957): risultati e deduzioni (Vatican City, 1948).

[99] For information about the post-conciliar reform and the preparation of the new *Liturgia Horarum*, cf. Bugnini, cha. 30–3.

sometimes quite detailed. The terminology, as usual, is extremely variable: *capitulare ecclesiastici ordinis, instructio ecclesiastici ordinis, breviarium ecclesiastici ordinis*. Sometimes the word *ordo* does not appear in the title at all; other times it is very clear, for example: *ordo processionis, ordo vel dununtiatio scrutinii*, etc. The length can vary from a few pages to fifty or sixty pages. Such a text is intended for the master of ceremonies and his assistants.

The *ordines* refer to the orations of a given liturgical action in various ways: (1) with a very general remark, such as *ut in sacramentario continetur*, (2) with the *incipit* of the prayer, or (3) with the entire prayer written out, but in such a case we have the precursor of a ritual, pontifical, or rubricated sacramentary.

3. *History*: In Andrieu's monumental work, fifty *ordines* are described and edited. Many of these originated in Rome as separate fascicles, and later made their way across the Alps to Franco-Germanic lands, where they were gathered together into collections. These collections date from the eighth-ninth centuries. A careful study of the texts enabled Andrieu to distinguish between the original Roman text of certain *ordines* (Collection A) and the Gallicanized adaptations of the same (Collection B). In addition, there are other Gallican collections not necessarily related to Collections A or B. These *ordines* treat a great variety of topics: the Mass (papal, episcopal, presbyteral), baptism, ordination, funerals, the crowning of the emperor, dedication of churches, the liturgical year, the liturgy of the hours, particular feasts, rituals for the monastic refectory, liturgical vestments, and so forth. These *ordines* are extremely valuable for a number of reasons. In some cases, they enable us to distinguish clearly between Roman usage and Franco-Germanic usage. They show a gradual codification of orations, readings, and chants. They give clues, which cannot be found elsewhere, as to how the various liturgical actions were carried out in that historical period. They give the reader some insight into the liturgical customs and the way of life of the Church both in Rome and across the Alps, in the eighth and ninth centuries.

II. ORDINALS

1. *Introduction*: The ordinal can be distinguished from the ordo in that it describes not only one liturgical action but many, throughout the entire course of the liturgical year, with the intention of establishing a

certain uniform usage. Because the ordinal is concerned with local and not universal custom, there is no standard collection of texts comparable to Andrieu's edition of the *Ordines*.[100] The ordinals date from the eleventh to the fifteenth centuries.

2. *Typology*: A document from the year 1208 defines an ordinal as: *Liber in quo continetur quid et quando et quomodo cantandum sit vel legendum, chorus regendus, campanae pulsandae, luminare accendendum*.[101] In other words, the ordinal is a book which regulates all the myriad details of an ordered liturgical life: whether that be Mass or Office or other ritual actions; whether it be for a religious order, a diocese, or one of the non-Roman western rites. In particular, the ordinal deals with certain complexities which require a guide, such as the relation between the temporal cycle and the sanctoral cycle and the alternation of fixed and moveable feasts. The intention is to codify liturgical usage and unify liturgical practice. Often the redaction of an ordinal is the result of a liturgical reform of some kind: this is frequently the case in the history of the new religious orders of the thirteenth century. When the ordinal serves this kind of purpose, it becomes the central element around which other liturgical books (missal, breviary) are organized.

The terminology is extremely varied. Sometimes cognates of the word "ordinal" are used: *ordinarius, liber ordinarius, ordinale*. Sometimes the title indicates the purpose of ordering the entire liturgical year: *breviarium sive ordo officiorum per totam anni decursionem, liber de ordinatione et officio totius anni, ordo ecclesiasticus per anni totius circulum*. Other expressions are: *liber consuetudinum, agenda, caeremoniale, directorium chori, mores, observantia, rituale, rubricae*. The ordinal is to be distinguished from a customary, which is a description of the usages of daily life for a collegiate church or monastery, containing far more than simply liturgical information.[102]

3. *History*: There are various types of ordinals, and here history and typology are intertwined. (1) The ordinal of a cathedral church and other churches dependent on the bishop: If the cathedral is in the

---

[100] Martimort, *Les ordines,* 53–61 gives an extensive list of ordinals, according to place of origin.

[101] Martimort, *Les ordines,* 62.

[102] For a discussion of the customary, cf. Palazzo, 221–7.

care of a group of canons regular, the ordinal may be that of the religious congregation. Otherwise, it would be compiled at the direction of the bishop, often with the purpose of establishing a model for the other churches of the diocese. (2) The ordinal of individual monasteries: The more important monasteries, such as Monte Cassino or Cluny, not only had ordinals of their own, but often exercised a considerable influence on the customs of smaller houses. (3) The ordinals of monastic congregations and the new religious orders: From the eleventh century and following, due to the vitality of various reform movements in the monastic world, many existing monasteries grouped themselves into congregations with more or less unified observances. New monastic orders, such as the Cistercians, were founded with a strong central authority, which meant that one ordinal would serve for the standard observance of all the houses of the order. The case is similar for the Premonstratensians, Dominicans, Carthusians, and Carmelites. Particularly noteworthy is the ordinal of the Franciscans, written by Haymo of Faversham in 1243–1244, because of its influence on the Roman rite. Haymo wrote both an *Ordo breviarii* and an *Ordo missalis*: when both were issued together the document was called *Ordinarium secundum consuetudinem Romanae curiae*. (4) The Roman ordinals: These documents form a kind of bridge between the *Ordines Romani* and the later ceremonials. The three most important are the *Liber politicus* (1140–1143), written by Benedict, a canon of the Basilica of St. Peter's;[103] the *Ordo officiorum vel consuetudinum* of Bernard, the prior of the Lateran Basilica (1139–1145);[104] and the *Ordo romanae ecclesiae curiae* compiled during the pontificate of Innocent III (1198–1216) describing the liturgy not of the Basilicas, but of the papal chapel.[105]

The history of this type of book can be divided into three periods. (1) The first ordinals which have come down to us are from the mid-eleventh century. Between the *Ordines Romani* and these early ordinals, it is difficult to find intermediaries; in monastic circles, however, there is greater continuity. (2) The twelfth-thirteenth centuries are

---

[103] P. Fabre - L. Duchesne, "Benedicti Beati Petri canonici Liber politicus," *Le Liber censuum de l'Église romaine . . .*, 3 vol. (Paris, 1910-1952), II,141–74.

[104] L. Fischer, *Bernhardi cardinalis et Lateranensis ecclesiae prioris Ordo officiorum ecclesiae Lateranensis*, Historische Forschungen und Quellen 2-3 (Munich, 1916).

[105] Van Dijk - Walker, *The Ordinal of the Papal Court* (Fribourg, 1975).

considered to be the "golden age" of the ordinal. In the centuries which follow, the document is improved, corrected, and made more precise. These indications become the *rubricae generales* of the missal and breviary. (3) When each community had a complete text of the general rubrics, plus the complete missal and breviary, the ordinal gradually lost its importance. It was enough to have a small booklet, or *breve* to supplement whatever was lacking in the rubrics. With the advent of printing, this *breve* becomes what we know as the yearly ordo, which resolves potential calendar conflicts for Mass and Office with directions for every day of the year.

III. CEREMONIALS

1. *Introduction*: The ceremonial can be distinguished from the ordinal in that it contains no liturgical texts, no incipits for the readings, prayers, or chants. It describes, with greater precision than the ordinal, the ceremonial practices of a given community throughout the liturgical year.

2. *Typology*: The typology of a given ceremonial can be determined by asking the question: Who was it written for? (1) The origins of the ceremonial are to be found in the twelfth and thirteenth-century development of the Roman curia and the necessity of writing down the rubrics for the complicated ceremonies and court etiquette of papal functions. It was important to know precisely who was responsible for what and how each person was to carry out his particular role. (2) Episcopal ceremonials followed, probably derived from papal ceremonial. For example, the Pontifical of the Roman Curia describes an ordination when the pope is not present: Thus bishops who were part of the papal court needed ceremonial directives too. The Pontifical of Guillaume Durand also contains a kind of ceremonial for the bishop.[106] (3) In addition, religious orders with a central government and a standardized liturgical observance might also have their own ceremonial. (4) Finally, those who followed various non-Roman western rites felt the need to codify their usages with a ceremonial, especially at the time of the Tridentine reforms, when in order to retain their customs it was necessary to demonstrate a tradition of at least two-hundred years.

[106] M. Andrieu, *Le Pontifical Romain au Moyen-Age: Tome III, Le Pontifical de Guillaume Durand*, ST 88 (Vatican City, 1940) 631–62.

3. *History*:

Papal ceremonial: Martimort traces the formation of the papal ceremonial as follows: (1) its beginnings in the twelfth century, (2) its development in the last quarter of the thirteenth century, (3) the changes brought about by the transfer of the papal court to Avignon in the fourteenth century, (4) the ceremonial in the period of the Great Schism, and finally (5) the period of the early Renaissance.[107] In this last period there were two important ceremonials published. The first was the *Caeremoniale romanum* of Peter of Burgos, the master of ceremonies of Pope Nicholas V (1447–1455). The second was *De caeremoniis Curiae Romanae libri tres* of Agostino Patrizi Piccolomini and John Burckard, who compiled their ceremonial at the request of Pope Innocent VIII (1484–1492) and submitted it to him in 1488. It was not published, however, until 1516, having been poorly re-worked by Cristoforo Marcello and dedicated to Leo X (1513–1521).

Episcopal ceremonial: In the fifteenth century, many bishops, with some ties to the Roman Curia, inserted details about ceremonial usages into their pontificals. These inserts were usually based on the earlier works of Latino Malabranca[108] and Guillaume Durand. Piccolomini and Burckard had more success with their episcopal ceremonial than with their papal ceremonial. Their *Pontificalis ordinis liber*, printed in 1485, includes an episcopal ceremonial, which became the basis for the official *Caeremoniale episcoporum* published in 1600 at the direction of Pope Clement VIII (1592–1605). With various corrections and additions, this text remained the norm until the post-Vatican II *Caeremoniale Episcoporum* of 1984.

BOOKS USED BY THE CELEBRANT FOR SACRAMENTS AND OTHER RITES

I. THE BISHOP'S BOOK: THE PONTIFICAL

Introduction: The orations that a bishop needed for the celebration of sacraments and other liturgical actions outside of the Eucharist were originally contained in the sacramentary. The rubrical directives for

---

[107] Martimort, *Les ordines*, 96–102.

[108] *Liber quando episcopus cardinalis missarum sollemnia celebraturus est* (ca. 1280), ed. Dymans, *Cérémonial* I, 220–63; cf. Martimort, *Les ordines*, 99.

the good ordering of these same services were contained in various *ordines*. It is easy to see why the bishop would find it more convenient to have both orations and rubrics gathered together in a single book.

Typology: There are both practical reasons and ecclesiological reasons for the development of the pontifical. The practical reasons are simply stated: in the cathedral, the bishop used the sacramentary and had all the other books necessary for the carrying out of those liturgical functions which pertained particularly to him. But when he was away from the cathedral, he needed something smaller and handier, a single book containing everything necessary. The ecclesiological reasons are related to the practical ones. In the ninth and tenth centuries the episcopal function in Christian society tends to expand and solidify: the role of the bishop acquires increasing importance both on the religious and social levels. The development of the pontifical as an independent liturgical book bears witness to these changes.

History:
The primitive pontificals: The oldest documents in the formation of the pontifical are *libelli*, dating from the second half of the ninth century, containing everything needed for the bishop to celebrate a single liturgical action: an ordination, the dedication of a church, the chrism Mass of Holy Thursday, the rites pertaining to a council or synod, etc.[109] With time, these *libelli* are gathered together in collections, the main characteristic of which is the lack of any fixed structure or content. These documents were compiled spontaneously according to the needs of the moment and were usually very modest and simple books, although occasionally splendid and luxurious books were produced as well.

The Roman-Germanic Pontifical of the tenth century: Just as the eucharistic liturgy arrives at a point of synthesis in the Gregorian-Hadrian sacramentary with its Gallican supplement, so also the

---

[109] There are also *libelli* containing episcopal blessings, deriving initially from the Mozarabic and Gallican rites, and entering the Roman rite with the Roman-Germanic synthesis of the 8th–9th centuries. This blessing, reserved to the bishop, was given not at the end of Mass, but before Communion. In that place it served the dual function of preparing communicants for receiving the Eucharist, and dismissing non-communicants from the liturgical assembly. Cf. E. Moeller, *Corpus Benedictionum Pontificalium*, 4 vol. CCL 162, 162a, 162b, 162c (Turnhout 1971–1979).

non-eucharistic liturgy reaches a new synthesis with the Roman-Germanic pontifical. The pre-emininence of the Gregorian Sacramentary was a result of Charlemagne's desire to unify his kingdom both politically and religiously. This pontifical also, a century or so later, is the product of the unification policies of the *Reichskirchensystem* of Emperor Otto I. It is an important book for the history of the Roman liturgy. It was compiled in the Benedictine monastery of St. Alban in Mainz between 950 and 962, when William, the son of Otto I was protector of St. Alban's, archbishop of Mainz, primate of Germany, and archchancellor of his father, the emperor. This pontifical is a substantial and complex book, and its sources are diverse: (1) the sacramentaries for euchological texts, (2) various families of *ordines*: Roman, Gallicanized-Roman, and pure Gallican, (3) didactic collections containing sermons, *expositiones Missae*, and explanations of the Our Father and the Creed. The first half of the pontifical includes such liturgical actions as the sacrament of orders, from the tonsuring of boys to the ordination of priests; consecration of virgins, deaconesses, and widows; blessing of abbots and abbesses; monastic profession; the consecration of a church along with special blessings for all the sacred vessels and other appointments; the election and consecration of a bishop; the consecration of the pope (recall that the Ottonian emperors had a vested interest in this matter); the blessing of the emperor or of a king; the convoking of a council; the explanation of the pontifical vestments; excommunications; reconciliation of the excommunicated; the order of Mass, along with an explanation of its parts. The second half is a kind of ordinal-sacramentary-ritual containing a description of the liturgical year (Andrieu's Ordo 50) and various other *ordines*, formularies for various Masses, and all manner of blessings. The entire complex is an adaptation according to the needs of the time and place, but done with the greatest of respect for the Roman tradition. The papal consecrations in 963 and 965 used the Roman-Germanic pontifical. Pope Gregory V (996–999) granted privileges to the monastery of Rheichenau (Saint Gall, Rheichenau, and Mainz had very close ties in this period) in exchange for liturgical books copied in the monastic scriptorium. These liturgical books, of course, were Roman-Germanic books. In the decades that followed, a number of German popes sat in the chair of Peter, using the same liturgical books which they had used north of the Alps. A century later, around 1150, the Ordinal of the Lateran Basilica cites this pontifical, giving it the name *Ordo Romanus*.[110] The Roman-Germanic pontifical was by then considered "Roman," and it became the basis for all later pontificals.

The Roman Pontifical of the twelfth century: It would be inaccurate, however, to suggest that the Roman-Germanic pontifical enjoyed uncontested sway. From the time of Pope St. Gregory VII (1073–1085) until the end of the twelfth century, various efforts at liturgical reform were made in Rome, including a reform of the pontifical. There is a great deal of variety in the manuscripts, and there is no one archetype which has come down to us. In making his edition of the twelfth-century pontifical, Andrieu classified the manuscripts according to their degree of similarity to the Roman-Germanic pontifical. The characteristics of this Roman adaptation are as follows: (1) the elimination of material considered too archaic or too German (certain *ordines*; the coronation of the king, which was not necessary in Rome; the didactic sections, certain blessings foreign to the Roman religious temperament, etc.), and (2) the simplification and elimination of some of the euchological selections. This new type of book had great influence in the Latin church, especially after the First Lateran Council in 1123, and the shoring up of ecclesiastical discipline.

The Pontifical of the Roman Curia of the thirteenth century: During the pontificate of Innocent III (1198–1216), the masters of ceremony of the papal household wished to adjust the pontifical to the needs of the pope and his curia. This pontifical went through three different recensions, the first during the pontificate of Innocent III in a version suitable also for episcopal celebrations, the last before the pontificate of Innocent IV (1243–1253), written for the use of the episcopal sees of Italy. It was this third version that came to dominate, and this was brought to Avignon in the first decade of the fourteenth century.

The Pontifical of Guillaume Durand (1293–1295): In the very same period, Guillaume Durand, bishop of Mende in France, compiled a pontifical to use in his own diocese.[111] The great advantage of his pontifical was its clarity of structure. The material is divided into

---

[110] Vogel, *ML* 239.

[111] Durand was born ca. 1230, became bishop of Mende in 1285, died in Rome on Feb.1, 1296, and is buried in Santa Maria sopra Minerva.

three parts: (1) ordination, consecration, and blessing of persons, (2) consecration and blessing of things, (3) other celebrations. In addition, he deliberately excluded those celebrations that pertained to an ordinary priest, reserving his book for episcopal ceremonies. As sources, he drew upon the Roman-Germanic Pontifical, the Roman Pontifical of the twelfth century, and the Pontifical of the Roman Curia, in addition to certain local customs. Because of its clarity and ease of use it soon came to dominate, and became the basis of all subsequent editions of the Roman Pontifical.[112]

The Pontificale Romanum: The *editio princeps* of the Roman Pontifical was published in 1485. It was a corrected and up-dated version of the Pontifical of Guillaume Durand, edited by Piccolomini and Burckhard: the same masters of ceremony who produced both a papal ceremonial and an episcopal ceremonial, as was mentioned earlier. This new edition involved suppression of out-dated materials (the expulsion of penitents on Ash Wednesday and their reconciliation on Holy Thursday, for example), the addition of rubrical directives, and the elimination of whatever was not exclusively the domain of bishops. A second edition was published in 1497 by Burckhard and Giacomo de Luzzi, containing various minor modifications. This edition was reprinted several times. Alberto Castellani, a famous editor of liturgical texts (who also produced a ritual, as we shall see below) took in hand a revision of the pontifical (1520) in order to insert once again certain chapters from the Pontifical of Guillaume Durand which had been omitted in the more recent editions. While there were several reprints throughout the sixteenth century, with minor variations, the text remained substantially the same. This *Pontificale Romanum* was promulgated for the entire Latin Church by Pope Clement VIII in 1595. There were some minor changes made by Urban VIII and Benedict XIV, but until Pope Paul VI, the pontifical remained basically that of Piccolomini-Burckhard, which was in substance the Pontifical of Guillaume Durand. In the post-Vatican II liturgical reforms, the various rites that pertain to the bishop were issued in separate fascicles. Thus, after a long history, the pontifical has reverted to the form of *libelli*.

---

[112] For the various pontificals between that of Durand and the *editio princeps* of 1485, cf. Dykmans, *Le Pontifical Romain*.

II. THE PRIEST'S BOOK: THE RITUAL

Introduction: The pontifical described the liturgical rites of great occasions when the bishop was present and presided. The ritual, on the other hand, the priest's book, describes the liturgical rites of everyday occasions in the humble setting of the local parish. Indeed, the local quality of the ritual (before the standardization of the sixteenth century) is one of its most salient characteristics. As such, this book provides priceless information about pastoral practice in a given place and period. At the same time, however, such diversity makes any general classification of texts difficult.[113]

Typology: The ritual contains all the texts necessary for liturgical actions outside of Mass and Office, which is to say all the other sacraments, rituals, and blessings which are not reserved to the bishop. The terminology is extremely variable, the most common names, aside from *rituale*, being *agenda, obsequiale, manuale, sacerdotale*, or *pastorale*. Since baptism is often the first ritual listed, the book is sometimes called a *baptisterium*. From the ninth century onward the parish becomes more and more important as an ecclesiastical entity distinct from the cathedral or local monastery, with subsequent changes in the style of pastoral ministry. There is a new emphasis on presbyteral liturgy (as distinct from episcopal or monastic) in all of its many sacramental forms: thus the need for a book with all the necessary liturgical texts for priestly ministry.

History:
Libelli: When for a given liturgical action, the orations from the sacramentary are put together with the rubrical directives from an ordo, the result is a *libellus* which acts as a kind of ritual. These early *libelli* were compiled mainly for the rites of penance, anointing of the sick, and funerals; these were occasions when the liturgy would not be celebrated in church, where the priest already had the necessary books, but in the home of the sick person, hence the need for a booklet which could be easily carried on such pastoral visits.

[113] Rituals are usually classified according to country or even city of origin: thus Vogel, *ML* 258–60 and Klöckener, "Die Ritualiensammlung," 38–54. For German-speaking lands, cf. M. Probst, *Bibliographie der katholischen Ritualiendrucke des deutschen Sprachbereichs*, LQF 74 (Münster, 1993). For France, cf. J. B. Molin - A. Aussedat-Minvielle, *Répertoire des Rituels et Processionaux imprimés conservé en France* (Paris, 1984).

Juxtaposed books: From the tenth-eleventh centuries a more complete ritual is often bound together with a collectar or a processional.[114] These juxtaposed books came primarily from monasteries, and show the connection between the conventual life and the pastoral care of souls. The monk-priest needed to have a book in which the orations he needed for the Divine Office, the rituals he needed for priestly ministry to his monastic confrères, and the prayers he needed for parish work outside the enclosure were all included. The content of such a book might include: (1) the collectar for Office, (2) the ritual, containing such things as rites for the sick and the dying, the funeral ritual, rites of monastic profession, of baptism, of penance, and of marriage, and (3) the processional, containing the Sunday blessing of holy water and the blessings for the various rooms of the monastery. Rituals were also bound together with sacramentaries, martyrologies, and other books.[115]

"Pure" rituals: From the twelfth century following, rituals independent of any other liturgical book became more common. The monastic influence is still strong, either because the monastery was engaged in pastoral work in the surrounding area or because the monastery had the scriptorium where the book was copied for the local diocesan priest. A well-known example of this type of book is the Ritual of St. Florian. During the thirteenth century, the rituals gradually moved out of the monastic context and became more parish-oriented. One of the reasons for this is the insistence of various diocesan synods which required the parish priest to have a *manuale*.[116] Also during the thirteenth century, as mentioned above, the pontifical excluded those

---

[114] A processional is a book of the prayers and chants which accompany various kinds of processions: the weekly Sunday procession between Terce and conventual Mass (connected with the blessing of various rooms if the context is a monastic one), or occasional processions which took place throughout the year. Cf. Gy, "Collectaire, Rituel, Processional," 466–9 and Palazzo 236–8.

[115] Gamber, *CLLA* II, 566–75. Salmon points out that the oldest juxtaposed rituals in the Vatican Library are the 10th-c. Rituale-Missale Bobiense (Vatic.lat.5768) and the 11th–12th-c. Rituale-Martyrologium (Archivio S. Pietro H 58). Cf. *Les manuscrits*, III, 86 and 60.

[116] The synodal statutes of Paris during the episcopate of Eudes de Sully (1200–1208) required that: *librum qui dicitur manualis habeant singuli sacerdotes parochiales ubi continetur ordo servitii extremae unctionis, catechismi, baptismatis et huiusmodi.* Cf. Palazzo, 203.

liturgical actions which were not reserved exclusively to the bishop. These texts were taken up, then, by the rituals. In the fourteenth century the diocesan bishop took greater responsibility for producing the ritual for his diocese. An example of this is the Ritual of Bishop Henry of Breslau (1301–1319). The fifteenth century continued to produce rituals, varying greatly in content, such that no two were exactly alike.[117] The sixteenth century, in contrast, was a time of standardization.

Printed rituals: Printed rituals before the Tridentine reform were very similar to their manuscript antecedents, but after the Council of Trent, the desire was for uniformity. There are three Italian editions which are in some way precursors of the *Rituale Romanum* of 1614: (1) the *Liber sacerdotalis* of Alberto Castellani (1523),[118] which is conveniently divided into three sections: sacraments, blessings, and processions, (2) the *Sacerdotale* of Samarino (1579) which was based on the work of Castellani, and (3) the *Rituale* of Santori (1584–1602).[119] Santori was commissioned by Pope Gregory XIII (1572–1585) to prepare a ritual which would respond more fully to the pastoral needs of the time and the norms of the Tridentine reform. Santori undertook the project, but the pope died in 1585. His successors Sixtus V (1585–1590) and Clement VIII (1592–1605) took an interest in the work, but Santori himself died in 1602, while the ritual was being printed. Pope Paul V (1605–1621) chose not to use the edition of Santori, but promulgated a simplified version (although using many elements of Santori's work): the *Rituale Romanum* of 1614.[120] However, this ritual was never made obligatory, and thus many local rituals continued to be used. In the twentieth century two new editions of the *Rituale Romanum* were made: one in 1925 by Pius XI, in order to incorporate the necessary changes occasioned by the 1917 Code, and in 1952 by Pius XII, when an appendix containing numer-

---

[117] Salmon, *Les manuscrits*, III, 55–93.

[118] E. Cattanew, "Il Rituale Romano di Alberto Castellani," *Miscellanea Liturgica in onore di S. E. il Card. G. Lercaro*, 2 vol. (Rome, 1967) II, 629–47.

[119] B. Löwenberg, *Das Rituale des Kardinals Julius Antonius Santorius* (Munich, 1937).

[120] B. Löwenberg, "Die Erstausgabe des Rituale Romanum von 1614," *Zeitschrift für katholische Theologie* 66 (1942) 141–7; B. Fischer, "Das Originalmanuskript des Rituale Romanum," *TTZ* 70 (1961) 244f; Idem, "Das Rituale Romanum," *TTZ* 73 (1964) 257ff.

ous blessings was added.[121] As with the pontifical, so also with the ritual: in the post-Vatican II liturgical reforms, the various rites that pertain to the priest were issued in separate fascicles.

CONCLUSION

The study of liturgical books is complex and very rich: books for Mass, for Office, for the good ordering of the liturgy, for the celebration of the sacraments and other rites. The books are many and varied, each one having its own specific typology and history. And yet the multiplicity of liturgical books has as its proper end the unity and beauty of liturgical prayer.

---

[121] P. Jounel, "The Pontifical and the Ritual," *The Church at Prayer: III, The Sacraments* (Collegeville, 1988) 6–8. For a description of the changes in the 1952 edition, see the review by E. Viale in *MD* 34 (1953) 164–7.

Bibliography

INTRODUCTION

Cabrol, F. *The Books of the Latin Liturgy.* Trans. Benedictines of Stanbrook. St. Louis, 1932.

Neuheuser, H. P. *Internationale Bibliographie "Liturgische Bücher"* = *International Bibliography on Liturgical Books.* Munich and New York, 1991.

Nocent, A. "I libri liturgici." *Anàmnesis* 2:129–183.

Palazzo, E. *Le Moyen Âge: Des origines au XIIIe siècle.* Histoire des livres liturgiques. Paris, 1993.

Scicolone, I. "Libri liturgici." *NDL* 701–713.

Sheppard, L. C. *The Liturgical Books.* New York, 1962.

Vogel, C. *Medieval Liturgy: An Introduction to the Sources.* Trans. and rev. W. Storey and N. Rasmussen. Washington, 1986.

Books Used for Mass

I. THE SACRAMENTARY

General Bibliography

Bourque, E. *Étude sur les sacramentaires romains.* 3 vols. Rome, 1948.

Chavasse, A. "Evangéliare, épistolier, antiphonaire et sacramentaire: Les livres romains de la messe, au VIIe e VIIIe siècle." *EO* 6 (1989) 177–255.

Deshusses, J. "Les sacramentaires: État actuel de la recherche." *ALW* 24 (1982) 19–46.

Gamber, K. *Sakramentartypen: Versuch einer Gruppierung der Handschriften und Fragmente bis zur Jahrtausendwende.* TuA 1. Abt., Heft 49/50. Beuron, 1958.

Metzger, M. *Les sacramentaires.* TS 70. Turnhout, 1994.

A. The Verona Sacramentary

Bourque, E. *Étude sur les sacramentaires romains*, 1:63–169. Rome, 1948.

Chavasse, A. "Le sacramentaire dit léonien conservé par le Veronensis LXXXV (80)." *SE* 27 (1984) 151–190.

Hope, D. M. *The Leonine Sacramentary: A Reassessment of Its Nature and Purpose.* Oxford, 1971.

Stuiber, A. *Libelli Sacramentorum Romani: Untersuchungen zur Entstehung des sogenannten Sacramentarium Leonianum.* Bonn, 1950.

B. The Gelasian Sacramentary

Chavasse, A. *Le sacramentaire Gélasien: Sacramentaire presbytéral en usage dans les titres romains au VIIᵉ siècle.* Tournai, 1958.

Coebergh, C. "Le sacramentaire Gélasien ancien: Une compilation de clercs romanisants du VIIᵉ siècle." *ALW* 7 (1961) 45–88.

C. The Gelasian Sacramentaries of the Eighth Century

Chavasse, A. "Le sacramentaire gélasien du VIIIᵉ siècle: Ses deux principales formes." *EphLit* 73 (1959) 249–298.

_____. *Le sacramentaire dans le groupe dit gélasiens du VIIIᵉ siècle.* 2 vols. Instrumenta patristica 14A–14B. Steenbruge, 1984.

Klöckener, M. "Sakramentarstudien zwischen Fortschritt und Sackgass." *ALW* 32 (1990) 207–230.

Moreton, B. *The Eighth-Century Gelasian Sacramentary: A Study in Tradition.* Oxford Theological Monographs. London, 1976.

Puniet, P. de. *Le sacramentaire romain de Gellone.* Rome, 1938.

D. The Gregorian Sacramentary

Chavasse, A. "L'organisation génerale des sacramentaires dits grégoriens." *RSR* 56 (1982) 179–200.

_____. "Le sacramentaire grégorien: Les additions et remaniements introduits dans le témoin P." *Traditio et Progressio: Studi liturgici in onore del Prof. Adrien Nocent, O.S.B.*, 125–148. SA 95. Rome, 1988.

Dehusses, J. *Le sacramentaire Grégorien*, 1:29–79. Fribourg, 1979.

E. The Mixed Gregorians of the Tenth and Eleventh Centuries

Bourque, E. *Étude sur les sacramentaires romains,* 2:251–274, 437–499. Rome, 1948.

Ebner, A. *Quellen und Forschungen zur Geschichte und Kunstgeschichte des Missale Romanum im Mittelalter: Iter Italicum,* 389–394. Freiburg, 1896. Reprint Graz, 1957.

Vogel, C. *Medieval Liturgy: An Introduction to the Sources,* 102–105. Trans. and rev. W. Storey and N. Rasmussen. Washington, 1986.

II. THE LECTIONARY

Chavasse, A. "Les plus anciens types du lectionnaire et de l'antiphonaire romains de la messe." *RB* 62 (1952) 3–94.

_____. "L'Épistolier romain du codex de Wurtzbourgh: Son organisation." *RB* 91 (1981) 280–331.

_____. "L'Evangéliare romain de 6645: Un recueil, sa composition (façons et matériaux)." *RB* 92 (1982) 33–75.

_____. "Aménagements liturgiques, à Rome, au VIIᵉ et au VIIIᵉ siècle." *RB* 99 (1989) 83–102.

_____. "Evangéliare, épistolier, antiphonaire et sacramentaire: Les livres romains de la messe, au VIIᵉ e VIIIᵉ siècle." *EO* 6 (1989) 177–255.

_____. "Après Grégoire le Grand l'organisation des évangélieres au VIIᵉ et au VIIIᵉ siècle." *Rituels: Mélanges offerts au Père Gy, O.P.,* 125–130. Paris, 1990.

_____. *Les lectionnaires romains de la Messe au VIIᵉ et au VIIIᵉ siècle: Sources et dérivés.* 2 vols. SFS 22. Fribourg, 1993.

Frere, W. H. *Studies in Early Roman Liturgy.* Vol. 2, *The Roman Gospel-Lectionary.* ACC 30. Oxford, 1934.

_____. *Studies in Early Roman Liturgy.* Vol. 3, *The Roman Epistle-Lectionary.* ACC 32. Oxford, 1935.

Martimort, A.-G. *Les lectures liturgiques et leurs livres.* TS 64. Turnhout, 1992.

III. THE ANTIPHONAL

Chavasse, A. "Les plus anciens types du lectionnaire et de l'antiphonaire romains de la Messe: Rapports et date." *RB* 62 (1952) 3–94.

_____. "La formation de l'antiphonale missarum." *Bulletin du Comité des Études de Saint-Sulpice* 32 (1961) 29–41.

_____. "Cantatorium et antiphonale missarum: Quelques procédés de confection: dimanches après la Pentecôte: graduels du sanctoral." *EO* 1 (1984) 15–55.

_____. "Evangéliare, épistolier, antiphonaire et sacramentaire: Les livres romains de la messe, au VIIe e VIIIe siècle." *EO* 6 (1989) 177–255.

Graduel Romain, Le: Vol. 2, *Les Sources.* Solesmes, 1957.

Huglo, M. *Les livres du chant liturgique.* TS 52. Turnhout, 1988.

Turco, A. *Il canto gregoriano.* 2 vols. Rome, 1991.

IV. THE CALENDAR

Bugnini, A. *The Reform of the Liturgy (1948–1975),* chap. 21. Trans. M. J. O'Connell. Collegeville, Minn., 1990.

Focke, E., and H. Heinrichs. "Das Kalendarium des Missale Pianum vom Jahre 1570 und seine Tendenzen." *TQ* 120 (1939) 383–400.

Frere, W. H. *Studies in Early Roman Liturgy.* Vol. 1, *The Kalendar.* ACC 28. London, 1930.

Jounel, P. *Le culte des saints dans les basiliques du Latran et du Vatican au douzième siècle,* esp. chap. 1. Rome, 1977.

Righetti, M. *Manuale di storia liturgica,* 1:240–243. 3rd ed. Milan, 1964.

Thurston H. "Calendar." *The Catholic Encyclopedia,* 3:158–166. New York, 1908.

Van Dijk, S.J.P. *The Ordinal of the Papal Court from Innocent III to Boniface VIII and Related Documents.* SF 22. Fribourg, 1975.

V. THE MISSAL

General Studies

Baudot, J. *Le missel plénier.* 2 vols. Paris, 1912.

Baumstark, A. *Missale Romanum: Seine Entwicklung, ihre wichtigsten Urkunden und Probleme.* Eindhoven-Nijmegen, 1929.

Bourque, E. *Étude sur les sacramentaires romains,* 2:439–544. Vatican City, 1949.

Ferreres, J. B. *Historia del Misal Romano.* Barcelona, 1929.

Van Dijk, S. "The Urban and Papal Rites in Seventh and Eighth-Century Rome." *SE* 12 (1961) 411–487.

_____. "The Old-Roman Rite." *Studia Patristica* V:185–205. TU 80. Berlin, 1962.

The Thirteenth Century

Andrieu, M. "Le missel de la chapelle papale à la fin du XIIIe siècle." In *Miscellanea F. Ehrle,* 2:348–376. ST 38. Rome, 1924.

_____. "L'authenticité du *Missel de la chapelle papale.*" *Scriptorium* 9 (1955) 17–34.

Azevedo, E. *Vetus Missale Romanum Monasticum Lateranense.* Rome, 1752.

Chavasse, A. *Les ancêtres du "Missale Romanum" (1570).* AL 20. Rome, 1995.

Gy, P.-M. "L'unification liturgique de l'Occident et la liturgie de la curie romaine." *RSPT* 59 (1975) 601–612.

Kennedy, C. "The Lateran Missal and Some Allied Documents." *MS* 14 (1952) 61–78.

Van Dijk, S. "Three Manuscripts of a Liturgical Reform by John Cajetan Orsini (Nicholas III)." *Scriptorium* 6 (1952) 213–242.

_____. "The Lateran Missal." *SE* 6 (1954) 125–179.

_____. "The Legend of the Missal of the Papal Chapel and the Fact of Cardinal Orsini's Reform." *SE* 8 (1956) 76–142.

_____. "The Authentic Missal of the Papal Chapel." *Scriptorium* 14 (1960) 257–314.

_____. *The Ordinal of the Papal Court from Innocent III to Boniface VIII and Related Documents.* SF 22. Fribourg, 1975.

Van Dijk, S., and J. H. Walker. *The Origins of the Modern Roman Liturgy: The Liturgy of the Papal Court and the Franciscan Order in the Thirteenth Century.* London, 1960.

_____. *The Origins of the Modern Roman Liturgy: The Ordinals by Haymo of Faversham and Related Documents (1243–1307).* 2 vols. London, 1960.

Editio Princeps, Milan 1474

Frutaz, A. P. "Due edizioni rare del "Missale romanum" pubblicato a Milano nel 1482 e nel 1492." *Miscellanea G. Belvederi,* 55–107. Rome, 1954.

Lippe, R. *Missale Romanum Mediolanensis anno 1474.* HBS 17/33. London, 1899/1907.

Missale Romanum 1570

Frutaz, A. P. "Contributo alla storia della riforma del Messale promulgato da san Pio V nel 1570." *Problemi di vita religiosa in Italia nel cinquecento,* 187–214. Padua, 1960.

_____. "Sirleto e la riforma del Messale Romano di S. Pio V." *Regnum Dei: Collectanea Theatina a clericis regularibus edita* 30 (1974) 84–111.

Jedin, H. "Das Konzil von Trient und die Reform des Römischen Messbuches." *Liturgisches Leben* 6 (1939) 30ff.

_____. "Das Konzil von Trient und die Reform der liturgischen Bücher." *Kirche des Glaubens, Kirche der Geschichte,* 2:499–525. Freiburg, 1966.

Missale Romanum 1970

Bugnini, A. *The Reform of the Liturgy (1948–1975)*, chaps. 24–29. Trans. M. J. O'Connell. Collegeville, Minn., 1990.

Fischer, B. "Vom Missale Pius V zum Missale Pauls VI." *LJ* 26 (1976) 2–18.

Books Used for the Liturgy of the Hours

BOOKS FOR THE CHANT

A. The Psalter

Palazzo, E. *Le Moyen Âge: Des origines au XIIIe siècle*, 145–150. Histoire des livres liturgiques. Paris, 1993.

Salmon, P. *Les manuscrits liturgiques latins de la Bibliothèque Vaticane*. Vol. 1, *Psautiers, antiphonaires, hymnaires, collectaires, bréviaires*. ST 251. Vatican City, 1968.

B. Antiphonal

Alfonzo, P. *L'antifonario dell'Ufficio romano*. Subiaco, 1935.

———. *I responsori biblici dell'Ufficio romano*. Lateranum, n.s., an. 2, n. 1. Rome, 1936.

Hesbert, R. J., and R. Provost. *Corpus antiphonalium officii*. 6 vols. Rome, 1963-1979.

Huglo, M. *Les livres du chant liturgique*. TS 52. Turnhout, 1988.

Palazzo, E. *Le Moyen Âge: Des origines au XIIIe siècle*, 145–150. Histoire des livres liturgiques. Paris, 1993.

C. Hymnal

Gneuss, H. *Hymnar und Hymnen im englischen Mittelalter: Studien zur Überlieferung, Glossierung und Übersetzung lateinischer Hymnen in England*. Anglia Buchreihe 12. Tübingen, 1968.

Gy, P.-M. "Le trésor des hymnes." *MD* 173 (1988) 19–40.

Huglo, M. *Les livres du chant liturgique*, 108–110. TS 52. Turnhout, 1988.

Palazzo, E. *Le Moyen Âge: Des origines au XIIIe siècle*, 156–158. Histoire des livres liturgiques. Paris, 1993.

II. BOOKS FOR THE ORATIONS

Gy, P.-M. "Collectaire, rituel, processionnal." *RSPT* 44 (1960) 441–454.

Palazzo, E. *Le Moyen Âge: Des origines au XIIIe siècle*, 159–162. Histoire des livres liturgiques. Paris, 1993.

Salmon, P. *L'Office divin au Moyen Âge: Histoire de la formation du bréviaire du IXe au XVIe siècle*, 23–26, 44–45, 50–60. LO 43. Paris, 1967.

III. BOOKS FOR THE READINGS

A. Scriptural Readings

Marot, H. "La place des lectures bibliques et patristiques dans l'Office latin." *La prière des heures*, 149–165. LO 35. Paris, 1963.

A.-M. Martimort, "Les livres des lectures de l'Office." *Les lectures liturgiques et leurs livres*, 69–76. Turnhout, 1992.

Palazzo, E. *Le Moyen Âge: Des origines au XIIIᵉ siècle*, 162–165. Histoire des livres liturgiques. Paris, 1993.

Righetti, M. *Manuale di storia liturgica*, 2:598–603. 3rd ed. Milan, 1964.

B. Patristic Readings

Barré, H. "Homéliaires, II: Homéliaires latins." *DSp* 7/1:597–606. Paris, 1969.

Grégoire, R. *Les homéliaires du Moyen Âge: Inventaire et analyse des manuscrits.* Rerum ecclesiasticarum documenta. Series maior: Fontes 6. Rome, 1966.

_____. *Homéliaires liturgiques médiévaux: Analyse des manuscrits.* Biblioteca degli Studi Medievali 12. Spoleto, 1980.

Martimort, A.-G. "La lecture patristique dans la liturgie des heures." *Traditio et Progressio*, 311–331. SA 95. Rome, 1988.

_____. *Les lectures liturgiques*, 77–96. TS 64. Turnhout, 1992.

Palazzo, E. *Le Moyen Âge: Des origines au XIIIᵉ siècle*, 166–169. Histoire des livres liturgiques. Paris, 1993.

C. Hagiographical Readings

De Gaiffier, B. "La lecture des Actes des Martyrs dans la prière liturgique en Occident: A propos du passionnaire hispanique." *AB* 72 (1954) 134–166.

Martimort, A-G. *Les lectures liturgiques*, 97–102. TS 64. Turnhout, 1992.

Philippart, G. *Les légendiers latins et autres manuscrits hagiographiques.* TS 24–25. Turnhout, 1977–1985.

Righetti, M. *Manuale di storia liturgica*, 2:608–609. 3rd ed. Milan, 1964.

Salmon, P. *The Breviary Through the Centuries.* Trans. Sister David Mary. Collegeville, Minn., 1962.

_____. *Les manuscrits liturgiques latins de la Bibliothèque Vaticane.* Vol. 4, *L'livres de lectures de l'office, les livres de l'office du chapître, les livres d'heures*, ix–xi. ST 267. Vatican City, 1971.

IV. THE BOOK FOR THE CHAPTER OFFICE

Chapter Office

Lemaître, J.-L. "Liber capituli: Le livre du chapitre, des origines au XVIᵉ siècle: L'exemple français." *Memoria: Der geschichtliche Zeugniswert des liturgischen Gedenkens im Mittelalter*, 625–648. Munich, 1984.

Salmon, P. *Les manuscrits liturgiques latins de la Bibliothèque Vaticane.* Vol. 4, *L'livres de lectures de l'office, les livres de l'office du chapître, les livres d'heures,* xi–xiii. ST 267. Vatican City, 1971.

Martyrology

De Gaiffier, B. "De l'usage et de la lecture du martyrologe: Témoignages antérieurs au XIᵉ siècle." *AB* 79 (1961) 40–59.

Dubois, J. *Les martyrologes du moyen âge latin.* TS 26, Turnhout 1978.

_____. *Martyrologes d'Usuard au martyrologe romain.* Abbeville, 1990.

Quentin, H. *Les martyrologes historiques du moyen âge: Étude sur la formation du martyrologe romain.* Paris, 1908.

Necrology

Huyghebaert, N. *Les documents nécrologiques.* TS 4. Turnhout, 1972.

V. THE BREVIARY

General Studies

Baudot, J. *The Roman Breviary: Its Sources and History.* London, 1909.

Bäumer, S. *Geschichte des Breviers.* Freiburg-im-Breisgau, 1895. French translation: *Histoire du bréviaire,* Rome, 1967; reprint 1967.

Battifol, P. *Histoire du bréviaire romain.* Paris, 1911.

Brinktrine, J. *Das römische Brevier.* Paderborn, 1932.

Leroquais, V. *Les bréviaires manuscrits des bibliothèques publiques de France,* 1:i–cxxxiii. Paris, 1934.

Martimort, A.-G. "La prière des heures." *EP 1983,* 4:167–293.

Piault, B. *La prière de l'Église, le bréviaire romain.* Paris, 1958.

Pinell J. "Liturgia delle ore." *Anamnesis* 5. Genoa, 1991.

Raffa, V. *La liturgia delle ore.* Brescia, 1959.

Righetti, M. *Manuale di storia liturgica,* 2:469–558. 3rd ed. Milan, 1964.

Salmon, P. "Aux origines du bréviaire romain." *MD* 27 (1951) 114–136.

_____. "La prière des heures." *EP 1961,* 789–876.

_____. *The Breviary Through the Centuries.* Trans. Sister David Mary. Collegeville, Minn., 1962.

_____. *L'Office divin au Moyen Âge: Histoire de la formation du bréviaire du IXᵉ au XVIᵉ siècle.* LO 43. Paris, 1967.

Sanchez, Aliseda, C. *El breviario romano.* Madrid, 1951.

The Thirteenth Century

Abate, G. "Il primitivo breviario francescano (1224–1227). *Miscellanea Francescana* 60 (1960) 47–240.

LeCarou, A. *L'office divin chez les Frères Mineurs aux XIIIᵉ siècle.* Paris, 1928.

Van Dijk, S.J.P., and J. H. Walker. *The Origins of the Modern Roman Liturgy: The Liturgy of the Papal Court and the Franciscan Order in the Thirteenth Century.* Westminster, Md., 1960.

The Sixteenth Century

Jungmann, J. A. "Perché la riforma del Breviario del Card. Quinonez è fallita?" *Eredità liturgica e attualità pastorale*, 310–330. Rome, 1962. Originally published as *Liturgisches Erbe und Pastorale Gegenwart.* Innsbruck, 1960.

Legg, J. W. *Breviarium Romanum a Francisco Cardinali Quignonio editum et recognitum iuxta editionem Venetiis A.D. 1535 impressam.* Canterbury, 1888. Reprint Farnborough, 1970.

_____. *The Second Recension of the Quignon Breviary.* HBS 35, 42. London, 1908, 1911.

Opfermann, B. "Das Reformbrevier des Kardinals Quinonez." *Bibel und Liturgie* 20 (1952) 307ff.

Vilnet, J. "Les réformes du bréviaire au XVIᵉ siècle." *L'ami du clergé* 64 (1954) 305–318.

Liturgia Horarum 1971

Ashworth, H. "The New Patristic Lectionary." *EphLit* 85 (1971) 417–33.

Braga, C. "Dal Breviarium alla Liturgia Horarum." *EphLit* 85 (1971) 184–205.

Gibert, J. "La nouvelle distribution du Psautier dans la Liturgia Horarum." *EphLit* 87 (1973) 325–382.

Pascher, J. "Il nuovo ordinamento della salmodia nella liturgia romana delle Ore." *Liturgia delle Ore: Documenti ufficiali e studi*, 161–184. Quaderni di rivista liturgica 14. Turin, 1972.

_____. "Dal Breviarium del Quignonez alla Liturgia delle Ore di Paolo VI." *Liturgia delle Ore: Documenti ufficiali e studi*, 289–363. Quaderni di rivista liturgica 14. Turin, 1972. 289–363.

_____. "Le intercessioni di Lodi e Vespri." *EphLit* 86 (1972) 41–60.

Pinell, J. *Las oraciones del salterio "per annum" en el nuevo libro de la Liturgia de las Horas.* BEL 2. Rome, 1974.

Raffa, V. *La nuova Liturgia delle Ore: Presentazione storica, teologica e pastorale.* Nuova collana liturgica 3. Milan, 1971.

_____. "L'ufficio divino del tempo dei Carolingi e il breviario di Innocenzo III confrontati con la liturgia delle ore di Paolo VI." *EphLit* 85 (1971) 206–259.

Books Used for the Good Ordering of the Liturgy

I. ORDINES

Text

Andrieu, M. Les *"Ordines Romani" du haut moyen âge*. 5 vols. Spicilegium Sacrum Lovaniense 11, 23, 24, 28, 29. Louvain, 1931–1961.

Studies

Martimort, A.-G. Les *"ordines," les ordinaires et les cérémoniaux. TS* 56. Turnhout, 1991.

Palazzo, E. Le Moyen Âge: Des origines au XIIIe siècle, 187–196. Histoire des livres liturgiques. Paris, 1993.

Vogel, C. *Medieval Liturgy: An Introduction to the Sources*, 135–224. Trans. and rev. W. Storey and N. Rasmussen. Washington, 1986.

II. ORDINALS

Martimort, *Les "Ordines,"* 49–85; Palazzo, 228–35.

III. CEREMONIALS

Text

Dykmans, M. *Le cérémonial papal de la fin du Moyen Age à la Renaissance*. 4 vols. Bibliothèque de l'Institut historique belge de Rome 24–27. Brussels-Rome, 1977–1985.

_____. *L'oeuvre de Patrizi Piccolomini ou le cérémonial papal de la première Renaissance*. 2 vols. ST 293–294. Vatican City, 1980–1982.

Studies

Martimort, A.-G. Les *"ordines," les ordinaires et les cérémoniaux*, 89–110. Turnhout, 1991.

Palazzo, E. Le Moyen Âge: Des origines au XIIIe siècle, 239–240. Histoire des livres liturgiques. Paris, 1993.

Books Used by the Celebrant for Sacraments and Other Rites

I. THE BISHOP'S BOOK: THE PONTIFICAL

Text

Andrieu, M. *Le pontifical romain au Moyen-Âge*: 1, *Le pontifical romain du XIIe siècle*; 2, *Le pontifical de la Curie romaine au XIIIe siècle*; 3, *Le pontifical de Guillaume Durand*; 4, *Tables alphabétiques*. ST 86, 87, 88, 99. Vatican City, 1939–1941.

Vogel, C., and R. Elze. *Le pontifical romano-germanique du dixième siècle.* 3 vols. ST 226, 227, 269. Vatican City, 1963–1972.

Studies

Dykmans, M. *Le pontifical Romain révisé au XVe siècle.* Studi e testi 311. Vatican City, 1985.

Leroquais, V. *Les pontificaux manuscrits des bibliothèques publiques de France,* 1:i–cliv. Paris 1937.

Palazzo, E. *Le Moyen Âge: Des origines au XIIIe siècle,* 204–220. Histoire des livres liturgiques. Paris, 1993.

Vogel, C. *Medieval Liturgy: An Introduction to the Sources,* 225–256. Trans. and rev. W. Storey and N. Rasmussen. Washington, 1986.

II. THE PRIEST'S BOOK: THE RITUAL

Texts

Castellani, A. *Liber sacerdotalis . . . .* Venice, 1523.

Franz, A. *Das Rituale von St. Florian aus dem zwölften Jahrhundert.* Freiburg im Breisgau, 1904.

_____. *Das Rituale des Bischofs Heinrich I von Breslau.* Freiburg im Breisgau, 1912.

Rituale Romanum. Rome, 1614.

Santori, J. A. *Rituale Sacramentorum Romanum.* Rome, 1584–1602.

Studies

Franz, A. *Die kirchlichen Benediktionen im Mittelalter.* 2 vols. Freiburg im Breisgau, 1909. Reprint Graz, 1961.

Gy, P.-M. "Collectaire, Rituel, Processionnal." *RSPT* 44 (1960) 441–454.

Klöckener, M. "Die Ritualiensammlung in der Bibliothek des deutschen Liturgischen Instituts." *LJ* 44 (1994) 33–61.

Molin, J. B. "Introduction à l'étude des Rituels anciens." *Bulletin du Comité des Études* 3 (1959) 675–692.

_____. "Pour une bibliographie des Rituels: Leurs divers intitulés." *EphLit* 73 (1959) 218–224.

Palazzo, E. *Le Moyen Âge: Des origines au XIIIe siècle,* 197–203. Histoire des livres liturgiques. Paris, 1993.

Vogel, C. *Medieval Liturgy: An Introduction to the Sources,* 257–265. Trans. and rev. W. Storey and N. Rasmussen. Washington, 1986.

16

Liturgical Books of the Non-Roman West

Not all Western liturgies have evolved in the same way. Some have developed themselves fully, while others never evolved completely. We cannot establish any concrete characteristics common to all the liturgies because the degree of evolution varies greatly from one liturgy to another. Some liturgies had scarcely developed when their evolution process was abruptly interrupted.

The liturgical books are a manifestation of this evolution process; some liturgies have a great abundance of liturgical production, while others are almost without documentation. In this article we will study the liturgical books of each of the non-Roman Western liturgies.

AFRICAN LITURGY

In spite of the fact that no liturgical books of the African liturgy have survived, there are some authors who, indirectly and above all through the works of St. Augustine, have nevertheless presented some fragments of the Lectionaries and a *laus cerei*, always within the realm of the hypothesis.

Thus, Godu, Bishop, and Willis have proposed some fragments of a lectionary;[1] Verbraken believes he is able to identify a *laus cerei* for the Easter Vigil among the sermons of Augustine.[2] This is all the in-

---

[1] G. Godu, *Lectionarium ecclesiae Hipponensis secundem Augustinum: DACL* 5/1, 857; W-L. Bishop, *The African Rite: JThS* 13 (1912) 263–4; G-G. Willis, *St. Augustine's Text Lectionary* = Alcuin Club 44 (London, 1962).

[2] P. Verbraken, *Una laus cerei africaine: RBén* 70 (1960) 301–13.

formation that we have of any possible lectionaries and liturgical African texts.

CELTIC LITURGY
Although the Celtic liturgy has not developed fully like other Western liturgies, it nevertheless has left us some liturgical books.

Sacramentaries
The Stowe Missal is the most representative sacramentary, although it is basically a Roman book with Gallican influences.[3] The Fulda Missal is another example of the Celtic liturgy, and is like the Stowe Missal. We also should cite the Missal of Corpus Christi College of Oxford.[4]

In addition to these missals, a considerable amount of sacramentary fragments also exist, like those of St. Gallen, Colmar, Reichenau, and Piazzenza.

The Gospel Books
Many Gospel books exist, with ages ranging from the second half of the seventh century until the eighth and ninth centuries.

Divine Office
In this area we have the psalter of St. Columba. This manuscript is important because it contains the titles of the psalms as well as some liturgical notes.

In this section of the Divine Office we also should mention the Antiphonary of Bangor,[5] and a book of hymns.[6]

Pontificals
Of this genre of liturgical books we only have some remains of the Celtic liturgy that are worth citing.[7]

---

[3] F-E. Warren (Ed.), *The Stowe Missal* = HBS 32 (London, 1920).

[4] F-E. Warren (Ed.), *The Manuscript Irish Missal of Corpus Christi College (Oxford)* (London, 1879).

[5] F-E. Warren (Ed.), *The Antiphonary of Bangor* = HBS 10 (1895).

[6] J-H. Bernard - A. Atkinson, *The Irish Liber Hymnorum* = HBS 13-14 (London, 1897–1898).

[7] L. Brou, *Le fragment liturgique Colmar 144 reste d'un pontifical irlandais du VIIIe. siècle: ButLitEc* 54 (1955) 65–71.

AMBROSIAN LITURGY

Writing an account of the Ambrosian liturgical books is arduous work because only a small portion of them are edited and it is impossible to follow the history and evolution of the manuscripts. This is due to the fact that the manuscripts from before the ninth century have been lost for reasons not having to do with the liturgy (invasions, moving to a different town, humidity of the area, etc.).

Sacramentaries

With the Ambrosian liturgy we not only should mention the sacramentaries, but the plenary missals as well, because in addition to the prayer texts they also contain readings and allusions to the songs. The edited manuscripts are from the ninth and tenth centuries. The unedited manuscripts are from the ninth to the twelfth century.

The oldest edited sacramentary is that of Bergamo,[8] from the year 850. From this same century comes the Sacramentary of St. Simpliciano,[9] from the tenth century are the Sacramentaries of Biasca[10] and Ariberto,[11] and finally, from the eleventh century we have the Triplex Sacramentary, which is a mixed sacramentary in which the Gelasian, Gregorian, and Ambrosian elements merge together.[12]

Lectionary

There are three kinds of lectionaries: the *capitulare lectionum*, the *capitulare epistolarum*, and the *capitulare evangeliorum*. To these we should

---

[8] P. Cagin (Ed.), *Codex Sacramentorum Bergomensis* = Auctarium Solesmense (Solesmes, 1900) 1–176; A. Paredi (Ed), *Sacramentarium Bergomense* = Monumenta Bergomensia VI (Bergamo, 1962).

[9] J. Frei (Ed.), *Das ambrosianische Sakramentar D 3-3 aus dem mailändischen Metropolitankapitel. Eine textkritische und redaktionsgeschichtliche Untersuchung der mailändische Sakramentartradition* = Corpus Ambrosiano Liturgicum 3: LQF 56 (Münster, 1974).

[10] O. Heiming (Ed.), *Das ambrosianische Sakramentar von Biasca* = Corpus Ambrosiano Liturgicum 2: LQF 51 (Münster, 1969).

[11] A. Paredi (Ed.), *Il Sacramentario de Ariberto*, in AA. VV., *Miscellanea Adriano Bernareggi* = Monumenta Bergomensia 1 (Bergamo, 1958) 327–488.

[12] O. Heiming (Ed.), *Das Sacramentarium Triplex. Die Handschrift C 43 des Zentralbibliothek Zürich* = Corpus Ambrosiano Liturgicum 1: LQF 49 (Münster, 1969).

317

add the Passion narratives, because in the feasts of the saints instead of reading from Book of the Prophets, the *lectio hagiographica* was read.

There are several editions of the Ambrosian Lectionary as a whole.[13] Besides these, other editions also exist that correspond to the triple division of the lectionary. Thus, of the *capitulare lectionum* there is an edition of a manuscript from the sixth and seventh centuries, for the section of epistles there is another edition,[14] and there is an edition of the gospels as well.[15]

Antiphonaries

In addition to the edited antiphonaries, above all in the sacramentaries, complete antiphonaries exist that contain the songs of the Mass and Office. Other antiphonaries only contain the antiphons for the Mass and for Vespers. The edition of the texts is found in the edition of Magistretti.[16]

Ordines

Although the term *ordines* is maintained, in the Ambrosian liturgy this term mainly referred to the celebration of Mass, but did not exclude other celebrations, like those of the Office. The most represen-

---

[13] P. Cagin (Ed.), *Lectionarium Bergomense* - Auctarium Solesmense (Solesmes, 1900) 187–192; this Lectionary also was edited by A. Paredi, *Sacramentarium Bergomense* - Monumenta Bergomensia 6 (Bergamo, 1962) 28-34; in addition we have information of a *corpus lectionum* placed apart in the section on the Master of Ceremonies, these readings were edited by P. Gagin, *Codex Sacramentorum Bergomensis. Accedunt tres indiculi sive Capitularia lectionum, Epistolarum et Evangeliorum antiqua* - Auctarium Solesmense 1 (Solesmes, 1900) 193–207.

[14] H. Quentin (Ed.), *Capitulare epistolarum Sancti Pauli*: RBén 28 (1911) 259-266; this edition was reproduced by G. Godu in: *DACL* 5/1 (Paris 1922); afterwards he again edited this manuscript A. Dold, *Die in Cod. Vat. Reg. lat.9 vorgeheftete Liste paulinischen Lesungen für die Messfeier* - TuA 35 (Beuron 1944).

[15] G. Morin (Ed.), *Un système inédit de lectures liturgiques en usage au VII/VIII siècle dans une église de la Haute Italie* :RBén 20 (1903) 375-388; this edition was reproduced by G. Godu in *DACL* 5/1 (Paris, 1922) 883-94; we also have an edition of an old gospel, N. Ghiglione (Ed.), *L'evangeliario purpureo di Sarezzano (s.VIII)* - Fontes Ambrosiani 75 (Venice, 1984).

[16] M. Magistretti (Ed.), *Manuale ambrosianum ex codice s. XI olim in usum Canonicae Vallis Travaliae* (Milan, 1904) 1–462.

tative manuscript is that of Beroldus,[17] to which we should also add the edition of the *Manuale Ambrosianum*.[18]

Divine Office
The already cited editions of the *Manuale* and the manuscript of Beroldus contain the section of the Ambrosian Divine Office.

Pontifical
The pontifical is a book that contains the celebration of the sacraments and of the sacramentals.[19]

Printed Missals
There are six incunable editions of the Ambrosian Missal, which range from the year 1475 to 1499. Starting in the sixteenth century the editions multiplied. We will cite only the edition of Puteobonelli of 1751, reedited some years later by Visconti.[20] From our century we should cite the edition of Cardinal Ferrari[21] and that of Cardinal Schuster, which was the last edition before the reform.[22]

Finally, the rite was revised according to the spirit of the Vatican II liturgical reform, and from this revision came the new Ambrosian Missal.[23]

[17] M. Magistretti (Ed.), *Beroldus sive ecclesiae ambrosianae mediolanensis kalendarium et ordines s. XII* (Milan, 1894).

[18] M. Magistretti (Ed.), *Manuale Ambrosianum* II-III=Monumenta Veteris Liturgiae Ambrosianae 2–3 (Milan, 1904–1905).

[19] M. Magistretti (Ed.), *Pontificale in usum ecclesiae mediolanensis necnon Ordines Ambrosiani ex codicibus saec IX-XV* = Monumenta Veteris Liturgiae Ambrosianae 1 (Milan, 1897).

[20] *Missale Ambrosianum. Joseph Cardinalis Puteobonelli Archiepiscopi auctoritate recognitum jussu Philippi Archiepiscopi novissime impressum. Typis Galeatiorum Impressorum Archiepiscopalium* (Milan, 1795).

[21] *Missale Ambrosianum ex Decreto Pii IX p. m. restitutum iussu SS. D. N. Leonis PP. XIII recognitum, Andreae Caroli cardinalis Ferrari Archiepiscopi auctoritate editum* (Milan, 1902).

[22] *Missale Ambrosianum iuxta Ritum Sanctae Ecclesiae Mediolanensis. Editio quinta post Typicam* (Milan, 1954).

[23] *Missale Ambrosianum. Iuxta ritum sanctae Ecclesiae Mediolanensis. Ex decreto Sacrosancti Oecumenici Concilii Vaticani II instauratum, auctoritate Ioannis Colombo, Sanctae Romanae Ecclesiae Presbyteri Cardinalis, Archiepiscopi Mediolanensis promulgatum* (Milan, 1981).

GALLICAN LITURGY

The sacramentaries and the lectionaries are the only books of the Gallican liturgy that have survived until our time. No testimony remains of the liturgical books that contain the other celebrations, like that of the Divine Office, the sacraments, etc.

Sacramentary

It is not possible to talk of a genuine or pure sacramentary in the Gallican Rite. All have been influenced by the Roman Rite, and for this reason the Roman elements and the purely Gallican elements are mixed in the sacramentaries.

The main Gallican Sacramentaries are: the *Missale Gothicum*,[24] the Bobbio Missal,[25] the *Missale Gallicanum Vetus*,[26] and the *Missale Francorum*.[27] All conserve the *ordo* of the Gallican Mass, although there is no uniformity among them; thus in the Bobbio Missal, the order of the Mass ends with the preface because this Missal adopts the Roman canon. The *Gallicanum Vetus* rarely includes the *post sanctus* and the *collectio post secreta,* but although the degree of Romanization of the *Gallicanum Vetus* is much more elevated than that of the Bobbio, it nevertheless offers us some authentically Gallican formulas for Holy Thursday, Good Friday, and the Easter Vigil. The degree of romanization of the *Missale Francorum* is so great that it does not even conserve the *ordo* of the Gallican Mass.

The name that we give to these liturgical books, "missal," does not describe the content well. It would be better to speak of a plenary book, because the name "missal" is given to those books that, in addition to the prayer text, also contain the readings. These liturgical books only contain the liturgical prayer texts. In addition to these

---

[24] L.-C. Mohlberg (Ed.), *Missale Gothicum* = RED. Series Maior. Fontes 5 (Rome, 1961).

[25] E.-A. Lowe (Ed.), *The Bobbio Missal. A Gallican Mass-Book* = HBS 58 (London, 1920).

[26] L.-C. Mohlberg (Ed.), *Missale Gallicanum Vetus* = RED. Series Maior. Fontes 3 (Rome, 1958).

[27] L.-C. Mohlberg (Ed.), *Missale Francorum* = RED. Series Maior. Fontes 2 (Rome, 1957).

missals we have a series of liturgical texts that are fragments of the Gallican prayer texts.[28]

The time span of these manuscripts is from the sixth century to the eighth. The oldest missal is the palimpsest of St. Gallen, and the most recent are the *Missale Gallicanum Vetus,* the Bickell fragment, and the *Missale Francorum,* all of which are from the second half of the eighth century.

Lectionary

The Gallican Lectionary is represented, more than anything else, by the palimpsest of Wolfenbüttel[29] and the manuscript of Luxueil.[30] To these we should add a number of shorter fragments and a list of pericopes, but the two cited lectionaries are the most complete.[31] The oldest document of the Gallican liturgy and the Western Latin liturgies is the palimpsest of Wolfenbüttel.

Both the Lectionary of Wolfenbüttel and that of Luxueil, each of which represent different traditions, agree about proposing three readings for the celebration of Mass: the first from the Old Testament, the second from the New Testament, and the third from the gospel.

HISPANIC LITURGY

The Gallican liturgical books are not abundant, as we have just seen, and we can reduce the liturgical books to just two kinds, the sacra-

---

[28] Among these fragments are found three palimpsests edited by A. Dold, *Palimpsest. Studien I - TuA* 45 (Beuron 1955); A. Dold - L. Eizenhofer, *Das irische Palimpsestsakramentar in Clm 14429 der Staatsbibliothek München - TuA* 43 (Beuron 1952); and two additional fragments of liturgical prayer texts edited by L. Eizenhofer, *Die Mone-Messen,* L.-C. Mohlberg, *Missale Gallicanum Vetus.* oc. 135–8; G. Bickell, *Ein Neues Fragment einer gallikanischen Weihnachtsmesse,* L.-C. Mohlberg, *Missale Gallicanum Vetus.* oc 95–6.

[29] A. Dold (Ed.), *Das älteste Liturgiebuch der lateinischen Kirche = TuA* 26/28 (Beuron, 1926).

[30] P. Salmon (Ed.), *Le lectionnaire de Luxueil = CBL* 7 (Rome, 1944).

[31] H.-J. White (Ed.), *The four Gospels =* Old Latin Biblical Texts. No III (Oxford, 1888) LIII-LV; A. Dold (Ed.), *Zwei Bobbienser Palimpseste mit frühesten Vulgatatext = TuA* 19/20 (Beuron, 1931) 64–66; G. Morin (Ed.), *Le lectionnaire mérovingien de Schlettstadt avec fragments du texte oriental des Actes: RBén* 25 (1908) 161–6; A. Dold (Ed.), *Die im Codex Vat. Reg. Lat. 9 Vorgeheftete liste Paulinischer Lesungen für die Messfeier = TuA* 35 (Beuron, 1944); D. DeBruyne (Ed.), *Les notes liturgiques du ms. 134 de la cathèdrale de Trèves: RBén* 33 (1921) 46–52.

mentary and the lectionary. The Hispanic liturgy has, on the contrary, an abundance of liturgical sources for all kinds of celebrations: Mass, Office, sacraments, benedictions, etc.

Lectionary

The lectionary in the Hispanic liturgy is called *Liber Commicus*. According to St. Julian of Toledo it should be called *commatus*, derived from *comma*, which means fragment. It is the book that gathers the pericopes (fragments) from the Bible that should be proclaimed at Mass. The *Liber Commicus* is mainly represented by five manuscripts, but other fragments of this lectionary exist as well.[32]

During Lent the *Liber Commicus*, in addition to the readings of the Mass, also carry the readings of the Cathedral Office, since during this time of the liturgical year there is a correlation between the readings of Mass and Office.

The composition of the *Liber Commicus* is mixed in the sense that the sanctoral is mixed with the temporal. The lectionary begins with the first Sunday of Advent and ends with the feast of the beheading of St. John the Baptist. The lectionary continues with the readings for the Masses of saints, followed by readings for some votive Masses and rituals, and concludes with the readings of thirty-one Sundays *De quotidiano*.

We should also mention that not all five manuscripts contain all of the readings for the whole liturgical year. Some of them are incomplete, but since the sources coincide in showing a similarly structured book, we are able to identify a complete lectionary.

The manuscripts of the *Liber Commicus* represent tradition A. The reading system of tradition B is found in the plenary missal edited by Cisneros.

Sacramentary (Liber Manuale)

This book, like the Roman Sacramentary, contains the nine liturgical prayer forms for the celebration of the Eucharist. The *post Gloriam* and the *completuriae* probably existed apart from each other. When

---

[32] G. Morin (Ed.), *Liber Commicus sive lectionarius Missae quo Toletana Ecclesia ante annos mille et duecentos utebatur* = Anecdota Maredsolana I (Maredsous, 1893); J. Perez de Urbel - A. Gonzalez y Ruiz-Zorrilla (Eds.), *Liber Commicus* = MHS. Series Liturgica 2-3 (Madrid, 1950–1955).

the plenary missals were made, these prayers were placed in their respective places. Only one example of this manuscript has been conserved, the 35.3 of the capitular library of Toledo.[33]

Antiphonary

This book includes the songs of the Cathedral office feasts and the songs for the celebration of Mass. We only have one example of this book, manuscript 8 of the Cathedral of Leon.[34]

Liber misticus

On the basis of the antiphonary, which contained the songs for Office and Mass, the plenary books were formed. These books were called *misticus*, a word derived from *mistus - mixtus*. The books are composed of the feast day prayer book, the hymnal, the antiphonary, the *Liber Commicus*, and the *Manuale*. Dom Ferotin gives them a name that describes them perfectly: *Officia et missae*. Because of the abundance of material, these books are divided in four parts: (a) from the first Sunday of Advent until Sunday *In carnes tollendas*; (b) Lent; (c) from Easter until Pentecost; and (d) the feasts of the Saints from June to November. There are no exact boundaries among the parts.

Liber orationum festivus

This book contains the liturgical prayer texts of the Cathedral Office. In the registry of the liturgical books donated to the Sahagun Monastery (960), a clear distinction is made between the feast-day prayer book and another prayer book that has the name of *psalmogravus* or *psalmographus*.

In addition to the conclusive *completuriae* of the Matins and Vespers, the feast-day prayer book contains the prayers that accompany the antiphons and responsories of Matins and the lesser hours of the penitential days, as well as the blessings. Two prayer book manuscripts exist, the oldest is the codex. LXXXIX of the capitular library of Verona, probably copied in Tarragon, and the other is

---

[33] M. Ferotin (Ed.), *Le Liber Mozarabicus Sacramentorum, et les manuscrits mozarabes* = MEL 6 (Paris, 1912); J. Janini (Ed.), *Liber Missarum de Toledo I* = Instituto de Estudios Visigótico-Mozárabes de Toledo. Serie Liturgica. Fuentes III (Toledo, 1982) 1–433.

[34] L. Brou-J. Vives, (Eds.), *Antifonario Visigótico Mozárabe de la catedral de León* = MHS. Series liturgica 5 (Barcelona/Madrid, 1959).

from the ninth century, copied in Silos, which today is in the British Museum add. 30.852.[35]

Psalterium - Liber Canticorum - Liber Himnorum
The antiphonary and the prayer book were not sufficient for the celebration of the Office; other repertories were necessary. These are the psalter, the book containing the psalms, the book of the Old Testament canticles for Matins, and the hymn book. There was a fairly well-spread tendency to regroup these three books (the psalter, the canticles, and the hymnal) into one single volume.[36]

Liber Orationum Psalmographus
P. Jordi Pinell reconstructed this Office book, which contains four series of psalm collections. These collections were used in the Cathedral Office, mostly in the non-feast day Office. A large part of the texts that compose this book were found scattered throughout the psalters that held the antiphones and the collections.[37]

The Passion Narrative
The Passion Narrative is a book for the liturgical celebrations of Office and Mass, because in the celebrations of the martyrs the story of their passion was read in Office and concluded in Mass.[38]

Liber Sermonum
This book contained the patristic homilies that were read after the gospel. Only one example exists in the British Museum add. 30.853, from the end of the ninth century. Using the title Homiliae Toletanae, G. Morin published this manuscript in his edition of Liber Commicus.

Liber Horarum
This was the plenary book that gathered the necessary formulas for the monastic celebration of Office, although it had to be completed with the psalter, the Liber Canticorum, and the Liber Hymnorum. Two

[35] J. Vives (Ed.), *Oracional Visigótico* = MHS Series Liturgica 1 (Barcelona, 1946).

[36] C. Blume, *Hymnodia Gothica. Mozarabischen Hymnen des altspanischen Ritus* = Analecta Hymnica Medii Aevi 27 (Leipzig, 1897), reedición (Frankfurt, 1961); M. Gilson (Ed.), *The Moazarabic Psalter* = HBS 30 (London, 1905).

[37] J. Pinell (Ed.), *Liber orationum psalmographus* = MHS. Series Liturgica 9 (Barcelona-Madrid, 1972).

[38] A. Fabrega (Ed.), *Pasionario Hispánico (siglos VII–XI)* = MHS. Series Liturgica 1-2 (Barcelona, 1953).

manuscripts of this book exist: the manuscript 7 of Silos, and the other is in the capitular library of Toledo 33.3.[39]

The Liber Ordinum

There are two kinds of *Liber Ordinum*, the *Sacerdotal* and the *Pontifical*. This book contains: (a) the ritual itself; (b) a compilation of the celebrations of the Triduum; (c) an appendix of votive Masses and Masses of devotional character.

This book is found in manuscripts 3 and 4 of Silos, and in the Emilianense 56. Manuscript 4 of Silos and the Emilianense correspond to the pontifical, and manuscript 3 of Silos corresponds to the sacerdotal.[40]

Liber Precum

Among the names listed in the old catalogs we find the *Liber Precum*, which is a book that cannot be identified with complete certainty, but it was probably a book that held the rhythmic prayers.

Printed Liturgical Books

Cardinal Cisneros, promoted to the Diocese of Toledo in 1495, was aware of the Hispanic liturgy's value, although it was in a state of great decadence because it lacked modern liturgical books. He ordered Canon Ortiz to prepare the edition of the Missal[41] and the breviary[42] that were published under his authority. For this edition of the missal and the breviary, Ortiz referred to the *Libri mistici*. In 1775

---

[39] This manuscript has been published in part by J. Pinell, *Las horas vigiliares del oficio monacal hispanico* - Liturgica 3 (Montserrat, 1966) 197–340. The critical edition of the remaining part of this manuscript, that is to say, the diurnal hours, has been presented as a doctoral thesis in the Pontifical Liturgical Institute, J-J. Flores, *Las horas diurnas del "Liber Horarum" de Silos. Introduccion y edicion critica* (Rome, 1995).

[40] M. Ferotin (Ed.), *Le Liber Ordinum en usage dans l'Eglise wisigothique et mozarabe d'Espagne du cinquième au onzième siècle* = MEL 5 (Paris, 1904); J. Janini (Ed.), *Liber Ordinum Episcopal* = Studia Silensia 15 (Abadía de Silos, 1991); J. Janini (Ed.), *Liber Ordinum Sacerdotal* = Studia Silensia 7 (Abadía de Silos, 1981).

[41] *Missale Mixtum secundum regulam beati Isidori dictum Mozarabes. Editado por el canónigo Alfonso Ortíz, por mandato del Cardenal D. Francisco Jiménez de Cisneros, Arzobispo de Toledo. Impreso en Toledo el mes de enero del año 1.500.*

[42] *Breviarium secundum regulam beati Isidori. Editado por el canónigo A. Ortíz, por mandato del Cardenal D. Francisco Jiménez de Cisneros, Arzobispo de Toledo. Impreso en Toledo en 1502.*

a new edition of the Missal came out in Rome, prepared by A. Lesley. This edition is reproduced in the PL.[43] In 1776 Cardinal Lorenzana made a new edition of the breviary, which was published in Madrid and also reproduced in the PL.[44] Some years later Cardinal Lorenzana also wrote a new edition of the missal.[45]

After Vatican II, in agreement with number 4 of the *SC*, and following the norms of the conciliar liturgical reform, Cardinal D. Marcelo Gonzalez Martin, primate of Spain, revised the missal another time. It was published in four volumes, two for the liturgical prayer texts, and two for the lectionary.[46]

[43] *Missale Mixtum secundum regulam beati Isidori dictum Mozarabes:* PL 85.

[44] *Breviarium Gothicum secundum regulam beatissimi Isidori:* PL 86.

[45] *Missale Gothicum secundum regulam Beati Isidori Hispalensis episcopi, iussu Cardinalis Francisci Ximenii de Cisneros, in usum mozarabum prius editum, denuo opera et impensa Eminentissimi Domini Cardinalis Francisci Antonii Lorenzanae recognitum et revissum. Ad Excellentiss. et Eminentiss. Principem et D. D. Ludovicum Borbonium archiepiscopum Toletanum, Hispaniarum Primatem. Romae, Anno MDCCCIV. Apud Antonium Fulgonium.*

[46] *Missale Hispano-Mozarabicum I-II* (Spanish Bishops' Conference, Archbishop of Toledo 1991–1994); *Liber Commicus I-II* (Spanish Bishops' Conference, Archbishop of Toledo 1991–1995).

Bibliography

African Liturgy

Gamber, K. *Codices liturgici Latini antiquiores,* 11–24. SFS 1. Freiburg, 1968.
_____. *Codices liturgici Latini antiquiores, Supplementum,* 39–49. SFS 1A. Freiburg, 1988.

Celtic Liturgy

Gamber, K. *Codices liturgici Latini antiquiores,* 101–177. SFS 1. Freiburg, 1968.
_____. *Codices liturgici Latini antiquiores, Supplementum,* 132–151. SFS 1A. Freiburg, 1988.

Ambrosian Liturgy

Gamber, K. *Codices liturgici Latini antiquiores,* 501–595. SFS 1. Freiburg, 1968.
_____. *Codices liturgici Latini antiquiores, Supplementum,* 259–286. SFS 1A. Freiburg, 1988.
Magnoli, C. "I libri liturgici ambrosiani 'riformati a norma dei decreti del Concilio Vaticano II.'" AA. VV., *Celebrare il mistero di Cristo,* 455–465. BELS 73. Rome, 1993. 455-465.

Triacca, A.-M. "Libri liturgici ambrosiani." *Anàmnesis* 2:201-217.

Gallican Liturgy

Gamber, K. *Codices liturgici Latini antiquiores,* 201–299. SFS 1. Freiburg, 1968.

_____. *Codices liturgici Latini antiquiores, Supplementum,* 156–192. SFS 1A. Freiburg, 1988.

Pinell, J. "Libri liturgici gallicani." *Anàmnesis* 2:185-190.

Hispanic Liturgy

Gamber, K. *Codices liturgici Latini antiquiores,* 301–395. SFS 1. Freiburg, 1968.

_____. *Codices liturgici Latini antiquiores, Supplementum,* 194–225. SFS 1A. Freiburg, 1988.

Pinell, J. "Libri liturgici ispanici." *Anàmnesis* 2:190-201.

_____. "Missale Hispano-Mozarabicum." *Not* 24 (1988) 670–727.

_____. "El Misal Hispano-Mozárabe: Nueva edición revisada." *Ph* 32 (1992) 367–380.

B. Interpretation of Liturgical Sources

Renato De Zan

17

Criticism and Interpretation of Liturgical Texts

1. INTRODUCTION

To study liturgical, or more precisely, euchological texts[1] means in the first place knowing how to contextualize them. Prayer texts, after all, have no life of their own but are situated within a celebration. Thus they must be studied within the context of a theological understanding of the liturgy.

The reflection on the liturgy begun by the council served as a bridge between the dynamic (though sometimes one-sided) research of the past and that of the present, which is active, systematic, and attentive to the various aspects of celebrating. As the council said, the science of liturgy must be understood, taught, and learned "under its theological, historical, spiritual, pastoral, and juridical aspects."[2]

---

[1] By liturgical texts we mean the body of texts that make up the ritual program or are linked to it. Liturgical texts are all those texts that were created by an act of the Church. Thus we have *Praenotanda, Instructiones,* rubrics, prayer texts, and poetic texts (hymns, responsories, tropes etc.). With regard to the biblical and patristic texts found in the liturgy, we rightly note that these texts are always "selected" and "cut" according to definite liturgical criteria. The simple fact that these texts are no longer found in their original literary-theological context, but have been cut and placed in a new literary-theological-celebrative context, makes them "liturgical texts" in the true and proper sense. Thus we would rightly distinguish a biblical or patristic passage in its original setting (the Bible or the writings of the Fathers) from a passage that forms part of a ritual program with its own shape and functions. In the first case, we should speak of biblical or patristic texts; in the second, we should speak of biblical-liturgical or patristic-liturgical texts. For a more traditional classification, see M. Augé, "Principi di interpretazione dei testi liturgici," *Anamnesis I*, 162–70.

[2] *SC* 16.

Putting these words into practice has meant that the scientific study of liturgy tries to present an overall view of the liturgical action with regard to texts, rites, and signs. It does this by studying the history of the liturgy, with special attention to the tradition of the Eastern Churches, by examining the very nature of the liturgy,[3] and by a respectful and discriminating use of "the sound results of modern human sciences, such as anthropology, sociology, linguistics, comparative history of religions, etc."[4] All this is possible because of a recent trend in modern research to do studies of a historical, theological, and pastoral nature.

2. A GRADUAL TREND

In the wake of the council, there have been not only general principles for interpreting the liturgy but also more specific principles for interpreting euchological texts.

The first proposal, quite interesting and well worked out, was that of F. Nakagaki.[5] Published in 1971, it was called the "integral method." Its five main elements are the liturgical, historical, literary, contextual, and unitary. Each element must be reunderstood in light of those that follow. The liturgical element considers the structure of the liturgical year, which influences rite and words (text). The historical element, on the other hand, is concerned with the euchological text's four coordinates: author, date of composition or use, place, and other things useful for situating the text in its cultural context. The literary element studies the words and phrases in their literary contexts, noting their structure and style, mindful that the words of a text acquire their full meaning from the rites (which are known through the rubrics) and the latter acquire their full meaning from the words of the text. The contextual element, closely associated with the historical, is its logical continuation. It studies the links between the text and the theological, historical, and literary contexts in which it originated. Lastly, the unitary element — which continues and

---

[3] See the 1979 Instruction on liturgical formation in seminaries, nos. 47, 49, 56, 58.

[4] Ibid., no. 59.

[5] F. Nakagaki, "Metodo integrale. Discorso sulla metodologia nell'interpretazione dei testi eucologici," A. Cuva (ed.), *Fons vivus. Miscellanea liturgica in memoria di don E.M. Vismara* (Zurich, 1971) 269–86.

completes the literary element —must be studied by situating the formula within its formulary so as to grasp its central ideas, as distinct from those which are secondary or accidental.

A few years later, in 1974, M. Augé took up the question again and presented his own principles for interpreting liturgical texts.[6] The scope of his research and the multifaceted nature of his investigation led him to extend Nakagaki's proposals considerably. He begins by excluding those areas that lie outside his study. He is not interested in the criteriology which plays a predominant role in liturgical reform and creativity; he passes over all liturgical sources ("the natural religious world, Sacred Scripture, the Fathers of the Church, the councils") except the liturgical books. He focuses on the euchological texts, dividing them into texts drawn from Scripture (scriptural readings and biblical songs) and texts created by the Church for worship (prayer texts, poetic texts, patristic texts). The liturgical texts, as sources, are studied in their historical identity (date, author, geographic setting, function, evidence from writers and quotations etc.) and their doctrinal identity (content, expressive power, specific liturgical meaning, link with patristic thought, and the theological climate of their respective period). For the biblical and patristic texts, he presents their type of use and distribution.

For the euchological texts, after a brief illustration of the doctrinal principles that guide their interpretation, he gives an ample presentation of his method of investigation. After clarifying the biblical roots of the liturgical texts and the peculiarities of the literary language (liturgical Latin), the author sets forth the three basic steps of his method: analysis of the text's objective elements or content; analysis of its structural elements or form of composition; analysis of its stylistic or rhythmic elements. The objective elements of euchology (theological content) are rooted in the world of the Bible (see the *berakah*) and are determined by Jesus. These three dimensions will be fundamental: remembrance with thanksgiving, sanctification of the gifts, and intercession for the Church. The structural elements of a prayer text are essentially the invocation, the petition (principal, introductory), the conclusion, the motive, and the introduction. The stylistic and rhythmic elements reveal human, religious,

---

[6] M. Augé, "Principi di interpretazione dei testi liturgici," *Anamnesis 1,* 159–79.

psychological, historical, and typological problems present in the text. These are among the most important elements listed by the author: amplification, binary succession, antithesis, parallelism (simple, antithetical), verbal redundancy, *cursus*, and concinnity. Every formula is part of a formulary and every formulary is situated within the liturgical year. Thus the context within which the prayer text must be interpreted becomes increasingly wider.

In 1977 A. Triacca and R. Farina looked at the question of methodology in the study and interpretation of the prayer book.[7] The study of euchology aims to examine the link between euchology and the theological climate of the time, the relationship between euchology and the historical setting, the relationship between euchology and the euchological school (stylistic criticism, redactional stratification, criticism of variants or textual criticism), euchology in itself (structuralist criticism), euchology and the literary system (formalist criticism), the relationship between euchology and the reader (believer, prayer, critical-literary scholar). This study will include four steps: historical-critical reading or analysis, etiological reading or analysis of the formulary, structural reading or analysis, and interpretive reading or analysis. Etiological reading or analysis of the formulary attempts to show "the motives or circumstances that over the centuries have caused a prayer formulary to be used in various ways in the various liturgical traditions." By structural reading or analysis the authors mean the combination of three methods: liturgical-contextual (analysis of the content of word and formula), linguistic-communicative (emphasis on the superficial formal structure of the structural analysis), and semiological or semantic. The latter is divided into four broad analytic steps with their respective subdivisions: linguistic grammatical analysis, analysis of the semantic function, semantic analysis of the syntagmatic unity, and analysis of the structural or formal elements of euchological texts. Finally, there is interpretive analysis of the text. This may be of two types: historical interpretation or exegesis (placing the prayer text and its compiler in contact with their spatio-temporal context), and existential interpretation (placing the prayer text and its compiler in contact with the "reader").

[7] A. Triacca and R. Farina, "Studio e lettura dell'eucologia. Note metodologiche," in C. Ghidelli (ed.), *Teologia, Liturgia, Storia. Miscellanea in onore di C. Manziana* (Brescia, 1977) 197–224.

The following year, 1978, the methodology of interpreting liturgical texts opened itself to structuralism with the contribution of R. Taft.[8] The author sketches his proposal, suggesting a plan for structural analysis of the celebration within which the texts are situated. The usefulness of his proposal is more apparent in the comparative-historical area than in the strictly textual.

A decisive turning point began nine years later, in 1987, with the full acceptance of the human sciences in the study of euchological texts. That year witnessed the publication of J. Schermann's doctoral thesis[9] as part of the series by the Innsbruck theological faculty. More than a real method, the Austrian scholar's research represents a linguistic-semiotic approach to the liturgy that we can no longer do without today. His study is divided into three parts. In the first, language is presented as an object and a means of communication. We note in the author's description the influence of structural linguistics, pragmatic linguistics, and the analytic philosophy of Oxford. In the second part, he gives an exact description of the liturgy understood as a dialogical interaction between God and humanity, with all the variables this can involve. Next he reflects on the science of communication, symbolic interactionism, and semiotics. His last part is a long list of linguistic acts present in the celebration: locutory, illocutory, and perlocutory.

The next year, 1988, works by two other authors began a dialogue between the human sciences — especially linguistics — and euchological texts. The work of M. B. Merz appeared in the series *Liturgiewissenschaftliche Quellen und Forschungen* of the Institute of the Abbey of Maria Laach.[10] It is also better in the case of Merz's study to speak of an approach rather than a method. His book is divided into four parts. After the first chapter in which he presents the characteristics of liturgical prayer and its modern theological interpretations, the author takes up questions that are more concerned with methodology: the linguistic perspective of the link and transition that takes place between the written text and the action by which it becomes spoken word, with all that flows from that. Three elements can come

---

[8] R. Taft, "The Structural Analysis of the Liturgical Units: An Essay in Methodology," *Wor* 52 (1978) 314–29.

[9] J. Schermann, *Die Sprache im Gottesdienst* (Innsbruck-Vienna, 1987).

[10] M. Merz, *Liturgisches Gebet als Geschehen* (Münster, 1988).

into play in the linguistic understanding of a written text that becomes spoken: pragmatics, textual linguistics, and communication. In the third and longest chapter, the author applies his methodology to the liturgical texts. He ends his work with a serious reflection on some of the elements that can become part of a new model for looking at things theologically in dialogue with the human sciences (especially those of a linguistic nature), applied to the Eucharistic Prayer.

The other work, by J. A. Zimmermann,[11] is a structuralist approach to euchological texts along the lines of Paul Ricoeur. His methodology has two basic aims: to understand the celebration through the form of the texts and through knowledge of the texts to understand the Christian life. This is possible because there is a strict relationship between text and celebration and an equally strict relationship between liturgy and life. The methodological process for understanding the texts involves the following steps: study of the words according to the linguistic criterion of synchrony (syntagmas, paradigms); study of the expressions or phrases as they are used in the text (relationship to the event; relationship to the performative, illocutory, and perlocutory; relationship to extra-linguistic reality); study of the text (structure, literary genre, and style); new study of the written text according to the criteria of written and read communication. In addition to the text there is its reference. What is required, therefore, is a pre-understanding (through a participation in the liturgical event), an explanation (through a distancing from it), and an understanding (through appropriation of the liturgical event).

A year later, in 1989, the work of S. Maggiani was published. Before dealing with the texts, he is particularly concerned with the "ritual program" as found in the liturgical book.[12] Underlying all hermeneutical research is the ritual program understood as significant praxis, capable of producing figures, texts, codified and traditional gestures, functioning at several levels and capable of as many manip-

---

[11] J. A. Zimmermann, *Liturgy as Language of Faith: A Liturgical Methodology in the Mode of Paul Ricoeur's Textual Hermeneutics* (Lanham-New York-London, 1988).

[12] S. Maggiani, "Interpretare il libro liturgico," *Il mistero celebrato. Per una metodologia dello studio della liturgia* (Rome, 1989) 157–92. The topic is taken up again in S. Maggiani, "Come leggere gli elementi costitutivi del libro liturgico," *Celebrare il mistero di Cristo. La celebrazione: introduzione alla liturgia cristiana*, vol. I (Rome, 1993) 131–41.

ulations (in a positive sense) and unlimited elaborations as there are expressive anthropological capabilities. By its nature the ritual program must be interpreted and understood in light of the anthropological dimension of the rite, the rituality, and of the anthropological-theological dimension of the sacrament. Today the ritual program is found in the typical editions of the liturgical books, which usually contain four elements: the *Constitutio Apostolica*, the *Praenotanda*, the *Ordo* and the *Ordines*, and possibly an *Appendix*. The *Constitutio Apostolica* (teaching) spells out the essence of the rite, sheds light on the sacramental meaning and its rituality. The *Praenotanda* or *Institutio* consists of a theological code (an exposition of the Church's teaching, which tells what should emerge and what a celebration ought to signify) and a rubrical code (which states the rubrical norms and emphasizes how the celebration must function if it is to achieve the effects signified). The *Ordo* contains the ritual program, inasmuch as it contains "the ritual description of the text (through explanations, verbal and non-verbal texts, etc.) as containing all that is needed for its own virtual carrying out, of which the liturgical actions or celebrations would be the variants." Interpretation of the ritual program can be done through several readings (linear reading, narratological and paraphrastic reading, performative-deictic reading, structural reading, symbolic-functional reading). "Within every ritual program are euchological texts" that can be interpreted by the classical methods (Nakagaki, Augé, Triacca, and Farina) or by modern methods (actantial, conversational, narrative structural).

The most curious principle regarding the interpretation of texts seems to be that of E. Mazza,[13] published in 1993. The author, a scholar of early liturgical texts, praises the historical-critical method. After stating, between polemic and paradox, how many times the word *oremus* conveys an excellent theology but has no impact on the celebration, he summarizes his ideas in a few simple sentences:

"In a celebration, what is being celebrated is the rite as such, in its globality, as a synthetic fact. In other words, the text is important not for itself, insofar as it is a text, but for its importance within the rite,

---

[13] E. Mazza, "Teologia liturgica centrata sul vissuto celebrativo," M. Midali and R. Tonelli (eds.), *Qualità pastorale delle discipline teologiche e del loro insegnamento* (Rome, 1993) 143–4.

that is, for its connection with what precedes and what follows, as well as with the totality of the rite insofar as it is a global fact. This is not to deny the validity of the text, but to situate it within the ritual context in which it is celebrated."

3. SOME FURTHER CONSIDERATIONS

Having explained some of the most important proposed methods for interpreting liturgical texts, we offer some further considerations. These may be grouped around the four basic notions of text, celebration, theology, and method.

When approaching a liturgical text, the scholar is confronted first of all by a *text*. This means that before a text can be approached as liturgy it must be approached as textuality.[14] Only by respecting the process that begins with a text's textuality and ends with its liturgicity do we respect its semantic and pragmatic dimensions. Textuality involves attention to several things. The first concerns the identity of the text. It is very easy to see that a formula in the *Sacramentarium Veronense* differs greatly from a text in the Missal of Paul VI. A formula from the *Sacramentarium Veronense* is expressed in a linguistic-cultural code that is homogeneous; it is very close to the linguistic-cultural code of the celebrating assembly. Indeed, the Latin used in formula was the homogeneous Latin of the period before the fall of the empire. Here was a language which, if not actually spoken by the assembly, was at least understood by it. Understood also were the cultural models found in the text. A formula from the Missal of Paul VI is expressed in a code that is dishomogeneous, artificial, and unconnected with the cultural code. It is dishomogeneous because many formulas are either a cento of fragments borrowed from early formulas or texts, or else they are very recent since they are new. It is artificial because Latin is a dead language. It is unconnected with the cultural code because the text is often linguistically dishomogeneous; since it must serve for the entire Church, it lacks a unique cultural and theological referent. The consequences of this first observation are clear. A formula from the Missal of Paul VI cannot be read as if it were a formula from the early liturgical tradition. The philological question is different, and the prescientific cultural referent, valid for

[14] See R. A. de Beaugrande and W. U. Dressler, *Einführung in die Textlinguistik*, M. Niemeyer (Tübingen, 1981).

texts prior to the Missal of Pius V, is no longer valid for texts from the Missal of Paul VI. And given the findings of linguistics, the question of translation is far from settled in the case of early texts. It is even more complex for texts from the Missal of Paul VI.

Once the textuality (historical-semantic dimension) of a text has been shown, attention must be paid to its liturgicity (pragmatic dimension). This means that the text must be properly situated within its liturgical-celebrative and linguistic-pragmatic contexts.

To situate a text within its celebrative context means to analyze it further relating it to the other texts of the rite, the gestures, the mystery being celebrated, and the liturgical season. In short, it means to situate the text within the total ritual program. The text is one fragment of a textual ensemble, which is formed by the lesser euchology from the other prayer and biblical texts of the formulary to which it belongs, by the greater euchology, and by the biblical texts of the lectionary. If the text is contemporary and is a Mass text, then its textual ensemble includes the texts that form the respective Liturgy of the Hours. The text is also part of a gestural ensemble that derives its meaning from the text, but when re-understood anthropologically, gives additional meaning to the text itself. The celebrative context is sustained by the mystery celebrated, which provides the ultimate framework for a complete understanding of the text. Finally, the liturgical season provides the setting within which to situate all the riches of the text brought out thus far. For texts from the conciliar reform, the *Instructiones* and *Praenotanda* in the liturgical books are a basic tool for the text's pragmatics.

Once the text has been situated within its linguistic-pragmatic context,[15] it is no longer approached as a written text but is understood as a linguistic event. To understand this natural aspect of prayer texts — which are created to be spoken and not merely written — we need to set up an interpretive grid: a text can be approached from a conversational point of view, or according to the laws of communication etc. In short, "speaking" becomes "doing."

The results of our interpretation of a liturgical text must converge in such a way that all the elements related to the text's semantic and

---

[15] J. Schermann, *Die Sprache im Gottesdienst* (Innsbruck-Vienna, 1987); M. Merz, *Liturgisches Gebet als Geschehen* (Münster, 1988).

pragmatic aspects can be organized and used to construct a liturgical theology. Such organization cannot be found in the division into tracts that is typical of dogmatic theology; it must be discovered in the world of the celebration. In other words, we must appeal to the great categories of anamnesis, epiclesis, doxology, and κοινωνία.[16] Then, within these categories, we must embrace the theandric, Christological-pneumatological, symbolic, and ecclesial dimensions.

Finally, we must say a word about methods. While these may seem to be infinite in number, in fact there are only a few. Our first point concerns the distinction between method and approach. It should be noted that the word "method" is used quite often to refer to both methods and approaches. Thus we have the liturgical-contextual method, the linguistic-communicative method, the semiological method, the actantial method, the conversational method, the narrative structural method, etc. A method is a body of scientific procedures, harmoniously and hierarchically related, whose aim is an understanding and explanation of the text. An approach, on the other hand, is a scientific study that is carried out according to a particular and limited point of view. That is why we have, for example, the historical-critical method and the semiotic method. There is no conversational or actantial *method* but rather a conversational or actantial approach. Our second point concerns the historical-critical method. The historical-critical method as understood today (free from any premise whose epistemological character is not in respectful relationship to its formal object) can no longer be stated as it was a few years ago. It has been greatly enriched by many contributions, especially of a linguistic or structuralist nature. Our third point concerns vocabulary. Authors rightly use the technical terms that are part of their respective disciplines, at times with nuances of meaning that can be lost on those who are not their disciples. This sometimes makes it hard to understand exactly what they mean. Our final point concerns examples. Certain methodological procedures, flawless from viewpoint of hermeneutic theory, often turn out to be muddled in practice and their results questionable.

Based on these observations, we can formulate a methodological proposal. Since the nature of the pieces in this book has already been

---

[16] E. Lodi, *Liturgia della Chiesa* (Bologna, 1981).

determined, our methodological proposal will stay within the framework of the historical-critical method. But we shall not neglect the findings of more recent methods and approaches.

4. A METHODOLOGICAL PROPOSAL

Liturgical texts[17] may be divided into two main groups: biblical texts (Scripture readings, psalms, and biblical songs) and texts composed by the Church (patristic, euchological, poetic, rubrical). Here we are interested in euchological texts,[18] which may be divided into *minor euchology* (brief and simple texts: opening prayer, prayer over the gifts, prayer after Communion, prayer over the people, psalm prayers, etc.) and *major euchology* (longer and more elaborate texts: prefaces, Eucharistic Prayers, solemn blessings, etc.). A single euchological text is called a *formula* (e.g., opening prayer), while an organic body of several euchological texts is called a *formulary* (e.g., entrance antiphon, opening prayer, prayer over the gifts, Communion antiphon, prayer after Communion).

In our study of the Church's euchological heritage, we must distinguish between the euchological deposit (euchology of the past) and contemporary euchology (euchology of the conciliar reform). Our proposed methodology looks at the characteristics of the euchological deposit and contemporary euchology, as well as at what scholars have said concerning method. Seeing our proposal, one may well object to its failure to distinguish between synchronic and diachronic analysis of the text. We would rather not accept this neat division, given the nature of euchological texts. These texts, after all, are not unique and fixed; they have been recycled again and again and are constantly in the process of becoming. A clear distinction between synchronic and diachronic analysis might well lead to a distortion of the text. While respecting the methodological identity of the two aspects, synchronic and diachronic, we prefer to see the results of the methodologies engage in dialogue within their common interpretive framework. For example, when analyzing the text's historical identity (diachronic analysis) we must answer the question, "Why and for

---

[17] See M. Augé, "Eucologia," *NDL* (Rome, 1984) 509–19.

[18] For interpretation of the biblical texts in the liturgy, see R. de Zan, *Bible and Liturgy*, in this volume.

whom was the text written?" This question can have a double context, past as well as present (consider an early text adopted in contemporary euchology). It is well to view the pragmatic and communicative approaches to the text from the framework of the context. While these are two synchronic moments, they are essential to understanding the meaning of the text, whether the latter is considered in its past or present use. In any case, let us keep in mind that while the euchological deposit can be subjected to the individual steps of the proposed methodological process, when it comes to an understanding of contemporary euchology, many of these steps are impracticable.

Finally, a methodological process for analyzing liturgical texts starts as a collection of several methods and approaches. It is important, after all, to answer the basic questions with what textual hermeneutics has to offer. Given the shape of euchological texts (texts that are evolving), we cannot follow the example of Procrustes and sacrifice the guest (the texts) to the bed (the methods and approaches). It is better to adapt the bed (the methods and approaches) to the guest (the texts). This gives us, then, a methodological process consisting of nine general steps which answer nine equally general questions:

a) What is the exact text being studied?

b) What is the meaning of this text?

c) What is its historical identity?

d) What is its communicative and pragmatic identity?

e) How has this text evolved historically through liturgical use?

f) What is its literary identity?

g) What is its contextual identity?

h) What is the text's theological value?

i) What is its new shape (translation) in a world that is culturally different from the one in which it originated?

The answers to these questions are to be found by a process of investigation that utilizes different methods and approaches.

a) The process always begins[19] with certitude concerning the text. Therefore we must begin with textual criticism, which enables us to work with a text that is certain and correct. We cannot, of course, use this step in the case of contemporary euchology, since here we have the *Editio typica*. We shall not illustrate this first step of the process here since it has already been illustrated in a separate article.[20]

b) Next we must analyze the text's meaning. Since it is written in Latin, we must first of all do a philological analysis. This will provide the meaning of the individual words, expressions, grammatical and syntatic constructions. It is only through philological analysis that we can make an initial translation and arrive at a first rough understanding of the text. Of course, a text from the euchological deposit is analyzed differently than a contemporary euchological text, as we shall see later.

Since at this stage of the process we are looking for the text's meaning, we may also use the semantic approach here, whether our text is early or contemporary.

c) Once we have analyzed the text's meaning, we must give it a historical identity. Analysis of its authenticity tries to establish, as far as possible, the text's author (and hence its theological and linguistic-literary current), its time and place of composition, and its purpose as intended by the author. Euchology reflects, in the various liturgical traditions, the socio-cultural and theological characteristics of its period of composition. Obviously, this part of the method does not apply to contemporary euchology.

d) A prayer text is not created to be written, but fundamentally to be spoken.

It is interesting to note how the purpose of the text gives us a chance to apply the pragmatic and communicative approach to it (whether it is early or contemporary). Euchology, too, is subject to the

---

[19] Anyone who wishes to undertake the study of euchology must first have a general bibliographical orientation. For this see M. Johnson (ed.), *Bibliographia liturgica* (Rome, 1992) — a brief review of the more important tools — editions of texts, periodicals, dictionaries, concordances, studies, etc. — which are useful for the science of liturgy; M. Zitnik, *Sacramenta. Bibliographia internationalis*, 4 vols. (Rome, 1992); the entries devoted to liturgy in the annual bibliography published by *Ephermerides Theologicae Lovanienses* may also be very useful.

[20] For textual criticism, see R. de Zan, *Textual Criticism*, in this volume.

linguistic law of the performative and thus to the law of illocutory and perlocutory acts.[21] To pray a euchological text during the celebration means not only to "say" it, but also "to do something" that is linked to its sender and recipient.

e) The study of the text's tradition leads us to examine how it may have evolved and assumed different functions — from its creation to its final redactional setting. In the past, this diachronic study of the text was often done through the use of textual criticism, which added the search for the correct text to the search for its sources, and the latter to the study of its tradition.

f) The fourth step concerns literary criticism. In this phase of the method we are looking for the sources of the liturgical text. These are basically two: the primary source, Sacred Scripture, and the material source, which is either the liturgy, the Fathers, or the magisterium (for contemporary euchology it could even be a question of newly-created texts). Besides the text's sources, literary criticism deals with the structure to which the question of literary genre is variously linked. Next is the stylistics, one of the important elements of meaning (philological-linguistic, semantic, and theological). From a study of the stylistics, we can, if we wish, move to a study of the text using the rhetorical method. This step concludes with an examination of the literary-liturgical context.

g) The text is part of a rite which is guided by a ritual program. There exists a ritual context within which the text is linked to other elements (gestures, spaces, objects, seasons). These give the text a shape which cannot be understood from textual, semantic, and historical-literary analyses alone.

h) All the data that have emerged from the process thus far must be organized and understood according to established rules. Since a celebration has intrinsic dimensions and foundations, the material must be organized according to its four dimensions (anamnesis, epiclesis, doxology, and κοινωνία) and its four foundations (theandric, Christological-pneumatological, ecclesial, and symbolic).[22]

i) After all these steps, which enable us to know and understand the text, we can finally begin the real work of translating it.

---

[21] J. L. Austin, *How to Do Things with Words* (Oxford-New York, 1975).

[22] E. Lodi, "La liturgia: teologia mistagogica. Introduzione generale allo studio della liturgia," *Liturgia della Chiesa* (Bologna, 1981) 21–226.

Obviously we cannot continue to act as if the text were an absolute, as if everything were contained in the Latin philology. We must try other ways that utilize whatever linguistics has to offer.[23]

5. THE MEANING OF THE TEXT

To speak of the meaning of the text means to speak of at least two things that are distinct: philological analysis and semantic analysis.

a) Philological analysis requires, first of all, knowledge of the language in which the text was written. Medieval Latin[24] inherited the riches and positive qualities of late imperial Latin and Christian Latin,[25] the latter having been created within the Latin of the Empire.[26] Liturgical Latin[27] is part of Christian Latin and linked to it in many ways. But it is also linked to the different cultures where Latin was spoken as a second language. Liturgical Latin represents one particular strain of Christian Latin with its own distinctive shape. Its vocabulary, for example, presents certain difficulties for those who are not experts in the field.[28]

All these studies are useful for texts from the euchological deposit, which are normally homogeneous, whereas contemporary euchological texts are usually dishomogeneous. In the case of the former, we

[23] See R. Jakobson, *Saggi di linguistica generale* (Milan, 1974) 185.

[24] See D. Norberg, *Manuel pratique de latin médiéval* (Paris, 1968); V. Paladini and M. de Marco, *Lingua e letteratura mediolatina* (Bologna, 1980); V. Väänänen, *Introduzione al latino volgare* (Bologna, 1982).

[25] See J. Schrijnen, *Charakteristik des Altchristlichen Latein* (Nijmegen, 1932); A. Dumas, *Manuel du latin chrétien* (Strasbourg, 1955); C. Mohrmann, *Études sur le latin des Chrétiens*, I–IV (Rome, 1958–1977).

[26] See J. B. Hofmann, *La lingua d'uso latina* (Bologna, 1985).

[27] See C. Mohrmann, *Études sur le latin des Chrétines, III: Latin chrétien et liturgique* (Rome, 1965).

[28] A. Blaise, *Dictionnaire latin-français des auteurs chrétiens* (Turnhout, 1962); A. Blaise and A. Dumas, *Le vocabulaire latin des principaux thèmes liturgiques* (Turnhout, 1966); see M. P. Ellebracht, *Remarks on the vocabulary of the ancient orations in the Missale Romanum* (Nijmegen, 1966). Countless monographs are studies of a single word or expression, for example, M. Steinheimer, *Die "ΔΟΞΑ ΤΟΥ ΘΕΟΥ" in der römischen Liturgie* (Munich, 1951); W. Dienzinger, *Effectus in der römischen Liturgie* (Bonn, 1961); B. Droste, «Celebrare» in der römischen Liturgiesprache* (Munich, 1963).

can do a classical philological analysis, and in the case of the latter, a philological analysis of a linguistic nature.

Classical philological analysis of euchological texts involves a few basic steps. The first concerns identification of the text's euchological source. Comparing the text with its source helps to situate it in its original context. This is valuable, seeing that the formula may reflect special dogmatic concerns (controversies, heresies) or troublesome civic and political situations. On the other hand, the original context provides the literary *entourage* with which to compare the formula and determine the meaning of the words[29] and of certain grammatical and syntactic constructions.[30] Next comes a consideration of the stylistic elements. These help determine the author or the euchologi-

---

[29] For the use of words in early texts, see P. Bruylants, *Concordance verbale du Sacramentaire léonien* (Louvain, 1945); see also J. Deshusses and B. Darragon, *Concordances et Tableaux pour l'étude des grands Sacramentaires*, 6 vols., Ed. Universitaires (Fribourg, 1982–1983).

[30] For the prayer over the gifts from the Mass for the Annunciation of the Blessed Virgin Mary (March 25), the *Missale Romanum ex Decreto Sacrosancti Concilii Tridentini restitutum Summ. Pontific. recognitum*, Editio sexta post typicam, Typis Polyglottis Vaticanis (Editio Typica 1920) gives the following text:

In mentibus nostris, quaesumus, Domine, verae fidei sacramenta confirma: ut qui conceptum de Virgine Deum verum et hominem confitemur; per eius salutiferae resurrectionis potentiam, ad aeternam mereamur pervenire laetitiam. Per. . . .

In the expression *conceptum de Virgine Deum verum et hominem confitemur*, we could stress the words *conceptum de Virgine*, giving us a translation more or less like this: we confess that he who is true God and man was conceived by a virgin. But knowing that the formula comes from the Gregorian Hadrian n. 142 and is not one of the earliest Roman orations — even though it can be dated to the fifth century — it becomes relatively easy to see that our proposed philological emphasis is wrong. The burning theological question of the fifth century was not the virgin birth but Christology (the Council of Ephesus, 431, and the Council of Chalcedon, 451; the first council opposed the Nestorian heresy and the second monophysitism). Thus what is emphasized in the text are the words *Deum verum et hominem*. The correct philological reading should be as follows: we confess that he who was conceived by the Virgin is true God and true man. The correct reading of the expression *verae fidei sacramenta confirma* is dependent on this reading. In the expression *verae fidei sacramenta*, the word *sacramenta* does not refer to "liturgical mysteries" but to "doctrinal mysteries." This reading is confirmed by the adjective *vera* which modifies *fides*. From this flows a correct understanding of the formula's *incipit, In mentibus nostris*, where the word *mens* may emphasize the intellectual more than the generic dimension "interior world." A possible translation of our first passage would be this: Increase in our minds, O Lord, a firm

cal school;[31] they also clarify the meaning of certain expressions.[32] Finally, we can make a rough translation. A full-fledged translation will come only after we know and understand all the dynamics of the text — in other words, at the end of the methodological process.

b) Semasiological analysis is another type of philological analysis in the broad sense.[33] It is used for prayer texts that are dishomogeneous, such as the contemporary Latin euchological texts. It is based on the contextual theory of meaning which requires only a context capable of codifying the use of the word we wish to analyze. For example, the euchological texts from the Missal of Paul VI provide the

---

acceptance of the mysteries of the true faith; by confessing the Son conceived by the Virgin, true God and true man, may we attain by the power of his resurrection. . . . (see B. Capelle, *Pour mieux comprendre les Oraisons du Missel: Cours et Conférences des semaines liturgiques*, vol. V (Huy, 1926) 135–45.

[31] G. Manz, *Ausdrucksformen der Lateinischen Liturgiesprache bis im Elfte Jahrhundert* (Beuron, 1941). While we do not always share the author's choices, the material is still useful.

[32] The text of the Sacramentarium Veronense n. 93 reads:
Da nobis haec, quaesumus, Domine, frequentata mysteria: quia quotiens hostiae tibi placatae commemoratio celebrantur, opus nostrae redemptionis exeritur. Per. . . .
Correcting the verb *celebrantur* to *celebratur*, the text presents no special difficulties except for the word *exeritur*. The textual tradition, in fact, proves that the text was not understood: the *Gelasianum* has *exercitum*, the Gregorian tradition has *exercetur*, the Gelasian of Angoulême has *exere*, and the Sacramentary of Prague (twice) has *exercitus* and *exercitur*. The verb *exero* is not commonly found in Christian Latin. But it is part of the style of St. Leo the Great, in whose writings it occurs at least six times. There *exero*, besides meaning 'to appear' or 'to manifest oneself,' also refers to the movement or action with respect to those to whom the reality that appears or manifests itself is addressed. The expression *opus nostrae redemptionis exeritur* means that "the work of our redemption (when the commemoration of Christ's sacrifice takes place) *is made present* to us *in order to affect* our life." See J. Pinell, "I testi liturgici, voci di autorità, nella costituzione «Sacrosanctum Concilium»," Congregazione per il culto divino (ed.), *Costituzione liturgica «Sacrosanctum Concilium». Studi* (Rome, 1986) 331–41.

[33] "The term semasiology, which prior to Bréal meant what today we call semantics, now has a narrower meaning. It refers to the study of significations or meanings or concepts, beginning from the words that name them. Making an inventory of all the meanings attributed to the semantic word is one of the problems of semasiology. On the contrary, the task of onomasiology is to make an inventory of the various names or significants that can be attributed to one and the same concept or meaning." See G. Mounin, *Guida alla semantica* (Milan, 1975) 8–9.

codifying context for use of the word *gloria* in formula 140-C2.[34] Semasiological analysis, which applies not only to the word but also to the sub-syntagmas and syntagmas, involves two steps: a search for associations and a search for commutations.

The search for associations also involves two steps: a search for the syntagmas[35] in which the word is found[36] and a cataloguing of these syntagmas (verbal, nominal, and determinative syntagmas) according to semantic areas.[37]

---

[34] The abbreviation 140-C2 refers to "the second collect on page 140 of the 1975 *editio typica altera* of the Missal of Paul VI." We can use this style of abbreviation until the *editio typica altera* has proven its validity and until the liturgical texts in the Missal of Paul VI are codified in a more serious form than has been attempted thus far.

[35] The word *gloria* from formula 140-C2 is chosen as an example. For the sake of brevity only the formularies from the Sundays of Advent are used here as a contextual area.

[36] Five syntagmas contain the word *gloria*: 132-C; 135-C1; 140-C2; 144-C; 149-So. Two of these, 135-C and 149-So, are omitted here because they present serious difficulties. For the solution, see R. de Zan, "La teologia liturgico-biblica della gloria in Avvento," and also A. Catella, *Amen Vestrum. Miscellanea di studi teologico-pastorali in onore di P. Pelagio Vaisentin OSB* (Padua, 1994) 345–76.

[37] The three syntagmas, 132-C, 140-C2, and 144-C should be divided and catalogued thus:

Associations:
    a) verbal   * area of eschatological movement
                      —PERDUCAMUR *ad gloriam resurrectionis:* 132-C
                      * area of revelation
                      —splendor *gloriae tuae ORIATUR in cordibus nostris:* 140-C2
                      —DIGNATUS ES REVELARE *splendorem gloriae tuae:* 144-C
    b) nominal   * area of revelation
                      —SPLENDOR *gloriae tuae:* 140-C2
    c) determinative   * area of revelation
                      —*gloriam RESURRECTIONIS:* 132-C
                      —*gloriae TUAE:* 140-C2

Complete analysis requires that each syntagma be analyzed at a stylistic level with respect to the entire formula of which it is a part. Such an analysis will enable us to discover the semantic meaning of the word in question.

Continuing the basic schema of associations, the search for commutations looks for other syntagmas[38] in the Missal of Paul VI belonging to the same semantic area as the preceding and corresponding to the same paradigm. These syntagmas contain the nominal sub-syntagma to be replaced[39] (equivalent or similar commutation) by the word in question.

[38] A basic work for this search is T. A. Schnitker and W. A. Slaby, *Concordantia verbalia Missalis Romani* (Münster, 1983).

[39] The process of commutations begins with the key word (verb, noun, determinative) printed in capital letters in n. 39. We look for other words, besides the word *gloria*, which are associated with the word in capitals. Then we examine the semantic area and paradigm to which they belong and decide whether they are commutable in an equivalent or similar mode with *gloria*.

Commutations:

a) verbal   * area of eschatological movement

— *PERDUCAMUR*	*ad gloriam resurrectionis:* 132C
— *perducas familiam tuam*	*ad dona superna:* 196-C
— *perducas nos*	*ad illam lucem in qua ipse es:* 199-C
— *perduxisti beatum Martinum*	*ad caelestem gloriam:* 638-C1
— *concedas perduci*	*ad veram patriam:* 881-C2

Already we can begin to see certain commutations, but it is worth completing the analysis with the determinative commutations.

* area of revelation

| — *splendor gloriae tuae* | *ORIATUR* | *in cordibus nostris:* 140-C2 |
| — *salutare tuum* | *oriatur* | *cordibus nostris. . .:* 173-C1 |

Splendor GLORIAE *tuae* and *salutare tuum* are two Christological titles typically found in the Bible and the liturgy. Their commutation is possible because we are dealing with the same person. But their equivalence is not complete, even though it is very extensive, because they are two different functions performed by Christ: one relative to God (in 140-C2 Jesus is the experiential manifestation of God with respect to human beings: see 374-C), the other relative to human beings (in 173-C1 Jesus carries out the saving will of the Father in favor of human beings). The nominal commutations are clearer.

b) nominal * area of revelation

— *SPLENDOR*	*gloriae tuae*	: 140-C2
— *splendor*	*animarum fidelium*	: 164-C
— *splendor*	*gratiae tuae*	: 209-Pc

c) Besides the words, expressions, and grammatical or syntactic constructions, we also have the text. Decodification of the text — through reading or hearing — is a backward process by which we retrace the production of the text. Here it is a question of discovering the relationships of meaning between the elements of the text. Theoretically speaking, this discovery is endless. On the one hand, the reader-hearer can always point out new relationships of meaning; on the other hand, the text becomes an area of multiple and possible meanings.[40] Various procedures exist for arriving at the semantics of the text, two of which we present briefly.

The first has three steps. First, the reader-hearer encounters a certain number of words (lexemes) and performs a semantic inventory

— *splendor*	*claritatis tuae*	: 311-C2
— *splendor*	*veritatis*	: 352-C
— *splendor*	*doctrinae et veritatis*	: 693-C1

In this series of words we must immediately exclude the expression *doctrina et virtus* (693-C1) because it clearly refers to realities predicated of a creature and not of God or Christ (see the meaning of *gloria* in the verbal commutations). A healthy dose of skepticism is called for with regard to the word *veritas*—whether to accept it or reject it. We cannot tell from the context whether it refers to a "body of data that are true" or to God himself (352-C). The syntagma *splendor animarum fidelium* in 164-C is a separate case since it corresponds to God himself. The other cases allow for a good commutation with *gloria*, even though not absolutely equivalent. For this reason we can say that the believer can see the *gloria* of God (140-C2) as *gratia* and *claritas* (note the presence of the possessive adjective *tuus* in all three sub-syntagmas). It is more questionable to see the same commutations with *gloria tua* when the sub-syntagma refers to Jesus Christ (144-C).

c) determinative   * area of (eschatological) movement
— *gloriam RESURRECTIONIS:* 132-C

The sub-syntagma *gloria resurrectionis* associated with *perduco* (132-C; 610-Pc) can be assimilated to the same sub-syntagma of 622-C2. In this case *gloria* takes on the meaning of "true state of the believer" or "true homeland" or "joys of eternal light."

[40] See A. J. Greimas, *Sémantique structural* (Paris, 1968); J. Courtès, *Introductions à la sémiotique narrative et discoursive* (Paris, 1976).

according to groups (or semantic areas). This provides a text's lines of meaning and its network of meaning.[41] The second step consists in recognizing the semantic oppositions.[42] The last step consists in initiating a dialogue between the lines of meaning and the oppositions in

[41] Euchological texts are usually short. Thus it is not easy to apply the method completely to texts of two or three lines or four or five *kommata*. The examples, which are continued in the following notes, are extremely schematic by reason of space. The text in question is 140-C2:

> *Oriátur, quaesumus, omnípotens Deus, in córdibus nostris splendor glóriae tuae,*
> *ut, omni noctis obscuritáte subláta,*
> *fílios nos esse lucis Unigéniti tui maniféstet advéntus.*

We can see at once that the text is very brief and the semantic inventory is very simple. In schematic form we have:

area of movement	area of stasis	area of divine realities
orior	*corda nostra*	*omnipotens Deus*
subfero	*omnis obscuritas noctis*	*splendor gloriae tuae*
adventus	*nos*	*Unigentius tuus*

Unigenitus	esse filii lucis	
manifesto		

The network of meaning is created by the divine action on behalf of the deixis "us." The objective is to make us children of God and reveal us as such. The divine action is manifold: it begins within God himself (*Unigenitus*), continues in an experience of drawing near (*adventus*), and is concretized in three quasi-simultaneous actions. The first is the "dawning" in the hearts of the suppliants; the second is the "dispelling" of night's darkness; the third is the "revelation" of the effect of the brightness of glory in the hearts of the suppliants. They are children of the light.

[42] In the same text we find clear oppositions in the expressed text and in the implicatures (what is not said but is implicit; in the schema these are the words in parentheses). The basic opposition is between the area of movement in which the area of divine realities is at work and the area of stasis in which the divine action manifests itself. In schematic form:

order to note the transformations present in the text.[43] For this final step we can use Greimas's semiotic rectangle or square,[44] which shows the relationship between the elements of meaning. But this is not necessary.

A second procedure, derived directly from A. Greimas,[45] is called actantial analysis. It involves rewriting the text according to the rules of the actantial model, which is made up of six actants: the Sender, the Object, the Recipient, the Assistant, the Subject, and the

the area of divine activity	the area of stasis
omnipotens Deus	(that which is not all-powerful:) *corda nostra*
splendor gloriae tuae	(that which is in darkness:) *corda nostra*
Unigenitus tuus	*nos*
orior	(locus of the action:) *in cordibus nostris*
subfero	(that which has dominated:) *omnis obscuritas noctis*
adventus	(that which is alone and waiting:) *nos*
manifesto	(that which is hidden:) *nos, filii lucis*
filii lucis	(that who were children of night's darkness)

With this schema of explicit and implicit semantic oppositions, the importance of the divine action, already described at the beginning as *omnipotens*, is much clearer.

[43] A comparison between what has been said in the two preceding notes shows us at once how the opposition between light and darkness is central. Within this opposition, which is the genotext, we see certain transformations. The condition of the suppliants before God intervenes is situated within the first opposition (darkness). When God intervenes, he intervenes as light (*splendor*) and he produces light (*filii lucis*). In short, our euchological text is a clear expression of Johannine theology (light-darkness), even though it uses the expression *splendor gloriae*, which is from Heb 1:3.

[44] A. Greimas, *Du Sens*, vol. I (Paris, 1970) 137; see A. Delzant, *La communication de Dieu* (Paris, 1978) 331–3.

[45] A. Greimas, *Sémantique structurale* (Paris, 1966); see S. Maggiani, *Interpretare il libro liturgico, Il mistero celebrato. Per una metodologia dello studio della liturgia* (Rome, 1989) 186–7; F. Isambet, *Rite et efficacité symbolique* (Paris, 1970).

Opponent.[46] The actants are not only the "actors" (God, the Church, the believer, the Evil One, etc.), but also all those realities which advance the action (faith, sin, grace, etc.). The procedure involves three operations: analysis of the initial situation,[47] identification of the three trials (qualifying, principal, glorifying),[48] and analysis of the final situation.[49]

[46] The names of the actants may also be as follows: Addresser, Object, Recipient, Assistant, Hero-Subject, and Opposer. The Sender charges a Subject with giving an Object to a Recipient. In carrying out his task the Subject seeks aid from the Assistant and is opposed by the Opponent. The schema is as follows:

Sender	→	Object	→	Recipient
		↑		
Assistant	→	Subject	←	Opponent

[47] Several questions must be asked of the text. What is the situation or missing object that initiates the action presented in the text? Who is presented as hero-subject? Who is the false subject or real opposer? In whose name or by whose mandate does the hero-subject act? How is the recipient defined? The initial situation can be summarized in schematic form as follows:

all-powerful God	to be children of light	→	"we"
	↑		
	your only Son/brightness of your glory	←	all of night's darkness

[48] A. Greimas and J. Courtes, *Semiotica. Dizionario ragionato della teoria del linguaggio* (Florence, 1986) 131. The qualifying trial is between Sender and Subject, the principal trial between Hero-Subject and Object, the glorifying trial between Object and Recipient. The three trials are situated within the schema thus:

Sender	→	Object	→	glorifying trial	←	Recipient
	↘	↑				
qualifying trial		principal trial				
	↘	↑				
Assistant	→	Subject			←	Opponent

In carrying out this step several questions must be asked. What is the trial (present or presupposed in the text) that qualifies the Hero-Subject as such? Who is the Assistant? In the case of the principal trial there are at least three questions. Where is the locus of the principal trial expressed or implied in the text? In what does it consist? How does it succeed in overcoming the Opposer? For the glorifying trial the essential questions may be reduced to two. When and how does the Hero-Subject make himself recognized as Hero-Subject who has overcome the

6. THE HISTORICAL IDENTITY OF THE TEXT

To search for the text's identity means to do a historical analysis (which has a complexity all its own) in order to articulate the data we wish to know. To search for the historical identity of a formula or formulary is equivalent to searching for the text's authenticity. This requires three operations: a search for the author of the text (or at least the theological school), a search for the time and place in which it written, and finally, its purpose.

a) A euchological text may be either a simple formula or a formulary. A group of formularies make up a document. Thus we must always distinguish the author of the text, understood as a formula or formulary, from the author of the document. The author of the document may have used texts composed by himself or texts composed by others. Scholars know the patience required to identify the author of a text. In doing this, it is very important to know the author's style and vocabulary. Neither can we forget that the great master often had disciples who imitated him. What might be attributed to one of the Fathers, could instead be the work of a disciple and imitator. This fact is not always taken into account.

b) Besides style and vocabulary, we must also pay attention to the milieu and historical setting in which the text is written. Indeed, historical setting and place may be the reason for certain theological choices made in the text itself. But we can also detect nuances of meaning that would otherwise be imperceptible.[50] Euchology carries

principal trial? How is the Object transmitted or how is the situation changed in favor of the Recipient?

[49] This last step of the procedure answers a single question: What transformation has taken place between the initial and final solution?

[50] If we wish to understand better n. 193 of the Gregorian Hadrian Sacramentary (*Deus, qui nos in tantis periculis constitutos, pro humana scis fragilitate non posse subsistere, da nobis salutem mentis et corporis, ut ea, quae pro peccatis nostris patimur, te adiuvante, vincamus*), it is not enough to know that it comes from Gregory the Great. See B. Capelle, "La main de S. Grégoire dans le Sacramentaire Grégorien," *Revue Benedictine* 49 (1937) 13–28. It becomes clearer if it is situated toward the end of the sixth century. We know, in fact, that the Lombards (who were Arians) laid siege to Rome in 593–594. See also the Christocentric emphasis of the Ambrosian prefaces. We cannot understand n. 193 unless we understand the anti-Arian environment in which these prefaces originated; see A. M. Triacca, *I prefazi ambrosiani del ciclo "de tempore" secondo il "Sacramentarium Bergomense." Avviamento ad uno studio critico teologico* (Rome, 1970).

within itself the socio-cultural and theological characteristics of the various liturgical traditions to which the text belongs and the time in which it was composed.

c) The expression "purpose of the text" is ambiguous and can be understood in several ways. The classical rule focuses on the author (or the later editor who modifies the text). Thus the search is devoted to the conceptuality and "speaking" of the author-editor. It starts with the presupposition that the author-editor meant to create a liturgical text that would express — in his own concrete historical situation — the specific and detailed need for salvation in a particular community and within a celebration that is making present to people the fulness of salvation. Thus the basic question is: what did the author-editor mean to say?

Obviously the answer must use the material obtained in a) and b) and develop it, with a rigorous search for words that can show the link between the author-editor and the literary and theological works of his time.[51]

7. THE TEXT AS EVENT AND COMMUNICATION

Linguistic studies today have discovered that although a text is linked to its author-editor, it also has a life of its own.[52] Consequently, we must look for motives within the text, using criteria that focus less on the "speaking" and more on the "doing" that is inherent in the very text.[53] The most important means for discovering this dimension involve an investigation of the text's performative and conversational dimensions.

a) We can do things with words. We need not automatically think of the text's performative dimension in its classical form, for

---

[51] See G.A.L. du Cange and L. Favre, *Glossarium mediae et infimae latinitatis*, vols. 1–10 (Graz, 1954) (anastatic reprint); A. Ernout and A. Meillet, *Dictionnaire étymologique de la langue latine. Histoire des mots* (Paris, 1959); A. Forcellini, *Totius latinitatis lexicon*, vols. I–VI, Padua (anastatic reprint); *Thesaurus Linguae Latinae, editus auctoritate et consilio Academicarum quinque Germanicarum, Berolinensis, Gottingensis, Lipsiensis, Monacensis, Vindobonensis* (Lipsiae, 1903).

[52] See E. D. Hirsch, *Validity in Interpretation* (New Haven and London, 1967).

[53] See J. Schermann, *Die Sprache im Gottesdienst* (Innsbruck-Vienna, 1987); M. Merz, *Liturgisches Gebet als Geschehen* (Münster, 1988); L. Sartori (ed.), *Comunicazione e ritualità. La celebrazione liturgica alla verifica delle leggi della comunicazione* (Padua, 1988).

example: "I swear." The text contains other elements that have to do with pragmatics.[54] For the sake of brevity, we simply mention how important are the illocutory[55] and perlocutory[56] of the formula or formulary.[57] Indeed, there is present in the text a "constativity" (to furnish information), an "intentionality" (to provide the text's purpose), and a "result" (in a text, the result is furnished in the recipient).[58]

b) The conversational dimension belongs to the sensitive side of communication. Here presentation of the conversational approach will be based exclusively on Grice's rules.[59]

8. THE HISTORY OF THE TRADITION OF THE TEXT

Once it has come to be, a euchological text embarks on a historical adventure. Reinterpretations by other editors different from the original author may have given rise to textual variants (voluntary changes) of a stylistic, cultural, or theological nature. In writing the

---

[54] See T. A. van Dijk, *Text and Context. Explorations in the Semantics and Pragmatics of Discourse* (London, 1977).

[55] "Illocutory" refers to the linguistic phonic or graphic act, examined through the intention of the text to modify the recipient. See J. L. Austin, *How to Do Things with Words* (Oxford-New York, 1975).

[56] "Perlocutory" refers to the linguistic phonic or graphic act, examined through the consequences of this act on the recipient (as intended by the editor of the linguistic act). The real extra-textual recipient is the object of sociological rather than linguistic study. See J. L. Austin, *How to Do Things with Words* (Oxford-New York, 1975).

[57] See R. A. de Beaugrande and W. U. Dressler, *Introduzione . . .*, 155–86.

[58] Austin's summary is well known by now: "We . . . can distinguish the locutory act 'he said that . . .' from the illocutory act 'he maintained that . . .' and from the perlocutory act 'he convinced me that . . .' " (Austin, op.cit., 77). Text 155-C reads: *Deus, qui hanc sacratissimam noctem veri luminis fecisti illustratione clarescere, da, quaesumus, ut, cuius in terra mysteria lucis agnovimus, eius quoque gaudiis perfruamur in caelo.* In this text, the constative (*qui in hanc sacratissimam noctem veri luminis fecisti illustratione clarescere*) is also a divine illocutory which has its direct human perlocutory (*cuius in terra mysteria lucis agnovimus*) and its indirect human perlocutory (*eius quoque gaudiis perfruamur in caelo*), the result of an implicature (the joy that arises from the fact that God has made the true light shine in this night filled with the mystery of salvation) of the divine illocutory.

[59] See G. Bonaccorso, "Le regole conversazionali di Grice: verifica su alcuni testi liturgici," L. Sartori (ed.), *Comunicazione e ritualità. La celebrazione liturgica alla verifica delle leggi della comunicazione* (Padua, 1988) 243–60.

history of the tradition of a liturgical text, we must retrace, at least in part, the historical stages of a theology that expressed itself in celebration. Variants may cause the text to assume different shapes at the literary-theological level and different functions within the ritual program.

a) A euchological text, created with a certain shape, was often taken up by later collections with conscious literary and theological revisions.[60] This process produced a text different from the original, and thus a "new" rather than an "erroneous" text. [61] The concept of the "history of the textual tradition" as understood in classical studies cannot be applied with impunity to the liturgy. The aim of the liturgy is not to "throw out" all subsequent changes to an original text so as to reconstruct the original. In liturgy, the history of the textual tradition shows how a text, created to become ever new, evolves and becomes incarnate in new historical-anthropological and theological situations.[62] At each new stage, the euchological text's historical identity would have been examined when possible, and historical data permitting, its new dimension as event and communication would also have been examined.

b) Besides changes of a stylistic, cultural, and theological nature, it is not uncommon for an earlier prayer text to have also undergone a change of function within the ritual program.[63]

---

[60] See, for example, how certain expressions typical of Gregory the Great (590–604), such as *flagella iracundiae tuae* or *a cunctis malis imminentibus* were originally used to refer to the barbarians who had laid seige to Rome. Later they referred to spiritual enemies (see Triacca and Farina, op.cit., 203, n. 32).

[61] We are speaking of deliberate changes in an original prayer text which cannot be classified as "errors," but which in liturgical textual criticism are classified as "variants."

[62] The most useful tool today for trying to reconstruct the history of the tradition of a text within the Roman liturgy is the work by J. Deshusses and B. Darragon, *Concordances et Tableaux pour l'étude des grands sacramentaires*, vols. 1-6 (Fribourg, 1982–1983). Johnson and Ward's work may also be useful to some extent (C. Johnson and C. Ward, *The Sources of the Roman Missal [1975], I. Advent Christmas*, in N 22 [1986] 441–747; C. Johnson and A. Ward, *The Sources of the Roman Missal [1975] II. Prefaces*, in N 23 [1987] 409–1009), which unfortunately contains many errors in its liturgical, patristic, and biblical citations.

[63] We may note, for example, how the opening prayer for Sixth Saturday of Easter (323-C) is taken from the embolism of the preface of the *quinta clausum*

9. THE LITERARY IDENTITY OF THE TEXT

Literary criticism is one of richest and most complex parts of the methodological process. A method in itself, it is an attempt to photograph the text on a surface level. Included in this step are the search for the sources, the identification of the structure, the identification of the literary genre, the search for the stylistic properties, and the analysis of the context.

a) The Search for the Sources

This is an essential step in the study of prayer texts. The investigation involves two distinct activities. First we must search for the primary sources, which are the biblical roots of the euchological text (see *SC* 24). Secondly we must identify the material sources, which are the text's ecclesiastical roots.

To search for the primary sources means to identify the biblical citations and allusions contained in the prayer text.[64] This means we must compare it to the Latin text of the Bible [65] with the help of concordances.

The search for the material sources is more complicated since it consists in identifying the patristic, liturgical, or material source from which the prayer is born. Unfortunately, the tools for these opera-

---

Paschae in the *Gelasianum Vetus*. In the ancient formulary, the embolism of the preface was part of a ritual program in which constant attention was paid to the gradual passage toward eschatology. The embolism of the preface, which today has become an opening prayer, loses its literary and theological-liturgical character and takes on a new shape that is hard to contextualize.

[64] In the case of a biblical citation, the euchological text contains one or more words identical to the biblical text. In the case of a biblical allusion, the euchological text expresses the same theme as the biblical text but in different words. It is well to keep in mind the extent to which the material sources of the euchological texts have been influenced by the interpretation of Scripture based on the method of *lectio* (*lectio, ruminatio* or *meditatio, oratio, contemplatio*, and perhaps also *collatio* and *actio*). A good help for understanding the game of biblical allusions in prayer texts is A. Blaise and A. Dumas, *Le vocabulaire latin des principaux thèmes liturgiques* (Turnhout, 1966).

[65] It would be a mistake to restrict ourselves to the Latin text of the *Vulgata*. This translation was not, in fact, as widespread and widely accepted as it would be after the year 1000. This means that we must also look at the *Vetus latina*, and if possible, other versions as well (the *Vetus hispanica*?).

tions are still inadequate.[66] Our search for the sources eventually discerns the variants between euchology and source (additions, subtractions, modifications, contaminations). It provides valuable material for our philological analysis, for the history of the tradition, and for the editorial history. But above all, it brings together the elements on which to base the liturgical theology of the text.

b) The Identification of the Structure

Despite a certain fluidity in formulating this part of the method, M. Augé's proposal prevails today.[67] With regard to the content of the euchological texts, these elements derive their origin from the prayer of Jesus at the institution of the Eucharist. The Jewish literary and cultural heritage (see the *berakah*) has passed over into Christian prayer, where it is used to express anamnesis of the *mirabilia Dei*, doxology, thanksgiving, sanctification of the gifts, κοινωνία, intercession for the Church, etc. These content-related data are also reflected literarily in the structure. There are eight basic structural elements, not all of which are found in a single text. Some are present in different literary genres, while others are specific to one literary genre in particular. The structural elements, of course, have various theological-liturgical functions. Here is a list of the most important structural elements:

* The introduction is usually expressed by an ablative absolute or a noun phrase.[68]
* The protocol and exocol are semi-fixed forms which begin and end the preface.[69]

[66] For the euchology of the Roman Missal of Paul VI, our first help is the notes by A. Dumas (A. Dumas, *Les sources du Missel Romain*, in *Notitiae* VII [1971] 37–42, 74–77, 94–5, 134–6, 276–80, 409–10). Johnson and Ward's work has already been mentioned. Bruylants' research on the Missal of Pius V is useful for some parts of the early euchology, P. Bruylants, *Les oraisons du Missel Romain. Texte et Histoire*, vol. I–II (Louvain, 1952). The *Concordances et Tableaux* by Deshusses and Darragon is always a good help.

[67] M. Augé, "Principi di interpretazione dei testi liturgici," *Anamnesis* 1, 159–79.

[68] Example of an introduction with an ablative absolute: *Accepto, Domine, pignore salutis aeternae . . .* (198-Pc). Example of an introduction with a noun phrase: *Sumentes pignus caelestis arcani, et in terra positi iam superno pane satiati . . .* (202-Pc1).

[69] Example of a protocol: *Vere dignum et iustum est, aequum et salutare, nos tibi semper et ubique gratias agere: Domine, sancte Pater, omnipotens aeterne Deus: . . .* (398-Preface). In the sacramentaries we find only the *incipit* of the protocol, often

* The embolism is the central part of the preface or canon, with a development that is either narrative and decidedly theological, or else the words of Jesus over the bread and wine in the canon etc.[70]
* The invocation, which always includes the divine name, is a complement to the vocation or call.[71]
* The amplification consists of a simple or compound apposition in simpler cases, or a relative clause in more complex cases.[72]
* The petition is usually expressed by a hortatory subjunctive or an imperative, which may be followed by an objective clause;[73] a euchological text may also have more than one petition.[74]
* The end or purpose of the petition is usually expressed by *ut* with the subjunctive or by *ad* with the accusative of the gerund.[75]

---

abbreviated. Example of an exocol: *Et ideo, cum innumeris Angelis, una te magnificamus laudis voce, dicentes: . . .* (401-Preface).

[70] Example of an embolism in the preface: *. . . Quia ipsum in Christo salutis nostrae mysterium . . . nova nos immortalitatis eius gloria reparasti . . . .* (398-Preface).

[71] Sometimes this may be reduced to a simple *Domine . . .* or *Deus . . . .* At other times it may be enriched by one or more elements (adjective; adjective + adjective; apposition + adjective): *Omnipotens Deus . . .,* (136-C2); *Praepara, quaesumus, Omnipotens sempiterne Deus . . .* (713-C); *Domine Deus noster . . .,* (136-C1).

[72] Example of an amplification by means of a simple apposition: *Exaudi nos, Deus, salutaris noster . . .* (708-C); example of an amplification by means of a compound apposition: *Deus, vita fidelium, gloria humilium, beatitudo iustorum, . . .* (318-C2); example of an amplification by means of a relative clause: *Deus, qui regnum tuum humilibus parvulisque disponis . . .* (619-C).

[73] Example of a petition in the hortatory subjunctive: *Accepto pignore vitae aeternae, te, Domine, suppliciter deprecamur . . .* (577-Pc); example of a petition in the imperative: *Exaudi, quaesumus, Domine, preces nostras . . .* (710-C2); example of a petition in the imperative with an objective clause: *Fac nos, quaesumus, Domine, his muneribus offerendis convenienter aptari . . .* (184-So).

[74] *Omnipotens sempiterne Deus, infirmitatem nostram propitius respice, atque ad protegendum nos dexteram tuae maiestatis extende* (183-C).

[75] Example of purpose expressed by *ut* with the subjunctive: *Omnipotens sempiterne Deus, deduc nos ad societatem caelestium gaudiorum, ut eo perveniat humilitas gregis quo processit fortitudo pastoris* (302-C); example of purpose expressed by *ad* with the accusative of the gerund: *Exaudi nos, omnipotens Deus, et familiae tuae corda, cui perfectam baptismatis gratiam contulisti, ad promerendam beatitudinem aptes*

* The motive is usually expressed by *quia* and the subjunctive, or else by a simple relative.[76]

c) The Identification of the Literary Genre

Analysis of the literary genre is based on three elements: form, content, and functionality. If we look at the form, we must say that the 'protocol' is never found in a *Collecta*. On the other hand, the *Collectae* from the Roman Missal of Paul VI always have the long ending, which is absent in the *Super oblata* and the *Post communionem*, where it is replaced by the shorter ending.[77] As for content, we may note that the most powerful themes of minor euchology are found in the collects and are often linked, more or less directly, to the Liturgy of the Word. On the other hand, the theological content of the prayer over the gifts will be less "ample" than that of the collect and will be related to its function as a prayer text associated with the offertory. Euchological texts come in a host of literary genres,[78] including antiphon, canon, collect, gradual, prayer after Communion, prayer over the gifts, prayer over the people, preface, responsory, trope, etc.

d) The Search for the Stylistic Properties

The term "stylistics" has acquired different meanings in the course of time.[79] However, by way of a beginning[80] it probably suffices to

---

aeternam. (294-Pc); example of two purposes with both constructions: *Excita, Domine, corda nostra ad praeparandas Unigeniti tui vias, ut, per eius adventum, purificatis tibi mentibus servire mereamur.* (137-C2).

[76] Example of motive with *quia* and the subjunctive: *Mentes nostras, quaesumus Domine, Spiritus Sanctus adveniens divinis praeparet sacramentis, quia ipse est remissio omnium peccatorum* (338-So); example of motive with a relative clause: *Tua nobis, quaesumus, Domine, miseratione concede, ut in his sacris mysteriis Dominum Iesum dignis obsequiis veneremur, in cuius nomine voluisti omne genu flecti, omnesque homines invenire salutem* (860-Pc). In this last example there is a double motive (1st: . . . *in cuius nomine voluisti omne genu flecti;* 2nd: *omnesque homines invenire salutem*).

[77] *Institutio Generalis Missalis Romani,* 32.

[78] For a treatment in greater depth see M. Augé, "Eucologia," *NDL,* 519, n. 23.

[79] See H. Lausberg, *Elemente der literarischen Rhetorik* (Munich, 1967); P. Guiraud and P. Kuentz, *La stylistique* (Paris, 1975).

[80] For the sake of brevity, we are skipping the phonological study (hiatus, harshness, alliteration, assonance, etc.), study of the figures of speech (metaphor, allegory, simile, irony, metonymy, synecdoche, hyperbole, litotes, antonomasia,

single out a few of the more important elements often found in eu-chological texts. These concern the rhetorical devices of addition[81] (parallelism, inclusion, hendiadys, and repetition or verbal redun-dancy), propriety of language (concinnity, the theological passive), and metrics (the *cursus*).

Parallelism means the repetition of two words, expressions, stichs, etc., which are capable of expressing the same concept by repeating it with different significants (synonymic parallelism).[82] It can also ex-press a concept with opposite significants (antithetic parallelism),[83] or it can express a concept in its completeness (synthetic parallelism, in which the second member completes the first or clarifies one element of the first).[84] Parallelism includes progression[85] and chiasmus.[86] Inclusion is a form of parallelism in which two elements are found at the beginning and end of the particular text.[87] Hendiadys, on the other hand, is a single concept expressed in two words.[88] It must not

---

euphemism), study of the rhetorical devices (apostrophe, epiphonema, question, prosopopoeia, personification, duplication, reticence, gradation, hypotyposis, pe-riphrasis, etc.).

[81] The rhetorical device of addition is characterized by the fact that one expres-sion is specified by another.

[82] This would be Augé's simple parallelism. The expression is no longer used. An example of synonymic parallelism: *Fac nos, omnipotens Deus, sanctis exsultare gaudiis, et pia gratiarum actione laetari . . .* (307-C).

[83] An example of antithetic parallelism: *. . . da, quaesumus, nobis eius divinitatis esse consortes, qui humanitatis nostrae fieri dignatus est particeps* (157-C).

[84] An example of synthetic parallelism: *. . . et ad intellegendum Christi proficia-mus arcanum, et effectus eius digna conversatione sectemur* (184-C).

[85] An example of synthetic progressive parallelism: *. . . quo lavacro abluti, quo spiritu regenerati, quo sanguine sunt redempti* (299-C).

[86] Chiasmic parallelism corresponds to the formula a - b + b' - a', as in the fol-lowing synthetic parallelism: *. . . sicut tuam cognovimus* (a) *veritatem* (b), *sic eam* (b') *dignis moribus assequamur* (a') (303-So).

[87] An example of inclusion: *Deus, per quem nobis et redemptio venit et praestatur adoptio, filios dilectionis tuae benignus intende, ut in Christo credentibus et vera tribu-atur libertas et hereditas aeterna.* (303-C). The double initial syntagma (. . . *nobis et redemptio venit et praestatur adoptio*) is met by an equally double final syntagma, with ellipsis of the verb (*tribuatur*) by the second element (. . . *et vera tribuatur lib-ertas et hereditas aeterna*).

[88] The expression *gratia et veritas* (grace and truth) is a hendiadys and is equiva-lent to *gratia veritatis* (the gift of truth).

be confused with polar expression, which is an attempt to express everything that is included between the two expressed elements.[89]

Repetition or verbal redundancy, which is similar to Jakobson's principle of equivalence, consists in the repetitive and emphatic addition of one term to another.[90]

Concinnity refers to the equilibrium and harmony of a sentence in which the formal symmetries correspond to the symmetries of content. It describes a literary statement in which the maximum of the concept resides in the minimum of the significants.[91]

The theological passive is a feature of the Semitic languages which has passed over into euchological texts. It refers to a verb which is passive in form but lacks a complementary agent; the complementary agent is understood to be God.[92]

Finally, the *cursus*[93] refers to the rhythm of the clausula of a phrase, stich, or *komma*. It is based on accent and is not quantitative. More precisely, according to Mocquereau, *cursus* refers to "a harmonious succession of words and syllables, which the Latin or Greek prose-writers adopted at the end of a phrase or semi-phrase, in order to produce cadences that are rhythmic and pleasing to the ear."[94] There are four types of *cursus: planus, tardus, trispondaicus,* and *velox*.[95]

---

[89] The expression *creatorem caeli et terrae* is a polar expression. It does not say that God is creator of the heavens alone and of the earth alone; he is creator of all that is included and found, according to ancient Jewish cosmology, within these two extremes or poles.

[90] See Augé's example (from the First Eucharistic Prayer): *Haec dona, haec munera, haec sancta . . .* (Augé, "Principi di interpretazione," 177).

[91] A short text with a good example of concinnity is perhaps 302-C: *Omnipotens sempiterne Deus, deduc nos ad societatem caelestium gaudiorum, ut eo perveniat humilitas gregis, quo processit fortitudo pastoris.*

[92] An example of the theological passive: *. . . per passionem eius et crucem ad resurrectionis gloriam perducamur* (132-C). The complementary agent is understood to be God (*a te, Domine*).

[93] For a bibliography on the *cursus*, see that of Mohlberg, which although dated by now, still remains a classic bibliography (L. C. Mohlberg, ed., *Sacramentarium Veronense* [Rome, 1956] LII–LIII).

[94] A. Mocquereau, "Le cursus et la psalmodie," *Paléographie musicale*, I/4 (Bern, 1974) 27 (anastatic reprint of the Solesmes edition of 1894).

[95] The *cursus planus* consists of five syllables (- - - - -) ($\leq$ _ _ $\leq$ _) and corresponds to the classical clausula made up of the sequence *creticus + choreus* (- ⌣ - + - ⌣): *libe-rán-te sal-vá-ri.* The *cursus tardus* consists of six syllables ($\leq$ _ _ $\leq$ _ _)

These correspond in certain ways with some of the classical *clausulae*.[96]

From an examination of the stylistics, we can, if we wish, go on to a study of the text using the rhetorical method, which is not presented here because of the difficulty in bringing together all the elements of the method in such short, oral texts.

e) The Analysis of the Context

Our study of the literary identity of the text concludes with a study of its literary-liturgical context. Analysis of the context is extremely important for understanding the most salient and significant biblical-liturgical themes. A formula is situated within a literary context which is proximate, remote, general, and complete. The proximate context is provided by the major and minor euchology as well as by the texts of the Liturgy of the Word. The remote context is provided by all the texts of the liturgical season, or by the particular part of the sacramentary or missal in which the formula in question is found. The general context is provided by the sacramentary or missal as a whole. The complete context, on the other hand, includes all contemporary liturgical texts.

10. CONCLUSION

At the end of this process it is important to note certain essential data that emerge from the methodology itself.

Prior to every method there is a hermeneutic. It is hard to do an exhaustive and definitive interpretation of liturgical data today, especially now that we have seen the beginning of a fruitful dialogue between the science of liturgy and the human sciences. As this dialogue gradually advances, it is proper that we should gradually open our methodology to the new.

To integrate several methods does not mean to eliminate the previous method. It is clear that the historical-critical method prevailed

---

and corresponds to the classical clausula made up of the sequence *creticus + creticus* (- ˇ - + - ˇ -): *sém-per ob-tí-ne-at*. The *cursus spondaicus* consists of six syllables (≤ _ _ _ ≤ _) and corresponds to the classical clausula made up of the sequence *paeon primus + choreus* (- ˇ ˇ ˇ + - ˇ): *adversi-tá-te li-be-rén-tur*. The *cursus velox* consists of seven syllables (≤ _ _ (≤) _ ≤ _) and corresponds to the classical clausula made up of the sequence *creticus + dichoreus* (- ˇ - + - ˇ - ˇ): *mé-ri-tis ad-iu-vé-mur*.

96 H. Lausberg, *Elementi di retorica*, Il Mulino (Bologna, 1969) 258–9 §462–3.

until a few years ago. Today many of its conclusions have been over-turned by linguistics, and what was once important has now been reappraised. Openness to the new takes place through integration as well as through reappraisal.

Linguistic hermeneutics offers many theoretical possibilities today. This does not mean that all of them can be applied to euchological texts. Indeed, there are certain peculiarities in prayer texts that do not always fit the theoretical data. The interdisciplinary dialogue be-tween liturgists and anthropologists is one in which neither side can claim an exclusive right to ask the questions or give the answers.

Finally, our methodological choices are always influenced by our aim. These few pages do not claim to exhaust all the textual riches to be found in the prayer book. Their only aim has been to begin to dis-cover further methods that will open the way to the riches of the eu-chological heritage and the contemporary euchology of the Church.

Bibliography

Augé, M. "Principi di interpretazione dei testi liturgici." *Anàmnesis* 1:159–179. Turin, 1974.

Catella, A. "Analisi filologica e critico-letteraria in ordine alla dinamica stor-ica della liturgia." *Celebrare il mistero di Cristo. La celebrazione: introduzione alla liturgia cristiana*, 1:121–130. Rome, 1993.

Maggiani, S. "Interpretare il libro liturgico." *Il mistero celebrato: Per una metodologia dello studio della liturgia*, 157–192. Rome, 1989.

_____. "Come leggere gli elementi costitutivi del libro liturgico." *Celebrare il mistero di Cristo. La celebrazione: introduzione alla liturgia cristiana*, 1:131–141. Rome, 1993.

Merz, M. *Liturgisches Gebet als Geschehen*. Münster, 1988.

Nakagaki, F. "Metodo integrale: Discorso sulla metodologia nell'interpre-tazione dei testi eucologici." A. Cuva, ed., *Fons vivus: Miscellanea liturgica in memoria di don E. M. Vismara*, 269–286. Zürich, 1971.

Schermann, J. *Die Sprache im Gottesdienst*. Innsbruck–Vienna, 1987.

Taft, R. "The Structural Analysis of the Liturgical Units: An Essay in Methodology." *Wor* 52 (1978) 314-329.

Triacca, A., and R. Farina. "Studio e lettura dell'eucologia: Note metodologiche." C. Ghidelli, ed., *Teologia, liturgia, storia: Miscellanea in onore di C. Manziana*, 197–224. Brescia, 1977.

Zimmermann, J. A. *Liturgy as Language of Faith: A Liturgical Methodology in the Mode of Paul Ricoeur's Textual Hermeneutics*. New York–London, 1988.

Renato De Zan

18

Liturgical Textual Criticism

A great teacher of Liturgy wrote:

"In order to perform correctly textual criticism, one must have broad erudition in several distinct branches of study, and likewise be endowed with great judgment for interpreting in the light of one's own learning the questions that arise during the *labor*: to make use of it at the right time; namely, always and only when a specific problem requires it."[1]

Liturgical textual criticism is indeed a science because of the approach that is taken toward the text and because of the scientific process necessary for the choices to be carried out. Yet it is also an art[2] because of the *esprit de finesse* that should guide the critic as he or she, first, becomes attuned to the author and the amanuensis and, thereafter, in evaluating what text is to be kept and what is to be left aside. This latter operation consists in evaluating rigorously what is an actual error to be corrected as opposed to what is a variant that

---

[1] J. Pinell, *Critica testuale. Corso di iniziazione per il buon uso delle edizioni critiche e diplomatiche liturgiche* (Rome, 1991[4]) 15 (lecture notes for the course in textual criticism at the Pontifical Liturgical Institute; abbreviation: Pinell, *Critica*). The critics of biblical texts also are set along the same line. Metzger states that teaching another person how to become a text critic is like teaching him or her to become a poet (B. M. Metzger, *The Text of the New Testament* [New York-London, 1964] 211. The third edition is from 1992).

[2] Cf. A. Passoni Dell'Acqua, *Il testo del Nuovo Testamento* (Leumann-Torino, 1994) 27–8.

should be respected, understood, and retained.[3] In contrast with the biblical (and profane) textual criticism that seeks to reconstitute, by eliminating errors and variants, the archetype or, if possible, the holograph itself of the author or of the final editor, liturgical textual criticism examines texts of a different kind: the liturgical variant does not separate the copy[4] from the exemplar,[5] but makes the copy a new text with respect to the exemplar. The copy, therefore, is to be corrected of errors and not of variants.[6]

A good critic of a liturgical text[7] in our time should possess some notions[8] that go beyond philology[9] and pure textual criticism: knowl-

---

[3] In 1994 F. Dell'Oro published in two articles a nearly complete list of editions of liturgical manuscripts from 1960 to 1992. F. Dell'Oro, "Recenti edizioni di Sacramentari della Liturgia occidentale," in *La preghiera della Chiesa* (Bologna, 1974) 261–78; F. Dell'Oro, "Recenti edizioni critiche di fonti liturgiche," *Liturgia delle ore. Tempo e rito* (Rome, 1994) 197–303.

[4] Manuscript copied from the exemplar.

[5] Manuscript that the amanuensis transcribes in his copy.

[6] Of interest is what the editors of the *Greek Barberini Euchology 336* write: "The edition of a euchological text, by its nature eminently oral, cannot be approached by the same criteria under which a classic text is critically published. What follows, then, is not a critical edition in the strict sense of the term, but rather an edition of the text of the Barberini Euchology that avails itself of other manuscripts only in the event that the reading of the codex evidently proves to be uncertain, corrupt or containing gaps." Eds. S. Parenti - E. Velkovska, *L'Eucologio Barberini gr. 336* (Rome, 1995) XXV–XXVI.

[7] See the interesting contribution of B. Baroffio on the nomenclature of liturgical books and of their parts: B. Baroffio, "I manoscritti liturgici," V. Jemolo - M. Morelli, *Guida a una descrizione uniforme dei manoscritti e al loro censimento* (Rome, 1990) 143–92 (abbreviation: Jemolo - Morelli, *Guida*).

[8] See the overview in A. D'Agostino, ed., *La critica dei testi medievali e umanistici* (Rome, 1984) trans. from the German of the collective work *Probleme der Edition mittel- und neulateinischer Texte* (Bonn, 1978).

[9] It seems unnecessary to point out that a good critic of liturgical texts should know, in addition to classical Latin, also the Christian and especially the medieval liturgical Latin. Cf. J. Schrunen, *Charakteristik des Altchristlichen Latein* (Nijmegen, 1932); C. Mohrmann, *Études sur le latin des Chrétiens*, vol. III: *Latin chrétien et liturgique* (Rome, 1965); M. P. Ellebracht, *Remarks on the Vocabulary of the Ancient Orations in the Missale Romanum* (Nijmegen, 1966[2]); V. Väänänen, *Introduction au latin vulgaire* (Paris, 1967[2]); D. Norberg, *Manuel pratique de latin médiéval* (Paris, 1968).

edge is also needed of codicology and paleography. The task of textual criticism, therefore, proceeds by stages, briefly summarized here.

1. Codicology[10] is concerned basically with the materials for writing which, by way of summary, are analyzed in line with this brief scheme:[11]

> a) Every manuscript has its own "shelf mark."[12] It is rare for a liturgical manuscript not to have a shelf mark, and therefore to be unknown.[13] It is necessary to assign one to it in order for it to be identified.

> b) A liturgical manuscript is normally a codex[14] consisting of two fascicles of sheets of parchment. Parchment is an animal skin (sheep or, less commonly, horse or cow), treated with lime, dried, and then smoothed with a pumice stone. It has a flesh side or side *c* (which adhered to the animal's flesh) and a hair side or side *p* (where the animal's hair lay). The flesh side is of a lighter color, the hair side of a darker color. As they age, the flesh side tends to become convex, and the hair side concave. The sheets were sewed together to form a fascicle so that the flesh side of a sheet would touch the flesh side of another sheet (preceding or following) and the hair

---

[10] Among the innumerable studies of codicology, mention should be made of A. Dain, *Les manuscrits* (Paris, 1975³); ed. J. Glenisson, *Le Livre au moyen âge* (Paris, 1988); J. Lemaire, *Introduction à la codicologie* (Louvain-la-Neuve, 1989).

[11] For a complete description of a manuscript, see Jemolo - Morelli, *Guida.*

[12] By "shelf mark" is meant the abbreviation and/or the number by which the manuscript is known in the library where it is kept. The *Reginensis latinus* 316 of the Vatican Library is the Gelasian Sacramentary, while the D. 47 of the Capitular Library of Padua is the *Paduense* Gregorian Sacramentary.

[13] Cf. K. Gamber, *Codices liturgici latini antiquiores*, vols. I-II (Freiburg, 1968²); K. Gamber, *Codices liturgici latini antiquiores / Supplementum* (Freiburg, 1988); (this is a completion of the work with contributions by B. Baroffio, F. Dell'Oro, A. Hänggi, J. Janini, A. M. Triacca).

[14] In the liturgical sphere a little less than twenty scrolls are known: the scrolls of the *Exultet*, the Ravenna scroll, the scroll with the *Benedictio fontis,* and the scroll of the pontifical for the ordination of a bishop. Cf. G. Cavallo, *Rotoli dell'Exultet dell'Italia meridionale* (Bari, 1973); G. Battelli, *Lezioni di paleografia* (Vatican City, 1949³) (there have been successive reprintings, without corrections: the eleventh was in 1991; abbreviation: Battelli, *Lezioni*) 142.

side, obviously, the hair side of the (preceding or following) sheet.[15]

c) The parchment was folded several times [16] and then cut. Normally every fascicle consists of four double sheets (eight sheets) and is called a *quaternion*.[17] Each sheet has a side called *recto* (for Latin books, it is the face of the sheet with the stitching on the left) and the other, called *verso* (for Latin books, it is the face of the sheet with the stitching on the right). The abbreviations are *r* and *v*. A formula usually indicates the composition and the state of the fascicle: IV R *r1v r2v* TP *r3v* | *r4v r5v r6v r7v* R. This is the fourth fascicle (IV) of the manuscript with the stitching reinforcement (R . . . R). This stands for a *quaternion*, which should have eight sheets. It has seven of them, three before the stitch (|) and four after, since the third sheet has been removed. The trace of this removal is the stub (T) of the lost sheet (P).[18] Every fascicle of a codex is examined and represented by a diagram such as the following:

[15] The philologist Casper Renatus Gregory noticed this order (the "face to face" rule) in 1885. His work of 1885, *Les cahiers des manuscrits grecs*, was reprinted in L. Gilissen, *Prolégomènes à la codicologie* (Ghent, 1977) 15–9 abbreviation: Gilissen, *Prolégomènes*. The "face to face" rule is called the Gregory rule, and it helps in seeing whether the manuscript is entire or if it has been subject to alteration (for example, by removal of a sheet or double sheet). The removal of just a sheet is unfortunately common. This appalling practice leaves a trace on the fascicle at the stub, a small strip of remaining parchment near the stitch. The small strip, however, that binds the fascicle from the outside, along the stitch, is called the reinforcement.

[16] The skin can be folded *in folio* (with one fold, yielding two sheets or one double sheet), *in quarto* (with two folds, yielding four sheets in two double sheets), *in octavo* (with three folds, yielding eight sheets in four double sheets).

[17] If the fascicle is composed of two double sheets (4 sheets), it is called a *binion*; composed of three double sheets (6 sheets), it is called a *ternion*; of four double sheets (8 sheets), *quaternion*; of five double sheets (10 sheets), *quinion*. Then there are a *senion*, a *septenion*, and an *octonion*. Thereafter it is said that a fascicle is composed of nine double sheets, of ten double sheets, etc.

[18] In applying the Gregory rule to the codicology formula, one notes that the flesh side of sheet 2v touches the hair side of sheet r3: R c1p p2c TP p3c | c4p p5c c6p p7c R.

R r1v r2v TP r3v | r4v r5v r6v r7v R

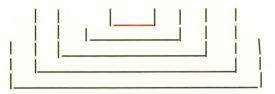

d) After the composition of the codex is determined in the individual fascicles, the cover and the back are also studied with their respective decorations or letterings.

e) Attention then shifts to the line pattern, which is the set of horizontal or vertical lines that delimit the writing frame. An old manuscript has provided us the general formula by which the amanuenses would proceed in setting the line pattern:[19] the page is made four units wide and five high (4/5);[20] the vertical line patterns: from the left side to the second vertical line, there should be 4/9 of a unit; the writing zone follows, delimited by a second vertical line that is a whole unit distant from the right margin; the horizontal line patterns: the first line lies 2/3 of a unit from the upper margin, while the last is a whole unit distant from the lower margin; between these two lines run the lines of writing within the frame in parallel order.[21]

f) Finally, the study of ink can yield more information for determining the place and time of a manuscript's composition.[22]

[19] The formula is contained in the ms. *Parisinus latinus* 11884.

[20] The criteria for line patterns have undergone various changes over the course of time, cf. J. Lemaire, *Introduction à la codicologie* (Louvain-la-Neuve, 1989); the ratio between width and height can also correspond to the golden section (0.618/1), to the Pythagorean rectangle (3/4), and to the proportions of Leonardo Fibonacci (5/8). These models almost never were executed exactly (Gilissen, *Prolégomènes*, 224–7).

[21] The mathematical formula of this simple line pattern is: (4/9:1) + (2+5/9:1) + (1/1) x (2/3:1) + (3+1/3:1) + (1:1). The first part of this formula comprises the horizontal reading, from right to left, of the vertical lines. After the x sign the vertical reading of the horizontal lines begins from the top.

[22] Cf. M. Zerdoun Bat-Yehouda, *Les encres noires au Moyen Age (jusqu'à 1600)* (Paris, 1983).

2. Paleography[23] is the science that studies and deciphers ancient writings. For liturgical texts, there are three especially important periods: the first (7th-9th centuries), during which the copying centers, the *scriptoria*, lie in the centers of Roman culture and the abbeys, is characterized by the survival of some handwriting forms of the previous period (especially cursive minuscule, half-uncial, and uncial) and by the use of new forms (Beneventan, Merovingian, Visigothic) of handwriting, the Carolingian and, in some particular places (Ireland, England) the insular script; the third period (13th-14th centuries) is dominated by the Gothic script that is used both by the abbeys and by the new copying centers that are the *scriptoria* of the universities. This simple classification aids in understanding the usefulness of knowledge of forms of writing which, together with a knowledge of inks and of other content elements, can lead to a good dating of a manuscript.

Each of these forms of writing, characterized by identifying letters, presents two large difficulties to the contemporary reader: the abbreviations and the ligatures. The former consist in reducing, according to a certain conventionality, the number of letters that make up a frequent word (Ds for *Deus*, IHS for *Iesus*, SPS for *Spiritus*, etc.). The latter are special ways of joining a sequence of letters one to another. In working with the writing on a manuscript, the following general rules should be observed in transcribing into typographic lower-case letters:

> a) A number is assigned to each liturgical text (from the euchological to the rubrical) of the codex under examination.
>
> b) Words are separated, abbreviations and ligatures are written in full.[24]
>
> c) Every letter is transcribed as it is recognized in the manuscript; it is more correct to write *j* as *i* and to distinguish between *u* and *v*.

[23] Among the numerous studies of paleography, noteworthy are: Battelli, *Lezioni*; A. Cappelli, *Dizionario di abbreviature latine ed italiane* (Milan, 1961⁶); G. Cencetti, *Paleografia latina* (Rome, 1978); G. Tognetti, *Criteri per la trascrizione di testi medioevali latini e italiani* (Rome, 1982); B. Bischoff, *Paläographie des römischen Altertums und des abendländischen Mittelalters* (Berlin, 1986).

[24] The accepted meaning is usually gained through the *Vere dignum*.

d) Attention is needed as to whether each line of writing has been done by one[25] or more hands[26] and whether there are corrections above the text or over an erasure.[27]

e) The interlinear and marginal glosses, when they belong to a text, are written between squared brackets È ⌣.

f) The upper case should be used: at the beginning of a text and after every period; for personal and place names; for names of peoples (and religions); for sacred persons (God, Persons of the Trinity, the Virgin . . .); for solemnities, feasts, and liturgical times; for *Ecclesia* (when it indicates the whole Church and not a particular church); *sanctus* and *beatus*, when they are applied to persons, should not be written with an upper-case letter.

g) It is preferable to employ modern diacritical signs: punctuation in manuscripts is almost always arbitrary.

h) During the transcription the sign of a page turn is placed in the text exactly where this action is done in a manuscript; the sign lies between brackets which contain the number of the sheet and its respective *recto* or *verso* [f.6v].

i) In the case of a text mutilated due to the decay of the writing materials, steps are taken for the hypothetical reconstruction of the text, by taking into account three basic elements:[28] the characteristics of the writing (abbreviations or ligatures) and its relation to the missing line pattern; the characteristics of the *kommata* or stichs (the length and the *cursus*,[29] when

---

[25] This concerns the text by the first hand.

[26] This concerns the text or additions by the second hand or the third, etc.

[27] The corrections can be by the first hand or by another hand. They are above the text when the mistaken word has been struck (but is still legible) and the correction has been made above it, by writing the correct word or whatever was deemed to be so. They are corrections over erasures when the mistaken word has been scraped off with a *scriptorium* knife, and the correct word or whatever is deemed to be so has been written over the erasure.

[28] J. Pinell, "Reliquias del Psalmographus," *Hispania Sacra* 25 (1972) 185–208.

[29] Cf. H. Lausberg, *Elemente der literarischen Rhetorik* (Munich, 1967[3]); A. Mocquereau, "Le cursus et la psalmodie," *Paleographie musicale*, I/4 (Berne, 1974) 27 (photomechanical reprint of the Solesmes 1894 edition).

possible); the connection of the text to be reconstructed with similar biblical, patristic, and euchological texts.

j) Particular attention is then paid to palimpsests.[30] The underlying text (*scriptio inferior*) is difficult to reconstruct given the possibility that the amanuensis might have altered, for whatever reason, the earlier order of the fascicles.

k) Musical notations[31] and decorations (capital letters, miniatures, etc.)[32] make up part of a special branch of paleography.

3. In the copying process, an *amanuensis* would perform textual alterations. There are involuntary alterations (errors) and voluntary ones (variants).[33] Errors can be due to sight (from two phenomena, *homeoarcton* and *homeoteleuton*,[34] there usually derive haplography and its opposite, dittography[35]), to hearing and to dictation (homophony, alteration of sound, and environmental phonetic conditioning[36]), to ignorance (grammatical, syntactical, and theological errors), and to psychological factors (inversions, metatheses, harmo-

---

[30] Alban Dold, O.S.B., has given particular attention to this kind of liturgical manuscript. See, for example, A. Dold, ed., *Palimpseststudien I* (Beuron, 1955); *II* (Beuron, 1957).

[31] Cf. M. G. Tedeschi, "I manoscritti musicali," in Jemolo-Morelli, *Guida*, 103–42. The bibliography is very good, albeit basic.

[32] Cf. L. Donati, *Bibliografia della miniatura* (Florence, 1972); G. Bologna, *Manoscritti e miniature. Il libro prima di Guttemberg* (Milan, 1994).

[33] The Gelasian textual tradition is marked by many errors and few corrections, while the Gregorian textual tradition counts few errors and many corrections (cf. Pinell, *Critica*, 17).

[34] *Homeoarcton* or *homeoarctia* is a graphic phenomenon that consists in two successive words (expressions, phrases, pericopes) beginning with the same letters (words, expressions, phrases). *Homeoteleuton* or *homeoteleutia* is the same phenomenon, but it involves the ending of words, expressions, phrases, and pericopes. The eye does not perceive two literary elements but just one.

[35] Haplography is the omission of the repetition of some element of writing (letter, syllable, word, expression, phrase, pericope when the correct form in the exemplar is double; dittography is the improper repetition of an element when the correct form in the exemplar is single.

[36] The copyist writes *preces* instead of *praeces*, or else *umanitas* instead of *humanitas* (homophony); he writes *monimentum* instead of *munimentum*; *creatur* instead of *creator* (alteration of sound); he writes *salba* or *mici* instead of *salva* or *mihi* (phonetic conditionings of the cultural environment within which he lives).

374

nizations[37]). Variants are voluntary alterations, due to the culture of the time and environment of the *amanuensis*. They make the text contained in the copy a new text with respect to the text of the exemplar. A comparative study (reasons that have led to: additions, deletions, expansions, modifications on a semantic, linguistic, stylistic, and theological level) between the text of the exemplar and the voluntarily modified text contained in the copy does not belong to the field of liturgical textual criticism. Rather, it belongs to the field of literary criticism of the sources, which liturgical textual criticism makes use of. These variants can be literary (stylistic perfecting or simplification of the text), hermeneutical (expansions, replacement of obsolete terms, alteration of meaning), and theological. When the variants present in the copy are drawn from an exemplar different from the one that the amanuensis is copying, there is the phenomenon of contamination; this phenomenon makes difficult the reconstruction of the lineage of the manuscript being examined.

Every manuscript has a genealogy behind it. Reconstructing this genealogy or lineage[38] is essential for non-liturgical textual criticism: only thus can the archetype of the text or even the original text be established. For liturgical textual criticism, precisely because of the characteristics of the text being examined, rather than reconstruct the lineage that leads to the archetype, one can normally reconstruct a segment of lineage that places the manuscript being examined within a family. A liturgical manuscript normally does not have an archetype but rather a model. The lineage is determined after a collection (*collatio*) of manuscripts close to the one being examined is made, and after examining the textual alterations (errors and variants). The errors-variants serve as guides. They are called conjunctive errors-variants when they are found in more manuscripts that make them related. They are called disjunctive errors-variants when they are present in some manuscripts

[37] The copyist writes *praecipio* instead of *percipio* (metathesis), *Iesus Christus* instead of *Christus Iesus* (inversion), or else he expands the text in the copy because, after reading some words, he thinks he remembers well the text of the exemplar, while instead he writes another text from memory.

[38] The classic text on lineage is P. Maas, *Textkritik* (Leipzig, 1957³). There is an Italian trans. by N. Martinelli of the second German edition, with a presentation by G. Pasquali: P. Maas, *Critica del testo* (Florence, 1972). The new feature of the third German edition, the *Rückblick* [retrospective], has been translated in *Belfagor* 23 (1968) 358–60.

but absent in others, thus creating a separation between one group and the other. By examining the textual alterations, conjunctive and disjunctive errors-variants, and by dating the manuscripts normally through the script and the ink, it is possible to reconstruct a segment of lineage (linear, divaricate, branched) where the capital letters of the Latin alphabet (A; B; C; etc.) indicate the real manuscripts, and the small letters of the Greek alphabet (α; β; γ; etc.) indicate the hypothetical manuscripts. It must be kept in mind that contamination often turns the lineage, or rather the segment of the lineage, into a very difficult task. At this point, the critic accepts the lesser evil: he or she carries out some simple comparisons among the texts he or she possesses, choosing a primary source for comparing with the others.[39]

4. The rules of textual criticism of a liturgical text basically involve the recomposition of a liturgical text, with errors corrected, according to the final redaction of the text itself. This simple statement has some consequences:

> — to restore a liturgical manuscript through textual criticism means to leave the order of the texts as it is, unless there are proofs to the contrary that emerge from codicology;
> — each text is respected for what it is and any comparison with texts of more archaic manuscripts serves for the correction of errors and not for the modification of variants; this can be useful for the delicate work of reconstructing a text containing gaps (cf. 2i).

> Liturgical textual criticism for certain aspects is simple: it involves correcting in general errors in spelling, grammar, and syntax. Rarely are there theological errors. More often there may be haplographs, dittographs, and metatheses. Even rarer are instances of a nonsensical reading. All these errors can be corrected, quite frequently, without resorting to parallel sources. Sometimes, however, it is necessary to refer to parallel sources: in this case, use is made of some rules, prudently applied. None of these rules, taken individually, is determinative for the choice of the *textus receptus* or the editor's read-

---

[39] "If the discrepancies between A and B are greater than between A and C, and furthermore C, with its particular variants, appears closer to B than to A, then C could be a good primary text" (Pinell, *Critica*, 9).

ing. Rather, it is the convergence of the entire set of these rules that is determinative. The external rules, that prescind from the content of the text, can be summarized as follows:

— the best-documented reading is the most original, taking into account the identity and the connection among manuscripts;

— the influence of parallel texts (euchological, patristic, biblical) of the connected readings and of the theological mentality must be taken into account;

— consideration must be given to the *cursus* and the *concinnitas* (grammar, syntax, phraseology, sentence division).

The internal rules, which take into account the content of the text, can be briefly presented as follows:

— the more difficult reading has the greater probability of being the original;

— the shorter reading has the greater probability of being the original;

— the preferred reading ought to be in harmony with the context;

— the other variants should be explained by the preferred reading.

Only in extreme cases (in case of a nonsensical reading) can recourse be made to conjectures.

5. The critical apparatus in the liturgical context has not yet assumed a canonical character inasmuch as a liturgical text cannot follow the rules of editions of biblical or profane texts.[40] A transition has been made from Mohlberg's skeleton notes to Canals' copious notes. The accumulated experience in these recent decades permits gathering some constants, capable of being summarized,[41] within the

[40] See note 7.

[41] By way of example, two publications may be read. For a calendar, see F. Trolese, "Usanze liturgiche del monastero de santa Giustina nel sec. XV: dal codice 1389 della Biblioteca Universitaria di Padova," in A. Catella, *Amen Vestrum. Miscellanea di studi liturgico-pastorali in onore di P. Pelagio Visentin o.s.b.*, (Padua, 1994) 13–68. For a sacramentary, see *Monumenta liturgica ecclesiae tridentinae*, vols. I–III (Trent, 1983–1985).

critical apparatuses of different published liturgical texts.[42] In the editor's reading, also called the *textus receptus*:

a) the identifying number of each text (liturgical, rubrical, musical) is placed in the margin;

b) the progressive line number is always placed in the margin (the number is written out every three lines: 3; 6; 9; etc.);

c) the sign of a page turn with brackets [], and the number of the sheet with the specification *r* or *v* are placed in the text; moreover brackets are used to enclose dittographs; acute brackets <> are use for enclosing haplographs; between squared brackets, È ᵕ, interlinear or marginal glosses are enclosed; a bar | can be employed for indicating in the *textus receptus* the point at which the *amanuensis* goes to the head of the manuscript.

At the foot of a page, however, two registers are normally placed: the one for parallel passages and the other for textual criticism. In the register of parallel passages, mention is made of the texts closest to the text being examined, or even the same text present in other manuscripts. In the register of textual criticism, however, these elements are usually found:

d) the line number written as an exponent to indicate where to find the problem of textual criticism that is sought for discussion;

e) written immediately thereafter is the word or expression of the *textus receptus* that is sought for discussion, followed immediately by a single bracket];

f) what comes next indicates the variant that was not chosen for the *textus receptus* but that is present in other manuscripts; for the Latin text, normal type is used, while for everything else (critical abbreviations,[43] abbreviations of codices, etc.) italics are used;

---

[42] The most important series of liturgical texts are: Henry Bradshaw Society, Liturgiegeschichtliche (Liturgiewissenschaftliche) Quellen und Forschungen, Rerum Ecclesiasticarum Documenta, Spicilegium Friburgense, etc.

[43] For example, *add.* (addition), *marg.* (marginal), *om.* (omission), *p.m.* (first hand), *ras.* (erasure), *s.m.* (second hand), *trans.* (transposition), etc.

g) the individual problem of textual criticism, whenever there might be more than one in one line, is enclosed by a vertical bar |; the double bar ‖ is used to enclose a problem or problems of textual criticism of a line of the *textus receptus*.

At the end of his or her work, the liturgical text critic is called to the true humility of the knowledge that is able to accept constructive criticism with gratitude. Indeed, it is difficult for the first edition of a liturgical critical text to be published without errors.

Bibliography

Agostino, A., ed. *La critica dei testi medievali e umanistici*. Rome, 1984.

Avalle, D. S. *Principi di critica testuale*. Padua, 1972.

Fränkel, H. *Testo critico e critica del testo*. Florence, 1969.

Pasquali, G. *Storia della tradizione e critica del testo*. Florence, 1952[2]. This is a classic manual for profane (and biblical) texts. Not all the criteria are useful for liturgical texts. It creates in the reader a good critical mindset, very useful for resolving typical cases of liturgical textual criticism. There is a reprint of the Italian edition: Milan 1974.

Pinell, J. *Critica testuale:. Corso di iniziazione per il buon uso delle edizioni critiche e diplomatiche liturgiche*. Rome, 1991[4] (lecture notes).

Reynolds, L. D., ed. *Texts and Transmission: A Survey of the Latin Classics*. Oxford, 1983.

Sabbadini, R. *Storia e critica dei testi latini*. Padua, 1971[2].

Salvatore, A. *Edizione critica e critica del testo*, Rome 1983.

Anscar J. Chupungco, O.S.B.

19

The Translation of Liturgical Texts

INTRODUCTORY NOTES

The liturgy uses a variety of texts, both biblical and extra-biblical. These texts are proclaimed as part of public worship and hence, together with the other ritual components of the celebration, contribute to the spiritual edification of the hearers. *Sacrosanctum Concilium* 33 teaches: "Not only when things 'that were written for our instruction' are read (Roman 15:4), but also when the Church prays or sings or acts, the faith of those taking part is nourished and their minds are raised to God." Liturgical texts are intended to nourish the faith of the assembly. That is why, they should be theologically rich and spiritually uplifting. At the same time they should be formulated that they serve as effective means of communicating the message of the liturgy to a given assembly.

It is useful at this point to compare liturgical texts with the other liturgical components. In a broad sense the texts and ritual elements of worship belong to the category of language: they all speak to the assembly and convey, in their particular way, the message of the liturgy. Both fall under the category of sign. They indicate the presence of God and of his salvation in the liturgical assembly. Some texts and ritual elements belong also to the category of sacraments. They "contain what they signify." Such are the sacramental formulas and gestures like the handlaying at ordination rites. Generally speaking, texts and ritual elements are plurivalent or open to a variety of interpretations. Exception should be made in those situations where they express a doctrine or perhaps even a dogmatic statement and hence must be interpreted according to the intention of the Church.

But there are differences. While non-verbal elements, such as symbols and gestures, address the assembly through the tactile and visual senses, liturgical texts are words that are communicated orally through aural contact.[1] While certain symbols and gestures are trans-cultural and do not need to be "translated" in order to be understood cross-culturally, liturgical texts require the use of the local assembly's words, phrases, and language patterns in order to pass on their message. In those instances — and today they constitute the majority of cases — where the texts originate in another epoch and in another theological and cultural milieu, translation becomes a necessity, unless new texts are composed locally. The decision of Vatican II to allow the use of the vernacular is surely one of its precious gifts to local churches.[2]

LANGUAGES USED IN THE LITURGY

We may presume that the first Christian community at Jerusalem worshiped in Aramaic, though it is expected that the scriptural readings were in Hebrew.[3] As the Church spread to other centers of the Roman Empire, a popular type of Greek became the language for worship. It was the language spoken throughout the major cities of the empire, including Rome itself. Greek κοινή, on the other hand, was the language in which the books of the New Testament were read. In Jerusalem the situation was somewhat different in the fourth century. The bishop spoke to the assembly in Greek while an interpreter translated into Syriac.[4] Eventually the biblical readings were translated also in Syriac and Latin for those who did not speak Greek.

But Christianity reached also the other parts of the world where Greek was less familiar. In the peripheries of Antioch people continued to speak Syriac and this became the established liturgical language. Alexandria spoke Greek, but by the sixth and seventh century

[1] K. Larsen, "Language as Aural," *Wor* 54 (1980) 18–35.

[2] J. Lamberts, "Vatican II et la liturgie en langue vernaculaire," *QL* 66 (1985) 125–54.

[3] A.-G. Martimort, "Essai historique sur les traductions liturgiques," *MD* 86 (1966) 75–105.

[4] Ethérie, *Journal de voyage* 47, SCh 21 (Paris, 1948) 260–3.

Coptic was introduced into the liturgy for nationalistic and sectarian, that is monophysite, motives. Today it uses Greek, Coptic, and Arabic. Ethiopia still celebrates the liturgy in ancient *Ge'ez*, which is a Semitic language, although the local Church was influenced by Coptic, Greek, and Syrian missionaries. Seleucia on the lower Tigris, the center of the Nestorian Church which brought the Gospel as far as India, Java, and China, used Syriac, the language in which Mesopotamia and Persia were evangelized. However, the missionary demands constrained the Nestorian Church to translate the biblical readings and its liturgical books into the local languages. Armenia which was evangelized in the third century and received influences from Antioch and Constantinople has kept its ancient Armenian language in the liturgy. Georgia still celebrates the Byzantine liturgy in the Georgian language. Lastly, most of the other churches in Eastern Europe from Bulgaria to Russia, which inherited the liturgy of Constantinople, continue to use Slavonic for their liturgical language.[5]

The use of native or local languages for the liturgy is thus a significant tradition of the early Church. The obvious motivation was clearly the absolute need to communicate the message to the liturgical assembly. In the second half of the ninth century the Thessalonian brothers Cyril and Methodius started their missionary work in Moravia by translating the Latin and Greek liturgies there into Slavonic. Their effort was met with hostility on the part of the Frankish clergy, the original missionaries of Moravia, who argued that God could be worshiped only in Hebrew, Greek, and Latin, the three languages in which Pilate wrote the cause for which he condemned Christ to the cross.[6] Such principle of "trilinguism" blatantly ignored both tradition and pastoral concern.

When the Christian community was established in Rome before the year 60, Greek was the dominant language among the inhabitants of the city. This is explained by the cosmopolitan and international character of the city which attracted the Orientals in great numbers. In fact during the first two centuries the Church of Rome raised ten

---

[5] T. Federici, "Le liturgie dell'area orientale," *Anàmnesis* 2 (Casale, 1978) 110–28.

[6] A. Dostal, "The Origins of the Slavonic Liturgy," *Dumbarton Oaks Papers* 19 (1965) 67–87.

Greek-speaking bishops to the throne of Peter. The Romans themselves learned and preferred to speak Greek as the language of culture and civilization.

The process of latinization in the liturgy began, not in Rome, but in the churches of North Africa.[7] The writers who contributed to the process were Tertullian, Cyprian of Carthage, Arnobius, Lactantius, and Augustine of Hippo. From them the Church in the West inherited such liturgical words as *sacramentum, ordo, plebs, disciplina,* and *institutio.* The first official Latin version of the Bible for use in the liturgy appeared in North Africa around the year 250. In his writings Cyprian constantly cited from this translation.

The first attempt to introduce Latin in the Roman liturgy was made during the pontificate of Victor I († 203), an African by birth. It was toward the year 250 when the Latin bible made its appearance in the city. By the second half of the third century, when the number of migrations from the oriental part of the empire dropped, Latin gained ascendancy. The Roman Church then adopted a bilingual liturgy: Greek for the Eucharistic Prayer, at least until the appearance of the Roman canon in the fourth century, and Latin for the biblical readings. This transitional stage lasted until the end of the fourth century, when Pope Damasus I († 384) initiated a definitive transition from Greek to Latin. He authored the famous Latin *epigrammata* and several Latin formularies that have been preserved in the Veronese Sacramentary. It is now commonly held that the shift involved the composition of new liturgical texts in Latin, not translation from Greek.[8] This was the way the Latin liturgical language evolved, thanks to the authorship of the Roman bishops, especially Pope Leo I († 461).

In the seventh century the Church of Rome returned to some form of bilingual liturgy to accommodate Orientals who poured back into the city. In fact from 638 to 772 nine popes were from the East. Rome's bilingual liturgy referred to the readings and to some rites of the catechumenate. Greco-Roman readings continued to be practiced in Rome for such occasions as Easter and Christmas, at the Vigils of

[7] C. Vogel, *Medieval Liturgy: Introduction to the Sources* (Washington, D.C., 1986) 294–7; T. Klauser, *A Short History of the Western Liturgy* (Oxford, 1979) 18–24, 37–47.
[8] C. Vogel, *Medieval Liturgy,* 295–6.

Easter and Pentecost, on Ember Saturdays, and at the Mass for the ordination of a pope.

In conclusion we recall that in the third century the liturgy of Rome was still in Greek, although the city spoke Latin. It took the Roman Church one century to adjust painfully to the inevitable, but it did so courageously, fully aware that it was abandoning the language of the apostolic times and the language of its martyrs. Yet the liturgy had to speak the language of the people, if the gospel message it contains was to be communicated at all. This same pastoral spirit came alive in the seventh century when the Roman Church shifted back to a bilingual liturgy in favor of migrants from the East.

It took the Roman Church several hundred years to adjust again to the fact that its liturgical assemblies no longer spoke nor understood Latin. This time it had to be a decision of an ecumenical council.

THE TRANSITION FROM LATIN TO THE VERNACULAR

When Vatican II approved the use of the vernacular in the Roman liturgy, it was implied that the Latin liturgical books would have to be translated into the local languages. This underpinned *Sacrosanctum Concilium* 36 whose formulation drew much debate in the council hall.[9] The final text is a classic example of the *via media* which reaffirmed, on the one hand, that "the use of the Latin language is to be preserved in the Latin rite," although the use of the vernacular may be extended, and empowered, on the other, the conferences of bishops "to decide and to what extent the vernacular may be used."[10]

While emotional attachment to the Latin liturgy on the part of some Fathers was present during the council discussion, the implications of a translated liturgy were not lost to others. Norms were needed to safeguard the liturgy's doctrinal purity as well as its authentic message. A petition was submitted to the conciliar commission to add a clause requiring that "translations from the Latin text into the mother tongue intended for use in the liturgy

[9] A. Chupungco, "The Translation, Adaptation and Creation of Liturgical Texts," *Not* 208 (1983) 694–700.

[10] For a 1979 listing of the various approved liturgical languages after the council, see J. Gibert, "Le lingue nella liturgia dopo il Concilio Vaticano II," *Not* 15 (1979) 387–520. See A.-G. Martimort, "L'Histoire et le problème liturgique contemporains," *Mens concordet voci* (Tournai, 1983) 177–92.

must be approved by the competent, territorial authority." The reason for the petition was "to avoid dangerous freedom and variety of translations which can threaten the true meaning and beauty of the texts."[11]

The first area of liturgy for which the vernacular was allowed is the divine office. In his celebrated *Motu proprio "Sacram Liturgiam"* of 1964 Pope Paul VI put into effect the use of the vernacular instead of Latin in the recitation of the hours. He defined the norm that the translated version should be drawn up and approved by the conferences of bishops and submitted to the Holy See for due approval, that is, confirmation. "This is the course to be taken whenever any Latin liturgical text is translated into the vernacular by the authority already mentioned."[12] In the same year the Consilium issued the Instruction *Inter Oecumenici* where it gave the criteria for vernacular translations.[13] Among other things, the Consilium made it clear that "the basis of the translations is the Latin liturgical text" (XI, 40a), that the work of translations should involve institutes of liturgy or persons who are experts in Scripture, liturgy, the biblical languages, Latin, the vernacular, and music (XI, 40b), that where applicable, "there should be consultation with bishops of neighboring regions using the same language" (XI, 40c), that "in nations of several languages there should be a translation for each language" (XI, 40d), and that the liturgy may be celebrated anywhere in the language of migrants, members of a personal parish, or other like groups (XI, 41).

In his address to the translators of liturgical texts in 1965 Pope Paul VI summed up the conciliar and postconciliar thinking on the matter.[14] The address is brief, but it covers the basic principles of liturgical translations. In many ways, the 1969 Instruction on the translation of liturgical texts is an elaboration of several of its points. First, the pope reminded the translators that the work of translation aims principally to promote active participation in the liturgy, as desired by the council. For this reason, the Church was willing to let go

---

[11] *Schema Constitutionis de Sacra Liturgia*, Emendationes IV (Vatican City, 1963) 15.

[12] *AAS* 56 (1964) 144.

[13] *AAS* 56 (1964) 877–900.

[14] *Not* 1 (1965) 378–81.

of its centuries-old Latin liturgy, permitting "the translation of texts venerable for their antiquity, devotion, beauty, and long-standing use." Yet active and devout participation stems chiefly from the understanding of the rites themselves. The sacrifice of so noble a heritage should thus be compensated by vernacular texts that are "within the grasp of all, even children and the uneducated." Translations should bridge the cultural gap between the Latin liturgy and the local churches everywhere.

Second, while the preconciliar translations assisted the faithful to understand the Latin rite, the official translations after the council "have become part of the rites themselves; they have become the voice of the Church." In other words, vernacular translations enjoy the same value and respect as the original version: they too are the Church's official languages in which God is worshiped. That is why, translated texts, approved by the local authority and the Holy See for liturgical use, "are as such to be held in all reverence." To take liberties with them is to disregard the nature of liturgical text as the prayer of the Church. After the council many new languages have been introduced for use in the liturgy. This does not mean that the Church has instituted new liturgical families. "The voice of the Church remains one and the same in celebrating the divine mysteries and administering the sacraments, although that voice speaks in a variety of tongues." In short, translations do not produce new rites.

Third, the type of language to be used in the liturgy "should always be worthy of the noble realities it signifies, set apart from the everyday speech of the street and the marketplace." This requires that translators "know both Christian Latin and their own modern language," and in view of a truly musical liturgy, also take the rules of music into account and so choose words that can be set to music suited to the culture of each people. At this point the pope once again reminds translators of the sacrifice the Church has made: "for pastoral reasons, the beauty and richness of Latin, which the Latin Church used for centuries for prayers, petitions, and thanksgiving to God, have been partially lost." The challenge for translators is to "make a similar clarity of language and dignity of expression shine forth in the vernacular translations of liturgical texts." The message or content should always be the chief consideration of translators. However, it is not enough to translate the message faithfully. In the tradition of the Latin texts, especially those belonging to the classical period of the Roman liturgy, translators should develop the kind of liturgical language that reflects the best in local culture. In their preoccupation to be faithful to the doctrinal message translators might lose sight of their obligation to be faithful to the artistic form or vesture of liturgical texts. The liturgy is not content alone nor form alone, but the interplay of both.

PRINCIPLES OF LITURGICAL TRANSLATION

A. A Definition of Translation

"If I translate word by word, it sounds absurd; if I am forced to change something in the word order or style, I seem to have stopped being a translator."[15] With these words St. Jerome articulated the experience of every conscientious translator. Word-by-word translation often does not make sense, but a change in the meaning of the word betrays the message. The translation of liturgical texts is perhaps the most delicate and complicated matter arising from the Council's decision to shift from Latin to the vernacular languages.

To define translation it is useful to review several of its components.[16] Translation consists basically of rendering into the receptor language the message of the source language. In our context the vernacular is the receptor language, while liturgical Latin is the source language. The message is the doctrinal and spiritual content of the Latin text, that is, the message which the Church intends to communicate to a particular assembly. This assembly is the addressee for whom the Latin text has been originally prepared.[17] In order that the assembly will grasp the full meaning of what is communicated, it is necessary that the content be expressed in the values, traditions, and linguistic patterns proper to the

---

[15] Jerome, *Eusebii Interpretata Praefatio*, Einleitung des Hieronymus, *Eusebius Werke* VII, 1, GCS 47, ed. R. Helm (1954) 2: *Si ad verbum interpretor, absurde resonat: si ob necessitatem aliquid in ordine, in sermone mutavero, ab interpretis videbor officio recessisse.*

[16] G. Venturi, "Fenomeni e problemi linguistici della traduzione liturgica nel passaggio da una cultura ad un'altra," *EphLit*, 92 (1978) 12–3; see also for background material, E. Nida - C. Taber, *The Theory and Practice of Translation* (Leiden, 1982) 12–4; P. Newmark, *Approach to Translation* (Oxford, 1981) 38–46.

[17] Consilium, *Instruction "Comme le prévoit,"* *Not* 5 (1969) 3–12. English text in *Documents on the Liturgy 1963-1979* (Collegeville, 1982) no. 6, 284–5.

assembly. This vesture is the cultural form with which the doctrinal content is expressed. It is through the form that the content is effectively communicated to the audience or assembly.

Although it is impossible to separate physically the doctrinal content from the cultural form, it will be necessary to make a mental distinction between them in order to allow the content to take on another cultural form. Sometimes the original text will undergo the process of what authors call "decomposition," "decoding," or "dehistorization," in order to establish the "kernel" or the basic doctrinal content. This process also aims to discover the relationship between the "kernel" and the other segments of the text or, in other words, its global historical, cultural, doctrinal, and literary context. The process concludes with the "recomposition" of the text in the new form of the receptor language.[18]

With its particular cultural and linguistic qualities the new form should be able to clothe the content in the same manner as the original form has done. It is implied that the new form possesses equivalent qualities wherewith the content can be adequately expressed. In a way, we can describe the process of translation as the passage of the content from one cultural form to another that represents equivalently the original form. A good translation is thus able to produce in the audience of the receptor language the same effect as the source language has on its original audience. In short, it achieves the same purpose as does the original text.[19]

This type of translation follows the theories of "dynamic equivalence," and has gained the approval of the Concilium in its 1969 Instruction *Comme le prévoit* on the translation of liturgical texts. The Instruction may be "dated," as some Church sectors snipe, but its value as guidelines for liturgical translation stands on solid scientific grounds. According to the Instruction, "a faithful translation cannot be judged on the basis of individual words: the total context of this specific act of communication must be kept in mind, as well as the literary form proper to the respective language."[20] The context, ac-

---

[18] N. Chomsky, *Syntactic Structures* (The Hague, 1964); see the application of this method in A. Echiegu, *Translating the Collects of the "Sollemnitates Domini" of the "Missale Romanum" of Paul VI in the Language of the African* (Münster, 1984).

[19] C. Rabin, *Cultural Aspects of Biblical Translation* (Jerusalem, 1971) 238.

[20] *Instruction "Comme le prévoit,"* no. 6.

cording to the Instruction, includes the message itself, the audience for which the text is intended, and the manner of expression.

The foregoing definition obviously discredits the type of translation that does not take into account the culture represented by both the source and the receptor languages. Such type merely renders the original text word by word or phrase by phrase, unmindful of the cultural underpinnings in them. It follows the method of "formal correspondence." Although it aims to be faithful to the original text, its fidelity centers almost exclusively on the surface level of the source language and on literal transference into the receptor language.[21] Sometimes formal correspondence tries to recast the system of the receptor language in order to conform to the source language. This often does untold violence to the receptor language. Apropos S. Marsili remarks: "We would not regard as scientific a translation based on the belief that the sense of a Latin text could be captured by a simple recourse to a dictionary and the study of the grammatical and logical form in question."[22] He points out that the text possesses a "genius" of its own, "which is in turn the genius of the people, the age, and the culture giving rise to the text."

B. Some Premises of Liturgical Translation

The work of liturgical translation rests on several premises. The first refers to the nature of translation as a scientific endeavor that follows a system of principles and procedures.[23] This involves two camps, namely linguistics and liturgy. Translators should possess adequate knowledge of the principles and structure of language. F. de Saussure, among others, has contributed immensely to the understanding of language.[24] Modern linguistics has moved away from the traditional notion of language as nomenclature, which means that the words used by different languages are regarded merely as sound labels for the same reality, and hence translation as only a matter of

---

[21] C. Kraft, *Christianity in Culture. A Study in Dynamic Biblical Theologizing in Cross-cultural Perspective* (New York 1979/1994) 265; see chapters 13–5, 261–312.

[22] S. Marsili, "Liturgical Texts for Modern Man," *Concilium* 2/5 (1969) 26.

[23] E. Nida, *Towards a Science of Translating with Special Reference to Principles and Procedures Involved in Bible Translating* (Leiden, 1964).

[24] F. de Saussure, *Course in General Linguistics,* trans. from the French *Cours de linguistique générale,* (Glasgow, 1974).

transferring names. On the contrary, every language has its distinctive cultural patterns and unique genius which the translators should know, respect, and work in terms of. The syntax, literary genres, and idioms manifest the receptor language's cultural patterns and linguistic uniqueness, while at the same time they provide the users of the language a prism wherewith to view reality.

The other camp is the liturgy. Translators work on existing liturgical texts. We know that these originate in different epochs of Church history, and were authored by various people for the use of a given assembly at a given occasion. Their authentic and original message will be understood better, if these considerations are known and kept in mind. In this connection, the Instruction *Comme le prévoit* (no. 8) exhorts that "to discover the true meaning of a text, the translator must follow the scientific methods of textual study as used by experts." Liturgical hermeneutics is now regarded as a foundational component of the study of liturgy. It consists, among other things, of philological analysis of the text, textual identification (authorship, theological and cultural ambient, literary qualities), and establishment of the redactional sources of the text and its ritual context. The Instruction (no. 10a) asks that "if need be, a critical text of the passage must first be established so that the translation can be done from the original or at least from the best available text." Such is the seriousness with which translations are to be made.

It is understood that translators read Latin. A translation from a translated text is anomalous, yet alas it is a regrettable reality in some local churches. The importance of Latin was vindicated by Pope Paul VI who himself "had taken every step to have all the modern languages introduced into the liturgy." He affirmed that "without the knowledge of Latin something is altogether missing from a higher, fully rounded education—and in particular with regard to theology and liturgy."[25]

The second premise is that liturgical translation is a work of art. It requires creative skill for producing translations that display form, beauty, and perception. Aesthetic in the best sense of the word is an integral element of Christian worship. Liturgical tradition has always put stock in the beauty and nobility of texts, ceremonies, vestments,

---

[25] "Address to Latinists," (1968) 144–5; *Documents on the Liturgy*, 282.

music, sacred images, books, architecture, and environment. A translation may be doctrinally faithful and linguistically correct, but if it lacks beauty or aesthetic form and is banal or trite, it is not suitable as a liturgical text. Prayers proclaimed in assembly should be pleasing to the ears, evoke beautiful images of God and his creation, and raise the hearts to what is sublime and noble. No wonder then that the Latin prayers, especially during the classical period, employed the finest rhetorical figures in the Latin language, such as redundancy, repetition, sound, vivacity, parallelism, argumentation, and imagery.[26] The Roman assembly took special pleasure in rhetorical devices like binary succession, antithesis, *cursus*, and *concinnitas* or symmetry. There is no reason to think that modern congregations are indifferent to the beauty and nobility of liturgical prayers said in their own language.

The third premise deals with the nature of translation as a living interpretation of a text in the context of a particular assembly. We are dealing, in other words, with the need for contextualized translation. Supposing that the critical text is established and the rules of hermeneutics are applied, translators should still pose the question whether the translated text communicates to a given assembly and in their own particular circumstances the message intended by the original text for its original audience. This seems to be the concern voiced out by the Instruction *Comme le prévoit* (no. 7), when it remarks that "in the case of liturgical communication, it is necessary to take into account not only the message to be conveyed, but also the speaker, the audience, and the style."

Liturgical texts have a performative quality which goes beyond the communication of doctrine. In liturgical celebrations they become actions expressing the relationship between God and the assembly in the here-and-now of a local Church. In the words of *Comme le prévoit* (no. 27), "a liturgical text is a linguistic fact designed for celebration." Thus, it is not enough to transmit the original message. It is essential that the message be contextualized, made alive and relevant to the particular ecclesial situation. After all, the liturgy is not an historical celebration nor is it merely a remembrance of what God did in ages past. It is also the celebration of what God does for the people gath-

---

[26] M. Augé, "Principi di interpretazione dei testi liturgici," *Anamnesis* 1, 174–8.

ered here and now. As the Instruction (no. 20) points out, "the prayer of the Church is always the prayer of some actual community, assembled here and now. It is not sufficient that a formula handed down from some other time or region be translated verbatim, even if accurately, for liturgical use. The formula translated must become the genuine prayer of the congregation and in it each of its members should be able to find and express himself or herself."

To achieve this the translated text must recreate or reshape the original message, though without departing from it, so that the assembly is able to perceive the vernacular text as if it had been thought out and written with their present situation and needs in mind.[27] Implied in this is the use of the current style of speech or the avoidance, where liturgically possible, of archaic and antiquated speech that creates the impression of transporting the assembly to some remote past. As Pope Paul VI exhorted translators, the vernacular texts should be "within the grasp of all, even children and the uneducated," though "set apart from the everyday speech of the street and the marketplace." Without this work of interpretation translated texts, especially from the earlier strata of the corpus of liturgical texts, will hardly speak in context to the assembly and enjoy ownership by the local Church.

The fourth premise, which is related to contextualized translation, is inculturation. The fact that good translations are generated by dynamic equivalence argues for the application of the principles of inculturation. The subject is broad, but the following couple of points may be useful.

Liturgical texts are shaped, already in original Latin, for public proclamation. They are meant to be recited aloud in the assembly and be attentively listened to. Unlike novena prayers which are recited in unison by the devotees, most liturgical texts, especially the presidential, are ministerially proclaimed. In other words, liturgical texts fall under the category of ritual language which is the type of speech employed for the performance of a rite.[28] Speech is composed of words

---

[27] A.-M. Roguet, "I generi letterari dei testi liturgici, loro traduzione e uso," *RL* 53 (1966) 19–31.

[28] G. Ramshaw, *Christ in Sacred Speech: The Meaning of Liturgical Language* (Philadelphia, 1986).

and phrases, but these are not independent units. They combine to create a denotation, a connotation, a context or, in short, a message.

In the liturgy ritual language assumes various forms. It can consist of formularies, acclamations, poetic compositions or hymns, and addresses in the form of homilies or instructions: in other words, of anything spoken, read aloud, proclaimed, or sung. By calling this type of language ritual we stress the fact that liturgical language is spoken language. It is primarily intended to be performed orally in celebrations with an assembly. Most of the liturgical texts, especially formularies and hymns, have been put down in writing. This should not lead us to regard them as literary pieces for private reading. Liturgical texts are always meant to be read or sung in public. The history of the sixth-century Veronese Sacramentary, for example, shows that its original was a folder wherein loose pages of Mass formularies had been inserted day after day in the course of the liturgical year. They were prayers written to be read aloud at papal Masses.

Vernacular versions should not obscure this trait of the liturgical texts. In every language there is a literary genre for speaking in large assemblies and on solemn occasions, or even in the intimacy of a family circle. Although the context often dictates the mode or style of recitation, the language itself stays on the level of ritual proclamation. Translated texts should thus be attentive to the local pattern of proclamation. Depending on the culture's oral and aural tradition, texts will opt for rhythmic cadences, use of rhyme or slightly poetic language, accent on key as well as final words in a line, and avoidance of too many unaccented syllables in a row.[29] In most cases the nature of public reading will call for the adoption of sense lines and of "user-friendly" words and phrases.

The depth of inculturation is shown in the way the receptor language employs idiomatic expressions and elements of local proverbs, maxims, and aphorisms. These are integral components of a people's

[29] The revised translations of the sacramentary by the International Commission on English in the Liturgy are attentive to the properties of formal spoken English: accent on key words, avoidance of internal rhyme and of too many unaccented syllables in a row, effort to end each line strongly on an accented syllable. These and the other properties of modern English language have in a number of instances resulted in English formularies that are akin to the original Latin in beauty and nobility.

linguistic patterns and reveal their innermost attitude toward God, history, and experiences of life. It is useful to remember that ritual language is not intended for making dogmatic statements on the faith of the Church. Although the *lex credendi* sometimes weighs heavily on the *lex orandi*, as in such feasts as the Corpus Domini and the Assumption of the Blessed Virgin Mary, ritual language is not constructed out of systematic theology. The only written element of the liturgy that can be considered dogmatic is the formula of the creed, but we know that it was not composed originally for liturgical proclamation. This does not mean that liturgical texts do not contain doctrine. However, the liturgy instructs, not in the language of systematic theology and speculative philosophy, but in the language used for acclamations and narrations. The liturgy is not primarily an exposition but a persuasion: we "remind" God of his deeds in order to persuade him to repeat them in our day. Persuasion is strongly captured by the translated texts by the way they use idioms and the elements of value language. Those who are excessively fastidious regarding the use of abstract and technical terms miss the basic premise that the liturgy is expressed in persuasive language.

In some local churches there is a tradition of popular religious language, which should be neatly distinguished from colloquial language. The language of popular religiosity, like those used for novenas, can be solemn, though often florid, discursive even to the point of rambling, and is vividly picturesque. The language of popular religiosity and that of the liturgy belong to different genre, but they are not enemies. In situations where the local people are more at ease with the language of popular worship it might not be altogether uncalled for to allow liturgical language to assimilate some characteristic traits of popular religious language.[30]

Finally, inculturation in certain receptor languages will necessarily touch the question of inclusive language. This is a delicate but basic matter which must be addressed by translators, and some conferences of bishops have already issued guidelines regarding the vertical language (when addressing God) and the horizontal (when

---

[30] A. Chupungco, *Liturgical Inculturation. Sacramentals, Religiosity, and Catechesis* (Collegeville, 1992) 95–133.

referring to humans).[31] The question is related not only to the evolution of verbal and lexical usage, but also to the cultural underpinning of modern society. Inclusive language is a modern protagonist of the centuries-old movement working for the recognition of the equality of human persons, male or female, and the promotion of their rightful place in Church and society. To ignore this amounts to a lamentable disregard of culture and the historical process.[32]

The fifth premise concerns the tradition of the Latin liturgical language. The Instruction *The Roman Liturgy and Inculturation* makes the timely reminder that "liturgical language has its own special characteristics."[33] Examples are its biblical content and inspiration and its possession of "certain Christian expressions that can be transmitted [by transliteration] from one language to another, as has happened in the past, for example in the case of: *ecclesia, evangelium, baptisma, eucharistia.*" The other details are laid out in the preceding Instruction *Comme le prévoit* (nos. 11–29). This document is an authoritative exposition of the criteria that govern the translation of those Latin texts which create special difficulties for modern languages. It recommends, however, that "in many modern languages a biblical or liturgical language must be created by use. This will be achieved rather by infusing a Christian meaning into common words than by importing uncommon or technical terms."

Conclusion

Translation was the immediate task that faced local churches after the council. Yet, the Instruction *Comme le prévoit* (no. 43) does not consider this the ultimate goal: "Texts translated from another language are clearly not sufficient for the celebration of a fully renewed liturgy. The creation of new texts will be necessary. But translation of texts transmitted through the tradition of the Church is the best school and

---

[31] M. Collins, "Naming God in Public Prayer, *Wor* 59 (1985) 291–304;
L. Roy, "Inclusive Language Regarding God," *Wor* 65 (1991) 207–15.

[32] It is useful to note that other receptor languages, especially outside the Western hemisphere, do not encounter this problem. In Tagalog language, for example, God in the third person is *siya*, which is inclusive. People are *tao*, brothers and sisters are *mga kapatid*, and sons and daughters are *mga anak*. These are all inclusive. To refer specifically to brother one needs to say *kapatid na lalaki*, and to sister *kapatid na babae*.

[33] Instruction *"The Roman Liturgy and Inculturation"* (Rome, 1994) no. 53.

discipline for the creation of new texts so "that any new forms adopted should in some way grow organically from forms already in existence" (*Sacrosanctum Concilium* no. 23).

Bibliography

D'Haese, P. "Traduction et version après Vatican II; à la recherche d'une langue maternelle liturgique." *QL* 73 (1992) 97–111.

Lamberts, J. "Vatican II et la liturgie en langue vernaculaire." *QL* 66 (1985) 125–154.

Lebrun, D. "Les traductions liturgiques: statut et enjeux." *MD* 202 (1995) 19–33.

"Les traductions liturgiques." *MD* 86 (1966).

Le traduzioni dei libri liturgici. Acts of the congress held in Rome, November 9–13, 1965. Vatican City, 1966.

"Problemas de lenguaje." *Ph* 10 (1970) 422–494.

Roguet, A.-M. "I generi letterari dei testi liturgici, loro traduzione e uso." *RL* 53 (1966) 19–31.

_____. "Essai historique sur les traductions liturgiques." *MD* 86 (1966) 75–105.

Venturi, G. "Fenomeni e problemi linguistici della traduzione liturgica nel passaggio da una cultura ad un'altra." *EphLit* 92 (1978) 5–75.

Frederick R. McManus

20

Liturgical Law

INTRODUCTION

Liturgical law is properly understood as an integral part of the canon law, in some ways the same as the rest of the Church's law, in some ways different. The purpose of this section of the *Handbook* is to explain the laws that govern liturgical celebration: their nature, kinds and sources, interpretation and force, and rationale or purpose. It is directly concerned with the Roman and other rites of the Latin or Western Catholic Church, not with liturgies of the Eastern Churches.

Liturgical history reveals orders or rules of celebration from ancient times,[1] whether these developed through the usage of the Christian community filled with the Spirit of God or were regulated at diverse levels of the Church, especially local and regional. This order of celebration may be governed loosely or rigidly, and it may be regulated by intervention or supervision on the part of those who hold the pastoral office. The latter preside over the celebrations themselves and exercise a corresponding role in proposing or accepting the rules (laws) of celebration. Our concern is with the existing liturgical law, in particular as this has moved in recent years from its post-Tridentine inflexibility to the norms of a renewed liturgy, one that has now been profoundly reformed and in the process made more flexible and open to creativity and inculturation.

---

[1] For the development of juridical sources, including liturgical sources, through the medieval period, see James A. Brundage, *Medieval Canon Law* (London and New York, 1995) especially chapters 1–3.

Liturgical law directly embraces the rule of celebration, affecting the actions (words, song, ritual acts) and the circumstances or environment (churches and baptisteries, furnishings, vesture, and the like). This legal or canonical scope presupposes an understanding of the holy liturgy itself: the divine act of sanctification and the public, corporate human response. It is the public worship of God by the Church, Christ the Head and his members — done through signs, the deeds and words that articulate communally the inward faith and worship and the divine gift or grace.

Large areas of church law related closely to sacraments and other liturgical services — from matrimonial dispensations to the requirements for ordination — are sufficiently extrinsic to the actual celebration of the holy mysteries that they are not counted as liturgical law in the strict or conventional sense. Despite evident overlapping between the norm of celebration and the church discipline related to the sacramental life of the Church, this distinction is useful. It is reflected in the name of the body within the Roman curia now responsible for the Roman and other Latin rites: the Congregation for Divine Worship and the Discipline of the Sacraments.

Another key to this distinction between the law of liturgical celebration and the discipline of the seven sacraments lies in canon 2 of the Code of Canon Law of the Latin Church (1983). This canon largely excludes the canon law of liturgical celebration from the code, noting that the liturgical laws lie outside it "for the most part [*plerumque*]." Nonetheless the code does contain many canons, chiefly definitions and foundational canons, that directly affect the liturgy's celebration.

The same canon 2 provides that "current liturgical norms retain their [canonical, juridically binding] force unless a given liturgical norm is contrary to the canons of the code." About two months before the 1983 code was to go into effect, the competent curial department issued a list of variations or emendations that had to be made in the new Roman liturgical books in view of the codification (decree, September 12, 1983). The variations, however, were largely minor or merely formalistic. (Something similar had happened earlier this century when the first code of the Latin Church was promulgated in 1917. That code had many norms derived from the existing liturgical books; the changes it made — the later law superseding prior norms — were then introduced into a new edition of the Roman Ritual in 1925.)

Despite differences between the liturgical law and other elements of the canon law, many canonical institutes are equally applicable to it. These include custom or unwritten law, the promulgation and interpretation of law, dispensations and commutations by church authority, concessions of privileges and indults, and the like. They are largely defined by the canons on general norms in Book I of the present code (especially canons 1–95 and 129–144).[2]

"NEW STYLE, NEW SPIRIT" IN LITURGICAL LAW

Contemporary liturgical law shares the pastoral approach of canonical revision in general, but often with a stronger base derived from the conciliar liturgical renewal. A postconciliar phenomenon called "new law, new spirit" demands that directly pastoral (and spiritual) dimensions be considered, such as the vast diversity among the assemblies where the liturgy is celebrated. Or it may be questions of the need for authenticity of celebration, distinctions between what is essential or truly necessary and what is worthwhile but not necessary, and the new ecclesiological insights of Vatican II, from collegiality to subsidiarity.

Another aspect is the artistic and esthetic dimension. In the liturgy this affects language, song and other musical forms, ritual gestures and actions, and material objects of every kind. On the one hand, it may be easy to state "norms" of beauty, dignity, intelligibility, pertinence to the reality of cult or sacrament, relationship of persons in celebration (ordained ministers who hold the pastoral office, special lay ministers, and the whole assembly), and more. On the other hand, these facets of the liturgy are less susceptible than other kinds of church law to strict or narrow regulation, which is a matter to be considered in attempting to understand the law and even to discern its canonically binding force.

All this, whether seen as new spirit or approach or even mindset, is amply confirmed by the way in which the revised liturgical books have been designed: the wealth of alternatives, the overall flexibility

---

[2] For these and other canons, see James A. Coriden et al., eds. *The Code of Canon Law: A Text and Commentary* (New York, 1985).

and openness to creativity, the choices allowed or encouraged among prayer texts and even more so among liturgical songs (especially by way of substitution), the opportunities afforded to employ "these or similar words," and the very language of prescriptions or precepts.

This new style may also be seen as a major development of older categories of liturgical decrees and other norms: the *facultative*, concessionary, or discretionary decrees, allowing for choice, as is now much more common; the distinction once made between *preceptive* norms and *directive* norms, the latter serving as important guidelines without the weight of a canonical precept.

SOURCES OF LITURGICAL LAW

The principal sources of the *general* law governing Catholic worship are the liturgical service books that are formally and officially approved, together with papal and curial documents that supplement the books themselves. *Particular* liturgical law, especially at the national level, has parallel sources in particular service books and in ancillary decrees or the like.

In the liturgical books themselves two styles of rule or regulation are ordinarily found: the rubrics that run through the prayer texts and rites themselves, determining both word and action, and the substantial introductions to each book. The introductions are called prenotes (*praenotanda*) or, in the most important books, general instructions (*institutiones generales*). In the post-Tridentine period the four principal liturgical books of the Roman rite were the missal, breviary, ritual, and pontifical. These categories were retained in the post-Vatican II reform as serial titles, although each one now covers multiple sections or volumes.

Besides the Roman books (in Latin), the particular liturgical books, whose "typical" or basic editions are in the various vernaculars, have the canonical approbation of individual conferences of bishops for the local churches or dioceses of their respective territories. Mostly they parallel the Roman books but may contain additional introductory matter, along with national or regional variations or adaptations, formularies for regional feast days, and supplementary, original prayer texts.

Sources outside the books themselves include papal documents (especially apostolic constitutions and apostolic letters on papal initiative, *motu proprio*) and a variety of curial documents, from directories and instructions to simple notifications. Only by exception are the latter counted as general decrees (laws): their juridically binding force cannot be presumed, but they may have their own obligatory weight. Today the principal category is the apostolic or papal constitution, used, for example, to approve the revised Roman Missal or to alter the central matter and form of sacraments, something reserved to the supreme authority of pope or council, as canon 841 states.

Particular liturgical law may take the form of general decrees of conferences of bishops and of individual diocesan bishops, although the latter do not promulgate liturgical books as such. It too may be supplemented by other documents, such as guidelines for celebration and doctrinal expositions concerning the liturgy.

In the mid-1960s the *Consilium ad exsequendam* or commission to implement the council's liturgical decisions had a project of codifying the general liturgical law, but the plan was not carried out. Instead collections of documents have been privately published in various languages.[3]

LITURGICAL LAW IN THE CONSTITUTION
SACROSANCTUM CONCILIUM

The conciliar constitution on the liturgy of December 4, 1963 is called *Sacrosanctum Concilium* (= *SC*).[4] It is a disciplinary constitution and contains decrees on both celebration and reform of the Roman liturgy, but it also has substantial expository material of a doctrinal

[3] A chronological collection in the original languages is edited by Reiner Kaczynski, *Enchiridion Documentorum Instaurationis Liturgicae* (Turin, vol. 1, 1975; vol. 2, 1988). An English collection in a topical arrangement, edited by the International Commission on English in the Liturgy (ICEL), is *Documents on the Liturgy 1963-1979: Conciliar, Papal, and Curial Texts* (Collegeville, 1982). Papal and curial documents are ordinarily promulgated in the official commentary of the Roman See, *Acta Apostolicae Sedis,* and also published in *Notitiae,* the journal of the congregation competent in this area.

[4] For commentaries on the constitution, see Joseph A. Jungmann, "Constitution on the Sacred Liturgy," *Commentary on the Documents of Vatican II,* ed. Herbert Vorgrimler (London, New York, 1967) 1:1–88; Annibale Bugnini and Carlo Braga, eds., *The Commentary on the Constitution and on the Instruction on the Sacred Liturgy* (New York, 1964); Congregazione per il Culto Divino, ed., *Costituzione Liturgica "Sacrosanctum Concilium"* (Rome, 1986).

nature. This follows the best canonical tradition of offering the rationale for the law and only then the "dispositive" norms or laws; a
similar pattern is followed in the prenotes of the service books already mentioned.

Most of the norms of SC in the formal sense are mandates for the
initial postconciliar reform of the Roman rite, which was largely
achieved through the revision of the Roman liturgical books in the
two decades following the council. The basic principles of reform in
SC continue in force, as do its other normative dispositions.

Besides the reform decrees, the principal areas of new church law
affecting worship in SC are (1) the broad norms for liturgical celebration and the promotion of better celebration and catechesis (parts 2,
4, and 5 of chapter 1); (2) a new determination of the locus of canonical power to moderate or govern the liturgy (especially article 22 of
chapter 1); (3) the articles on future cultural adaptation (now called
inculturation: SC 37-40 , in chapter 1). These norms of Vatican II are
unaffected by the subsequent Code of Canon Law (1983) or other legislation. Some fundamental texts of SC, however, are also redacted in
canons like 834–839 at the beginning of Book IV of the code, which is
about the sanctifying (worshiping or priestly) office in the Church.

SC 22, §1

The first paragraph of article 22 determines that the moderation, ordering, and governance of the liturgy belong to the Church, that is,
not to some non-ecclesial agent such as a civil authority; this law is
not new. The text, however, goes on to alter radically the post-
Tridentine rule (ultimately embodied in canon 1257 of the 1917 code)
that reserved the regulation of the liturgy exclusively to the Roman
See and placed the diocesan bishops in the position of mere enforcers
of the liturgical law (canon 1261 of that code). Now this power resides in the Roman pontiff "and, in accord with the law [*ad normam
iuris*], the [diocesan] bishop."[5]

Although the diocesan bishop may add to the general liturgical
law and dispense from it, his power still remains limited. The very
extent and breadth of the law in the revised liturgical books weaken
the presumption of subsidiarity, namely, that the diocesan bishop has

[5] See Ignatius Gordon, "Constitutio de Sacra Liturgia et Canones 1256–1257,"
Periodica 54 (1964) 89–140; 352–405; 517–82.

all the power required to exercise his pastoral office unless the Roman pontiff withdraws that power by reservation. [6] It is impossible to foretell how the two authorities, primatial and diocesan, will resolve future conflicts or liturgical tensions, but the change in *SC* 22, §1, is radical in its recovery of the nature of the particular or local church, shepherded by its bishop.[7]

SC 22, §2

Equally radical is the new determination of an intermediate authority in paragraph 2, namely, the national or regional conferences of bishops — although the conferences are only a new form of the conciliarity that was found in the ancient Church long before the assembly of the episcopal college at the ecumenical council of A.D. 325. This second paragraph recognizes "territorial bodies of bishops" (in practice, episcopal conferences) as also having the same governing power as in paragraph 1, but only "within certain defined limits." Thus these bodies are not presumed to possess binding authority over liturgical celebration unless this is somehow defined: by liturgical or other general laws, by new papal concessions, or by custom. In many such areas, however, the responsibility of the conferences is substantial and extensive, above all in the approbation of liturgical books (below).[8]

An additional note to both paragraph 1 and paragraph 2 of article 22: Both conventionally and in canonical tradition, the distinction between the liturgy itself and other forms of devotional life, both public and private, has been made explicitly on the basis of inclusion in, or exclusion from, the official liturgical books. While this distinction between liturgical and non-liturgical continues to be important, it does not affect the moderating or governing power within the church

---

[6] To appreciate this point, it is necessary to study the text of the conciliar decree *Christus Dominus*, October 28, 1965, n. 8, and, for *SC* 22, §2, nn. 36–8 of the same decree. The two matters may also be pursued in commentaries on canons 381 and 447–59, respectively, of the present code, as these canons are applicable to the enactment of liturgical laws at local and regional levels.

[7] See dogmatic constitution *Lumen gentium*, chap. 3 (nn. 18–27).

[8] See Hervé Legrand et al., eds., *The Nature and Future of Episcopal Conferences* (Washington, D.C., 1988; also *The Jurist* 48 [1988] 1–412); Thomas J. Reese, ed., *Episcopal Conferences: Historical, Canonical, and Theological Studies* (Washington, D.C., 1989).

community, as envisioned in the first two paragraphs of article 22. *SC* 13 (and now canon 839) makes clear that "pious" devotions of the Christian people (especially when ordered by the Roman See) and "sacred" devotions (mandated by bishops) are equally subject to church regulation or law.[9] They are important to the Church's cultic life, but "the liturgy by its very nature surpasses any of them."

SC 63

Another specific matter is the power of the conferences of bishops to give their approbation to particular (national, regional) liturgical books in the respective vernaculars, which are to be "in harmony with the revised Roman Ritual" in the case of sacraments and sacramentals and, an important decree, are to include the pastoral, ecclesial, canonical, and doctrinal prenotes from the Roman books.

Of critical canonical significance is the further requirement that the books (or, for that matter, other particular liturgical laws of conferences and councils, but not of diocesan bishops) receive a canonical recognition (*recognitio*) or confirmation by the Roman See before they may be promulgated. The nature of this review is formally determined by *SC* 35, paragraph 3, in the context of the vernacular concessions: it is a species of approval best described as confirmation, that is, it adds a further juridical and moral weight to the decrees of the conferences of bishops but is different from any Roman approbation or enactment. A decree promulgating a vernacular liturgical book thus emanates from the lawmaking power of the conference of bishops, not that of the Roman See which reviews it. The distinction is a close one but of major significance in the relationship between the Apostolic See and the group of local churches that make up a given episcopal conference.

SC 37-40

The distinction becomes sharper when *SC* defines the responsibility for future cultural adaptation or liturgical inculturation.[10] A careful

---

[9] Another example is indulgenced prayers and practices. See canons 992–7, derived from Paul VI's reform of teaching and practice about indulgences, in the apostolic constitution *Indulgentiarum doctrina*, January 1, 1967: *AAS* 59 (1967) 5–24.

[10] See Anscar Chupungco, *Cultural Adaptation of the Liturgy* (New York, 1982); *Liturgies of the Future: The Process and Methods of Inculturation* (New York, 1989); *Liturgical Inculturation: Sacramentals, Religiosity, and Catechesis* (Collegeville, 1992).

division is made between, first, the "legitimate variations or adaptations to different groups, regions, and peoples" within the "substantial unity of the Roman rite" (*SC* 38–9) and, second, more profound or radical developments (*SC* 40). The former adaptations, foreseen and spelled out in the reformed Roman liturgical books, all fall within the competence of the conferences of bishops, which may enact them as law. The latter, on the other hand, require not simple Roman recognition or confirmation but the consent or canonical approbation of the Roman See — and thus are papal particular laws.[11] (Going even further toward liturgical inculturation, *SC* 4 acknowledges the possibility of new non-Roman rites with the same, equal right and dignity as the existing rites of East and West.)

LITURGICAL AUTHORITIES AND STRUCTURES: GENERAL

If the power to supervise or regulate liturgical celebrations belongs to the Roman pontiff and the diocesan bishop, as well as to the conferences of bishops, institutional structures both old and new play an executive or at least consultative role in the liturgical law and its carrying out.

In the modern period, as the bishops of Rome carried out the decrees of the Council of Trent, a commission of cardinals supervised the preparation of the new Roman breviary and missal. The commission was succeeded, in the complete structure of curial congregations reformed by Sixtus V, by the Congregation of Sacred Rites, SRC. This curial department or dicastery was established in the bull *Immensa aeterni Dei* of January 22, 1588, and its competence embraced, among other matters, "vigilance for the observance of sacred rites . . . [continuing] reform and correction of the liturgical books . . . canonization of saints."[12] Throughout its long history (until 1969), the member cardinals, with a cardinal prefect at their head, dealt with two broad

---

[11] A document of the Roman Congregation for Divine Worship and the Discipline of the Sacraments has further defined this doctrine and discipline: "The Roman Liturgy and Inculturation: IVth Instruction for the Right Application of the Conciliar Constitution on the Liturgy (nn. 37–40)" January 25, 1994: *AAS* 87 (1995) 288–314.

[12] See Frederick R. McManus, *The Congregation of Sacred Rites* (Washington, D.C., 1954).

areas: the liturgies of the Latin Church and the processes or causes of saints.

In his general reform of the Roman curia, Pius X partially restricted the breadth of SRC's venerable competence (constitution *Sapienti consilio*, June 29, 1908). Matters of sacramental "discipline" were transferred, for example, to the new Congregation for the Discipline of the Sacraments, and the older body's role was restricted to "matters pertaining *proximately* to sacred rites." The full 1908 definition of the congregation's responsibility was carried over into canon 253 of the 1917 code.

It was only later that the two chief areas of SRC's competence were formally recognized as two separate sections of the dicastery (1914): one for the causes of saints, which had long been the principal occupation of the congregation, the other for "sacred rites." The latter section had become so weak that Pius X's predecessor, Leo XIII, had to establish ancillary commissions for liturgical matters. Finally, in 1930 a third "historical" section was added by Pius XI, to provide historical research in the causes of saints and for the revision of liturgical books.

Over the centuries since 1588 the Congregation of Rites oversaw new editions of the liturgical books, but its work was also represented by its decrees, both general and particular, which were (selectively) collected and published — first, in private collections, then officially under Leo XIII as *Decreta Authentica Congregationis Sacrorum Rituum* (five volumes, 1898-1901; two later volumes, 1912, 1927). Because most decrees were addressed to particular dioceses, religious institutes, etc., the classifications of *general* or universal, *particular*, and *"equivalently general"* decrees arose — the latter being particular decrees judged as general because of their nature and thus considered binding universally. This helped add even greater narrowness to liturgical law, since commentators and rubricians treated particular responses to minute questions like precedence as if they were universal law.

When the reform of the Roman liturgy, left dormant after Pius X, was taken up again by Pius XII, he created a commission of general liturgical restoration in 1948, ancillary to SRC.[13] In effect, the work of

[13] For the 1948 commission and later curial developments through 1975, see Annibale Bugnini, *The Reform of the Liturgy 1948–1975* (Collegeville, 1990) esp. "The Beginning of the Reform," 3–95.

this important reform body was taken over by John XXIII's liturgical commission preparatory to the council (1960–1962), which drafted *SC*, and in turn by the conciliar commission (1962–1963). After the general conciliar debate on the draft, the commission revised it for many votes and ultimate enactment by Vatican II.

Next in sequence was the postconciliar commission created by Paul VI in January 1964. This *Consilium* of implementation had the responsibility of preparing the new Roman liturgical books and many documents of reform; it also reviewed the decrees of the conferences of bishops. An anomaly was that the *Consilium* had to submit its revised texts for at least nominal acceptance by the Congregation of Rites, which then received authorization from the pope to issue the individual liturgical book or other document. This structural situation was ultimately resolved by the suppression of SRC in 1969 by Paul VI. In succession to SRC and the *Consilium* the new Congregation for Divine Worship was created; matters of beatification and canonization were transferred to a new Congregation for the Causes of Saints.

Although this appeared to be a final resolution, other structural changes followed: Paul VI merged the new Congregation for Divine Worship with the Congregation for the Discipline of the Sacraments, resulting in the Congregation for Sacraments and Worship (1975); the Congregation for Divine Worship was restored to separate status by John Paul II (1984); finally, the same pope again merged the departments as the present Congregation for Divine Worship and the Discipline of the Sacraments (1989).

Today the liturgical competence of the congregation includes "moderation and promotion of the sacred liturgy, first of all the sacraments," with the specific details listed in the most recent reform of the Roman curia by John Paul II (constitution *Pastor bonus*, June 28, 1988, articles 62–70). In part these are responsibilities going back to 1588, such as the maintenance of liturgical order and the extirpation of abuses, preparation of liturgical texts, examination of particular calendars, and the like. Others are contemporary additions, such as the review of adaptations made by authority of the conferences of bishops. The promotional function introduced in 1969 — relating to commissions, institutes, associations, etc. — is only occasionally carried out.

LITURGICAL AUTHORITIES AND STRUCTURES: PARTICULAR

On the particular diocesan and supradiocesan levels, papal and other efforts culminated in various determinations of Vatican II. *SC* 44 recommends that national liturgical commissions (desirably assisted by an institute or center) be set up to direct pastoral liturgical activity, with whatever executive (but not legislative) power as may be delegated by the episcopal conference. The role of such commissions is defined in a Roman instruction of September 26, 1964 (*Inter oecumenici*, n. 44).

Other supradiocesan structures exist, such as the joint or ("mixed") international commissions in the several major language groups. Their power or responsibility depends on the action of the episcopal conferences that create them. Such commissions propose liturgical texts, books, and adaptations to the participating conferences of bishops of a given language, which approve them and then individually transmit them for recognition or confirmation by the Roman See; alternatively, a joint commission may assemble the national decrees of approbation within a given language group and submit all of them directly to the Roman congregation.

Culminating papal injunctions of six decades, *SC* 46–47 requires diocesan (or interdiocesan) liturgical commissions and, if possible, commissions on music and art, either acting collaboratively or being combined.

CUSTOM AND LITURGICAL LAW

Many liturgical laws, like rites and texts themselves, have their ultimate origin in the usage and practice of local communities under the movement of the Spirit of God, with greater or less initiative or intervention by church authorities. The code of the Eastern Catholic Churches (1990) expresses it best by speaking of Christian custom insofar or inasmuch "as it responds to the action of the Holy Spirit in the ecclesial body" (canon 1506, §1).

Canonically the institute of custom, understood as unwritten law, is now determined by canons 23–28 of the Latin Church's code: (1) to govern the custom by which a community gives itself additional norms of church order and (2) to govern the customs by which a community alters or abrogates the written law. In particular, the canons define the period of uninterrupted usage necessary for the unwritten canon law. These terms are also applicable to unwritten liturgical law.

Beyond this, it is not uncommon for the liturgical books to speak of custom (or usage or tradition) in contexts that do not mean the canonically enforceable customs referred to in the regulatory canons of the code. Instead they are the factual or actual usages, of whatever duration, that simply show how the Christian people act in their common worship. Technically these are called *consuetudines facti:* they may be simply the ongoing practice of the Church or of local churches or even congregations, and they are acknowledged in church documents that otherwise may seem fixed and inflexible. The matter is expressed in the new edition of the *Ceremonial of Bishops* (1984): the directions given in that book are qualified by the clause: "in such a way that the traditions and requirements proper to each place can be retained."

INTERPRETATION OF LITURGICAL LAW

The purpose of interpretation is to enable the Christian, affected by or bound to observe church law, to uncover the genuine meaning of a law.[14] To begin with, the canons themselves embrace the venerable rule, which began as a medieval aphorism, that the custom or usage of the Christian community is the "best interpreter of laws" (canon 27) — a canon of direct and obvious application to the law of the liturgy that is celebrated by the whole community.

Another significant rule for interpretation has been repeatedly emphasized for the canons of the present code, beginning with the apostolic constitution of promulgation, *Sacrae disciplinae leges* (January 25, 1983). It is that the canons are always to be understood in the light of the Vatican II conciliar documents and their spirit, not vice versa. The same principle works for liturgical laws as well, for example, those found in the liturgical books or in postconciliar documents: these too are to be understood in the light of Vatican II's decisions, not vice versa.

[14] See Ladislas Örsy, "The Interpreter and His Art," *The Jurist* 40 (1980) 27–56; John M. Huels, "Interpretation of Liturgical Law," *Wor* 55 (1981) 218–37; idem, *One Table, Many Laws: Essays in Catholic Eucharistic Practice* (Collegeville, 1986), chap. 1.

Words in Text and Context

When the text or language of any church law is examined for its genuine meaning, the formal norm is that laws "are to be understood in accord with the proper meaning of the words considered in their text and context"; if this fails, then "recourse is to be taken to parallel passages [of the law], if such exist, to the purpose and circumstances of the law, and to the mind of the legislator" (canon 17). Another fundamental rule, also applicable to liturgical laws, is that a strict interpretation (that is, limited to the smallest number of cases) is to be followed for laws which ". . . restrict the free exercise of rights or which contain an exception to the law" (canon 18); the burdens of the law must be minimized, especially as they may limit the rights of believers. Ordinarily, for example, the language will make it clear whether a norm is a canonically obligatory law as opposed to an exhortation or recommendation. By exception, the running rubrics of liturgical books are usually couched in descriptive language (that is, in the indicative mood) rather than preceptively; such rubrics are presumed to be precepts to carry out the action described.

The sense of the rule about "text and context" is evident. Although individual words may have several meanings, ordinarily there is a simple, conventional meaning of words and phrases used in church law, including of course liturgical law. The immediate context of the legal text, in this case liturgical laws, is again evident: the language that surrounds the given text, the important expository statements made in the prenotes of the respective liturgical book, the placement of a norm in a larger section or complete document, and the other rubrical directions in a rite.

This primary determination may suffice. But often it may be useful or necessary to examine analogous legal texts, legislative history (when this is available, as with the decrees of Vatican II and sometimes with the drafts of liturgical books), the language of superseded laws (most likely deliberately abrogated or replaced), as well as what stands behind the law: the purpose (expressed or unexpressed) and circumstances, the mind of the legislator (again, expressed or unexpressed). Yet it is always the responsibility of the legislator (or legislature) to express clearly this "mind" or intent: none of the Christian people is bound by a law that remains truly doubtful (canon 14).

The Broader Context

A recent development in the understanding of the canon law has been greater appreciation that laws exist in a much broader context, one already suggested as new style and spirit.[15] This allows for (1) the important theological (and even philosophical) underpinnings of the law, especially sacramental theology and ecclesiology in the case of liturgical law; (2) the findings of the social sciences, especially the anthropology of rites and ritual; (3) the time and culturally conditioned nature of the period to which a written law or unwritten custom belongs; (4) the changing reasonableness or unreasonableness of a law (which is an "ordinance of reason"); and (5) the form or type of law, now clearly normative, now hortatory.

THE BINDING FORCE OF LITURGICAL LAW

Once the meaning of a law has been determined, the question of its canonically binding force may arise.[16] On the face of it, church laws presumptively bind the members of the community, each with his or her own responsibility. Even when a law is clear and certain (rather than "doubtful and obscure"), this may not speak to the relative weight or force of the law, much less to the moral (as compared to the canonical) obligation of observing the law. It may be that there is a real but lesser weight or binding force in documents that are executory in nature but not laws in the strict sense, namely, the laws that are found in the liturgical books or papal documents or general decrees of episcopal conferences and diocesan bishops.

The question of the degree of gravity of violating a law or the sin of transgressing the law is ordinarily a matter of moral theology, left to the moralists to define and propose. An example in which the liturgical law carefully avoids the judgment of degree of gravity is found in the canonical mandate for the ordained and others to celebrate the liturgy of the hours. Instead of saying that the failure to pray morning or evening prayer is a grave moral transgression, the general instruction on the office carefully states that these hours "should not be omitted except for a serious reason" (n. 28).

---

[15] See Ladislas Örsy, *Theology and Canon Law: New Horizons for Legislation and Interpretation* (Collegeville, 1990).

[16] See Walter J. Kelly, "The Authority of Liturgical Laws," *The Jurist* 28 (1968) 397–424; John E. Rotelle, "Liturgy and Authority," *Wor* 47 (1973) 514–26.

In certain circumstances a law may become, in the course of time, unreasonable or obsolete — and thus no law. To take small examples, the so-called Sanctus-candle and the handing around of the "instrument" of peace became obsolete in the centuries after the issuance of the 1570 Roman Missal. Nevertheless the primary concern must always be to understand the law as it is; only then does it become possible to discover its application or non-application in particular circumstances.

The new tone and spirit of postconciliar liturgical law implicates more than mere interpretation or a better context for determining the relative weight of liturgical precepts. The fresh spirit may help to relieve the pastoral burden of some laws, along with very traditional means.[17] Among these traditional means are some principles inherent in the law: (1) Matters so minute or insignificant as not to be the proper object of the lawmaking power -— the principle is *de minimis non curat lex* — will not be true law. (2) In some cases there is only an exhortation, recommendation, expression of a preferable course of action, or purely descriptive rather than prescriptive or preceptive language. (3) Another, already mentioned in a different context, is what canonists call the intrinsic cessation of law — when the law ceases through total lack of purpose or reasonableness or reasonable applicability. (4) Other means may involve the decision of church authorities, like dispensation or commutation of laws, based on the conciliar norm that moderation of the liturgy is now attributed presumptively to the diocesan bishop in the particular church. (5) Still other instances may arise from moral principles such as the existence of excusing causes sufficiently grave in relation to the purpose of the law. (6) Even the virtue of epiky may be exercised, with the effect of rendering virtuous the non-observance of law, in particular cases and for genuine cause.

This elaboration of reasons for mitigating the obligatory weight of the law should not be taken to minimize in any way the significance of the Church's liturgical law. In particular, the reasons for such order (below) work to the contrary: they favor exact observance of the law as it is. The same holds for recognizing the human self-deception of finding reasons to weaken the force of law in favor of oneself or one's

[17] See Frederick R. McManus, "Liturgical Law and Difficult Cases," *Wor* 48 (1974) 347–66.

community. The principle is that no one is a (sound) judge in his or her own case (*nemo iudex in propria causa*). Thus the starting point must be the greatest effort to discern what the law truly means, with the expectation and likelihood that it may be feasibly and responsibly followed by pastoral officeholders and other members of the Christian community.

THE RATIONALE OF THE LITURGICAL LAW

Since many norms affecting liturgical celebration are far from essential either to the genuineness (validity) of sacraments or to the integral nature or unity of the several rites, it may seem that a strong presumption of freedom from law might often prevail. The purpose of this final section is to balance legitimate freedom with the case for observance of the law, namely, its aim and reasonableness. (This is said authoritatively in *SC* 22, paragraph 3, derived from the 1947 encyclical *Mediator Dei*: "Therefore no other person [other than the Roman pontiff, the diocesan bishop, or a conference of bishops — in accord with *SC* 22, paragraphs 1-2], even if a priest [*sacerdos*], may add, remove, or change anything in the liturgy on that person's own authority.")

A prenote is needed. Although in recent centuries canonists have placed most weight upon the "will of the legislator" (extrinsic authority) as determining the law, it is the law as ordinance of reason that has the greater tradition and substance. This is why the church authorities are understood as publishing or promulgating the canon law, including the liturgical law, for the common good of the Christian community. Paul VI made this point in the promulgation of the revised liturgy of the hours: Those mandated to celebrate the daily ecclesial prayer "should celebrate the hours not only through obedience to law, but should also feel drawn to them because of the intrinsic excellence of the hours and their pastoral and ascetic value" (constitution *Laudis canticum*, November 1, 1970).

1. Relationship of the Pastoral Office and Liturgical Presidency

The act of presiding over the eucharistic and other assemblies of worship, whether by the bishop or by the presbyter who takes his place, is closely related to the episcopal pastoral office known as oversight (ἐπισκοπή). It is not necessary to resolve the question whether those who exercise that pastoral office therefore preside over the Eucharist or whether those who preside over the liturgy on that account shepherd the community of Christian believers.

The relationship between the offices or roles is attested to in *SC* 41. There the participation of the whole assembly "in the same eucharist, in a single prayer, at one altar at which the bishop presides surrounded by his college of priests and by his ministers" is seen as "the preeminent manifestation of the Church." The role of the bishop is not monarchical: the full sign is the assembly of believers, where the bishop presides together with the order of presbyters and the other ministers. Nor is the ordinary, parochial assembly neglected as the authentic sign of the Church, that is, the local congregation headed by "a pastor taking the place of the bishop" (*SC* 42). And the episcopal power is expressed canonically by describing the bishops as "principal dispensers of the mysteries of God" and equally "moderators, promoters, and custodians of the whole liturgical life of the church committed to them," together with the presbyters, who also "exercise the office of sanctifying . . . under the authority of the [diocesan] bishop" (canon 835, paragraphs 1–2).

This is a recovery of eucharistic ecclesiology, or at least of the eucharistic dimension of ecclesiology, although not at the expense of baptismal or communion ecclesiology. It helps explain and support the enactment of liturgical laws by the pope and the other bishops individually or by the bishops gathered in conference or council.

2. Public Order and Common Good

Like the rest of the canon law, liturgical law is directed toward the common good and the public order of the church community when the Church is assembled in a given place and at a given time for divine worship. If anything, supporting this order of the church community is all the stronger reason for law in the case of the celebration of rites, words, and actions, since that cultic activity needs to be externalized if it is to be the public and communal act of the community in union with its head, the Lord Jesus.

The need for order or discipline may thus be equated with the so-called incarnational principle. Despite past rubricism, which seemed to identify the liturgy with externals or even rubrical directions, the relationship of the external signs and symbols with the internal faith, cult, and devotion, demands that those things which can be touched by law — the externals of church order and discipline — be subject to legitimate moderation or regulation.

3. The Quality of Liturgical Celebration

This may be the most elusive of the reasons why liturgical laws are necessary or useful. The goal is surely desirable, that each celebration of the mysteries should be of the highest quality possible in the circumstances and within the capabilities of the individual gathering. Thus, in matters that are proper to a worthy and suitable liturgical service, laws may govern the rite. These include the active participation of all the members of the assembly, each in his or her own role or ministry; the choices of prayer and song that are allowable; the material elements that provide the setting for the action; etc.[18]

Yet there is an inevitable degree of subjectivity in judgments concerning the quality of celebration, especially given the language, musical, and visual arts involved. It is nearly impossible to make effective legislative decrees about the excellence of carrying out liturgical services or liturgical catechesis and other preparations or planning. No lawmaker can by fiat insure a high quality of preaching or song, of art or architecture. Paradoxically this goal of worthy celebration may be most important, but one not easily pursued legally with any specificity or effectiveness.

Nevertheless, it is possible to introduce desirable prohibitions into the liturgical law; these are perhaps weightier than affirmative prescriptions. They may proscribe aberrational practices (for example, the needless giving of the Holy Eucharist in Communion from preconsecrated elements) or outlaw unsuitable forms of music or art. The law can prohibit specific kinds of abuses, some of which may arise from sheer liturgical and theological ignorance. Or the law may offer normative direction, affirmative or negative, for the specific responsibilities of the ordained ministers of the Church to foster excellence in celebration and communal participation.

---

[18] For a history of the law of liturgical music, see Robert F. Hayburn, *Papal Legislation on Sacred Music 95 A.D. to 1977 A.D.* (Collegeville, 1979). For contemporary commentaries on the law of what is now called the liturgical environment, see G. Thomas Ryan, *The Sacristy Manual* (Chicago, 1993); Mark G. Boyer, *The Liturgical Environment: What the Documents Say* (Collegeville, 1990).

4. Manifestation of the Common Christian Faith

The entirety of the Christian liturgy is a confession of Christian faith, from the eucharistic anaphoras to the core of the other "sacraments of faith," from the celebrations of the inspired word of God to the explicit creeds or symbols that define faith, from the communal singing and acclamation to the prayers to which the people give assent by the common Amen. The need to express authentic and orthodox faith calls or may call for norms and interventions by church authority — for non-liturgical public devotions as well, but far more for the holy liturgy itself (SC 13).

This is an aspect of the fifth-century axiom, "law of prayer, law of belief" (*lex orandi [supplicandi], lex credendi*).[19] In recent times the effort to characterize this ancient assertion as demanding that the rule of faith be prior and determinative has been confusing and problematic: the liturgy is itself a source in which the traditional, received faith is professed and in which the articulations or understanding of faith may be found.

Perhaps it is best to see the relationship of prayer or liturgy to the orthodox determination of faith as reciprocal. Nonetheless, the relationship gives rise to the possibility or need for the liturgy and its forms to be judged by the received doctrine of faith and then governed by church authorities and law.

5. The Communion of Churches

Possibly communion, a sense of the Church recovered by Vatican II both in the abstract and in the concrete formula of the People of God, is the chief reason for liturgical law and order. Communion is maintained within a diversity of liturgical rites and uses of East and West, but nothing can be done or permitted that weakens such communion. This in turn gives rise to the need for moderation and direction by law.

Within the particular church shepherded by the diocesan bishop, it is a matter of communion among parishes, congregations, communities, and other liturgical assemblies, one with the other and all with the bishop. The degree of the essential unity in the liturgical celebrations may differ, as an allowable and valuable diversity may dictate,

[19] See Geoffrey Wainwright, *Doxology: The Praise of God in Worship, Doctrine, and Life* (New York: Oxford, 1980) chaps. 7–8, 218–83.

but both guidance and supervision may be required lest diversity offend communion or unity.

The same considerations of communion prevail among the local churches of a region (province, nation, or larger area of church life) or of a rite — and with the full *ecclesia*, which is the communion of churches represented by the college of bishops together with its head, the chief bishop. Again, diversity may be most desirable in the forms of liturgy, especially as this is inculturated in innumerable ways, but even this diversity (for example, within a rite such as the Roman) may also demand the kind of governance found in liturgical laws of celebration.

Somewhat analogous to this communion of the Church and churches is the need for some continuity of ritual actions and commonly used prayer texts.[20] This is in accord with anthropological findings about the human nature of repetitiveness in rites and ritual and may be the occasion for law. While not necessarily a matter of communion, the point is strongly affirmed in *SC* 23, which demands that change should somehow "grow organically from forms already existing."

The quantity or rigidity of liturgical laws is not truly at issue, and judgments on this point are necessarily subjective. Most would see in the preconciliar liturgical law an extreme and needless rigidity, probably greater in the previous hundred years than in the immediate post-Tridentine period. Nevertheless, in the postconciliar Church, for all its moderation and openness to variation and change, much liturgical law of substance remains, and nothing in the reform should be seen as any repudiation of law or acceptance of antinomianism.

The principal reasons or justifications for liturgical law do not prejudge the objective value and worth of specific laws, much less the desirable mean between greater and lesser firmness, between uniformity (an excess as opposed to unity) and a near total absence of law. A willingness to understand and observe the liturgical law as it is, along with all the postconciliar openness to change and creative growth, is a true sign of liturgical renewal.

[20] See Aidan Kavanagh, *Elements of Rite: A Handbook of Liturgical Style* (New York, 1982).

Bibliography

Huels, J. M. *Liturgical Law: An Introduction.* Washington, D.C., 1987.

Manzanares Marijuan, J. *Liturgias y decentralizacion en Concilio Vaticano II.* Rome, 1970.

Martimort, A.-G. "Structure and Laws of the Liturgical Celebration." Martimort, ed., *The Church at Prayer*, 1:113–129. Collegeville, Minn., 1987.

McManus, F. R. "Book IV: The Office of Sanctifying in the Church [cc. 834-1253]." *The Code of Canon Law: A Text and Commentary*, ed. J. A. Coriden et al., 593–642, 673–712, esp. 593–614. New York, 1985.

Richstatter, T. *Liturgical Law: New Style, New Spirit.* Chicago, 1977.

Schmidt, H.A.P. *Introductio in liturgiam Occidentalem*, 140–147. Rome, 1960.

Seasoltz, R. K. *New Liturgy, New Laws.* Collegeville, Minn., 1980.

Subject Index

The following pages list the more commonly treated subjects that are pertinent to the introductory study of the liturgy. This index does not contain the names of persons, events, and places recorded in this volume.